THE GRAHAMS
& THE DONALDS

Edited by
Rab Anderson and Tom Prentice

SCOTTISH MOUNTAINEERING CLUB
HILLWALKERS' GUIDE

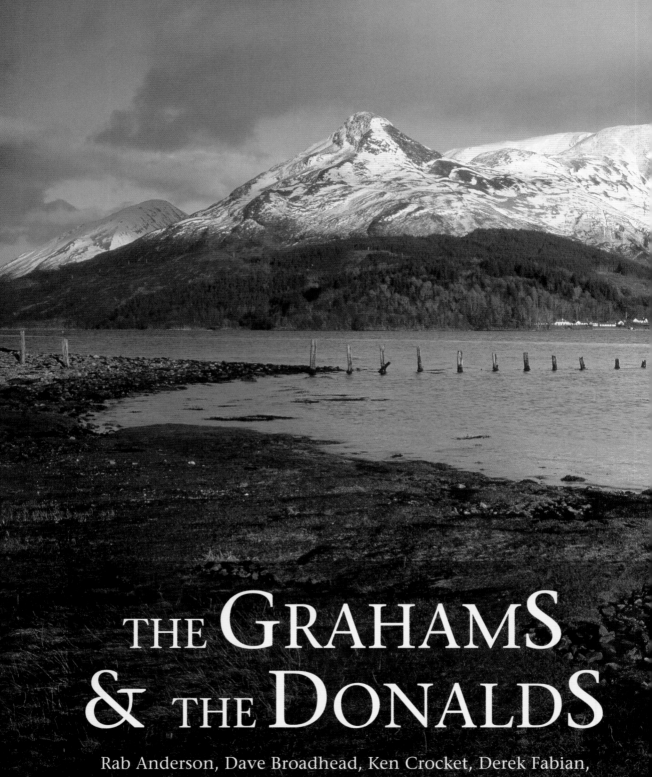

THE GRAHAMS
& THE DONALDS

Rab Anderson, Dave Broadhead, Ken Crocket, Derek Fabian,
Andrew Fraser, Alec Keith, Graham Little, Grahame Nicoll,
Andy Nisbet, Meryl Marshall, Colin Moody, Fran Pothecary,
Tom Prentice, Matt Shaw and Noel Williams

First published in Great Britain by the Scottish Mountaineering Trust

First Edition 2015

ISBN 978-1-907233-19-7
A catalogue record of this book is available from the British Library

SMC ® and Munro's Tables ® are registered trade marks of the Scottish Mountaineering Club
Some maps are derived from Ordnance Survey OpenData™ © Crown copyright and database right 2010

Front Cover: Stac Pollaidh   *Rab Anderson*
Title Page: Beinn na Caillich (Broadford), Skye   *Rab Anderson*
This Page: Sgòrr na Ciche (Pap of Glencoe)   *Cubby Images*

Produced and designed by Tom Prentice for Scottish Mountaineering Trust (Publications) Ltd
Maps: Bernard Newman

Printed & bound in India by Replika Press Pvt Ltd
Distributed by Cordee Ltd (t) 01455 611185 (w) www.cordee.co.uk

Beinn Mheadhonach from Pt. 619m, Ben Starav in the distance (Rab Anderson)

Culter Fell and Chapelgill Hill from the flanks of Gathersnow Hill (Rab Anderson)

This guidebook to *The Grahams & The Donalds* follows in the footsteps of the Scottish Mountaineering Club's guides to *The Munros* and *The Corbetts*.

Most people, and not just hillwalkers, have heard of The Munros, the collective name given to the 282 mountains in Scotland above 3000ft which came into being following the 1891 publication by SMC member Sir Hugh Munro of his *Tables Giving All the Scottish Mountains Exceeding 3000ft in Height*. No one could have anticipated the influence Munro's Tables would have on generations of hillwalkers and that more than a century after their publication, they would still be the inspiration for many people's hill climbing activities.

In 1935 another hill listing came into being when Percy Donald published his *Tables Giving All Hills in the Scottish Lowlands 2000ft in Height and Above*. Donald was also a SMC member and, as with Munro, the hills on his list became known as The Donalds.

It wasn't until 1952 that the next listing was established with the posthumous publication of John Rooke Corbett's *List of Scottish Mountains 2500ft and Under 3000ft in Height*. Again Corbett was an SMC member and, as with the other two, these hills became known as The Corbetts. Where his list differed from the others was that it included a height separation criterion based on a set number of map contour rings. This was subsequently interpreted to mean that the hills on his list had to involve a re-ascent of 500ft (152.4m) on all sides, thereby illustrating a hill's prominence, or what has become known as its drop.

Despite these early lists it was some time before a definitive listing of Scottish hills in the 2000ft to 2500ft range was finalised. Perhaps this should have occurred with William McKnight Docherty's listing of hills. Docherty, another SMC member, published a list of some 900 British and Irish Mountain Tops in 1954, followed by two supplements in 1962. These publications included all but four of what we now know as The Grahams, although his means of separating them was not the same as that used for the current listing.

But, unlike Munro, Donald and Corbett, who all published their lists in the Scottish Mountaineering Club Journal, Docherty published his lists privately. Perhaps if he had published them in the SMC Journal, then these hills would now be known as Dochertys? Over the following years, others produced lists which included the 2000ft hills, but none of them became accepted.

In 1992, Alan Dawson produced his book *The Relative Hills of Britain*. This lists all of the hills in Britain, regardless of height, so long as they have an all-round relative height of at least 150m compared to the surrounding land. In other words they had to be at least 150m high and have a 150m drop, or prominence. Numbering over 1500, these hills were named The Marilyns and in Scotland included all the hills in the 2000ft to 2500ft range, known at the time as Lesser Corbetts, abbreviated to LCs and known as 'Elsies'.

All of The Corbetts are listed as Marilyns, since the generally accepted height separation criterion for the Corbetts is 500ft (152.40m). However, not all of The Munros are Marilyns because Munro's selection was subjective, rather than based on a specific height separation criterion. Over the years, the fact that Munro set no absolute method of determining what is, and what is not, a Munro has been a cause of consternation to many.

Also in 1992, Fiona Torbet (née Graham) published her own list of Scottish hills in the 2000ft to 2500ft height range in the Scottish based hillwalking magazine *The Great Outdoors*. Dawson and Torbet subsequently met and agreed on a definitive drop based listing for hills in this category with Torbet's maiden name of Graham being given to them; The Torbets no doubt too easily confused with The Corbetts!

In 1995 TACit Press published a booklet of Tables which included The Grahams and in 1997 a new and updated edition the SMC book *Munro's Tables* was published which included, along with Tables of Munros, Corbetts and Donalds, the list of Grahams as compiled by Alan Dawson. 1997 also saw publication of the first Grahams guidebook; *The Grahams A Guide to Scotland's 2,000ft Peaks* by Andrew Dempster.

The Grahams had become firmly established and accepted by the hillwalking community.

The Donalds

In compiling his Table of Lowland Hills, Percy Donald visited every elevation over 2000ft in what he considered the Scottish Lowlands, over a five month period starting in December 1932. It was an impressive achievement, especially since he mainly used public transport, walked all bar one hill on his own and the choice of attire for all his walks was the kilt.

The format of Donald's Tables was similar to that of Munro's Tables where summits were originally classified as Hills and Tops, but are now known as Munros and Munro Tops. Likewise, the summits in Donald's Tables are now known as Donalds and Donald Tops and there are 140 hilltops made up of 89 Donalds and 51 Donald Tops. The inclusive nature of the Table means that it contains all of the Lowland Corbetts (7) and all of the Lowland Grahams (23). Donald's Tables, together with an explanation can be found on page 324.

The formula Donald chose to distinguish between those points which he classified as Hills and those which he considered to be Tops has, like Munro's Tables, been the subject of some discussion ever since!

Unlike the Munros though, where the majority only climb the principal Hills and perhaps less than 20% climb the Munro Tops as well, most of those bagging The Donalds actually climb all 140 Hills and Tops on the list. Much of the challenge of The Donalds is the logistics required to incorporate the outlying Tops into the day's walk. By their nature, Donald rounds are generally substantial undertakings.

Confusing matters slightly is what are known as the New Donalds. Donald's formula and his categorisation into Hills and Tops was not neat enough for some, so a rigid drop-based criterion was applied to create this new list of hills in the Scottish Lowlands over 2000ft.

Regardless of this, as with The Munros, the challenge is in completing Percy Donald's original and historic listing, so the New Donalds are seen as something of an aberration. In any case, climb all 140 Donalds and Donald Tops and by default you climb all of the New Donalds.

The Donald rounds described in this guidebook are by their nature generally quite long, but they are attainable to a fairly fit and competent walker. They can easily be broken down into smaller walks if required and they can also be extended into larger outings for those seeking to complete the list more rapidly. These Lowland hills might not have the same form and rocky nature as those of the Highlands but they do have a charm all of their own and will undoubtedly provide the walker with an entertaining and thoroughly enjoyable experience.

The Grahams

The Grahams are defined as Scottish hills over 2000ft (609.60m) and under 2500ft (762m) in height, which have a distinct all-round height separation of at least 150m.

Fiona Torbet's original list only included hills in the Highlands and involved a drop based criterion of about 150m, together with a distance based criterion of a listed hill being the highest all round point for about two miles. Dawson's list included all of Scotland and was based purely on a 150m drop.

Following Fiona Torbet's death in 1993, Alan Dawson has continued to maintain the official list of Grahams and details of this can be found through his *Relative Hills of Britain* (RHB) website and the *Database of British and Irish Hills* (DOBIH) website. The list has been presented differently in this book to fit with the section numbers already established in the SMC's guidebooks to *The Munros* and *The Corbetts*. The list used for this book is that originally agreed between Alan Dawson and Fiona Torbet and contains 224 Grahams which are listed in the Table starting on page 318.

Rather than just describing the ascent of a particular Graham, this guidebook aims to provide the walker with details of the best available route for a day's hillwalking. In many cases the Graham is combined with another nearby hill to produce a logical round and a number of Graham and Corbett combinations are described.

Since the 23 Lowland Grahams are also Donalds they have been incorporated into the Donald rounds. For the walker solely interested in The Grahams, brief Graham only details have been given where relevant.

As more walkers compleat The Munros and The Corbetts, attention is being focussed on The Grahams. However, it is still fairly unusual to see anyone apart from on the most popular of Grahams. This lack of traffic also means that there are few distinct paths to follow, so despite their stature many Grahams provide quite arduous outings. The smaller nature of these hills means that their summits provide interesting perspectives of their larger neighbours and some of the dullest looking Grahams provide some of the finest viewpoints. Whilst there are Grahams that number amongst the most well known of Scottish peaks, there are a great many obscure ones that will be a revelation.

Oireabhal and Bidigidh above Loch Chliostair, Harris (Noel Williams)

ROUTE DESCRIPTIONS
Hill Heights

Height information has been taken from the Ordnance Survey as the national mapping authority responsible for the maintenance of the definitive record of Britain's geographic features. The SMC is aware of independent surveys undertaken by others. Where these surveys remain unratified by the OS it is the SMC's view that they cannot be deemed to be official. However, the SMC recognises that this unratified survey data might well be accurate and is therefore of relevance to hillwalkers. Where necessary a note of such information is made either in the walk description or in the lists at the back of the book.

Grahams are referenced G1 (Beinn Talaidh) to G224 (Ladylea Hill), depending upon height. A full list of Grahams in order of height is given at the back of the book, together with a table listing all the Grahams laid out in order of SMC Sections which matches the chapters in this book.

Donalds are similarly referenced, D1 (The Merrick) to D89 (Innerdownie). Donald Tops have not been referenced in order of height and are simply identified – DT. A full list of Donalds and Donald Tops in order of height is given at the back of the book, together with Donald's Tables listing all the Donalds and Donald Tops.

Mapping

Route maps illustrate route descriptions and serve as aids to planning and have been drawn from out of copyright mapping suplemented by on-the-ground observation. The detail on these maps is not complete and they should not take the place of a proper map.

The recommended maps for hillwalking are the Ordnance Survey 1:50k Landranger Series and in the heading for each walk the letter L followed by a number, denotes the relevant OS map. The OS also produce an Explorer Series of maps at a larger scale of 1:25k. The heights of features are generally taken from either the OS 1:50k maps series or the 1:25k series.

Harvey Maps' 1:25k Superwalker and 1:40k British Mountain Maps series are on waterproof and tearproof paper and cover a number of popular mountain areas. Harvey also publish a number of summit map enlargements.

UK mapping uses metric measurements, so distances and heights in the text are in kilometres (km) and metres (m). Distances when approaching by car are sometimes in miles to aid measurement via a car mileometer.

Six figure grid references identify certain locations and are preceded by two OS grid letters to provide a unique reference to within 100m.

The maps in this book use the following symbols to indicate the status of a summit:

◆ **Graham** (224); 2000ft (609.6m) to below 2500ft (762m); minimum 150m drop

◇ **Graham Top** (776); 2000ft (609.6m) to below 2500ft (762m); minimum 30m drop

■ **Donald** (89); Lowlands, over 2000ft (609.6m) Note: 23 Donalds are also Grahams and 7 Donalds are also Corbetts. Others are Graham Tops and Corbett Tops. In all of these instances the 'other appropriate symbol' has been placed within the Donald symbol.

☐ **Donald Tops** (51); Lowlands, less distinct summit heights over 2000ft (609.6m). Some Donald Tops are also Graham Tops. In these instances the Graham Top symbol has been placed within the Donald Top symbol.

▲ **Munro** (282); 3000ft (914.4m) and higher

△ **Munro Top** (227); 3,000ft (914.4m) and higher, less distinct summit heights

● **Corbett** (220); 2500ft (762m) to below 3000ft (914.4m); minimum 500ft (152.4m) drop

○ **Corbett Top** (450); 2500ft (762m) to below 3000ft (914.4m); minimum 30m drop

⊗ Other summit

Distances, Height Gain & Time
Distances and heights have been rounded up to the nearest 500m and 10m respectively. Ascent times are calculated on the basis of 4.5km per hour for distance walked, plus 10m per minute (1 hour per 600m) for climbing uphill. Times have been rounded up to the nearest 5 minutes.

Timings are a close metric approximation to Naismith's rule. No allowance has been made for stops but an allowance has made for difficult ground and for steep or difficult descents during the walk. This has been based on Langmuir's method of adding 10 minutes per 300m of difficult descent, a timing which has been applied a little more liberally and is particularly relevant to long descents at the end of the day.

Where descriptions relate to the traverse of two or more hills, the distance, height gain and time at selected summits are cumulative from the start. The overall distance, height gain and time has been highlighted in blue.

Parking, Roads, Tracks & Paths
Three levels of parking have been identified on the maps. 🅿 indicates an official, or publicly maintained car park, or a parking area such as a layby. 🅿 indicates that there is adequate off-road parking. 🅿 indicates that parking is limited or restricted, such as in small pull-offs or verge parking.

Throughout the text, road means a tarmac surface, usually public. Where a surfaced road is private, as in some estate roads, this is mentioned. Track means any unsurfaced way such as used by forestry or estate vehicles; usually private. Atv track means any less distinct route on the hill used by all-terrain-vehicles such as quad bikes. Tracks can usually be biked, whereas it is unlikely that atv tracks can be. Path means a clear pedestrian route on the ground, often a stalkers' or hillwalkers' path.

Routes
Continuous red lines on the maps indicate the principle routes and dashed lines some alternatives.

The objective of this book is to describe routes to the Grahams and the Donalds. However, the nature of these hills means that it is often possible to extend routes to take in nearby hills and routes have been described with this in mind. Without stating it every time, it will often be possible to shorten a walk after the principal objective has been climbed, either by returning via the route of ascent, or by some other route. Where extensions are logical these have normally been described or mentioned with full distances and times given.

Routes have generally been described to take in the principal objective first then perhaps a neighbouring higher hill. However, these are only suggestions. On the day, a reverse approach to the one described might better suit the conditions or the party.

MOUNTAIN SAFETY & WEATHER
Participation Statement
The Mountaineering Council of Scotland recognises that hillwalking, climbing and mountaineering are activities with a danger of personal injury or death. Participants in these activities should be aware of and accept these risks and be responsible for their own actions and involvement.

Navigation, Equipment & Planning
Good navigation skills, equipment, clothing and forward planning can all help reduce the chance of an accident. While mobile phones and GPS can help in communications and in locating your position, the former do not work over all of Scotland and both rely on batteries and electronics which can fail or be easily damaged. Consequently, they can never be a substitute for navigation skills with map and compass, first aid or general mountain skills. The potential hazards of winter conditions, rivers in spate, or challenging navigation from changes in weather should always be remembered.

Weather Forecasting
Although weather forecasting has improved over the years, it is not a precise science. The smaller nature of the hills covered in this guidebook means that they are generally less affected by low cloud and bad weather than the higher hills. The downside to this though is that many of the hills in this book have less defined routes and less defined features than their higher counterparts, so navigation in poor weather can prove challenging. There are many forecasts available but a few are worth mentioning. The Mountain Weather Information Service (MWIS) has forecasts covering Scotland in five areas. The Meteorological Office (Met Office) also has Mountain Weather forecasts covering the main mountain areas of Scotland in two areas. Links to MWIS and the Met Office are also available through the MCofS website. In addition, BBC TV and Radio forecasts, which at times include a walkers' forecast, also have regularly updated web based forecasts. These are all available for mobile phones, together with other mobile phone app forecasts.

Avalanches

Avalanches occur with great regularity in the Scottish hills. The lower nature of the Grahams and Donalds means that for much of the time they can be less susceptible to avalanche risk than the higher hills. However, avalanches can happen wherever there is snow lying on ground of sufficient angle, so these lower hills are not avalanche risk free. Winter walkers should familiarise themselves with the principles of snow structure and avalanche prediction.

While the ability to make your own assessment of risk is vital, snow and avalanche predictions for the major mountain areas are produced by the Sportscotland Avalanche Information Service (SAIS) and are readily available throughout the winter. As well as on the SAIS website, which can also be linked to from the MCofS website, these reports can be found at police stations, sports shops, tourist information centres and on display boards in mountain areas. The About Avalanches section on the SAIS website makes useful reading. *A Chance in a Million?* is the classic work on avalanches and is recommended reading for anyone venturing onto the Scottish hills in winter.

Mountain Rescue

In the event of an accident, contact the police, either by phone (999) or in person. It is often better to stay with the casualty but in a party of two, one may have to leave to summon help. If the casualty has to be left, leave them in a warm, comfortable, sheltered, and well-marked place. Further information is available on the Mountain Rescue Scotland website.

Midges, Clegs, Deer Ked & Ticks

Biting insects such as midges, clegs and deer ked can make things unpleasant at times. Ticks however can carry Lyme disease and incidents appear to be increasing, so it is worth reading up on them. The MCofS, the BMC and Lyme Disease Action UK all have relevant information.

OTHER USEFUL INFORMATION

Access

The Land Reform (Scotland) Act 2003 gives everyone statutory access rights to most land and inland water including mountains, moorland, woods and forests, grassland, paths and tracks, and rivers and lochs. People only have these rights if they exercise them responsibly by respecting people's privacy, safety and livelihoods, and Scotland's environment. Equally, land managers have to manage their land and water responsibly in relation to access rights. The Outdoor Access Scotland website and the Scottish Outdoor Access Code provide detailed guidance on these responsibilities.

Stalking, Shooting & Lambing

Deer management takes place during many months of the year but the sensitive period is the stag stalking season, from 1st July to 20th October. Few estates actually start at the beginning of the season and most stalking takes place from August onwards. Hinds continue to be culled until 15th February. Requests may be made to either avoid areas where stalking is taking place, or to keep to standard routes and ridgelines. Stalking does not normally take place on Sundays, although requests to avoid disturbing deer on the hills may still be made. There is no stalking on National Trust for Scotland land.

Heading for the Scottish Hills provides information and contact phone numbers to help hillwalkers and climbers find out where red deer stalking is taking place over the stag stalking season. This can be found online by entering Heading for the Scottish Hills into a search engine. A link is also available from the MCofS website.

The grouse shooting season is from 12th August until 10th December. If you are heading onto the hills with a dog it is important to avoid disturbance to sheep, especially during the lambing season between March and May.

Footpath Erosion, Cairns & Memorials

It is the responsibility of all walkers to minimise their erosive effect on the mountain landscape. The proliferation of navigation cairns detracts from the feeling of wildness and may be confusing rather than helpful as regards route-finding. The indiscriminate building of cairns and memorials on the hills should be discouraged.

Bikes, Cars & Transport

A number of routes in this book advocate the use of mountain bikes for approaches along estate and forestry tracks. Bikes can cause erosion when used on footpaths and open hillsides and should only be used on prepared surfaces such as vehicular or forest tracks and some stalkers' paths. Access rights do not extend to vehicles being driven up private roads without permission.

Most walkers will arrive by car. For those using public transport, then up-to-date timetables are best found via the internet. Transport Scotland, Traffic Scotland and Traveline Scotland (free app) are all useful.

Bothies

The Mountain Bothies Association maintains about 80 bothies on various estates throughout Scotland. None of these are owned by the MBA, but belong to estates which generously allow their use. A number of bothies are closed during the Stalking Season. Visit the MBA's website for further information.

Mountaineering Council of Scotland (MCofS)

The MCofS is the representative body for climbers and hillwalkers in Scotland. One of its primary concerns is the continued free access to the hills. Information about bird restrictions, stalking and general access issues can be obtained from the MCofS. Any hill user encountering problems regarding access should contact the MCofS.

Scottish Mountaineering Club

The SMC produces guidebooks for Hillwalkers, Scramblers and Climbers. All profits from these guidebooks go to the Scottish Mountaineering Trust (SMT) and provide much of the SMT's revenue – see opposite.

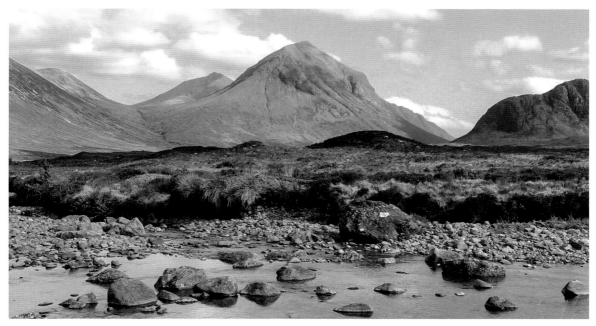

Marsco and the Allt Dearg Mòr (Tom Prentice)

Scottish Mountaineering Trust

All profits from the sale of this publication go to fund the Scottish Mountaineering Trust. All grants given by the Trust benefit mountains or the people who enjoy them.

Since 1990, the Trust has granted more than £1 million for causes such as:

Scottish Mountaineering Trust

* Renovation of Club Huts
* Footpath construction and maintenance
* Land purchase, such as John Muir Trust acquisitions
* Supporting visually impaired people to attend Glenmore Lodge courses
* Mountain Rescue
* Supporting young people to go on expeditions
* Supporting access
* Supporting environmental conservation

Our funds come from Trust publications, such as Scottish Mountaineering Club guidebooks, as well as donations and bequests from the public.

If you would like to donate to the Trust, or to see how the trust could help you or your organisation, please go to: *www.smc.org.uk/trust/* or email: *trust@smc.org.uk*

SECTION 0a
Galloway & The Lowthers

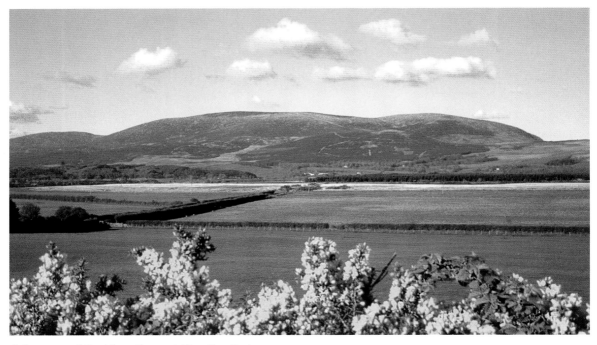

Cairnsmore of Fleet from the west (Tom Prentice)

Knee of Cairnsmore; 657m; DT; L83; NX509656

Cairnsmore of Fleet; 711m; (G79); (D28); L83; NX501670; *moor of cairns, above the Fleet. There are two prehistoric cairns on the plateau*

Meikle Mulltaggart; 612m; DT; L83; NX512678

A massive whalebacked granite intrusion, this southernmost Graham dominates the western reaches of the Solway Firth. In addition to Cairnsmore of Fleet itself which is also a Donald, it includes the Donald Tops of Knee of Cairnsmore and Meikle Mulltaggart. On a clear day the views south from these hills extends to the Lake District, the Isle of Man and the Mountains of Mourne in Ireland.

A circular and relatively dry route taking in all three tops starts at the Big Water of Fleet Viaduct (NX557642). This is reached from Gatehouse of Fleet via the B796 north beside the Water of Fleet from where a minor road leads to the Nature Reserve Information Centre then along a track for 1km, to a parking area just after the viaduct. The viaduct is an imposing 20 arch structure which once carried the former Dumfries to Stranraer line and featured in the Hitchcock film

of John Buchan's book *The Thirty Nine Steps*.

Take the track on the west side of the river and follow it north into the

forest, past a turn-off right to Meikle Cullendoch, then west to exit the forest. Continue across trackless ground to climb the east ridge of the

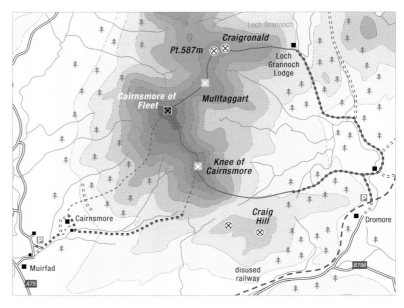

Knee of Cairnsmore. The OS 1:25k and 1:50k maps show the top at a cairn at NX509654 but the 1:10k map shows a point 200m to the north to be 1m higher. A faint path leads along the ridge, across the Nick of Clashneach, then up to the summit shelter and trig point on Cairnsmore of Fleet (**8km; 650m; 2h 50min**).

Immediately before the summit is a granite memorial to the crews of eight aircraft which crashed on the hill between 1940 and 1979, the earliest a Luftwaffe Heinkel bomber and the latest a USAF Phantom jet. The cairns on both Cairnsmore and the Knee are of Bronze Age vintage. The desolate corrie to the east hosts the remote Spout of the Clints Waterfall and is a National Nature Reserve; an example of open moorland ecosystem, common before blanket afforestation. On the north side of the hill lies Billy Marshall's Cave, used for smuggling by the legendary gypsy king who died in 1792, aged 120!

Drop north-east to Nick of the Saddle and climb Meikle Mulltaggart, picking up an atv track. The top is unmarked and the track bypasses the summit to the west of it (**9.5 km; 700m; 3h 15min**).

The return is made via Loch Grannoch Lodge at the end of Loch

South to Knee of Cairnsmore (Rab Anderson)

Grannoch. Trackless, rough going leads northwards over an unnamed 587m top, then east down the ridge of Craigronald. Cliffs immediately above the lodge can be avoided either north or south of it. From the lodge, follow the forest track south, taking a right turn after 2.5km, then another right after 2km at the house of Meikle Cullendoch, followed by a left shortly thereafter to reach the start (19km; 720m; 5h 35min).

Cairnsmore of Fleet can be climbed by itself via the path from Cairnsmore Farm near Newton Stewart, reached from the signposted parking area at NX464632 (**6km; 690m; 2h 30min**); (12km; 690m; 4h). Meikle Mulltaggart and Knee of Cairnsmore can easily be added, climbing the former first then gaining the latter by back-tracking to pass beneath the summit of Cairnsmore of Fleet. Descend south-west off the Knee to gain the rough track which starts at NX506641 and leads to the farm (17km; 900m; 5h 35min).

Descending to Meikle Mulltaggart from Cairnsmore of Fleet (Keith Fergus)

Curleywee, left, and Lamachan Hill over Loch Dee (Andrew Fraser)

Larg Hill; *676m; (D49); L77; NX424757; shank hill. Gaelic 'lorg', shank, thigh, leg (in shape)*
Lamachan Hill; *717m; (G71); (D26) L77; NX435769; hill above Lamachan (farm). Mapped as Lommachan Hill (1654). Perhaps from Gaelic 'lomach', bare place*
Curleywee; *674m; (D51); L77; NX454769; hill of the eagle? The burn in the northern corrie was mapped as Korreilleury Burn in 1654: maybe Gaelic 'coire', corrie, or 'corr', pointed hill, with 'na-h'iolaire', of the eagle*
Millfore; *657m; (G169); (D62); L77; NX477754; cold hill from Gaelic 'meall fuar'. Mapped Mullfear (1654)*

Lying between the A712 to the south and Loch Trool and Loch Dee to the north, these hills offer fine high-level ridge walking. They can be done in one long outing as described, although the inclusion of Millfore adds considerably to the day. Millfore can be climbed separately, and if so, is better approached from Craigencallie or the Black Loch, as described at the end. Start at the Bruce's Stone car park at the east end of Loch Trool. The stone commemorates Robert the Bruce's victory in 1307 at the Steps of Trool, the battle which opened the war of independence.

From the car park, follow the track down then eastward past the Falls of Buchan and Glenhead and across the vehicle bridge to the south side of the Glenhead Burn. Continue south-east on the forest track (National Cycle Route 7), rising through the trees for 1km until it crosses the Shiel Burn at NX435790. Leave the track here and follow the line of the burn then its right

fork up to Nick of the Lochans, between Mulldonach and Lamachan Hill.

If omitting Larg Hill it is best to take the ridge to the left or east of the Shiel Burn which leads to Bennanbrack. A wall then leads right to the summit of Lamachan Hill.

To take in Larg Hill from Nick of the Lochans, climb the steep slope to the south onto Cambrick Hill until it starts to level out then traverse south along the western side of Lamachan Hill to gain the Nick of the Bushy col. A wall can then be followed south-west

Curleywee, left, and Millfore from Lamachan Hill (Tom Prentice)

along the ridge to Larg Hill (**7km; 620m; 2h 35min**). Larg Hill was the site of an airship crash in 1917.

Return to Nick of the Bushy and follow the wall onto the summit plateau of Lamachan Hill. The main ridge now switchbacks for 2.5km of fine ridge walking, first east-north-east to Bennanbrack then south-east

past Nick of Corners Gale and Nick of Curleywee to the shapely Curleywee (**11km; 920m; 4h 5min**). Known as the 'Matterhorn of the South' this peak is finely situated above Loch Dee.

If omitting Milfore, descend north over White Hill then drop through rough terrain either direct or via an atv track to pick up the route of the

Southern Upland Way west of Loch Dee which leads back to the start (**17.5km; 1010m; 5h 45min**). If continuing to Millfore, take the ridge south for 800m to a wall which is followed south-east to the Loup of Laggan; the col between the Pulnee and White-Laggan Burns. From here it is 2km of

▶

Millfore from the south (Jim Teesdale)

complex but interesting ground east to Millfore with its trig point (**14.5km; 1200m; 5h 25min**). The ascent passes first the Black Loch then the White Lochan of Drigmorn. The White Lochan was used for curling in the 19th century, the stone structure on its northern shore having been being built by soldiers stationed at Newton Stewart during the Crimean War.

From Millfore the quickest descent is north-west for 2km, crossing the upper reaches of the Black Laggan Burn, over a small subsidiary ridge, then continuing downhill to the path on the west side of the White Laggan Burn. This leads past White Laggan bothy to join the forest track, which is followed west for 2.5km to the col between Loch Dee and Loch Trool. From here, either follow the Southern Upland Way north of the Glenhead Burn or continue along the forest track on the south side of the burn, used on the approach. Both lead past Glenhead to the car park, the track being quicker and drier but less scenic (**24.5km; 1300m; 8h**).

Millfore can be climbed by itself by starting at the right-angled corner (NX503774) about 600m south of Craigencallie at the end of the minor road, which leaves the A712 and runs round the west side of Clattering-shaws Loch. Follow the burn up the edge of the forestry, go over Cairngarroch then past the Nick of Rushes (fence with stile at NX485769) and the bizarrely named Buckdas of Cairnbaber to reach Millfore (**4km; 560m; 1h 50min**).

Either return the same way or descend east-north-east for 1km to gain a forest track which leads back to the start (**7.5km; 560m; 2h 50min**). Another route from the south starts at the Black Loch car park (NX499730) and follows a forestry track to a saddle then climbs the south-east ridge (**5km; 500m; 2h**); (**10km; 500m; 3h 25min**).

Another option is to bike to the south side of Loch Dee, quicker and easier from Craigencallie, then make a circuit of these hills, or both Grahams, via White Laggan bothy with Curleywee being climbed only the once then bypassed on its south side on the traverse between the Grahams.

Galloway Hills

The main group of Galloway Hills effectively comprises 19 Donalds and 7 Donalds Tops, of which 5 are Grahams and 3 are Corbetts, including the highest hill in the South of Scotland, The Merrick. It is a fairly complex group of hills which is covered here in six walks although there are many other ways of climbing the various hill groups, either in shorter, or more extended outings.

Those interested in climbing just the Grahams can tackle these as two pairs and a single. Cairnsmore of Fleet is easily split from its two attendant Donald Tops and quickly climbed via the path from Cairnsmore to the south-west, as mentioned in the route description. Lamachan Hill and Millfore can be tackled from any of the starts described in the route description, omitting Larg Hill, however Curlywee lies between them and although this can be avoided it is perhaps better to take it in. Similarly, Craignaw and Mullwharcher can be split from the Donald round which includes The Merrick, however the reality of the terrain and the fact that a good path leads to, or from, the summit of The Merrick means that there is in fact little to be gained in doing so.

The main northern group of hills is formed by three distinct south to north running parallel chains which lend themselves to long ridge walks along the crests, although getting back to the start points can prove a logistical problem due to forests and burns, unless transport can be arranged at either end, or overnight stays are made in bothies or by camping.

The seven hilltops on the western chain from Caerloch Dubh to Benyellary, of which five are known as The Awful Hand (Benyellary being the thumb and The Merrick the forefinger), can be climbed in a linear traverse from the Stinchar Bridge car park in the north to the Glen Trool car park in the south (18km; 940m; 6h 15min). A circuit of these seven tops is also possible from the Kirriereoch car park via the principal route described for Shalloch on Minnoch by continuing from Kirriereoch Hill over The Merrick to Benyellary. Either descend Kirn Brae (steep) or the north-west ridge to gain a forest track at NX386855 which leads back to the car park (27.5km; 1300m; 8h 45min). A descent can be made off The Merrick down the west ridge to gain a track at NX388868. These hills, in whole or in part, can also be climbed from Forest Drive via the forest track down the west side of Loch Riecawr, which opens up the possibility of extending the round to include Craignaw, Dungeon Hill and Mullwarchar with the Tunskeen bothy (NX425906) perhaps being of use.

The eastern chain of nine hilltops from Corran of Portmark to Meikle Millyea is known as the Rhinns of Kells and although covered here in two walks, the ridge can be climbed in one linear outing. This can be done from Green Well of Scotland, as for the route taking in Meaul and Carlin's Cairn then continuing south to Meikle Millyea. There are three possible descents from here. The first is as for the route described for the Corserine to Meikle Millyea round to gain the Forrest Lodge car park (23km; 1130m; 7h 30min). The second gains the Southern Upland Way then the car park at NX558826 (22.5km; 1130m; 7h 25min). A third option is to continue over Little Millyea and Darrou to go down a rough firebreak directly to the Southern Upland Way and the River Dee crossing at NX496794 from where the road end can be reached at Craigencallie (24.5km; 1200m; 8h). This traverse relies on a secondary means of transport being available. It is possible to climb all these hills as a round from the Forrest Lodge car park. This is done by starting with Meikle Millyea then climbing the ridge northwards to Corran of Portmark then returning over Bow to climb Cairnsgarroch. A descent can be made from here south past Craigchessie then down a firebreak to gain a forestry track which is crossed to descend a felled area where the Polmaddy Burn can be crossed and followed east to a stile to reach another firebreak leading to a forest track which runs south then south-east back to the start (30km; 1340m; 10h). Further clear felling of the forest may open up the routes to the various tracks and provide other routes across the Polmaddy Burn.

Looking across Loch Enoch to The Merrick, left, and Kirriereoch Hill (Andrew Fraser)

Benyellary; 719m; (DT); L77; NX414839

The Merrick; 843m; (D1); L77; NX427855; branched or spreading mountain. Bin Maerack (1654), i.e. Gaelic 'beinn meurach'. Beinn was lost, replaced by "The" from 1755

Mullwharchar; 692m; (G116); (D39) L77; NX454866; hill of the lapwing. Gaelic 'meall na h-adharcan' or the hunting horn 'adhairce'. Mapped Mayllhorkun hill (1654), Millwharchar (1797)

Dungeon Hill; 620m; (D83); L77; NX460850; hill above the Dungeon lochs, there being another of the name 6km east. Perhaps from the rocky fastness appearance of the hill

Craignaw; 645m; (G180); (D68) L77; NX459833; Craggy hill of the rock. Gaelic 'creag na h' aill'. The hill's surface is a mass of rocks, including the Devil's Bowling Green. Mapped Kraigna (1654), Kraignall (1755). Possibly 'creag an atha', cliff of the ford, from the crossing of the Silver Flowe below

---

This superb route combines The Merrick as the highest hill in Southern Scotland with the Dungeon of Buchan range as this area's most rugged and arguably finest hills. The first half to The Merrick is on good paths and easy walking, the Dungeon section is pathless and rough going. This reflects the different geology, metamorphic on The Merrick and granite on the Dungeon, the junction being clearly visible on the descent from The Merrick to Loch Enoch. It is possible to split the traverse into two equally fine walks, as described at the end, but the nature of the terrain means there is little to be gained in terms of time or effort by doing so.

Start at the Bruce's Stone car park at the end of the road in Glen Trool, where a path is signposted to The Merrick. Follow this for 2km, first above the Buchan Burn then in forestry to the basic bothy at Culsharg. From here the path climbs Benyellary for 2km, the ascent being steep but on delightfully dry and short grass. Thereafter follow the wall across the ridge of the Neive of the Spit, then north-east across The Merrick's gently rising summit plateau to the top where a trig point sits above the steep northern face (**6.5km; 770m; 2h 45min**). The views are extensive, with the distant peaks of England's Lake District, the Mourne Mountains of Ireland, Arran and the Highlands all visible.

From here on is largely pathless. Descend to Loch Enoch by heading east-south-east at first to gain Redstone Rig then head for the north-west corner of Loch Enoch. The butterfly-shaped Loch Enoch is notable for a number of reasons. It is the highest and at 39.3m, the deepest loch in Southern Scotland. In *his book The Merrick and Neighbouring Hills*, J.McBain describes how in 1918 he drilled holes in the partly frozen loch to check the depth by plumbline. The island on the loch has its own loch-in-loch and in former years the fine silver sand was a prized commodity for sharpening scythes. The remains of a 1940

▶

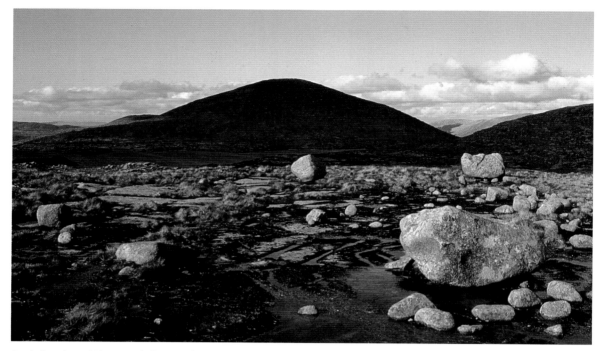

Loch Enoch and the rounded cone of Mullwharchar from the south (Tom Prentice)

Whitley bomber lie on the southern shore.

To the north-east rises the cone of Mullwharchar, the remotest hill in Southern Scotland and the first of the Dungeon of Buchan range. The ascent involves weaving a line up through grass and rock (**9.5km; 970m; 4h**). Mullwharchar became the unexpected focus of environmental protest in the early 1970s when a proposed nuclear waste repository on the hill was defeated at public inquiry.

From Mullwharchar descend rough ground south to the Pulskaig Burn outfall from Loch Enoch, then head south-east onto the north ridge of Dungeon Hill, known as the Brishie. The summit (**11.5km; 1090m; 4h 50min**) gives a fine view south down the valley of the Cooran Lane, surely a prime candidate for 'rewilding' with the removal of forestry and tracks to reinstate a previous wilderness. The concentric rings of the floating bog of the Silver Flowe are prominent. This is a National Nature Reserve and home to the fine azure hawker dragonfly.

Descend west to the foot of the rise up to Craignairny then cut down the side of this to the Nick of the Dungeon col. Climb the increasingly rocky north–west ridge of Craignaw to the Deil's Bowling Green, an area of flat granite littered with boulders. Beyond, a steep rocky slope leads past a northern top to the summit (**14km; 1240m; 5h 45min**). This gives excellent views of The Merrick and Loch Enoch, as well as east to the Rhinns of Kells. Some 200m to the south-west of the summit, below a steep cliff, is a memorial to the crew of an American F1-11 jet which crashed here in 1979.

Descend south for 600m then head down rough ground to cross the Mid Burn between Loch Neldricken and Loch Valley to gain a path. The path gives difficult and boggy going, past Loch Valley then down and

Dungeon Hill from the flanks of Craignaw (Rab Anderson)

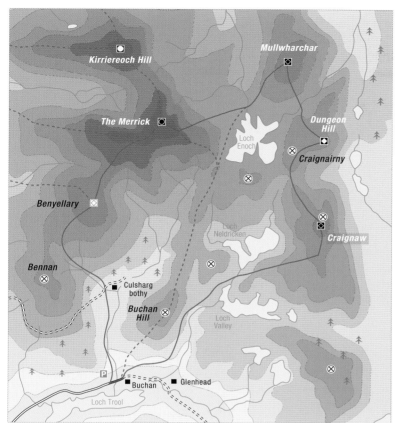

around the side of Buchan Hill above the Garland Burn. Gain the track at Buchan farm and follow this past the Falls of Buchan back up to the car park (20km; 1260m; 7h 45min).

The Merrick and the two Graham's of the Dungeon hills can be done as separate walks. For both routes it will be necessary to gain or descend from the south-west end of Loch Enoch, either by the good but boggy path past Loch Valley and Loch Neldricken, or by Buchan Hill. Points of interest on the former are the rock face of the Old Man of The Merrick at NR437846 and the Murder Hole of Loch Neldricken. This latter is a grim eye of water immortalised in S.R.Crockett's book *The Raiders*.

The route via Buchan Hill starts on the east side of the Buchan Burn, immediately after the bridge on the road to Buchan farm. This is a drier, more scenic but perhaps rougher walk than by the lochs and leads over Buchan Hill to the Rig of Loch Enoch. From the south-west corner of Loch Enoch The Merrick is easily climbed by Redstone Rig while Mullwharchar can be accessed via the rough west side of Loch Enoch.

South to Craignaw from Craignairny (Tom Prentice)

Shalloch on Minnoch; 775m; (D13); L77; NX407905; hunting place on the middle hill? Gaelic 'sealg', hunt and 'meadhonach', middle. Mapped Shellach of Meannock (1654), Shalloch Cairn (1775)

Caerloch Dhu; 659m; (DT); NX400920

Tarfessock; 697m; (D35); L77; NX409891; bearded, shaggy hill. Gaelic 'tòrr feusagach'. Mapped Torfessock (1797)

Tarfessock South Top; 620m; (DT); L77; NX413886

Kirriereoch Hill; 786m; (D11); L77; NX420870; hill of the greyish quarter (or corrie). Gaelic 'ceathramh' (or 'coire') 'riabhach'. The hill seems to be named from Kirriereoch farm: 'ceathramh' is a land measure

These hills form the northernmost fingers of the Awful Hand, the ridge of hills of which The Merrick (the forefinger) is highest. A 4km forest track approach is more than compensated for by an interesting and characterful route. Access is via the unclassified road between Straiton and Glentrool Village which bounds the hills on their west side.

About 4.5 miles (7.5km) north of Glentrool Village, and 2.5 miles (4km) south of the Barr road junction at Rowantree Bridge, turn onto a track signed Kirriereoch and park at a Forestry Commission picnic site by the Water of Minnoch (NX358867). The once popular route via Shalloch Farm from the Rowantree Bridge car park, is overgrown with forestry and no longer recommended.

From the parking area continue

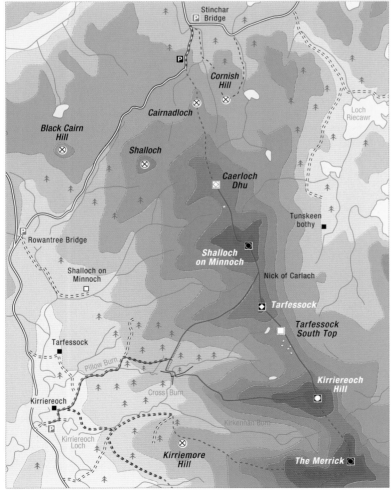

along the track and turn sharp left followed by a sharp right just short of Kirriereoch farm. After 300m a track comes in from the right. The return route from The Merrick and Benyellary (see the Galloway Hills information panel on p18) takes this track. Continue straight ahead and on for another 1.8km to cross a bridge over the Pillow Burn. About 250m beyond the bridge, keep right where the track forks and follow it to its end (NX389881). Providing The Merrick and Benyellary are not being included in the round, a mountain bike would assist this section since the track has only moderate inclines.

Just before the track ends, turn left onto a path beside old wooden fence posts and ascend the clearing between the plantations. It is worth noting that the return route ascends the continuation of the clearing and fence posts immediately below the track.

Head up the hill to gain gloriously easy walking on the west ridge of Tarfessock. Rather than follow the ridge, take a rising traverse northeast to gain the Nick of Carclach, the col between Tarfessock and Shalloch on Minnoch. After a further 800m the summit plateau of Shalloch on Minnoch is gained. The 775m summit is clearly marked on the 1:25k map and lies near the corrie edge, about 300m south-east of the 768m trig point (**7.5km; 560m; 2h 40min**).

The Donald Top of Caerloch Dhu is unhelpfully situated to the north and requires an out and back trip to attain its summit. This is the westernmost hill on Donald's List and is gained by descending the broad ridge north of the trig point (**9km; 590m; 3h 5min**). Whilst it only involves an ascent of 30m or so, it requires a more substantial 140m climb back to the trig point on Shalloch on Minnoch.

Kirriereoch Hill, left, Tarfessock and Shalloch of Minnoch from the south-east (Tom Prentice)

From Shalloch on Minnoch return south to the Nick of Carclach then continue onto Tarfessock. Rough and rocky ground studded with lochans leads over Tarfessock South Top to a fence at the col below Kirriereoch's screes. Avoid these on the left by a steep ascent on grass to arrive at a wall which straddles the hill. The high point probably lies on the rounded ground about 180m south-east of the wall, but the OS 1:10k map indicates two 786m points here, some 100m apart (**15km; 1020m; 5h 15min**).

It is possible to extend this walk to The Merrick and perhaps Benyellary see the Galloway Hills information panel on p18 for details.

To descend, return to the wall and follow intermittent paths down the west ridge. Where the wall turns sharply south, pass through it and follow a rough path beside metal fence posts to reach a fence surrounding forestry in the glen. Follow the fence west towards the Cross Burn to an old stile on the right. Go over the fence here and follow the path north to meet the burn. Ford the burn and continue between a fence on your left and forestry on your right,

to where the plantation ends. This is the clearing below the track, identified on the ascent. The start of the clearing is extremely marshy, but the track is soon gained and followed back to the start (**22.5km; 1030m; 7h 15min**).

These hills can also be traversed via an out and back route from the north, using an atv track which starts from a passing place at NX394947, just south of where the road exits, or enters the forestry. There is parking at Stinchar Bridge 1km further north, and some limited off-road parking

closer to the start. The track leads for 4km over Cairnadloch and Caerloch Dhu to Shalloch on Minnoch.

Tarfessock then Kirriereoch Hill are included as above (**10km; 740m; 3h 40min**) with a return along the tops (**20km; 1040m; 6h 50min**). A variation could also be made over Cornish Hill (NX404941) using the waymarked trail to or from the Stinchar Bridge car park. A linear traverse to Glen Trool can also be made and is described in the Galloway Hills information panel on p18.

Descending to Caerloch Dhu from Shalloch on Minnoch (Tom Prentice)

Carlin's Cairn, Meaul, centre, and Bow from the flanks of Corran of Portmark (Andrew Fraser)

Corran of Portmark; 623m (D80); L77; NX509936; pointed hill, above Portmark (on Loch Doon), from Gaelic 'corr', pointed. Alternatively Gaelic 'corran', sickle, from shape of late snow wreath seen from Carsphairn. Mapped Corran (1797)

Bow; 613m; (DT); L77; NX508928

Meaul; 695m; (D37); L77; NX500909; hill. Gaelic 'meall', lumpy hill. At one point it would have had an adjective – e.g. 'meall buidhe', yellow hill, which perhaps explains the adjacent hill Bow 'buidhe'

Carlin's Cairn; 807m; (D8); L77; NX496883; the old woman's cairn. Scots 'carline'; in honour of a miller's wife who sheltered Robert the Bruce

Cairnsgarroch; 659m; (D60); L77; NX515913; pointed from Gaelic 'càrn sgòrach', or possibly, cold and windy, hill 'càrn sgàireach'. Mapped Kingswell Hill (1654), Cairnsgorroch (1797)

Lying on the eastern edge of the Galloway Forest Park, the Rhinns of Kells ridge runs for 18km, not falling below 620m for 10km. This route takes in the hills of the northern part of the ridge and offers open walking with superb views north to Cairnsmore of Carsphairn and west to The Merrick. Once on the tops the hills are generally grassier than the southern section of the ridge, but the descent north from Cairnsgarroch is rocky, rough and wet and gives slow going. The Galloway Hills information panel (see p18) includes details of the full Rhinns of Kells traverse.

Parking is available at a bend on the A713 at Bridgend – Green Well of Scotland. This is just south of the bridge over the Water of Deugh and one mile (1.6km) north of Carsphairn village. Cross the bridge, turn left down the access road to Holm of Daltallochan and follow the track beyond for 2km to Garryhorn. In the 18th century, Garryhorn was the local headquarters of Grierson of Lag, whose dragoons hunted and killed numerous Covenanters. Believed to be in league with the devil, at his funeral a black corbie perched on the hearse all the way to the grave.

Continue for 1.8km to the abandoned Woodhead Lead Mines. In its heyday between 1839 and 1873, this had a population of 300 with its own school. All that remains are numerous ruined buildings and 11 shafts, the deepest of which is reputed to be 95m. Follow the track to the tree surrounded highest ruins, the track fades as you get close, then take a clearer track on the right which leads north past a fenced-off ventilation shaft to a gate in a wall before a conifer plantation. Go through the gate and turn left onto an atv track which ascends the flanks of Knockower and on to Corran of Portmark (named Coran on OS maps). Leave the atv and ascend to the summit cairn, one of the finest viewpoints in Galloway (**6km; 430m; 2h**).

Cross the fence and follow another atv track on its west side over the Donald Top of Bow towards Meaul. At NX500917, near the atv track on the

Section 0a – Galloway & The Lowthers

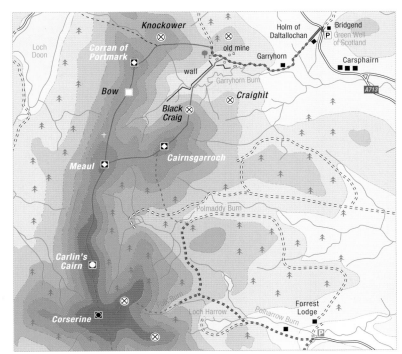

a miller's wife, who in return for aid offered to a fugitive Robert the Bruce was granted land in Polmaddy to the east. From Carlin's Cairn it is possible to continue south to the Donald and Corbett of Corserine by way of the col known as the Riders' Gap then return to Carlin's Cairn; add (2.5km; 210m; 1h).

Retrace the route north to Meaul then pick up a wall and follow this down eastwards then up onto Cairnsgarroch (**17km; 970m; 5h 20min**). Descend Cairnsgarroch initially northeast down a broad, rough and mostly pathless ridge, then in a more northerly direction to Black Craig. From here descend the rough and tiring slopes east of the crags to a point where the Garryhorn Burn is crossed by a wall at NX524930. Here the girders of a ruined footbridge can be used to cross the burn. About 350m downstream a log carries the fence from the col between Cairnsgarroch and Craighit over the burn, and this can also be used to cross over. Follow the wall towards the mine ruins to join the outward track and follow it back to the start. Great care should be taken in the vicinity of the mines as deep vegetation may obscure open shafts from view (**23.5km, 980m; 7h**).

northern flank of Meaul overlooking Loch Doon, a single upright stone and plaque mark the spot where Covenanter John Dempster is said to have been shot in 1685, following a long chase by Lag's dragoons. A trig point marks the summit of Meaul (**9.5km; 610m; 3h**). Descend to a col which once formed part of a drove road between the Ken and Girvan valleys by way of Loch Doon. An easy climb now leads to Carlin's Cairn (**12.5km; 790m; 4h**). Legend attributes the building of the large cairn here to

Carlin's Cairn, left, Meaul, Corran of Portmark and Cairnsgarroch, right, from Corserine (Rab Anderson)

Corserine from the ridge of the Rhinns of Kells (Rab Anderson)

Corserine; *814m; (D6); L77; NX497870; crossing point of the Rhinns (of Kells, the parish). Gaelic 'crois na rinne'. Corserine lies athwart this north-south range (Gaelic 'rinn', point as in its eastern spur Craigrine; and its western spur Craigtarson, from Gaelic 'tarsuinn', transverse). Mapped Krosrang (1654)*

Millfire; *716m; (DT); L77; NX508847*

Milldown; *738m; (D18); L77; NX511839; brown hill. Gaelic 'meall donn'. Mapped Milldoon (1797)*

Meikle Millyea; *746m; (D15); L77; NX518828; big (grey) hill. Scots 'meikle' and Gaelic 'meall', plus possibly 'liath', so perhaps 'grey hill'. Mapped Mekle Mulle hill (1654). Locally pronounced Millyae*

Corserine, the second highest hill in Galloway, and its attendant hills form the southern part of the Rhinns of Kells ridge, and can be climbed in a fine circuit of Loch Dungeon. The summits alternate between rough grass and rocky outcrops, character-istic of the granite underlying much of the area. The ridge gives tremendous views west over the Silver Flowe to craggy Dungeon Hill and Craignaw, backed by The Merrick.

Start at a car park at the end of the Forrest Lodge road, accessed off the A713 some 2 miles (3.5km) north of St John's Town of Dalry, or just beyond where the road crosses the Polharrow Burn if approaching from the north. The Galloway Hills informa-tion panel contains details of a long return circuit of all the hills on the Rhinns of Kells ridge from this car park, together with a complete linear traverse from Green Well of Scotland to the north, starting as for the previous walk.

Head north towards Forrest Lodge then go left (west) up the forest track, named Birger Natvig Road to pass the house at Fore Bush. After 2km take a right turn at a junction, Robert Watson Road, and cross the Polharrow Burn. Continue straight ahead at another three junctions until after a further 1.5km the track swings right at NX525874. Take to a track on the left and after 200m or so, follow a path off left into the forest on the south side of the Folk Burn, which is crossed (not immediately obvious) after a few hundred metres.

Once it emerges from the forest the path continues west onto Craigrine, the north-east ridge of Corserine, which is climbed to the summit plateau. The summit trig point can be difficult to locate in mist but by keeping the edge of the northern corrie just in sight to the right, it should be spotted on the left (**6.5km; 680m; 2h 35min**).

Carlin's Cairn lies just to the north and is an easy optional diversion with a return to Corserine, add (**2.5km; 200m; 1h**). From Corserine, descend the ridge south-south-east for 1.7km to the col below Millfire.

In the valley to the west of this can be seen the former shepherd's house at Backhill of Bush which was last inhabited in the 1940s and is now a bothy. Prior to forestation, this was a truly remote spot, reached from Forrest Lodge by way of this col. All supplies, even funeral corteges had to come this way, transported on sleds pulled by ponies. The serious-ness of this route in winter is highlighted by a cairn 1km to the east, which commemorates shepherd boy Ralph Forlow who died here in the blizzard of 27th January 1954.

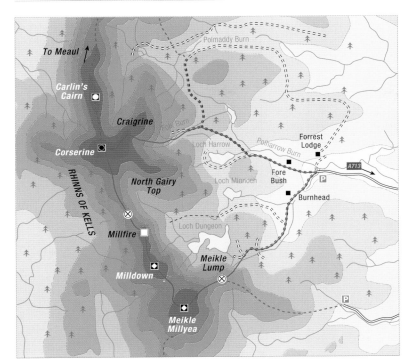

northern top has a trig point and is the 746m highpoint given by the OS. However, Harvey Maps give a highpoint of 749m at NX516825 some 400m further along the wall to the south-south-west. The prudent should visit this too (**11.5km; 920m; 4h 10min**).

From the trig point, descend the north-east ridge of Meikle Lump. A dyke that joins the one followed on the ascent runs down the ridge, swinging east then north-east towards the forestry and a track beyond.

It is best to follow the wall almost to the edge of the forest where the track can be gained by going left over a burn to a stile (NX534838). Turn right at the junction and descend past a wooden watch tower. Alternatively, follow the boggy forest edge right for 500m where a break leads to the track.

Descend the track, named Prof. Hans Heiberg Road, for 3.5km, keeping straight ahead at all junctions, past Burnhead Farm to reach the car park (**17km; 920m; 5h 40min**).

Pass easily over the craggy Donald Top of Millfire and make the short ascent onto Milldown beside a drystane dyke. Thereafter drop to the Lochans of Auchniebut and follow the dyke up Meikle Millyea. The

Millfire from the north-west (Rab Anderson)

Cairnsmore of Carsphairn, Beninner, Moorbrock Hill and Windy Standard from the south-east (Andrew Fraser)

Beninner; 710m; (DT); L77; NX605971

Cairnsmore of Carsphairn; 797m; (D10); L77; NX594979; moor of cairns, above Carsphairn (carse of alders). Mapped Kairnsmoort (1654), Cairnsmuir upon Deuch (1755), Cairns Moor (1797)

Keoch Rig; 611m; (DT); L77; NX617999

Moorbrock Hill; 650m; (D65); L77; NX620983; mapped Kornsleu Hill (1654), Cornsclia (1797), Cornsolue (1826). Probably Gaelic 'cor an sliabh', point on the moor

Together with its neighbouring hills, Cairnsmore of Carsphairn forms part of a distinctive group towards the southern end of the range that to the north includes Blackcraig Hill and Windy Standard, both of which are Grahams and covered on the next pages. Being a Corbett, Cairnsmore of Carsphairn is the highest point in the range, as well as the highest of the three Cairnsmores, as celebrated in the old Galloway doggerel 'There's Cairnsmore of Fleet and Cairnsmore of Dee, but Cairnsmore of Carsphairn is the highest of the three'.

Together with the adjoining Beninner, the round of this southern group of hills includes Keoch Rig and Moorbrock Hill on the opposite side of the valley. Windy Standard can be added as an extension, however despite being a fairly compact group this walk is probably tough enough for most as it is.

The round is started from the valley of the Water of Ken, reached by the dead end single track road which branches north from the B729 Carsphairn to Moniave road at Stroanfreggan Bridge. Drive up this road to Craigengillan where a forestry track starts next to a cottage at NX637948. There is limited parking on the verge next to the wall around the cottage, which at the time of writing was acceptable to the owner; there is also room to squeeze off the road in a passing place just before this. A gated estate track to Moorbrock 500m further north has a No Parking sign at the entrance.

Follow the track north next to the Polifferie Burn and when the track swings left into the forest, continue ahead over an old bridge by an overgrown route to join the estate track at the entrance to Moorbrock. At the byre in front of the estate house, it is

possible to go west beside a wall then up the break in the forestry on the north side of the Poldores Burn which is crossed to gain the open hillside. However, this gives tortuous going through deep tussocks and perhaps a better route, though slightly longer, is to stay with the track, taking the left branch uphill just beyond the estate house. This track traverses around Green Hill and from its lowest point the second firebreak can be descended to cross the burn and gain the hillside. Whichever route is chosen, either climb directly up the steep slope left of Beninner Gairy then go up left by an obvious break through the minor rock outcrops in the upper section, or traverse across to the left of the steep ground before ascending to the summit of Beninner (5km; 540m; 2h; 10min).

Descend north-west to the Nick of the Lochans then continue up to the

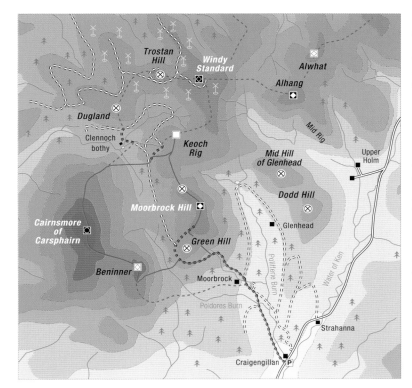

immediately to climb steeply up the spur of Alwhat onto the flat top of Keoch Rig, or continue to the burn then climb onto the spur of Hog Hill and swing round to the top (**11km; 910m; 4h 5min**).

To include Windy Standard, go to Clennoch bothy and follow a track north to where it forks then leave it to ascend steeply north onto Dugland (608m). From here the ridge is followed across the south side of Trostan Hill past the wind turbines to gain the trig point on top of Windy Standard. The windfarm access road crosses most of this ground and can be used as much or as little as possible. From the summit, follow the wide ridge south and descend past the Deil's Putting Stone then go south-west onto Keoch Rig; an additional 3.5km; 150m; 1h.

From Keoch Rig, a rough atv track can be followed south-west then south to a col from where the ascent is made onto the long summit ridge of Moorbrock Hill (**13km; 1040m; 4h 45min**).

From the southern end of the summit ridge, descend a track for a short way towards the saddle, then short-cut directly downhill to the south-east by the Poltie Burn to rejoin the track. Descend to a junction, turn right across the burn and return past Moorbrock (**17.5km; 1040m; 5h 50min**).

trig point on the granite boulder studded summit of Cairnsmore of Carsphairn (**7km; 700m; 2h 45min**). The view is extensive down the Ken and Dee valleys, with the Rhinns of Kells particularly prominent.

Descend north onto Currie Rig then drop north-east off this towards Clennoch bothy, situated in the floor of

the glen at the junction of the Bow, Clennoch and Hog Hill Burns. Near the bottom, swing right to go through a gate in the fence at NX603998, then cross the Bow Burn and ascend rough ground around the left side of a forestry plantation to gain a track junction. Take the higher track to the left and either break off right almost

Moorbrock Hill, right, from the estate track to Moorbrock (Rab Anderson)

Blackcraig Hill and Glen Afton from Cannock Hill (Tom Prentice)

Windy Standard; 698m; (G109); (D33); L77; NS620014; windy hill with cairn. Scots 'standard', hill cairn: there are nine Standard hills in Galloway and Ayrshire

Alhang; 642m; (D71); L77; NS642010; from Gaelic 'allt', mountain stream (original meaning – steep slope): the river Afton rises on its north slope. Aldhing (1654), Alhinge (1797). Second element possibly Gaelic 'cumhaing', narrow

Alwhat; 628m; (DT); L77; NS646020

Meikledodd Hill; 643m; (DT); L77; NS660027

Blacklorg Hill; 681m; (D45); L77; NS653042; black shank-shaped hill. Gaelic 'lorg', shank, thigh, leg (in shape)

Blackcraig Hill; 700m; (G105); (D30); L71, 77; NS647064; black cliff hill. Mapped Black Craig (1755)

Upper Glen Afton is surrounded by rolling hills including two Grahams, which offer a straightforward and pleasant high-level route round the Afton Reservoir. Lower Glen Afton, celebrated in song by Burns, is still an unexpected gem. Unfortunately, the same cannot be said of the ever expanding windfarm on Windy Standard, although by walking this round in an anti-clockwise direction, its visual intrusion can be minimised and a sense of the area's former tranquillity partially restored.

From New Cumnock take the B741 west for a few hundred metres then turn left into Afton Road (signposted Burns Cairn) and ascend Glen Afton to the end of the public road where there is a parking area (NS627054) across a croncrete bridge on the left,

just beyond the Afton Water Treatment Works.

Follow the track south for 200m towards the dam then take a waymarked path on the right, past the rocky knoll known as Castle William, which has connections to William Wallace, to gain a higher track. This track leads left to a junction above the Afton Reservoir dam where the right branch is followed towards the grassy ridge which rises south-east towards Wedder Hill, Millaneoch Hill and Windy Standard.

At the time of publication, plans had been submitted for 14 wind turbines on this ridge, with accompanying access tracks. Follow the earth access track towards Wedder Hill, it is possible to leave it after a while for a

grassy atv track beside the fence, to gain the rounded summit. Leave the earth track at this point, cross to the western side of the fence and follow a clear path onto Millaneoch Hill. Descend to a col with a wooden gate, then ascend Windy Standard to its turbine surrounded trig point (**5.5km; 400m; 1h 50min**).

Return to the col and wooden gate and descend south-east beside the fence to the marshy col below Alhang. Continue beside the fence up and over Alhang, then north-east over the Donald top of Alwhat to a fence junction below Meikledodd Hill. The ill-defined summit of this Donald top is gained by a short diversion southeast beside the right-hand fence (**11km; 710m; 3h 40min**).

Descend back to the junction and

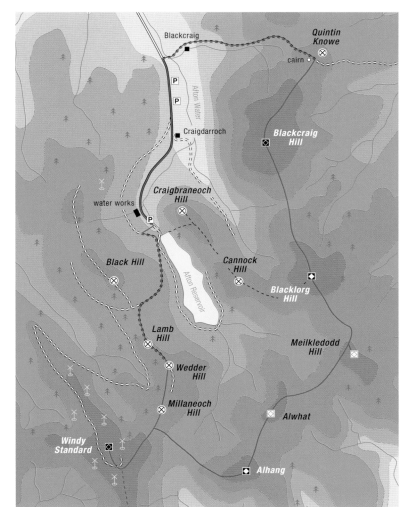

continue north-west round the head of the Montraw Burn, from where a steady ascent gains the cairned top of Blacklorg Hill and a stile. Cross over and continue north-west, with occasional waymark posts to the peat hag covered col below Blackcraig Hill, which is best crossed via atv tracks on its west side, well away from the fence. Ascend to the summit trig point which lies a short distance west of the fence (**15km; 970m; 5h**).

To descend from Blackcraig Hill, rejoin the fence and follow a path on the north ridge to Quintin Knowe. Go north-west, then west following a path down the north side of the Langlee Burn which turns into a track leading past Blackcraig farm to the road. Turn left and follow the road up the glen for 2.8km back to the start (**22km; 1060m; 7h**).

Blackcraig Hill can be climbed on its own from one of the many long laybys on the Glen Afton Road, south of Blackcraig Farm, by reversing the descent described above (**4.5km; 440m; 1h 45min**). Return the same way (**9km; 440m; 2h 50min**).

Although Windy Standard can be climbed from the south-east via Holm of Dalquhairn, the road up the Water of Ken is more awkward to access. It is therefore best climbed on its own from Glen Afton via the ascent route described above with a return the same way (**11km; 440m; 3h 10min**).

Approaching the summit of Windy Standard (Tom Prentice)

Queensberry from Gana Hill (Rab Anderson)

Queensberry; *697m; (G111); (D34); L78; NX989997; the second element is probably from Old English 'beorg', rounded hill. Recorded as Queensberry (1633), Queinsberg (1648). First element obscure, though it may refer to a queen*

Earncraig Hill; *611m; (D88); L78; NS973013; eagle crag, from 'erne' Scots for eagle and crag. Mapped Sergan Law (1773) or Sergeant Law (1817), from Scots word for a sheriff's officer*

Gana Hill; *668m; (D54); L78; NS954010; hill above Gana Burn on its north slope. Another Gana Burn 5km north-west (see also Ballencleuch Law), might suggest a form of Scots 'kennel', channel (for a burn)*

These three hills, one Graham and two Donalds, form the southernmost part of the high ridge of the Southern Lowther Hills. Although they can be tacked onto a large round from Daer Reservoir (see following route), they are more conveniently climbed in a good round from the farm at Mitchellslacks to the south-west. This is reached by a loop of the unclassified road to the east of Thornhill on the A702. There is limited parking on the verge at NX964961 beside a Scottish Rights of Way signpost, a little north of the access track to Mitchellslacks. Locations around Mitchellslacks were used in the 1978 adaptation of John Buchan's spy story *The Thirty Nine Steps* starring Robert Powell.

Cut down the bank onto the access track to Mitchellslacks and follow this over the Capel Water then swing left past the farm to head northwards through the fields. When the track forks after the last gate leading out onto the open hillside, the right-hand track is followed uphill, past a track off right, then across to the foot of the distinctive small hill The Law. Take the track on the right which contours The Law then cuts back downhill to a series of sheep pens in the valley floor. Loop around to the north of the pens on a rough track then cross the burn to the side of them and follow atv tracks south-east then east heading for the prominent cairn on High Church, which lies above an interesting rocky defile with a pond at its entrance. The ridge leads north-eastwards onto Craih Hill then down and across a gap where a short but steep climb gains the trig point on top of Wee Queensberry. Head north-east along the top on an atv track then drop down across a boggy area and continue on up the long slope of Peace Knowe to the top of Queensberry (**6km; 570m; 2h 20min**).

Descend north to pick up a fence and follow this as it swings north-west onto Penbreck. Earncraig Hill sits directly opposite but there is a deep and narrow glen in-between which has to be circumnavigated north then west beside the fence. Cross the col at Capel Yetts then head south-west up Berry Rig to meet a wall at the summit of Earncraig Hill (**9.5km; 730m; 3h 25min**).

The route continues westwards beside the wall, dropping quite steeply to the col at Daer Hass where the wall turns away north. Now climb west up the slope across rough

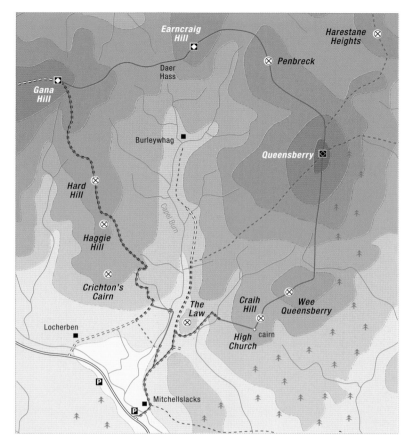

track south to flatter ground. After dropping down the banking the Capel Burn can be crossed to gain the track on the other side then the gate in the wall. Continue through the fields past Mitchellslacks back to the start (**18.5km; 950m; 6h**).

Queensberry itself can be climbed more directly, but less interestingly, by keeping left where the track forks at the foot of The Law and continuing up the glen above the Capel Burn. After crossing a side burn an atv track, signposted to Queensberry, can be followed up right to the top of the hill (**5.5km; 490m; 2hr**), (**11km; 500m; 3h 30min**).

Another option for climbing Queensberry on its own is from the north-east above Beattock on the M74. The route starts from the end of the road which climbs past Beattock Hill; there is room to park before the bridge over the Kinnel Water at Kinnelhead (NT033016). Following Scottish Rights of Way signposts, initially take the track towards Kinnelhead then take another track back south-west to Lochanhead. Cross the burn just east of the cottage, then cross boggy ground and follow the edge of the forestry plantation uphill past the Pot of Ae (the head of the Water of Ae) to the summit of Queensberry (**5.5km; 450m; 2h**). Rather than return the same way (**11km; 450m; 3h 20min**) the route can be varied by taking a slightly longer descent over Harestanes Heights and Craighoar Hill to the north-east.

ground and pick up a fence which runs south-west then swings round to head north-west up the shoulder of Gana Shank. Join a track then go through a gate in another fence and stay on the track as it cuts the corner away from the fence to rejoin it again where it passes over the summit of Gana Hill (**12km; 910m; 4h 20min**).

Return along the track and follow it south down the spur of Gana Shank. At the foot of this the track swings round from one side of the ridge to the other, through a col, to pass over Hard Hill where it then descends along the upper slopes of the valley of the Capel Burn. Shortly after a right-hand hairpin bend the track crosses a burn then drops a little to where it makes another right-hand turn at NX968978.

At this point it is possible to cut down the steep slope on the left to re-cross the lower part of the burn just crossed to find a bridge at NX970978 which enables the Capel Burn to be crossed below The Law.

Follow paths south beside the burn to a track which rises to meet the outward track at the gate in the wall just north of Mitchellslacks.

Another option is to continue on the track on the west side for a short way and where this swings towards Locherben leave it and follow an atv

North to Burleywhag bothy and Earncraig Hill (Tom Prentice)

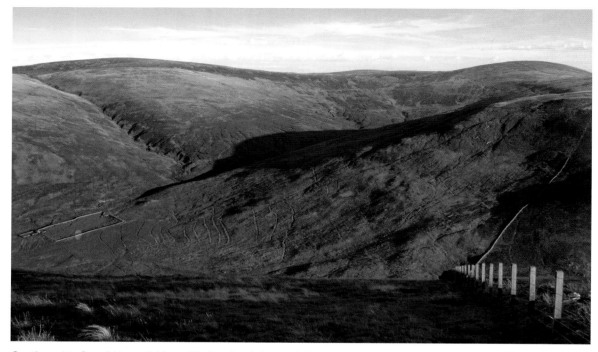

South-east to Scaw'd Law, right, and Ballencleuch Law, left, from Well Hill (Andrew Fraser)

Glenleith Fell; 612m; (DT); L78; NS922023

Wedder Law; 672m; (D52) L78; NS938025; lamb hill. Scots 'wedder', castrated male sheep, usually a yearling lamb

Scaw'd Law; 663m; (D58); L78; NS922035; speckled, scabby or patchy hill. Scots 'scald', 'scawd', scabby, patchy. A common southern hill name

Ballencleuch Law; 689m; (G119); (D42); L78; NS935049; hill above Ballen Cleuch, the stream gorge (Scots 'cleuch') east of the summit. Mapped Ganaw hill (1755), the Gana Burn draining to the west

Rodger Law; 688m; (DT); L71, 78; NS945058

Comb Law; 645m; (D67); L71, 78; NS943073; arched ridge hill. Mapped Netherburn Hill (1755), from the burn on the west side, then as Comb Law in 1817: nearby is Coom Rig. Pont maps a Coom Head (1590s), which may be either

The Southern Lowther hills comprise an area of elevated grouse moor, the summit ridge of which stretches some 14km from Ballencleuch Law in the north to Queensberry in the south, only once falling below 500m in altitude. Ballencleuch Law, also a Graham, is the highest hill in the northernmost part of this ridge which also includes three Donalds and two Donald Tops. Queensberry and the southern part are described on the previous pages.

The principal route described accesses these hills from the attractive village of Durisdeer. Parking is available in the village next to the church, although is likely to be in short supply on a Sunday morning. While now a sleepy hamlet, Durisdeer is strategically positioned at the southern end of the Well Path, a Roman road which for centuries was the principal route through these hills. There has been a church on this site since at least the 13th century and the present one contains a remarkable marble-carved mausoleum to the Dukes of Queensberry, underneath which lies a vault containing lead coffins of the Douglas family.

From Durisdeer, walk south back down the main road for 200m and turn left immediately before the cemetery onto a track leading to Glenaggart. Follow the track for 800m to a junction just after the burn at Glenimp then take the track on the left. This track traverses the hillside then climbs steadily to gain the ridge-line on the shoulder of Scaw'd Law, 500m south of its summit.

The Donald top of Glenleith Fell lies to the south and is easily reached, either across deep heather, or by descending the track a short way, passing through a gate, then taking another track that cuts across the slope to pass just beneath the top, which is gained by a short climb west (4.5km; 470m; 1h 45min).

Return to the main track and follow this south-south-east downhill past a shed then quite steeply uphill to the

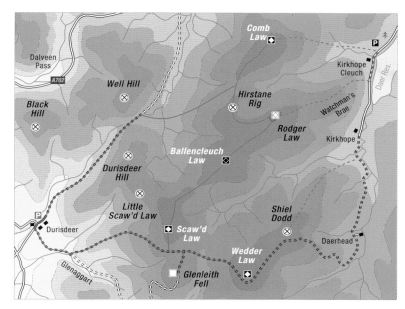

Well Path. This is followed south-west for 4km back to Durisdeer, past an elevated Roman fortlet reckoned to be one of the best preserved in Britain (**23km; 950m; 6h 50min**).

Those seeking to bag the Graham of Ballencleuch Law as quickly as possible can do so from Daer Reservoir by climbing over Rodger Law via Watchman's Brae (**4km 390m 1h 30min**); (**8km; 430m; 2h 30min**). There is parking just before Kirkhope Cleuch at a track entrance at NS967073.

It is also possible to climb this round of Donalds from this parking spot. Follow the south side of the wall around a forestry plantation to gain Comb Law then reverse the above route to Wedder Law. From here, continue north-east on the track to Shiel Dod then either follow the track back, south-east and east down Sheil Dod (easier and drier but a little longer), or cut more directly down the north-east ridge of Ewe Gair and rejoin the track in the floor of the valley. The track leads back to the reservoir (**21km; 720m; 6h 20min**).

It is possible, though a much bigger undertaking, to extend the walk from Wedder Law to take in Ganna Hill, Earncraig Hill and Queensberry returning past the ruin of Daerhead (**31km; 1280m; 10h**). This long route could also be split over two days by utilising the bothy at Burleywhag at the head of the Capel Burn west of Queensberry (see Queensberry map).

top of Wedder Law, the summit being located at a fence just north of the track (**7km; 620m; 2h 30min**). By this stage, signs of the intensive use of these hills for grouse shooting will be evident. While perhaps less visually intrusive than say, windfarms this particular track is a good argument as to why planning control of such tracks is necessary, if only to control the use of non-native materials and to provide for eventual restoration.

From Wedder Law, the simplest option is to return via the track, back through the gate in the fence just below the shoulder of Scaw'd Law, then branching off right on a grassy atv track where the main track swings left. On reaching a wall, go through a gate and climb onto the top of Scaw'd Law (**9.5km; 760m; 3h 20min**). The purist could take the more scenic route a little to the north by following the fence and wall line through the well-named Carsehope Middens, past rows of shooting butts.

Follow the wall, or the atv track just out from it, and where the wall veers off after 400m continue easily north-east beside or just out from the fence onto Ballencleuch Law and continue on to the 1m lower Roger Law, which sports a trig point (**13km; 890m; 4h 20min**). The visual impact of the massive Clyde Valley windfarm to the north-east can be fully understood from here whilst to the north-west the

Northern Lowther Hills are more pleasing on the eye, as is Queensberry to the south east, standing out over Earncraig Hill.

This now leaves the awkward outlier of Comb Law and although this lies to the north, one has to first backtrack south-west for about 300m to pick up the fence again then follow this down the spur north-west. The fence swings round down Hirstane Rig then continues north-east to a junction of fences on top of Comb Law (**16.5km; 950m; 5h 10min**).

To descend, return to the col with Hirstane Rig then drop west-south-west down the hillside to gain the

Ballencleuch Law from Scaw'd Law (Rab Anderson)

Looking across Wanlockhead to Lowther Hill, right, and Green Lowther (Andrew Fraser)

Cold Moss; *628m; (DT); L71, 78; NS898094*

Lowther Hill; *725m; (D23); L71, 78; NS890107; an obscure name, unless it be a decomposed form of Gaelic 'meall odhar', dun-coloured hill: there are two hills called Me(a)lowther in south Scotland. Mapped Loders Hill (1654)*

East Mount Lowther; *631m; (D76); L71, 78; NS878100; 1944 summit indicator states previously named Auchenlone Hill; possibly after a farm, now lost, called Auchenton or Auchenlon. Southern ridge still mapped as Auchenton Shank, 'shank' being the Scottish equivalent of Gaelic 'lurg', leg. Roy's map shows two farms with auchen-names further down the Mennock Water. Present name first recorded by the OS c.1850. Most westerly of the Lowther range and 'mount' very unusual in the Border hills*

Green Lowther; *732m; (G44); (D21); L71, 78; NS900120; green for its vegetation to distinguish it from Dun Law and White Law just along the range. To south-west is Green Trough*

Dun Law; *677m; (D48); L71, 78; NS916136; dull brown hill. Its neighbours include White Law, Black Law, and Green Lowther*

Lousie Wood Law; *618m; (D86); L71, 78; NS931152; hill above Lousie Wood Burn (and the burn from a wood, now lost) on its west. Pont's map (1590s) seemed to name it Wadderlaw (hill of wedders, lambs)*

Lowther Hill's huge air traffic control 'golf ball' radome makes it a conspicuous landmark, although the highest point on this long upland ridge is actually Green Lowther, the sole Graham in the massif. An access road joins the two peaks and while these intrusions make neither hill particularly attractive, the full traverse of the ridge is still a satisfying and enjoyable outing.

The start is at a height of just over 300m, to the north of the top of the spectacular Dalveen Pass. Ample parking is available on a section of old road at NS931100, 500m to the north of Overfingland, where the Southern Upland Way (SUW) leaves the A702. Walk south up the road past Overfingland and Troloss Cottage then take the signposted SUW to the west. This waymarked route climbs uphill to the south of a small forestry plantation, passing through a gate then crossing a stile, before climbing over Laght Hill then Comb Head and the Donald Top of Cold Moss to ascend Lowther Hill (**5.5km; 570m; 2h 10min**). A fenced compound surrounds the radar station and there is no access to the highest point.

East Mount Lowther is an outlier to the south-west, climbed by an out and back route. Follow the SUW left over a stile before the compound is reached then skirt south of the summit to a stile over a fence by a small hut. Cross over to gain the

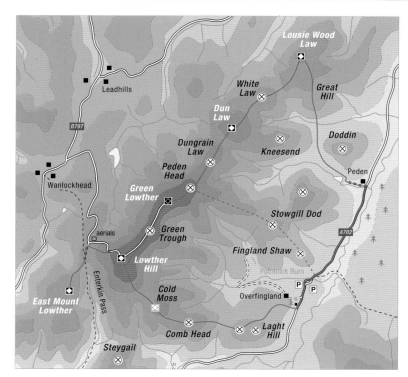

valley to Tinto and Culter Fell with Hart Fell to the east. This 5km ridge only has two main drops, either side of Dun Law. They are the Big and Little Windgate Hass, the origin of whose names possibly reflects the presence of Lake District miners in the area. The fence crosses the unmarked summit of Dun Law while the top of Lousie Wood Law is marked by a trig point 100m north-north-west of where the fences join (**16km; 1150m; 5h 35min**).

The descent is south by way of Great Hill then following faint tracks across rough ground between Kneesend and Doddin to reach paths on the north side of the Peden Burn. The A702 is met at Peden from where it is a 3km walk back along the road to the start (**22.5km; 1180m; 7h 10min**).

Although the quickest way of climbing Green Lowther is to use the access road from Wanlockhead, a more enjoyable route starts from the parking north of Overfingland. Follow the road north over the Potrenick Burn then ascend Fingland Shaw where an atv track leads to Stowgill Dod. From here a fence is followed to Peden Head then Green Lowther (**4.5km; 450m; 1h 45min**); (**9km; 480m; 2h 50min**).

access road and follow this for a very short distance then cut back left to the fence and descend to gain a track opposite another aerial compound. Descend the track south-west to the head of the Enterkin Pass, then ascend beside the fence to the summit of East Mount Lowther (**7.5km; 650m; 2h 45min**). There are fine views down the Nith Valley to the Lake District and westwards to Arran.

It is now necessary to reverse the route back to Lowther Hill which gives good views to Wanlockhead, at 425m the highest village in Scotland. Lead has been mined here since Roman times and gold was discovered during the reign of James IV.

Either follow the road up and around the north side of Lowther Hill and on towards Green Lowther, or retrace the outward route south round the compound to gain an atv track on the east side of the fence beside the road. Follow this over Green Trough to Green Lowther (**11km; 880m; 3h 55min**). The trig point stands below a collection of rusting masts, surrounded by wind-blasted fencing and concrete bunkers.

Fortunately the rest of the route over Peden Head and Dungrain Head

to gain the two Donalds, Dun Law then Lousie Wood Law, gives pleasant, unobstructed high-level walking following a fenceline. There are fine views to the village of Leadhills and north-east up the Clyde

Approaching the summit of Lowther Hill (Tom Prentice)

SECTION 0b
The Borders

Tinto from Lamington Hill to the south-east (photo Rab Anderson)

Tinto; *711m; (G80); (D29); L72; NS953343; Fiery hill. Gaelic 'teinnteach', suggesting a beacon hill where fires were lit in times of danger. Mapped Tintok Hill (1590s), reflecting old local name Tintock*

Tinto stands proud and dominates the local landscape with its pointed profile and red coloured screes. It occupies a solitary position north of the main Southern Uplands, rising above the flat lands between the Clyde and Douglas valleys. A large prehistoric cairn known as The Dimple adorns the summit, dwarfing the trig point, which stands to one side. Tinto's prominence and accessibility makes it a popular hill and its summit provides fine panoramic views which include the Lake District peaks, Arran and Lochnagar.

The hill is roughly shaped like a cross with ridges running to the four points of the compass and the simple up and down ascent of any ridge is just a short walk. However, if the hill is traversed a longer, more interesting walk can be constructed utilising quiet country roads to north and south.

The northern approach is by far the most popular with a major path all the way. Start from the minor road that runs north of Tinto. There is a car park near Fallburn at NS964374, close to the junction with the A73, where there is a convenient tea room. The path passes an iron-age fort with concentric ramparts, over Totherin Hill then up to the summit cairn (**3.4km; 480m; 1h 35min**). Descend the same way with fine views over the Midland Valley (**6.8km; 480m; 2h 30min**).

An ascent from the south is perhaps the most pleasant, and relatively unfrequented. Start at Wiston Lodge YMCA hostel (NS958322). There is limited parking on the roadside but, if courteous, visitors should be able to drive into the grounds and park near the hostel.

Walk due north by an avenue of trees, past a house and a water supply building.

Pass through a gate and follow the edge of the field north, aiming directly for the peak. Large zigzags gain the top of Pap Craig where the path becomes less distinct in a mix of heather and red scree. Alternatively, a fenceline on the right leads direct to the summit (**2.9km; 440m; 1h 25min**). Descend the same way (**5.8km; 440m; 2h 15min**).

The west ridge has a secluded feel and starts at Howgate Mouth, a col that can easily be gained either from the south, from NS925331 on the B7055 road, or from the north by parking at NS919349 at the end of the public road just south of the houses at Howgate. A pleasant grassy walk over Lochlyock Hill leads to the summit (**3.5km; 440m; 1h 30min**); descend the same way (**7km; 490m; 2h 30min**). This west ridge also makes a pleasant descent if climbing the hill from the north or south.

The east ridge is probably the least climbed, partly because parking is difficult. The path starts from near Broadlees (NS984352), but the safest parking is probably on the minor road to Symington, 450m to the south. Walk through a field onto the ridge crest. A bulldozed track comes in from the north before zigzagging its way up to Scaut Hill. Either descend slightly from the crest to pick up this track, or turn to the south-west and ascend the ridge crest (**4km; 500m; 1h 45min**). Descend the same way (**8km; 530m; 2h 50min**).

Ascending Tinto's west ridge; Culter Fell in the distance (Rab Anderson)

Culter Fell from Congrie Hill (Rab Anderson)

Chapelgill Hill; *696m; (D36); L72; NT066303; hill above Chapel Gill, a stream and farm (now lost names) on the east. 'Gill' is a Middle English word for stream in a ravine, and it and 'chapel' suggest an incomer from north England*

Cardon Hill; *675m; (DT); L72; NT065314*

Culter Fell; *748m; (G15); (D14); L72; NT052290; hill above Culter. Originally recorded as Fiends Fell early 17th century. Name changed late 17th century to that of the parish – Culter*

This trio forms the northern group of the Culter Hills and is prominent when viewed from the north, with the highest hill in the area, the wedge-shaped Culter Fell (pronounced Cooter), forming a backdrop to Cardon Hill's rounded summit. A pleasant and fairly short circuit of the three hills can be made from Glenkirk near the head of the Holms Water valley, south of Broughton. There is parking on grass at the end of the public road just before the house (NT079294). Follow the track on the right before the house to a barn and skirt it on its left side to gain the south-east ridge of Chapelgill Hill. The ascent is a sustained pull but easy underfoot. Higher up a fence is joined coming up from the east. A small cairn marks one of several possible summits on the flat, grassy top (**2km; 430m; 1h 10min**).

Cardon Hill is a short diversion to the north over the minor top of Birnies Bowrock (un-named on OS 1:50k map) from where easy ground leads to the summit; the views to the north are beautiful. In poor visibility the fence at the top of Chapelgill Hill runs to a T-junction from where a right

(north-east) turn along the fence leads to Cardon Hill. Culter Fell is gained by retracing your steps southwards following the watershed, and the fence which runs all the way, over

Chapelgill Hill, right, from Culter Fell (Tom Prentice)

tussocky, boggy ground around the head of Hope Burn and over Kings Bank Head. Continue up the north ridge to the summit where there is a trig point; on a clear day the views are excellent (**6km; 650m; 2h 25min**).

The shortest route back to Glenkirk is to return down the north ridge before dropping eastwards to gain a grassy track which runs down the ridge between the Glenharvie and Hope Burns then over Congrie Hill (**10km; 660m; 3h 30min**). This walk can be pleasantly extended to the south via Leishfoot Hill, or Holm Nick, the col at the head of Glenholm, to gain Holms Waterhead.

An alternative route of ascent for Culter Fell, together with Cardon Hill and Chapelgill Head if required, can be made from the Culter Water valley to the west. There is limited parking beyond Culter Allers farmhouse at NT031312 and beside the Culter River at NT031311, before the public road ends. Walk south along the road for about 700m before turning east and following the track beside Kings Beck. A small footpath continues pleasantly up the burn beyond where the main track ends and the beck can be followed in its entirety to emerge beneath the north ridge of Culter Fell which is climbed beside the fence to the summit (**4km; 500m; 1h 45min**).

The quickest descent is down the north-west ridge, Fell Shin. However, a better walk can be had by descending south to Holm Nick and then taking the track down to Coulter Reservoir. This track can also be gained from Culter Fell by a south-west descent over Knock Hill. A pleasant 4km walk leads back down the glen from the reservoir (**13km; 530m; 4h**).

The quickest ascent of both Grahams in this group on their own is made by approaching Culter Fell from Glenkirk via the grassy track over Congrie Hill (**4km; 480m; 1h 45min**), followed by the onward link to Gathersnow Hill beside the fence up Glenwhappen Rig (**8km; 720m; 3h**). The best descent is over Coomb Hill then down the ridge to Holms Waterhead (**13km; 760m; 4h 20min**). The ascent of both Grahams from the Culter Water side is longer (**16km; 750m; 5h**).

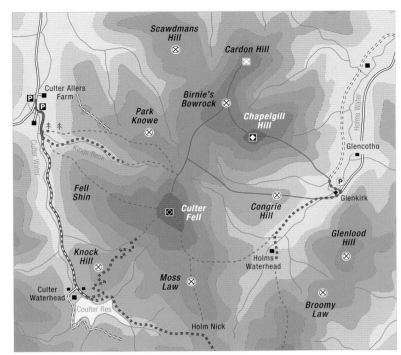

Culter Hills

This fine range of rolling hills lies on the watershed between the major valleys of the River Clyde and the River Tweed, the former draining into the Atlantic on one side of the country and the latter draining into the North Sea on the other side. Lying almost equidistant from Glasgow and Edinburgh and being encircled by the main roads of the M74, the A701 and the A702, the hills are readily accessible.

The range as a whole falls into three distinct groups; Culter Fell and its two northern outliers, the Gathersnow Hill group in the south and the western outpost of Hudderstone. Intruded into by a number of major valleys, which provide the access routes, it is a complicated group of hills with numerous ways of attaining the various summits. The routes described here are for tackling each of the three principal groups separately although it is possible to link the hills, or even combine them into one longish outing.

The extended outing of five Donalds and three Donald Tops (which includes the two Grahams, Culter Fell and Gathersnow Hill) starts and finishes from the parking just beyond Culter Allers Farm in Culter Glen. Start by ascending towards Culter Fell up Kings Beck, or the path up its northern rim. Branch out north to visit the outliers, Chapelgill Hill and Cardon Hill, then double back south over Culter Fell. Another diversion is needed to visit Coomb Hill before the rest of this group is traversed; Gathersnow Hill, Hillshaw Head then the outlier Coomb Dod. After returning to Hillshaw Head the lonely tramp out to Hudderstone is not for the fainthearted, taking in some wet, tussocky ground. However, the descent at the end of the day from Hudderstone via Cowgill Rig is very pleasant.

At the time of writing there is a proposal to extend the massive 152 turbine Clyde Valley Wind Farm by 57 turbines and this will encroach onto the section of the walk between Coomb Dod and Hudderstone. However, once construction has been completed the proposed turbine access road may be used to ease the going on this rough section, although the purist can always opt for the wet and tussocky ground on the other side of the fence! (29km; 1350m; 9h 30min).

Gathersnow Hill viewed from the north-west across Coulter Reservoir (Tom Prentice)

Coomb Hill; *640m; (DT); L72; NT069263*

Gathersnow Hill; *688m; (G121); (D43); L72; NT058257; the hill holds snow until late. Mapped Gathersnow (1755). There is a Snowgill Hill 3km west*

Hillshaw Head; *652m; (D63); L72; NT048246; top above the hill wood. Hillshaw Burn on east: Scots 'shaw', small (natural) wood. Mapped Hillshaw Browhead (1775) and Culter Stane Hill (1817)*

Coomb Dod; *635m; (DT); L72; NT046238*

The Gathersnow Hill group of hills can be climbed from the Kingledoors valley to the south-east. The primary route described is that from Kingledores Farm at the foot of the glen. A small loop of old road at the east entrance to the farm affords good parking (NT109281). Walk up the tree-lined driveway, then turn left and walk through to the far end of the farmyard. From here there is a choice of routes to Coomb Hill.

The route up the glen follows the track across the burn to gain the access track to the Glenkerie Wind Farm (11 turbines) and this leads on up the glen to ascend Kingle Rig onto Broomy Law. Continue on the track up the glen to reach the white farmhouse of Hopehead. From here ascend a track west and then north towards the small col behind Point 429m (Glengary Knowe) and make a direct ascent of Coomb Hill on easy ground. The summit is delightfully grassy.

Easy walking then leads south-west along the grassy ridge following the fence to the main peak of Gathersnow Hill, marked by only a few stones (**7km; 500m: 2h 20min**). The high tableland of the Manor Hills dominates the view to the east whilst the view to the west and south-west is met by the 152 wind turbines of the Clyde Wind Farm. At the time of writing there are plans to add a further 57 turbines to this wind farm which will extend onto Hudderstone, Hillshaw Head, Coomb Dod and Glenwhappen Dod and impinge upon the next section of the walk.

Continue easily alongside the boundary fence separating Scottish Borders from South Lanarkshire, to Hillshaw Head, marked by a small pile of stones east of the fence, and then down and up to reach Coomb Dod with its trig point (**9.5km; 590m; 3h 5min**). The easiest return from here is to drop eastwards into the Kingledoors valley and walk along the track back to the start (**18.5km; 590m; 5h**).

From Kingledores Farm, the ridge on the north side of the glen can be gained by following the path north-west of the farm onto Cocklie Rig Head. To reach this path, follow the track to just beyond the farm where it crosses the burn, then break off right and climb north past a stand of Scots Pines. The path gradually ascends above the Benshaw Burn, passing by two lonely rowan trees, after which it becomes indistinct. It is probably now easier to head onto the spur on the

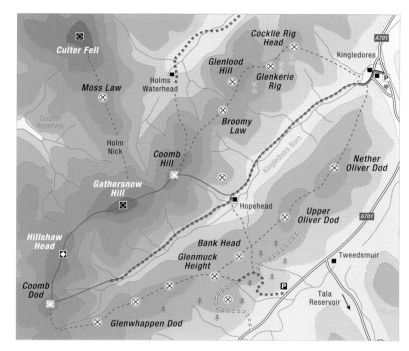

700m south of the junction of the Talla Reservoir road with the A701. There is some space for parking at the start of the forest track.

The track curves gently up the hillside. Just past the high point, close to the ridge crest, a junction is reached to the south-east of Bank Head. From here, leave the track and cross due north over rough ground for a short way, passing a small pond, to pick up the line of the burn dropping north into the Kingledoors valley. The burn follows a narrow defile before opening up into flat fields, which are crossed to the farmhouse of Hopehead; a bridge by the house crosses the Kingledoors Burn. From here follow the route already described over Coomb Dod to Gathersnow Hill (**6km; 560m; 2h 20min**) and onwards to Coomb Dod (**8.5km; 630m; 3h 5min**). The direct return to Tweedsmuir is made by continuing around the horseshoe over Glenwhappen Dod, but the going is distinctly tussocky and slow. Join a forest track just south-east of Glenmuck Heights and turn left (north-east). This track gains the junction passed on the ascent, from where a right turn leads back down to the start (**15km; 700m; 4h 45min**).

The quickest Graham only option is to combine Gathersnow Hill with Culter Fell, the other Graham in the group, and make the ascent from Glenkirk (see Culter Fell on p42).

left to gain the wind turbine access road and follow this up left then right to the top of Cocklie Rig Head and step over the fence. Once on the ridge, stick to the crest following the fence all the way over Glenlood Hill and Broomy Law onto Coomb Hill, then Gathersnow Hill (**8km; 670m; 3h**). Follow the previous route to Coomb Dod (**10.5km; 760m; 3h 45min**), then either descend as for that (**19.5km; 760m; 5h 40min**), or continue along the chain of the hills forming the southern side of the glen to complete the Kingledoors Horseshoe (**19.5km; 1000m; 6h 15min**). However, despite the lesser height of the hills the terrain on this side is much more difficult and time consuming.

At the time of writing there are plans to extend the Glenkerie Wind Farm by erecting nine turbines on the Holms Water side of the ridge with three turbines on Glenlood Hill, two on Broomy Law and two on Coomb Hill. These will be accessed using the existing track up Broomy Law. Those who may wish to avoid the intrusion of the wind turbines as much as possible may wish to opt for the route from Tweedsmuir, although the more pessimistic could see the gap between the proposed Clyde Wind Farm and the Glenkerie Wind Farm

being filled at some point, as well as the ground on the south side of the Kingledoors valley.

The round of these hills can also be started from near Tweedsmuir on the A701 and although shorter this involves crossing the Oliver Dod ridge first. The path marked on the OS 1:50k map running north-west from the village has all but disappeared, not least because of some recent forestry planting. Instead, take a new forestry track from NT091240 some

Gathersnow Hill from Coomb Hill (Rab Anderson)

Hudderstone; 626m; (D78); L72; NT022271; stone in the heather, probably. Hill mapped Hatherstone (1817 and 1840) and Heatherstane Law (OS, 1860): 'hather' and 'hadder' are Scots renditions of heather

Hudderstone is a remote outlier to the west and north-west of the main Culter hills group and being awkward to contrive into a reasonable Donald round with them, is generally climbed on its own. Although an ascent can be made using the surfaced road up the Culter Water valley, then crossing the Coulter Reservoir dam wall to ascend Snowgill Hill, both the route and the parking are better from the road up the Cow Gill valley.

On the road in from Coulter, fork right just past the entrance to Culter Allers farm and pass Birthwood Farm to park on the verge about 1km further on, just before a bridge over the burn (NT020306). Walk over the bridge, then in front of a cattle grid follow a track on the left uphill and round into a walled field. Leave the track and climb uphill on a grassy atv track which leads up the edge of the field to pass through a gate and gain the crest. The atv track passes just beneath the top of Ward Law and is followed over Woodycleugh Dod then uphill beside a fence to the top of Hudderstone (**4.5km; 470m; 1h 50min**).

What the summit lacks in drama is more than made up for on a clear day

by its superb view: Culter Fell to the east with the high tablelands of the Manor Hills beyond, Broad Law over the shoulder of Gathersnow Hill then Hart Fell to the south-east, the distant Lake District fells to the south, Arran to the west and Tinto close by to the north-west.

Several obvious options exist for extending this outing but the simplest route is to return back down the north-west ridge beside the fence to pick up the obvious track which leads over Cowgill Rig to regain the road close to the start (**8.5km; 490m; 3h**).

Bodesbeck Law; *665m; (D55); L79; NT169104; hill above Bodesbeck (farm). Mapped Bodgeback Law in 1775; 'beck' is northern English for a stream*

Mid Rig; *616m; (DT); L79; NT180122*

Bell Craig; *623m; (D79); L79; NT186128; bald cliff. Scots beld (sometimes bell), 'bald': Bald Craig is the cliff just west of the summit*

Andrewhinney Hill; *677m; (G137); (D47); L79; NT197138; obscure. Scots 'hinney' honey (as endearment). Known by farmers on west side as Andrew Whinny Hill which might suggest whin-covered*

Trowgrain Middle; *628m; (DT); L79; NT206150*

Herman Law; *614m; (D87); L79; NT213157; mapped Herskey Law (1755) perhaps Scots 'harsky' rough? Later Hermans Law (1773). OS Name Book states may be "a contraction of Herd Man". Farmers on west called it Hirmont Law, according to OSNB, which may be Britonnic 'hyr monith', long hill*

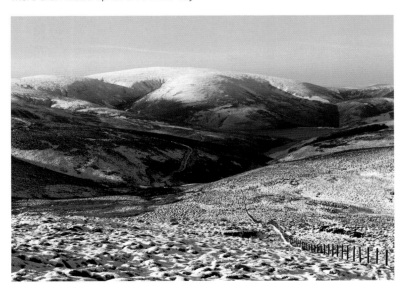

Hudderstone and Coulter Reservoir from Gathersnow Hill (Rab Anderson)

The broad summit of Andrewhinney Hill seen from the flanks of Bell Craig to the south-west (Rab Anderson)

the Hart Fell hills around Black Hope.

Ahead a wall and fence run along the grassy crest to the aptly named Nowtrig Head (Pt.608m on the OS 1:50k map) where the wall turns away right. Continue beside the fence over Mid Rig (also unnamed on the OS 1:50k map) to Bell Craig. The hills on the opposite side of Moffat Dale are now Carrifran Gans and White Coomb. The highpoint of the day, Andrewhinney Hill, is easily gained after a short descent and a 100m ascent (**8km; 510m; 2h 40min**). Loch Skeen and its surrounding hills, with the Grey Mare's Tail below, captivate the view on the other side, although one has to descend a little to the west to see the waterfall.

A choice of ridges gives an escape route from here back to the Ettrick valley, however the minor bump of another Mid Rig then Trowgrain Middle offer little resistance on the easy walk out to the final summit of the day; Herman Law (**10.5km; 580m; 3h 20min**).

Head south from here and descend the narrow ridge between the waters of the Black Grain and Back Burn to reach the road at the white cottage of Brockhoperig. From here 6km of road leads pleasantly alongside the Ettrick Water, gently uphill, following the route of the Southern Upland Way to provide an end to an enjoyable and satisfying day (**20km; 700m; 5h 40min**).

A swift ascent of Andrewhinney Hill itself can be made from Birkhill at the top of the A708 above Moffat Dale; parking just to the north-east of the farm. Take the signposted route at the farm, straight up the steep hillside beside the fence onto Herman Law then follow the fence over Trowgrain Middle and Mid Rig to Andrewhinney Hill. Return the same way or descend from the col before Trowgrain Middle to pick up a rough track that drops to Birkhill (**8km; 440m; 2h 40min**).

A chain of eight high-level grassy hilltops runs along the ridge between the valleys of the Moffat and Ettrick Waters opposite White Coomb and the Grey Mare's Tail waterfall. This ridge contains four Donalds and two Donald Tops, of which Andrewhinney Hill, a Graham, is the principal summit. Although the full traverse of the ridge, together with the return along the road, is fairly long it is a straightforward outing, especially since the start is at an altitude of 378m.

Drive up the Ettrick valley to the end of the public road and park considerately at the edge of the turning area, as much off the road as is possible. Head north-west on the right-hand track through the gate and follow this as it climbs, uphill through the forest above the Longhope Burn. The track zigzags out of the trees into the open onto a grassy shoulder where it becomes a grassy hill track which is followed westwards to swing round onto the top of Bodesbeck Law (**3km; 290m; 1h 10min**). On the other side, across the deep trench of Moffat Dale lie Under Saddle Yoke and

Capel Fell, left, Ettrick Pen in the distance and Wind Fell from Croft Head (Rab Anderson)

Ettrick Pen; *692m; (G115); (D38); L79; NT199076; head point of Ettrick(dale). Mapped Penn of Ettrick (1654): also known 16th-18th centuries as Penn of Esdaile Moore, because it also stands at head of Eskdale, to south*

Hopetoun Craig; *632m; (DT); L79; NT187067*

Wind Fell; *665m; (D56); L79; NT178061; windy hill. The pass beside it on the west was Windy Hass (1804), later Windy Nick (1860)*

Loch Fell; *688m; (D44); L79; NT170047; no loch present here, so the name is obscure*

West Knowe; *672m; (DT); L79; NT163052*

Croft Head; *637m; (G188); (D72); L79; NT153056; hill above Crofthead (farm). Scots 'croft', smallholding*

Capel Fell; *678m; (G133); (D46); L79; NT163069; horse hill? Scots 'cappell, capul', horse. Horses roamed wild on hills*

Smidhope Hill; *644m; (DT); L79; NT168076*

White Shank; *622m; (DT); L79; NT169083*

These nine hills are clustered around and close to the afforested headwaters of the Ettrick Water. They can be conveniently combined into a very fine extension of the classic Border round known as The Ettrick Horseshoe. The walk described is one of only a few where three Grahams can be climbed in one logical outing.

Drive up the Ettrick valley to the end of the public road and park considerately at the edge of the turning area, as much off the road as is possible. Take the left-hand track and follow this, the route of the Southern Upland Way, south-west past Potburn and cross the bridge over the Ettrick Water to reach the bothy at Over Phawhope. Break off left just beyond the bothy, cross the Entertrona Burn and head uphill on another track through a break in the forest. Where the track ends, climb steeply up the rounded spur to reach the splendid viewpoint of Ettrick Pen (**3.5km; 320m; 1h 20min**). To the south the view extends from The Cheviot on one side of the country to the Solway Firth on the other.

The regional boundary continues around much of the high-level part of this walk and is marked on the ground by a fence, then a wall, which act as navigational aids. A long south-westerly section alongside the fence leads over Hopetoun Craig then onto Wind Fell. Descend to where the fence splits and drop down beside the left-hand fence to Wind Fell Nick, then follow the fence up the long spur to reach a junction of fences and the trig point on top of Loch Fell (**8.5km; 570m; 2h 50min**).

Take the right-hand fence to gain West Knowe where the next objective, Croft Head, can be seen on the opposite side of the valley with the sizeable drop and ascent in between fully revealed. Descend steeply beside the fence towards the edge of the forest for a short way then break away from this to cut steeply down and across the slope to gain a sheep fank on the valley floor. Pause for breath, cross the Southern Upland Way, then climb the path which ascends the fine and narrow east ridge via some zigzags to gain the Cat Shoulder leading to the top of Croft Head (**11km; 790m; 3h 50min**). Savour the splendid view then return to the valley floor.

Now follow the Southern Upland Way up the right side of the narrow

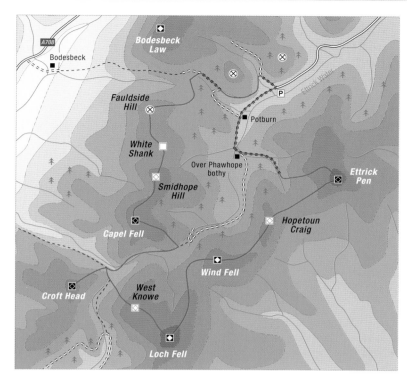

valley opposite the Craigmichen Scar. Beds of sedimentary rock have been exposed here and shaped by the forces of nature into an impressive unstable high-angled hillside and a gorge through which the Selcoth Burn flows. The burn is crossed higher up by a bridge to gain Ettrick Head, the col where the path descends into the Ettrick valley. Climb north-west beside a fence onto the third Graham, Capel Fell (**14km; 1020m; 5h**).

Although there is still some distance to cover, the going becomes easier and the views ahead to Hart Fell, Carrifran Gans and White Coomb can be fully appreciated. Descend north-east beside the fence to the col to meet a wall which now indicates the boundary and follow this over Smidhope Hill then onto White Shank. Swing round beside the wall over the bump of Fauldside Hill then drop down to meet a track at the col in front of Bodesbeck Hill. Now heading back to the valley floor on the track, descend through a break in the forest to reach a sheep fank where the main track dog-legs off right to Potburn. Continue straight ahead on a grassy track which leads into the forest and contours the hillside. On emerging from the trees, cross the burn by a footbridge and descend another track back to the road (**20km; 1100m; 6h 30min**).

A slightly shorter Graham only route starts as for the described route onto Ettrick Pen (**3.5km; 320m; 1h 20min**) and continues to Wind Fell. Drop down to Ettrick Head then follow the Southern Upland Way and ascend Croft Head (**9.5km; 680m; 3h 15min**). Return to Ettrick Head then ascend Capel Fell (**12.5km; 910m; 4h 25min**) and return to Ettrick Head. Follow the Southern Upland Way back to the start (**17.5km; 910m; 5h 30min**). A route of a similar length can be made from Sailfoot in Moffat Dale but the ascent involved is greater.

Capel Fell from Loch Fell (Rab Anderson)

Nether Comb Craig; *724m; (DT); L78; NT129109*

Swatte Fell; *729m; (D22); L78; NT120115; obscure. The OS Name Book suggests Anglo-Saxon 'swaete', sweated. More likely is Old English 'swað', which developed to 'swathe', sward of grass*

Falcon Craig; *724m; (DT); L78; NT122127*

Hart Fell; *808m; (D7); L78; NT113135; hill of the stag. Hills named after stags are found in the Lakes (Harter Fell), the Hebrides (Hartaval) and elsewhere in Nithsdale*

Under Saddle Yoke; *745m; (D16); L78, NT142126; saddle shaped like a yoke. Mapped Coripheran Yoke (1775), the Yoke (1790s), Saddleback (1820), this hill together with Saddle Yoke, form a classic narrow saddle*

Saddle Yoke; *735m; (DT); L78; NT144123*

Forming a natural circuit around the Blackhope Burn and the Black Hope valley, these hills can be conveniently climbed in one superb outing known as the Black Hope Round. This is one of the classic Border hillwalks. There are no Grahams on this round but the highest point is Hart Fell, a Corbett.

The circuit starts at Blackshope cottage in Moffat Dale, 5.5 miles (8.8km) to the north-east of Moffat. Blackshope is the white cottage on the north side of the A708, just east of the farm at Capplegill and the bridge over the Blackhope Burn. Parking is possible at the north-east side of this cottage around the grassy edge of the gated track into the Black Hope valley, as well as on the grass verge opposite. Take care not to block the track, or access to the garage.

Walk 200m or so west along the road over the Blackhope Burn, to a gate into a field, just past a small building. Walk up the right bank of the Hang Burn towards the obvious cleft on the hillside; Hang Gill. Pass through a gate and follow a sheep track steeply up the side of Hang Gill. Just above the waterfall, go through a gate at first one fence (electrified) then right through a gate in another fence. Head up rightwards to pick up a path which leads up the broad ridge running up the side of Black Craig to gain the top of Nether Coomb Craig (**2.5km; 580m; 1h 35min**). The slope on the right plunges steeply down into Black Hope and there are fine views across to Saddle Yoke.

A fence and dyke run from here all the way to Hart Fell but unless this navigational aid is required the better route is closer to the edge. Follow this edge, dropping down then up onto Swatte Fell, then head leftwards for 300m or so to go through a gate in the fence and try and find the top. The OS 1:25k map gives a height of 729m at the grid ref stated in the heading above, whist the 1:50k map gives a height of 728m at NT118114, some 200m to the south-west. This latter point is likely to be the actual summit in the light of a recent unratified survey, which gives a height of 730m at this point.

Go back through the gate and follow the wall and fence over Falcon Craig, a cairn on the other side of the fence marks the top. At the narrow neck, the Hass o' the Red Roads, the wall turns and descends south–west down a fine valley, down which the Auchencat Burn flows into the River Annan. Continue uphill beside the fence then along the broad summit to reach the trig point on Hart Fell

Hart Fell, left, and Under Saddle Yoke, right, from Croft Head (Rab Anderson)

Under Saddle Yoke, left, and Saddle Yoke from Hart Fell (Rab Anderson)

(**6.5km; 760m; 2h 40min**).

Those in a hurry to tick the Donalds might opt to pick up the outlier, Whitehope Heights, to the north-west but this involves a big drop-off and re-ascent, adding 2h to the day. It is also

off the natural round and better collected via a separate walk on the other side and albeit this climbs Hart Fell again, it takes in the Devil's Beef Tub and provides another enjoyable outing. The Whitehope Heights and

Hart Fell route is described on p52.

Continuing with the circuit, swing around the head of the Black Hope valley following the fence north-eastwards then eastwards above Saddle Craigs and descend over Hartfell Rig. Break away from the fence just before the col with Cape Law then cut across the head of Whirly Gill and contour the slope southwards to another col. Ascend the broad ridge to the top of Under Saddle Yoke (**10.5km; 910m; 3h 50min**).

Descend steeply to a narrow col then back up the narrow ridge on the other side onto Saddle Yoke. Pause for breath, savour the view to the Ettrick Hills in front, Carrifran Gans and White Coomb to the side and the Eildons in the far distance, then plunge down the splendid long south ridge into Moffat Dale. Just before the foot of the ridge, head right to reach the track at a gate and follow this back (**14km; 970m; 5h**).

See following page for map

> **Moffat Hills**
> *The Moffat Hills contain no Grahams but there are 10 Donalds and 11 Donald Tops, which as their highest points include the Corbetts White Coomb and Hart Fell. Collecting these hills in a satisfactory logical fashion and in accordance with Donald's original list proves a little more awkward than it seems at first sight, due to a number of outlying Donald Tops. However, given that statistics show the majority of Donaldists opt to compleat Donald's original list in full then part of the attraction is in deciding how to tackle these outliers. All of the Moffat Hills on Donald's List could essentially be climbed in two big rounds with some significant out and back detours to pick up the outliers, which the fit and those in a hurry to compleat might elect for. However, this would miss out on some particularly fine walks and for this reason The Moffat Hills are described here in four logical walks and although these include two out and back detours these are not particularly significant. These rounds do overlap in places and some hills appear twice, however there is no great hardship in climbing hills such as White Coomb and Hart Fell from two different direc-tions and the majority should hopefully enjoy the experience. It is also possible to tackle the hills described here in smaller or indeed different rounds to suit weather conditions and levels of fitness.*

Whitehope Heights across the head of Annandale (Rab Anderson)

Whitehope Heights; *637m; (D73); L78; NT095138; height above Whitehope (Burn). Scots 'hope', small upland valley. Whitehope Top (1775)*

Hart Fell; *808m; (D7); L78; NT113135; hill of the stag. Hills named after stags are found in the Lakes (Harter Fell), the Hebrides (Hartaval) and elsewhere in Nithsdale*

Whitehope Heights is a Donald that can truly be classed as an outlier, being separated from Hart Fell, its nearest Donald neighbour, by a walking distance of 2.6km, a drop of 281m and an ascent of 110m. It can be climbed as a somewhat lengthy and arduous detour off the Black Hope Round, the preceding route, and a time is given in that walk for its inclusion. However, it is off the natural round and it could be argued that it detracts from that classic horseshoe walk.

For this reason Whitehope Heights is perhaps best left for an ascent on its own and the walk to its summit from the west, together with an ascent of Hart Fell and a return by the Devil's Beef Tub, makes a fine round. The Beef Tub is a natural steep-sided corrie bowl at the head of Annandale where Border reivers hid stolen cattle.

At the top of the Devil's Beef Tub on the A701 some 5 miles (8km) north of Moffat, park considerately around the entrance to a gated track (NT055128) at a height of 395m. There is further parking downhill a little. The initial part of the route to just beyond Chalk Rig Edge is followed by the Annandale Way long distance footpath.

Cross the fences to the side of the gate by stiles and climb to the trig point on top of Annanhead Hill (478m) then continue over to Great Hill (466m) with the slopes below falling steeply into the Beef Tub. Continue along the grassy crest of the ridge beside the fence, over Chalk Rig Edge (500m), then drop slightly and climb towards the top of Whitehope Heights. Cross the stile in the deer fence to gain the cairn (**5km; 420m; 1h 50min**), then return back over the fence.

Tick done, the simple option is to return, however much the better walk is to continue on to Hart Fell whose vast bulk dominates the view ahead. Drop gently north-east through an odd corridor created by a sheep fence on the left and the deer fence on the right, then more steeply east to a narrow col. Draw breath and make a long, steep ascent beside the fence to reach the flat summit of Hart Fell (**7.5km; 710m; 2h 55min**) where there are splendid panoramic views.

Follow the fence south for 200m and where this swings away south-east, head south-west on an atv track down a long, grassy shoulder over Arthur's Seat. Go through a gate in the deer fence and continue down the narrow spur of Well Rig, through the gap between the burns, to pass above Hartfell Spa, a chalybeate spring felt to have health giving iron salt properties. At the bottom, go right

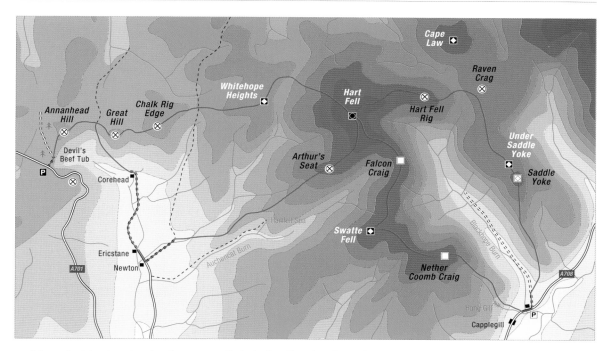

and through gates to gain a track leading to the minor road up the floor of the glen at Newton.

Turn right and follow the road around the east side of the buildings at Ericstane, then on to the buildings at Corehead, which are rounded in an anti-clockwise direction. A number of gates are passed through to gain an indistinct path which rises up the side of the Devil's Beef Tub to the heights above. This is certainly one of the highlights of the round and the final airy traverse to reach the col proves somewhat of a surprise and not just for weary knees weakened by the ascent! All that remains is a short re-ascent of Annanhead Hill, beyond which lies the road (**17.5km; 1020m; 5h 55min**).

Great Hill, left, Whitehope Heights and Hart Fell from the Devil's Beef Tub (Tom Prentice)

Lochcraig Head; *801m; (D9); L79; NT167176; hill above the cliff of the loch (Skene)*

Nickies Knowe; *761m; (DT); L79; NT163191*

Firthhope Rig; *800m; (DT); L79; NT153153*

White Coomb; *821m; (D4); L79; NT163150; white arched ridge. A cornice often forms in winter over Coomb Craig, facing east. Mapped White Coom Edge (1775)*

Carrifran Gans; *757m; (DT); L79; NT159138*

This is an excellent and scenic Donalds circuit of Loch Skeen, taking in the Corbett White Coomb as its highest summit.

Park in the National Trust's pay and display car park at the foot of the Grey Mare's Tail waterfall, off the A708 in Moffat Dale. Follow a good path up the steep slope on the east side of the waterfall. Height is gained rapidly and the path soon traverses the hillside to easier ground beside the Tail Burn which leads pleasantly to picturesque Loch Skeen. Lochcraig Head rises resplendent above the far end of the loch.

Walk along the east side of the loch for about 200m then break off right across heather to pick up a fence which is followed across a couple of boggy sections towards Lochcraig Head. Any other line is likely to prove more difficult. The fence and an old wall running beside it lead up the right side of the steep slope before swinging round and traversing across the flat summit area a short distance south of the actual top itself, which is easily gained alongside another fence (**4.5km; 570m; 2h**). Most people walk to the edge for the splendid view over Loch Skeen to the Graham Andrewhinney Hill on the ridge running above Moffat Dale.

The Donald Top of Nickies Knowe is an outlier to the north, easily picked up by following the fence to where it splits on Talla East Side then following the left-hand fence with a drop to a wide saddle and a short climb to the top (**6km; 600m; 2h 25min**).

Return to the saddle then pick up a sheeptrack which rises slightly then contours the hillside to reach the wall and remnants of the fence just above Talla Nick; the deep col between the hills. In poor visibility it might be better to keep to the fencelines.

From the col, ascend onto the top of Firthybrig Head to meet another wall and fence that run along the flat ridge then follow a vague atv track south-west. There is an imperceptible rise over Donalds Cleuch Head and another slight rise to reach the Donald Top of Firthhope Rig (800m). Now make a right-angled turn to the left and head south-east on the atv track, alongside a fence and the remnants of wall. Where the fence makes a right-angled turn to the south-west and the wall carries

White Coomb from Andrewwhinney Hill to the south-east (Rab Anderson)

Lochcraig Head and Loch Skeen from Andrewhinney Hill (Rab Anderson)

straight on, cut diagonally across to the rounded summit of White Coomb (**11.5km; 790m; 4h**).

The Donald Top of Carrifran Gans is an outlier less than 1.5km to the south and is easily included by descending south-west to a broad col with a tiny lochan then making a short ascent to the summit (**13km; 830m; 4h 25min**).

The first of the two descent options is to follow an atv track down the broad east ridge towards the forest. At a cairn, either drop northwards with the atv track to reach the head of a track through the forest, or continue down the crest to descend a break in the trees and gain the forest track lower down. Descend the track past a branch off left, then after crossing a burn take the left fork to gain the road and follow this for 2.5km back to the start (**18.5km; 870m; 5h 45min**).

The second option is to return to White Coomb and take the standard descent from there by heading north a short way to the wall, then following this down the east ridge over the bump of Upper Tarnberry to reach the Tail Burn well above the waterfall. The crossing may well entail getting wet feet. Descend the path to the car park (**17.5km; 940m; 5h 45min**). It is also possible to traverse across to the outflow from Loch Skeen from the dip in front of Upper Tarnberry.

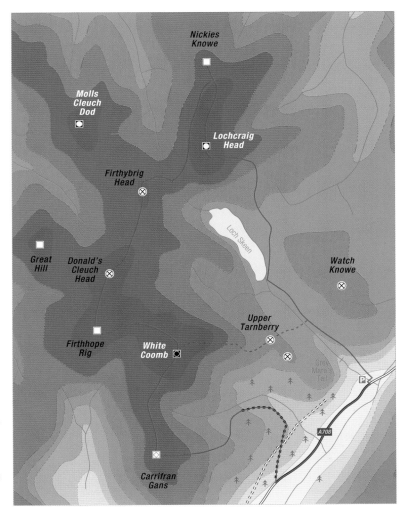

Garelet Hill; 680; (DT); L72; NT124201

Lairds Cleuch Rig; 684m; (DT); L78; NT125195

Erie Hill; 690m; (D41); L78; NT124187; mapped Earickle (1775). Possibly from Gaelic 'elrick', a narrow pass used to trap deer

Garelet Dod; 698m; (D32); L78; NT126172; lump of the grassy stripes? Scots 'gair, gare', green grassy stripe on hillside where water has suppressed heather: east of the top is Speir Gairs

Din Law; 667m; (DT); L78; NT124156

Cape Law; 722m; (D24); L78; NT131150; coping-stone hill? Scots 'cap'e can mean such a stone. The south end of the summit plateau was mapped Three Lairds Cairn (1775), indicating estates junction

White Coomb; 821m; (D4); L79; NT163150; white arched ridge. A cornice often forms in winter over Coomb Craig, facing east. Mapped White Coom Edge (1775)

Carrifran Gans; 757m; (DT); L79; NT159138

Firthhope Rig; 800m; (DT); L79; NT153153

Great Hill; 774m; (DT); L78; NT145163

Molls Cleuch Dod; 785m; (D12); L79 NT151179; lump above Molls Cleuch. Scots 'cleuch', ravine, possibly with a personal name. Mapped Maulscleuchshank (1775)

Carlavin Hill; 736m; (DT); L78; NT142188

Taking in all of the hills on Donald's List which lie around the Games Hope valley, this is one of the bigger Donald rounds. It provides a superb day out as well as a true test of stamina. There are no Grahams but if desired (and most will no doubt do so) the Corbett of White Coomb can easily be included, perhaps with Carrifran Gans. These two hills are also on the round of Loch Skeen, described on the preceding pages.

Start at the south-east end of Talla Reservoir, beyond the farm at Talla Linnfoots. There is ample verge parking just before the bend where the road starts to climb out of the valley (NT134202). Walk down the road for 100m or so and cross the footbridge over the Games Hope Burn. Ahead is a steep grassy slope which provides an unrelenting but brutally satisfying climb, leading directly to the trig point on Garelet Hill. Stay to the right of the Witch Linn burn, stepping over a fallen fence part way up and make best use of sheep tracks on firm ground up the slight ridge. If the fallen fence is ever fixed, there is a gate some 200m away on the other side of the burn (**1km; 380m; 50min**).

Step over the boundary fence which runs along the crest and walk south beside this onto the slightly higher Lairds Cleuch Rig then descend to the shallow col in front of

the next hill. Break away from the fence here and make the short ascent to the top of Erie Hill before descending off the back to rejoin the fence. A gradual climb beside the fence leads up the spur of Common Law then around onto Garelet Dod, the top of which lies just out from the fence and wall (**4.5km; 620m; 2h**).

Drop off the back, cutting down and across steeply to rejoin the fence and follow this over Ellers Cleuch Rig to the rocky head of Ellers Cleuch, level with the head of the small Gameshope Loch. Head up the other side and climb to the rocky knoll that is the top of Din Law; the top is about 100m out from the wall. Rejoin the wall and follow this down then up to Cape Law.

Follow the wall along a level section out to Pt.709m. The slopes here are those skirted on the Black Hope Round on the way to Saddle Yoke from Hart Fell. Continue following the wall and fence towards Saddle Yoke, dropping to a small dip. The wall can be seen going over a

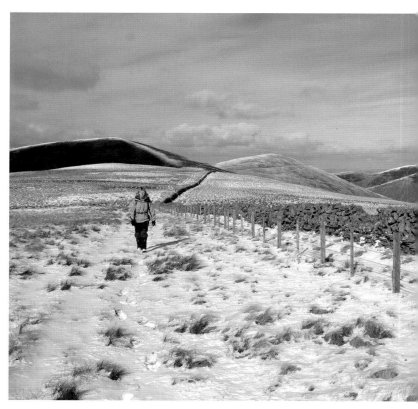

Erie Hill, left, and Lairds Cleuch Rig with Broad Law to the right (Rab Anderson)

slight rise ahead, then across the head of Rotten Bottom and up to Firthhope Rig. Just before the rise it is possible to cut the corner and rejoin the wall at the foot of Firthhope Rig, saving some time and distance.

Two options exist from here. The first is to cross flat ground, still following the wall and fence and make the steep climb up then across to a junction of fences on top of Firthhope Rig. From here, White Coomb is an easy short detour, gained by dropping down slightly and following what is left of the wall and the fence gently uphill. Where these diverge cut across to the top of White Comb (**11.5km; 1070m; 4h 30min**).

The second picks up Carrifran Gans by cutting eastwards across the slope from here to swing round and make a rising traverse above the burn to gain the col, between White Coomb and Carrifan Gans. A fence leads to the summit. Return to the col then climb beside the fence to White Coomb. This detour only adds 1km, 20m of ascent and 15min over the

first option.

Follow the wall and fence back to Firthhope Rig and stay with these onto Donald's Cleuch Head, an imperceptible rise. Leave the fence and head north-west along an old fence-line onto Great Hill, then return to the fence and continue to Firthybrig Head. There is a junction of walls and fences here with the right-hand wall dropping to Talla Nick beneath Lochcraig Head. The fit and the determined could detour to take in Lochcraig Head and Nickies Knowe, however this is likely to involve a return time of about 1h 45min.

Now on the home run, drop down then gradually up beside the left-hand wall and fence to the top of Molls Cleuch Dod (**17.5km; 1210m; 6h 5min**). There are two cairns, one next to the wall and another 100m to the north-east. Continue beside the wall and fence, down then easily up to the

final summit of Carlavin Hill.

For the descent, follow the wall downhill a short distance then head north away from this as it drops into a shallow basin at the head of a burn that descends to the valley floor.

If the wall is followed it crosses the burn and traverses the hillside to an area of rock where it stops and a line of old fence posts drops down alarmingly steep slopes directly to the valley floor. This should be avoided. If one chooses to descend this way it would perhaps be better to follow the south side of the burn down into the valley, although this is still very steep.

Better and safer is to either descend north down the burn of Gates Cleuch to reach the road, or head away from the wall just after the summit and follow the northern shoulder of the hill down to the road, which is followed downhill to the start (**21km; 1230m; 7h 15min**).

Broad Law and Cramalt Craig, right, from Molls Cleuch Dod to the south (Rab Anderson)

Talla Cleuch Head; 691m; (D40); L72; NT133218; hill above Talla Cleuch, the cleuch (ravine) dropping to Talla Reservoir. Talla is probably Gaelic 'an t-alla', the crags, or 'talla' rocks, on account of the striking cliffs above the reservoir and Talla Water

Broad Law; 840m; (D2); L72; NT146235; broad (flat-topped) hill. Mapped Braidl Hill (1654) from Scots 'braid', and Hairstane Broad Law (1755), after the farm (now) Hearthstane at its foot

Hunt Law; 639m; (DT); L72; NT150264

Cramalt Craig; 831m; (D3); L72; NT168247; cliff above the Cramalt (Burn). The burn name is probably Gaelic 'crom allt', crooked torrent. Mapped Black Dody (1775), 'the black lump'

Clockmore; 641m; (DT); L72; NT183228

Another Donald round with no Grahams, this walk has the Corbett Broad Law, the second highest hill in the Southern Uplands, as its highest point. As with many Donald rounds there are two outlying Donald Tops which make the outing a little more difficult, though not unduly so.

Start from the high point of the road (450m) that crosses between Talla and Megget Reservoirs. There is space for a few well-parked cars at the cattle grid beside the Megget Stone boundary marker. Given that a return is made along the road, various other places to park can be found to the east.

Ascend an atv track up the hillside to the right of the fence above the cattle grid, onto Fans Law. Cross flat ground and swing round beside the fence continuing uphill a short distance before crossing the fence and cutting north-west up and across the slope to reach another fence coming down off Cairn Law. Follow an atv track just out from the fence to avoid boggy ground on the broad col and climb to the top of Talla Cleuch Head; the high point lies on the east side of the fence about 100m beyond where it makes a right-angled turn (**2.5km; 250m; 1h**). There are fine views across to the hills around the Games Hope Burn.

Return downhill then follow the fence uphill to join the fence left earlier on Cairn Law and make a gradual 2km ascent alongside this to gain the trig point on top of Broad Law (**6km; 460m; 2h 10min**). Swing around north-east beside the fence, passing the crown-like aircraft beacon that adorns the summit, then pass one aerial to join a track and go through a gate to reach two larger aerials.

Descend east beside the fence, with the great bulk of Cramalt Craig lying ahead. The Donald Top of Hunt Law lies to the north and although well off to the side it is easier to take in than it looks. Rather than traverse directly to this from the col, it is

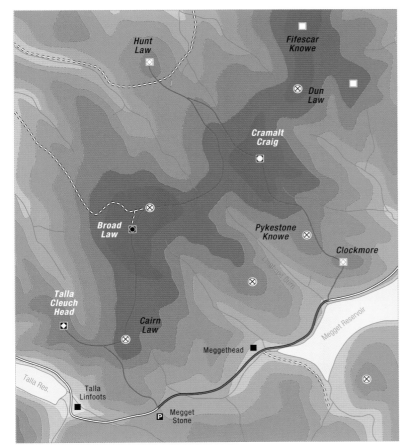

Manor Hills
Named after the Manor Valley which cuts into their midst, the Manor Hills occupy the area of hill country south of Peebles. They are separated from the Moffat Hills by the Megget and Talla Reservoirs and lie between the River Tweed on the west and the Yarrow Water on the east. There are 13 Donalds and 9 Donald Tops out of which Dun Rig is the solitary Graham and Broad Law, a Corbett, the highest point. All these hills can conveniently be climbed in four reasonable outings.

and make the short ascent to the top of Clockmore.

Megget Reservoir lies below and after dropping southwards for a bit, the road bridge across the Linghope Burn comes into view. Descend steeply south-south-west down Appletree Brae towards the bridge and at the bottom pass beneath the power lines to go through first one, then another gate to reach the road.

Cross the bridge and follow the road past Meggethead at the end of the reservoir, then gradually uphill beside the Megget Water back to the start. The walk back along the road takes about 45min (**20.5km; 970m; 6h 30min**).

perhaps better to climb partway up the hillside next to the fence before stepping over and descending towards it. Pick up a rough atv track which descends from the summit of Cramalt Craig and follow this over the boggy col. Cross the bulldozed track which links the valleys on either side then continue up an atv track to the top of Hunt Hill. To the west across the Tweed Valley are the Culter Hills, then north the Drumelzier hills with Fifescar Knowe and Dollar Law to the east.

Return across the boggy col and follow the rough atv track all the way up the spur to gain the summit of Cramalt Craig (**13km; 810m; 4h 20min**). This hill is only 9m lower than Broad Law and until 1984 was classed as a Corbett, however the drop is c146m.

Head southwards from the summit across flat ground following an atv track which descends the shoulder then swings to the south-east before

dropping to cross rough ground just to the east of the shepherds' cairn on Pykestone Knowe. Cross a shallow col

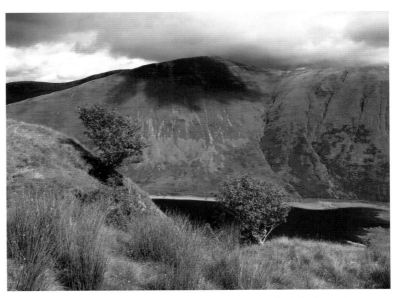

Talla Cleuch Head and Talla Reservoir from the south (Rab Anderson)

Pykestone Hill, left, to Drumelzier Law, right (Rab Anderson)

The Scrape; *719m; (DT); L72; NT176324*

Pykestone Hill; *737m; (D19); L72; NT173312; hill with pointed stones. The summit is scattered with many pointed boulders. Mapped Pikestone Craig (1755), and Pykitstane Hill (1775)*

Middle Hill; *716m; (D27); L72; NT159294; middle hill, between the high points Pykestone Hill and Dollar Law: also, viewed from Tweed valley, midway between Glenstivon Dod and Taberon Law*

Taberon Law; *636m; (DT); L72; NT146288*

Drumelzier Law; *668m; (D53); L72; NT149312; hill above Drummelzier. Mapped Great Law (1755 and 1775)*

This round of Donalds and Donald Tops starts from Drumelzier, alleged to be the burial place of the wizard Merlin of Arthurian legend fame, the spot at NT134345 being marked by a plaque. The walk starts from a small parking area on the left just beyond the village hall, a short distance up the access road 100m west of the telephone box, on the south side of the B712 Peebles to Broughton road.

Rather than use the track past the farm, cross the burn by a footbridge and go left around the side of Old Mill house to pass through a gate and follow a grassy path into the valley for

400m. Go through another a gate then cross the burn by a footbridge to regain the track and continue along this.

After crossing a bridge and climbing through a break in a small forestry plantation, take the right-hand track which rises up the side of the spur of Dens Knowe. A little higher take the left-hand track and continue to just below the summit of Pykestone Hill. Break off left here and contour to the fence then cross Broad Moss and make the short climb to the junction of fences on the broad, rounded summit of The Scrape. Return across Broad Moss and climb

to the trig point on top of Pykestone Hill (**7km; 580m; 2h 30min**).

Descend south onto the line of the old drove road, the 'Thief's Road', which is followed for a short way, over the bump of Grey Weather Law, before leaving it to continue beside the fence onto Long Grain Knowe. The old drove road heads south up onto Dollar Law.

At the junction of fences on Long Grain Knowe, a right-angled turn to the right leads across boggy ground beside the fence to a left turn to gain the top of Middle Hill whose summit is covered in a lovely mossy carpet. The actual top lies 50m to the south lies south of the fence. On the other side of the Stanhope valley to the south is Hunt Law, the outlier on the Broad Law Round (see preceding route), whilst across the Tweed, Gathersnow Hill and Culter Fell stand out. Return to the top of Middle Hill then step over the fence and head north on the now fenceless ridge to the shepherds' cairn on Glenstivon Dod. Continue for a few hundred metres then drop north-west to a col and climb onto shapely Drumelzier Law (**15.5km; 910m; 5h**).

Descend to the north-west and follow an atv track which swings west then north along the ridgeline onto Logan Head. On this section there are fine views up the Tweed valley and across to Broughton Heights. The track swings around again here and is followed north-east down Finglen Rig to a gate in the corner of a field.

Go through the gate and take either of two grassy tracks, the upper gives better views, to regain the track in the floor of the glen. Cross the footbridge and return past Old Mill house to the start (**20km; 1160m; 6h 15min**).

of the fence (**10km; 670m; 3h 20min**).

Now for the 55min there and back deviation to pick up the outlying Donald Top of Taberon Law, which lies 1.5km away to the south-west above afforested slopes. Keep to the atv track which avoids the boggy ground at the col to gain the top which also

Drumelzier Law from Middle Hill (Rab Anderson)

Black Cleuch Hill, left, and Black Law (Rab Anderson)

Black Cleuch Hill; *675m; (DT); L73; NT222290*

Black Law; *698m; (D31); L73; NT222279; black hill. From its heather cover. Mapped Blake Law (1775), from Scots 'blake', black*

Conscleuch Head; *624m; (DT); L73; NT220262*

Deer Law; *629m; (DT); L73; NT222255*

Greenside Law; *643m; (D70); L72; NT197256; hill with the green side. A contrast with its eastern nose, Black Rig*

Notman Law; *734m; (DT); L72; NT185260*

Fifescar Knowe; *811m; (DT); L72; NT175270*

Dollar Law; *817m; (D5); L72; NT178278; high meadow? Mapped Duillard hill (1654) and Duller Law (1755) might suggest Brittonic or Gaelic 'dol ard', meadow on the height. It has a broad flat grassy top*

Grouped around the head of the lovely Manor Valley, these Donalds and Donald Tops provide another sizeable outing. Begin not far from the end of the road up the Manor Valley where there is a good parking on the right, next to the bridge over the Kirkhope Burn (NT199307) and just beyond a white cottage.

Walk south along the road across the bridge, go over a cattle grid then go left across the field and cross the Manor Water by a wooden bridge (there is another bridge a little further up by a Scottish Water facility). Climb steeply up the hillside, initially following sheeptracks, to gain the top of Langhaugh Hill (533m) and 100m beyond this pick up an atv track. Either follow this along the south side

of the hill where it does swing round to the top, or break up onto the shoulder at some wooden shooting butts to reach a fenceline and follow this to a fence on the otherwise featureless top of Black Cleuch Hill (named as this on the OS 1:25k map, but Blackhouse Heights on the OS 1:50k map). Swing round then drop south to a col and climb onto Black Law (**4.5km; 450m; 1h 45min**); the summit is on the first rise.

Continue south-west to the second slight rise, which is 2m lower, and go through a gate to follow the fence which leads off at right-angles. This leads downhill to a col then easily over Conscleuch Head onto Deer Law where the fence swings away eastwards. A finger of rock cairn marks

the top, 100m to the south-west.

Greenside Law is the next objective and lies to the west, on the other side of Glengaber Burn valley. Either head downhill cutting north-west across the slope on very tussocky terrain, aiming to the right of the summit of Greenside Law, or return to the col with Conscleuch Head then descend west down the slope. Cross the Glengaber Burn at around NT211260 and climb up the other side through deep heather on Black Rig, passing a wooden shed, to gain the through track between the Manor Valley and Megget Reservoir. From a cairn at the high point of the track, leave it and climb to the top of Greenside Law which lies on the other side of a fence (**10km; 700m; 3h 30min**).

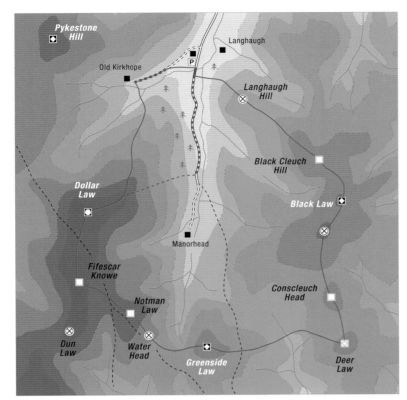

Head then up onto Notman Law.

Drop off the back and either follow the fence, or the grassy track. Where the fence swings left and the track passes through it by a gate, follow the fence uphill away from the track. Join another fence and an old wall then follow these north onto Fifescar Knowe. After a short descent cross the track which heads across to Pykestone Hill and continue easily to the cairn and trig point on the summit of Dollar Law (**14.5km; 1010m; 5h**).

There are two descent options. One follows the fence and wall north-east all the way downhill to the southern end of the forest, then gains the road which is walked back to the start. The other follows the wall and fence gradually downhill for 600m before crossing over and heading off at right-angles beside another fence that runs down the north spur, along the top edge of the forestry plantation.

At the bottom, cross the bridge and go round the side of the sheep pens at the Old Kirkhope steading then follow a track back towards the road, passing a cross and font stone in a field on the left. Where the forestry ends, just before the white cottage, go through a gate and follow the burn back to the car (**19km; 1010m; 6h 20min**).

Descend south-west on an atv track alongside the fence and swing around the steep-sided corrie which forms the head of the valley where there are fine views down the Manor Valley. There is a rough track on the other side of the fence, marked as a path on the map, but this passes beneath the top of Notman Law. The direct route beside the fence is the better option, steep initially, over the bump of Water Head or Shielhope

Greenside Law, far left, and Dollar Law from the north (Rab Anderson)

Dun Rig; *744m; (G22); (D17); L73; NT253315; dull-brown ridge. Mapped 1775 as Coom or Blackcleugh Head*

Glenrath Heights; *732m; (D20); L73; NT241322; heights above Glenrath (glen, farm). Gaelic 'gleann ràth', glen with a old fort: the farm lies beside a prehistoric fort called Macbeth's Castle*

Stob Law; *676m; (D50); L73; NT230332; mapped Sandy Know Head (1775). Scots 'stobis' a stake, tree trunk or boundary post: there is no boundary here and the flat top is cairn-less*

Birkscairn Hill; *661m; (D59); L73; NT274331; cairn above Birks (farm). Mapped Birks Cairn (1775) by Armstrong who described "a remarkable large and regular built pile of stones". Scots 'birk', birch*

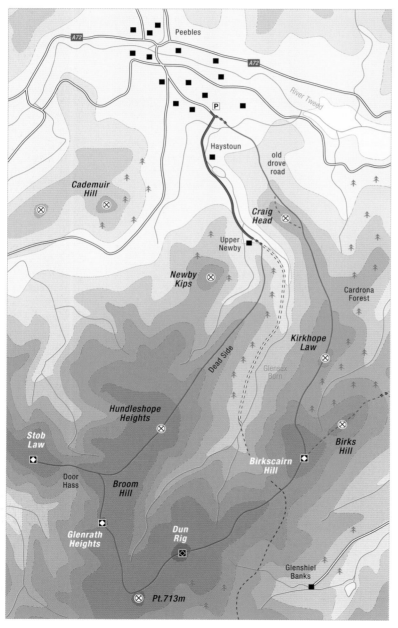

As well as being a Donald, Dun Rig is the only Graham in the Manor Hills. It sits in a commanding position at the head of the Glensax Burn and when climbed as part of a round with its neighbouring Donalds, it gives a long but fine circuit. Park on the south-eastern edge of Peebles, at the end of Glen Road (NT260393), gained from Springhill Road.

Walk past the road off right to Haystoun, which is the return route, and take the Tweed Trails signposted track straight ahead. Cross the Glensax Burn via the bridge and follow the route up the hillside past fields then uphill through the trees where the track (an old drove road) runs between two drystane dykes for a way. When the walls open out either skirt Craig Head on the drove road or go over its top on a path. Continue uphill to meet the top edge of the Cardrona Forest, then with fine views opening up all around climb over Kirkhope Law (537m) and leave the forest behind to climb Birkscairn Hill.

Drop south-west to where the drove road starts the descent towards the

Hundelshope Heights, left, Glenrath Heights and Stob Law from the Manor Valley to the north (Rab Anderson)

Yarrow Water and St Mary's Loch then head up over Stake Law on increasingly boggy ground through peat hags to reach the trig point on the flat top of Dun Rig (**10km; 700m; 3h 20min**). The OS show the high point a little further south-west.

Descend south-westwards then break away from the fence on a boggy path that contours below Pt.713m and swing round to rejoin the fence where it drops north to a col. Climb onto Glenrath Heights (named as Middle Hill on OS maps) and continue beside the fence, descending slightly then passing through a gate to follow the left-hand fence onto the spur of Broom Hill. Drop north-westwards to a col, Door Hass, then easily climb the outlying Stob Law (**14.5km; 860m; 4h 40min**).

Return to Broom Hill then cut the corner to rejoin the other fence and follow this north-east onto Hundleshope Heights (685m) where there is a trig point. Break away from the fence here and follow an atv track down the long north-east spur of Dead Side to join the track along the floor of the glen. The track becomes surfaced and leads along the Glensax Burn past the farm of Upper Newby then a pond and the large house at Haystoun, back to the start (24km; 1000m; 7h 15min).

A shorter Graham only route is possible starting at NT305336 beside the Quair Water to the east, using the road to Glen House, the hill track onto Birks Hill to gain Birkscairn Hill, and on to Dun Rig (**7km; 620m; 2h 35min**), (**14km; 680m; 4h 20min**). From the same start it is also possible to bike to Glenshiel Banks and climb the hill via its south ridge.

Dun Rig, left, and Hundleshope Heights from near Craig Head (Rab Anderson)

Blackhope Scar from Bowbeat Hill (Rab Anderson)

Blackhope Scar; *651m; (G174); (D64); L73; NT315483; common grazing land of Blackhope (farm). Scots 'hope' upland valley*

Bowbeat Hill; *626m; (D77); L73; NT292469; hill for summer grazing for cows. Scots 'bow', cattle and 'beat', hill-grazing*

Dundreich; *623m; (D81); L73; NT274490; hill-fort with a good outlook, perhaps, from Britonnic 'din drich' or, less likely, Gaelic 'dùn dreach', hill-fort on the (hill)face. There are ancient earthworks on top*

The Moorfoot Hills lie to the north of the Manor Hills above Peebles and present a steep north-west facing scarp slope towards Edinburgh. The highest points on this scarp slope, though not the highest point in The Moorfoots which is Windlestraw Law, are formed by the Graham Blackhope Scar and its neighbouring Donalds, which sit around the headwaters of the River South Esk. It is a distinctive skyline hereabouts and the round of all three hills gives a scenic and varied outing.

Start from the car park at NT292528 at the southern end of Gladhouse Reservoir. Walk south-east along the road into the farmyard at Moorfoot, then swing round to the right and follow the track towards the valley formed by the River South Esk. Pass Gladhouse Cottage then cross the South Esk and break off the track to climb up onto the narrow spur of Hirendean Hill, passing the remains

of Hirendean Castle. A steep climb up the grassy crest gains the top then easy ground followed by a short climb onto The Kipps (541m).

Drop off the back and head east-

wards above the head of a track to pick up the fence which runs up the shoulder of Blackhope Scar. The going is generally better on the left of the fence and there is a small path

Hirendean Castle ruins above the South Esk (Rab Anderson)

through the heather. However the going can be slow and some back and forth crossings of the fence will be required to avoid boggy bits, of which there are many. The fence leads to the summit where there is a trig point at a junction of fences (**6km; 410m; 2h**). The view over Edinburgh and the Forth Valley is fabulous and extends to Beinn a' Ghlo and the Cairngorms, readily seen, especially when snow capped.

Follow the fence which swings round south-west and descend Long Edge to reach Kings Road Nick in front of Emly Bank and the Bowbeat Windfarm. Climb south-west to easily take in Bowbeat Hill; purists may wish to flounder along on the north side of the fence whereas the sensible will use the turbine access roads. Swing around the head of the Bowbeat Burn onto Bowbeat Rig, moving easily or floundering depending on which side of the fence one sits! Leave the wind-farm behind and climb north-west following the bleak high ground, then swing south-west near the fence between Dundreich and Jeffries Corse, to cross a fence ascending from below and gain the cairn and trig point on the summit of Dundreich (**12.5km; 690m; 4h**). Although this route is clear on the ground the featureless terrain means it might not be so obvious in snow and mist. In

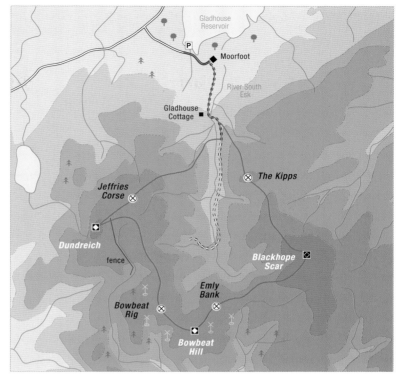

these conditions it is possible to descend west from the high ground to gain a fence beside a burn. This leads to the summit slope and is the fence crossed in the above description.

Continue north-east to Jeffries Corse then break away from the fence to pick up an atv track which

leads downhill to the north-east to swing east between burns and climb onto a small grassy knoll. Descend the fine ridge of Long Shank which leads to a crossing of the River South Esk and the track running beneath Hirendean Castle, back to the start (**18km; 710m; 5h 30min**).

Jeffries Corse and Dundreich (Rab Anderson)

Windlestraw Law; *659m; (G162); (D61); L73; NT371430; hill covered in windlestrae (grass). Scots 'windelstrae', long spindly grass such as crested dogstail or tufted hair-grass*
Bareback Knowe; *657m; (DT); L73; NT362420*
Whitehope Law; *623m; (D82); L73; NT330445; hill above Whitehope (farm). Scots 'hope', upland valley*

Although it is the highest point in the Moorfoot Hills, the Graham Windlestraw Law is an elusive summit which remains hidden from view from the roads which surround it. The hill only reveals itself to those travelling the B709 which runs through the middle of The Moorfoots along the secluded glen between Heriot and Innerleithen. It is from the north side of the Glentress Water in this glen that the route to it's summit begins. Despite the drop back to the floor of the glen, it is easy to include an ascent of the Donald of Whitehope Law on the opposite side.

Start from the B709 at NT348434 some 400m south of Blackhopebyre and the obvious grassy track that leads onto the hill just south of these buildings. There is ample off-road

parking beside the fence on the west side of the road, a little down from a wooden pole bridge over the Glentress Water, which is the return route, if doing Whitehope Law.

Walk northwards up the road and about 100m or so before Blackhopebyre, go through a gate onto the grassy track on the east side of the road. Follow the track up Gentress Rig, initially on a long traverse to the right, then east up the spur keeping to the more obvious tracks leading up Wallet Knowe. Higher, the track becomes less distinct and swings right to pass along a line of shooting butts to reach a fence and where this reaches the fence on top, cross over then go left for 100m to the trig point (**4km; 380m; 1h 30min**).

Descend easily south-west along-

side the fence then make the short climb onto the summit of Bareback Knowe, a Donald Top. Continue following the fence along the crest to reach another fence coming in from the left, go past this for a short way and then cross over the fence and head westwards to pick up a fence then an atv track which leads down the north-west shoulder. There is a notable contrast between the heathery ground on the right side of the fence and the grassy ground on the left.

Just before the col with Dod Hill, take the less obvious left-hand atv track down the side of the fence and go through a gate to follow an atv track down the left side of the fence. Ignore a gate into the field on the right and continue to another fence then follow this left a short way to its end then cut straight down to the road a short distance south of Glentress cottage; about 1km from the start.

Looking across to Whitehope Law from this descent a large circular sheepfold will have been seen, to the right of a small forestry plantation; an objective on the ascent. Also spotted will be a bridge over the burn at NT337430 with some obvious sheep tracks leading from it. Walk south-west along the road for 200m beside a wall and fence then go through a gate into the field to cross the bridge and follow the sheeptracks that zigzag uphill to the sheepfold. Above this the going becomes more tedious through generally trackless heather and eventually leads up the shoulder to a fence then the summit of Whitehope Law (**10.5km; 780m; 3h 45min**).

On the way down, tussocky and awkward initially, simply head for the track up Glentress Rig on the opposite side and descend directly to the pole bridge by the parking area (**12km; 780m; 4h 15min**).

Above: Windlestraw Law from Whitehope Law (Rab Anderson)

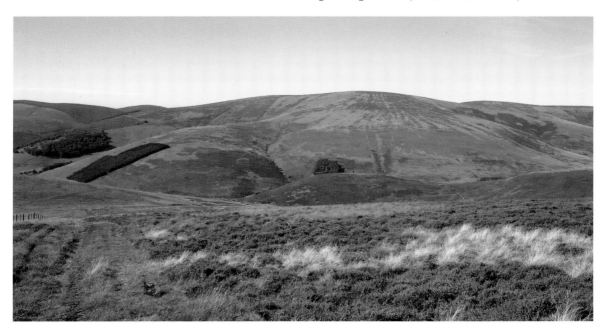

Whitehope Law from Bareback Knowe (Rab Anderson)

Cauldcleuch Head (Rab Anderson)

> **Cauldcleuch Head;** *619m; (G209); (D84); L79; NT456006; hill above the Cauld Cleuch. Scots 'cauld cleuch', cold gully, ravine, which runs north from the top*

S itting in splendid isolation, Cauldcleuch Head forms the high point in the relatively unfrequented Border hills between Hawick and the Muckle Toon of Langholm. This Graham is a great whaleback of a hill, the ascent of which provides a fine and scenic round. The start is reached along a minor road through the lovely glen that runs eastwards off the A7 and down which the Carewoodrig Burn flows. There is parking at the entrance to a forest track at the high point of this road at NY439978, between Carewoodrig and Billhope.

Walk west along the road for 100m, then go through a gate and climb the hillside just out from the edge of the forest, initially following an atv track, then a fence to gain the trig point on the 599m high Tudhope Hill (**2km, 310m; 1h**). With the bulk of the climbing behind and a clear view of the great rounded slopes of Cauldcleuch Head in front, follow the fence over to Millstone Edge, then swing around onto Langtae Hill at the head of the Billhope Valley. After a short descent, climb up and around peat hags, still beside the fence, to reach the flat top of Cauldcleuch Head (**6km; 470m; 2h 10min**). Although the ground underfoot gives rough going at times, especially when wet, the splendid views more than compensate for any hardship. In all directions, as far as the eye can see the landscape is a soothing blend of rounded green hills, glens and forest.

Descend south onto Muckle Land Knowe then break away from the fence and cross rough ground, passing over the minor bumps of Pennygant Hill, to reach the narrow top of Stob Fell. Just beyond the summit, drop off west and descend the prominent ridge of South Mid Hill to gain a track beside the Billhope Burn, at a cottage. A short walk south along this track leads to the road at Billhope and this is followed uphill back to the start (**11km; 560m; 3h 30min**).

> **Windy Gyle;** *619m; (D85); L80; NT855152; mapped Windygate Hill (1770). The OS had Windygate until 1907 (3rd edition); thereafter Windy Gyle, perhaps from 'ghyll', gully. There is a gate at the summit where the border is crossed*
>
> **Cairn Hill West Top;** *743m; (DT); L80; NT895193*

W indy Gyle is a solitary Donald in The Cheviot Hills and sits on the border with England. It can be combined with a walk along the border via the Pennine Way to Cairn Hill West Top. This hill appears in Donald's List as a Donald Top and the highest point on the border. However Cairn Hill West Top is not really a summit, merely a south-west top of The Cheviot, the highest summit in The Cheviot Hills. Due perhaps to some odd quirk, the border with England does not run along the high point of The Cheviot as might be expected and the summit of The Cheviot lies wholly within England. However, its western flanks spill onto the Scottish side of the border, so it makes sense to combine it with an ascent of Windy Gyle.

Start from Cocklawfoot at the end of the road up the Bowmont Water valley, gained from the B6401 about 1km south of Town Yetholm. There is ample off-road parking in the vicinity of the road end where an onward track goes to Cocklawfoot via a bridge and ford over the river (the return route) and a track off right is the approach past Kelsocleuch.

Take the track on the right and follow it past the farm at Kelsocleuch to where it divides. Go right through gates onto a track through a small plantation and exit to open pasture. Follow the grassy track past a shed and ascend the steepening hillside to the ridge of Kelsocleuch Rig. Here expansive views around the whole circuit open up, with the imposing bulk of The Cheviot at the end.

The route heads up around the edge of a grassy corrie bowl onto Windy Rig then climbs south-east to the large cairn (Russell's Cairn) and trig point at the summit of Windy Gyle (**4.5km; 390m; 1h 40min**).

Descend north-east along the ridge passing another large cairn. The long, broad and featureless frontier ridge stretches into the distance across ground which can be incredibly boggy and tiresome when wet. Any temptation to stay on the Scottish side of the fence is soon dispelled, especially when the Pennine Way path on the other side becomes a slabbed walkway. This may be a somewhat strange intrusion on the landscape however it does prevent erosion and certainly makes the going easier. The pavement soon crosses the ancient cross border route of Clennel Street coming up Cock Law to the north and for those satisfied with their Donald tick, a return could be made to Cocklawfoot down this.

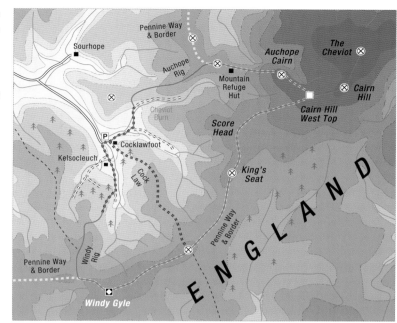

Continuing, swing north past the trig point on King's Seat to reach Score Head then climb north-east to Cairn Hill West Top, a mere bump but the highest point on the entire border. The Pennine Way makes a hairpin turn to the north-west here, however a short extension leads east up to Cairn Hill itself then north-east up to the elevated trig point on the great, rounded peaty dome of The Cheviot (**13km; 600m; 4h**); at 815m the highest hill hereabouts.

Return to Cairn Hill West Top and follow the Pennine Way to the cairns on Auchope Cairn then descend steeply beside the fence to the Mountain Refuge Hut. The valley on the right opens up to reveal the fine and craggy defile that is the Hen Hole. Continue along the Pennine Way for 500m or so, go through a gate to leave England, then follow a fence down the long ridge of Auchope Rig, south-west to a small flat col at the junction of four fences. Drop to the Cheviot Burn in the floor of the valley via the grassy track and follow this through the farm at Cocklawfoot back to the start (19km; 620m; 5h 40min).

Looking south to Cocklawfoot farm, Windy Rig, right, and Windy Gyle, centre (Rab Anderson)

SECTION 0c
The Midland Valley

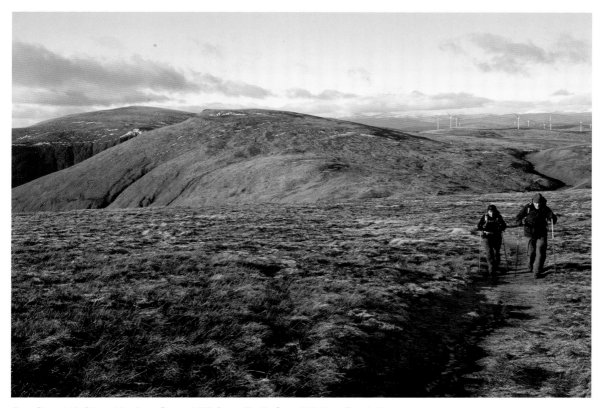

Ben Cleuch (left) and Andrew Gannel Hill from King's Seat Hill (Ken Crocket)

King's Seat Hill; 648m; (D66); L58; NS933999; also known as Innercairn (1769)
Andrew Gannel Hill; 670m; (DT); L58; NN918006
The Law; 638m; (DT); L58; NS910996
Ben Cleuch; 721m; (G62); (D25); L58; NN902006; stony mountain. Gaelic 'beinn clach'. Mapped Benclach (1783)
Ben Ever; 622m; (DT); L58; NN893001

The Ochil Hills occupy a prominent position in the centre of the Midland Valley with the rounded dome of Ben Cleuch forming their highest point. The first of two routes described is a longer walk which as well as climbing Ben Cleuch takes in the other four of its attendant hills that appear on the list of Donalds. The second route is a more direct there and back ascent of Ben Cleuch via The Law. Both routes conveniently start from Tillicoultry, at the entrance to Mill Glen which is signposted from the west end of the town. There is parking at the top of Upper Mill Street, or nearby, just below the stepped entrance to the Glen.

Where the road swings left over the burn, turn right up a track signposted to Blackford and after 50m, turn left up the hill to follow a stepped path, which then zigzags up the open hill-side. This provides a view down into the disused quarry on the opposite side above Mill Glen and leads to a fork. The left fork leads to the burn at the foot of The Law. Instead, take the higher fork on the right which contours the hillside above the lower path. After rounding the spur, climb uphill on the path and shortly after crossing a burn take the right-hand fork to continue up the spur; the lower path heads for the col between the hills. Part way up, a cairn (shown on OS maps) is passed and further on the path swings round onto the top of King's Seat Hill with its open views to the Lomond Hills and across

the Forth to the Pentland Hills (**4km; 600m; 2h**). The highest point lies at the north-west end of the high ground, not at the large cairn to the south-east.

Head north-west and take the path that drops to the col then make the short ascent to Andrew Gannel Hill. The summit is beside the fence, but a little nose just off to the side provides an excellent position overlooking the route. This is en route to Ben Cleuch and easily taken in, however The Law requires a relatively short diversion although it does entail some descent and re-ascent. Follow the fence towards Ben Cleuch with a short drop then climb to where it joins another fence. Cross over and descend south beside the fence to gain the top of ▶

The Law. From here Andrew Gannel Hill and King's Seat Hill are prominent, with Tarmangie Hill peeping over between the two. Return north to the junction of fences then swing left and climb to the rock strewn top of Ben Cleuch (**8.5km; 870m; 3h 30min**). A stone wall round the trig point provides shelter in bad weather. The view to the west and north-west is particularly fine. Arran is visible on a good day and moving round north, the Arrochar Alps, Ben Lomond, the Crianlarich hills, the Ben Lawers group and the Cairngorms are all well seen.

Descend north-west on a path and swing round south-west to pick up the fence which leads to a col, an intersection of fences which is crossed, then a grassy track leading to the top of Ben Ever. Continue along the south ridge on the grassy track to reach a fork then take the right fork which leads past sheep pens into Silver Glen and a farm track. Turn left, go over a gate, and continue down the track, now zigzagging, until a sign marked Public Footpath after the second zag left indicates a gate into Wood Hill Wood. Follow this path across the burn and on for about 1.5km, passing the Ochil Hills Woodland Park car park, which is an alternative starting point for the walk, to exit the wood above the golf course. Turn right at a tarmac road and go through shrubs on the left-hand side to gain Scotland Street which leads back to Upper Mill Street (15km; 920m; 5h 10min).

The direct route to Ben Cleuch normally passes through Mill Glen, however at the time of writing damage caused by rockfall has caused the Council to close this popular path. Funding has been found to rectify this but work has not yet begun. Instead, turn right at the top of Mill Street and follow the previous route for a short way to the fork in the path after the zigzags, then take the left fork. This contours above the glen then makes a short and steep scramble down to a wooden footbridge which crosses the Gannel Burn just before its confluence with the Daiglen Burn.

Now follow the well-trodden path up the slender ridge ahead, steeply at first then easing somewhat to gain the summit of The Law. Continue north beside the boundary fence over easy ground to eventually meet another fence then swing north-west to Ben Cleuch (**4km; 700m; 2h**). Return via the route of ascent (8km; 720m; 3h 20min).

The Ochil Hills

The name Ochil comes from the ancient Cambric 'uchel', meaning high. When viewed from the south this is understandable, for The Ochils suddenly rear up to the north of the flat estuary of the River Forth. Due to the proximity of these hills to the major centres of population, a large number of routes breach this steep introductory slope to gain access to the gently rounded and grassy high ground linking the various hill tops. The highest point in the Ochils is Ben Cleuch (721m), the only Graham of the range.

Lying south of the Highland Boundary Fault Line, The Ochils are classified as being in the Lowlands and are therefore included in Donald's Tables, there being five Donalds and four Donald Tops. These hills are covered here in three principal walks, although anyone interested in exploring this fine range of hills these could break these down into smaller or different outings. The full 'Round of Nine' can be done in one outing starting at Menstrie and ending at Glendevon (25.5km; 1200m; 8h 30min).

Blairdenon Hill from Sheriffmuir (Tom Prentice)

Blairdenon Hill; 631m; (D75); L58; NN865018; Gaelic 'blàr' means plain or flat ground; 'denon' is obscure

Blairdenon Hill lies at the western end of the Ochil Hills and is set back from the steep frontal scarp slope containing all the other main high points. As a result it is more difficult to link into a circuit with these hills and is therefore generally climbed on its own, although there are a few principal ways of attaining its summit.

The most direct route from the south starts at Menstrie and takes in Colsnaur Hill, an usually quiet hill and a good viewpoint. Turn north off the A91 at the Hollytree Inn and go up Park Road into Ochil Road where there is parking. At the end of the cottages follow the gated track through a kissing gate and onto a farm track that zigzags up the hillside. Follow this track which has been well-engineered to allow a steady pace up the steep escarpment.

At about 2.5km the First Inchna Burn is crossed and some 30m further on, leave the vehicle track at a small burn and follow an atv track up the unnamed south-west spur of Colsnaur Hill. Keep right at any junctions to reach a final path leading to the 553m summit, which has a small cairn and sheltered hollow.

Continue north along the ridge, following an atv track beside a drystane dyke and fence, then just a fence, across Menstrie Moss. Some 2km from Colsnaur Hill a slight descent is made to cross the Old Wharry Burn. Keep left of the fence and ascend to the flat top of Blairdenon Hill and a junction of fences, beyond which lies the actual summit, marked by a small cairn (**6.5km; 650m; 2h 40min**).

Retrace your steps across the Old Wharry Burn to regain the wall and follow it to a high point at approximately NN862004. The next section definitely requires micro-navigation in poor visibility. Go due west from the wall over the knoll of Pt.545m to gain an atv track and follow it south of Pt.541m, keeping right at junctions to gain a shallow col above the Third Inchna Burn and below Big Hunt Hill.

Future afforestation plans for Menstrie Glen have not yet begun (2014). Until they do, keep to the high ground south to Jerah ruin, otherwise, turn south-west along an atv track to about 200m east of Pt.453, where a future forestry track should be picked up and followed south towards Jerah ruin. From Jerah go south-east over two pastures to gain the path on the north side of the Menstrie Burn. This section through the old wooded glen is in complete contrast to the higher ground, and is particularly attractive in spring and summer before the bracken rises. It leads over the three Inchna Burns to gain the initial farm track which is followed back to the start point (15km; 700m; 5h).

An alternative route starts from the west, at the car park on the north side of the Sherrifmuir Inn (NN827021) and is a circuit of Glen Tye. Walk down the road for 100m and go through a rickety gate onto the moor, then head across rough ground towards the entrance to Glen Tye, making best use of sheep tracks. Stay on the higher ground above the burn in the floor of the glen, then where the wall and fence start to climb the hillside go through a rickety gate to gain the burn. Keep to the left bank until above a small cascade then cross over. Now climb the slope on the opposite side past the base of a forestry plantation and continue up onto Little Hunt Hill (431m). Beyond this, cross a fence then ascend rough ground up and leftwards onto the top of Big Hunt Hill (520m). Now head south, then south-east to pick up an atv track and follow this round Pt.541m and Pt.545m to gain the wall and fence (the 'Menstrie' route in reverse). Follow the fence north across Menstrie Moss and over the Old Wharry Burn to the top of Blairdenon Hill (6km; 450m; 2h 20min).

Continue west beside the fence passing a memorial to a crashed aircraft onto Greenforet Hill then swing round north-west onto Mickle Corum (594m). Break away from the fence past the remains of a rectangular enclosure and descend the slope westwards to a col then climb onto Glentye Hill (481m). A rough track now leads down the shoulder to the burn where a gate allows the fence to be followed towards a small stand of trees beside the road. Just before the trees, cross the fence and walk down a line of standing stones on the moor, back to the Sheriffmuir Inn (11km; 500m; 3h 40min).

Innerdownie summit and Whitewisp Hill, left, from the south (Tom Prentice)

> **Innerdownie**; *610m; (D89); L58; NN966031; obscure. There is another Innerdouny Hill 8km to the north-east*
> **Whitewisp Hill**; *643m; (DT); L58; NN955013*
> **Tarmangie Hill**; *645m; (D69); L58; NN942014; hillock abounding in fawns. Gaelic 'tòrr mangaich'. Mapped Tarmangie Carn (1779)*

These grassy hills offer an enjoyable high level round with fine views east to Loch Leven and the Lomond Hills and south to the Forth. From the Glen Sherup Forestry Commission car park in Glen Devon, ascend the signposted path to gain a forest track beyond Whitens and follow it to where the Reservoir Trail (the return route) is signposted off right to Glensherup Reservoir dam. Just beyond this, turn left at a track junction and contour the hillside east down Glen Devon through felled and forested sections.

At NN975041, near the end of the track, a Scotways marker indicates a narrow firebreak on the right, which is followed south-east through the conifers to a gate on the northern flanks of Innerdownie. Follow the wall to the cairned summit of Innerdownie (**5km; 390m; 1h 45min**) and views south to rounded Whitewisp Hill, more pointed Tarmangie, and distant Ben Cleuch. Continue beside the wall over the ill-defined bump of Bentie Knowe to a col, from where a steady ascent beside a fence gains a stile and the broad summit of Whitewisp Hill. Return to the wall and fence and

follow them to the summit of Tarmangie Hill (**8.5km; 510m; 2h 45min**), gained by a gate in the fence or a stile further on. Descend keeping right of the fence to a gate in the deer fence below Cairnmorris Hill, from

where an atv track begins. The atv track can be followed all the way to the base of Ben Shee, but it is worth making a short diversion en route to the top of Scad Hill with its large summit boulder.

As Ben Shee is approached, more and more seedlings line the route. Since buying the high ground from Cairnmorris to Ben Shee, Woodland Trust Scotland have removed the sheep, controlled deer numbers and planted millions of birch, oak, rowan and other native trees and shrubs. The atv track skirts Ben Shee to the west, but a sign indicates a path to the summit which is easily gained (**12.5km; 610m; 3h 55min**).

Descend to regain what is now a gravel track and follow it over the ridge and down into Glen Sherup. Two options are now possible. Remain on the track to where the rough scrub on the right ends, then descend right to the road in the glen floor. Alternatively, descend through the scrub to a ladder stile at NN963047 visible in the deer fence below, to gain the road. Both options now follow the road back up to the reservoir and Glen Sherup House. Cross the dam over the reservoir, ascend to the track and turn left back to the car park (**16km; 620m; 4h 40min**).

Uamh Bheag, background, with Am Beannan in the foreground (Rab Anderson)

Meall Clachach; *621m; (DT); L57; NN688125*
Uamh Bheag; *664m; (G156); (D57); L57; NN691118; little cave;*
Uamh Bheag East Top *(twin); 664m; L57; NN696119*
Beinn Odhar; *626m; (DT); L57; NN714127*
Beinn nan Eun; *631m; (D74); L57; NN723131; mountain of the birds*

Positioned just south of the Highland Boundary Fault, these hills lie in the Scottish Lowlands and as such, fall within the geographical boundary of The Donalds. However, they were not included in Percy Donald's original list. Uamh Mhòr on the southern flanks of Uamh Bheag sports an impressive rock cleft at NN 687111, described by Walter Scott as "a great den, or cavern... said, by tradition, to have been the abode of a giant. In latter times, it was the refuge of robbers and banditti...". It is well worth a visit if time allows.

Unfortunately, these mountains are rather less interesting than their history. The finest hill on the round is shapely Am Beannan, an unclassified peak of 574m, which displays steep conglomerate common with other points along the Highland Boundary Fault such as the Menteith Hills, Conic Hill and Inchcailloch island.

Uamh Beag is pleasant enough, but peat hags, bog and rough grass dominate the tops of Meall Clachach, Beinn Odhar and Beinn nan Eun, while the southern flanks of the latter two support wind turbines visible from most of the Forth valley.

Park at the car park below Glen Artney church and walk down the glen to the bridge over the Water of Ruchill. Go through the gate before the bridge and follow sheep and cattle paths along the south side of the river towards the Allt Ollach, with Am Beannan obvious ahead.

Ascend either side of the fence before the Allt Ollach to a bridge. Cross over and make a steep ascent of Am Beannan to arrive unexpectedly on its rounded top (**4km; 420m; 1h 35min**). A broad hag-strewn ridge leads to Meall Clachach and a fence which is followed through more hags to the summit of Uamh Bheag, marked by a cairn at the intersection of three fences (**6km; 570m; 2h 15min**). For the single Graham, return the same way (**12km; 610m; 3h 50min**).

The southerly fence leads to Uamh Mhòr and the cleft on its southern slopes. Continuing east, a short descent and ascent gains the lower trig point at Pt.662m. Some 150m north, the OS 1:25k marks a second 664m high point which is worth including for completeness, although an unratified survey indicates it is only 663.4m. From here make a rough descent by a fence, boundary cairns and wind turbines to a col, followed by a heathery ascent to the featureless summit of Beinn Odhar (**9.5km; 720m; 3h 20min**).

Descend eastwards to a shallow col and ascend peat trenches to the summit of Beinn nan Eun (**10.5km; 770m; 3h 35min**), marked by a fence post in a pile of stones on a flat, peat-hag summit riven with pools. Head off down the north ridge past grouse butts to sheep pens and cross the Allt na Caillich to a track. Follow the track left to white gates, then turn left down the road to the car park (**14.5km; 770m; 4h 45min**).

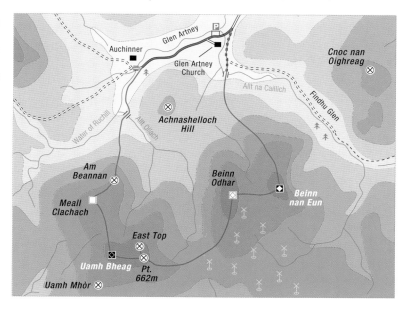

SECTION 1a
Loch Fyne to Loch Lomond

Cruach nan Capull from the Glen Lean approach past Corrachaive (Tom Prentice)

Cruach nan Capull; 611m; (G220); L63; NS095795; heap of the horses

Surrounded on three sides by Loch Striven and the Firth of Clyde, Cruach nan Capull lies at a similar latitude to Glasgow and Edinburgh, making it the most southerly Graham in the Highlands. The mountain can be climbed from Glen Lean to the north or from Inverchaolain on Loch Striven to the south. For the general approach see the Cowal Hills panel on p81.

The northerly route starts from a large layby on the B836 about 400m west of the access track to Corrachaive. There is also limited parking at the start of the track. Follow the track, going left at a Y-junction to reach a gate. Cross the burn and continue through conifer plantations towards Cruach nan Capull, to a point where the track turns west and crosses the Corrachaive Burn. Just before the next and smaller Midhill Burn, turn left into the conifers (NS098808) onto an overgrown grassy track (shown on the OS 1:25k map).

Zigzag up the hillside on this track then make long, straight contours first south, then north to gain the shoulder of Mid Hill, from where the summit of Cruach nan Capull is easily gained (**4km; 510m; 1h 45min**). Descend by the same route (**8km; 520m; 2h 45min**).

The southern route starts from a small parking area in front of Inverchaolain church, gained via the A815 south from Dunoon and a minor road north along Loch Striven. Go north up the road to the first track on the right and follow it past Stronyaraig to open hillside, from where the impressive Sròn Dearg is gained and climbed to a fence leading to a trig point on the rounded, grassy summit of Pt.572m.

A long, grassy ridge then leads to the summit of Cruach nan Capull (**5km; 610m; 2h 10min**). Descend steeply east still following the fence and go over a slight rise turning south-east to Leacann nan Gall (568m). Continue south-east over Green Knap to the Bealach na Srèine on the old coffin route from Inverchaolain to Glen Kin and Glen Lean.

Black Craig (522m), a rounded Sub 2000ft Marilyn, lies to the south and can be included with a return to the bealach, although most will wish to simply descend steeply west into Inverchaolain Glen, crossing the burn to pick up the track in the glen floor. Keep right where the track divides, to gain a higher track and follow this back past Stronyaraig to the start (**12km; 690m; 4h**).

An approach is also possible from the east using forest tracks above Dunoon to gain Bishop's Seat and the Bealach na Srèine, as well as via the coffin route up forested Glen Kin.

Beinn Ruadh; *664m; (G155); L56; NS155883; red mountain*

Beinn Ruadh's lower flanks are steep and forested, limiting access points and making circular routes awkward. The easiest approach is from the Forestry Commission Scotland Inverchapel car park (NS145865) on the east side of the A815, a few hundred metres north of the Stratheck holiday chalets at the southern end of Loch Eck.

Cross the footbridge over the Inverchapel Burn, then turn right onto a waymarked path and ascend beside the burn. Keep left at a junction and zigzag up to join a higher path and follow it left towards a viewpoint over Loch Eck. Before reaching the viewpoint, gain the hillside at a wooden kissing gate and follow assorted animal tracks to a fence. Cross over and make a steep right traverse below the craggy south-west face to gain the south ridge.

The cairn on Pt.623m is soon reached, from where an intermittent old fenceline leads over the knobbly ridge, with fine views over Loch Eck to gain the summit trig point (**3km; 650m; 1h 45min**). Descend by the same route (6km; 635m; 2h 45min).

The mountain can also be climbed from the north, starting from the minor road which crosses the north end of the hill from Loch Eck to

Ardentinny. Park on the north side by a gate at NS150924 where the Loch Eck cycle route crosses over. On the south side of the road the obvious cycle path leads to a track. Go left and descend to a fork, then right onto

another track which is followed to its end, from where a path leads off left.

Cross over the burn and keep ascending on a path which leads up and round to a wide, grassy firebreak beside the burn. Follow this for a short distance to another burn and firebreak coming in from the left and go up these to open hillside beyond.

Go over a fence to gain the top of Sligrachan Hill, marked with a prominent tall cairn. An old fenceline leads up Beinn Ruadh's craggy north ridge to the summit trig point (**5km; 620m; 2h 20min**). Descend the same way (10km; 720m; 3h 50min)

An approach is also possible from the east via a Forestry Commission track (NS174896) near Drynain at the north end of Ardentinny. Ascend the track, keeping right where it divides to reach a higher track. Follow that right to a junction, then turn hard left and ascend to a turning area. A rough track goes sharp right to exit the forestry, from where an intermittent track leads to sheep pens in Drynain Glen. Head north-west to clear the trees at a fence and stile before the Drynain Burn, then turn due west and ascend to the north ridge and the summit (**4km; 650m; 2h**). Descend the same way (8km; 650m; 3h 10min).

Approaching the summit of Beinn Ruadh above Loch Eck. The Corbett Beinn Bheula is in the distance (Tom Prentice)

Beinn Mhòr, left, and Beinn Bheag, right, in shade, from Beinn Ruadh (Tom Prentice)

Beinn Bheag; 618m; (G210); L56; NS125932; little mountain
Beinn Mhòr; 741m; (G29); L56; NS107908; big mountain

Loch Eck's western shore is dominated by a 10km wall of steep, rocky hillside and impressive corries. The northern end is capped by the rocky tops of Beinn Bheag and the unnamed Pt.568m with its trig point. The southern end is the vast sprawling bulk of Beinn Mhòr. As with most mountains in the area, steep hillsides and conifer plantations limit access points.

The well-established route from Glenmassan to the south suits an ascent of Beinn Mhòr by itself, but continuing to Beinn Bheag necessitates a rather tedious 370m re-ascent over Beinn Mhòr, and for this reason it is hard to recommend. The other popular route via Bernice on Loch Eck is more accommodating.

From the car park at Benmore Botanic Garden on the A815, cross the bridge over the River Eachaig, turn right and follow the track north round the garden to a right turn onto the track up the west side of Loch Eck. Pass Bernice after 7km, continue uphill to a junction then turn left and take the track up Bernice Glen, leaving it at its high point where it swings left (**8km; 160m; 2h**).

Ascend first on the right, then cross to the left side of the burn and climb to a faint path at the edge of the felled forest. Cross a fence and follow it down right to regain the burn and ascend to the Bealach Bernice. The col is marshy, so it is worth trying to cross the two fences on the right before arriving. Ascend north and east to skirt Pt.534m and Meall Breac, then continue to the west of Pt.601m to Beinn Bheag's summit cairn (**10km; 620m; 3h 15min**).

Return to the bealach, cross back ▶

Cowal Hills
Despite their proximity to Greenock and Glasgow, the Firth of Clyde complicates access to these hills, the most southerly of the Highland Grahams.

Although Cruach nan Capull, Beinn Ruadh and Beinn Mhòr are all clearly visible across the Firth, potential suitors from the central belt face a long drive north, west and then south via lochs Lomond, Fyne and Eck The alternative for anyone with easy access to the M8 or the rail network, is the 20 minute ferry ride from Gourock or Greenock to Dunoon.

The total journey by ferry can take almost as long as driving, but makes a much more satisfying approach to the mountains, especially in summer when tourist traffic on Loch Lomond can significantly slow the journey.

Cars can be taken on the ferry, but it is also possible to leave the car at Greenock and use bicycles to access all five Cowal hills, although the Loch Striven approach to Cruach nan Capull and the Glenbranter approaches to Creag Tharsuinn, Beinn Mhòr and Beinn Beag involve longer distances.
Western Ferries: *<www.western-ferries.co.uk>, Gourock to Dunoon (vehicle). A second vehicle service is expected to start in 2014-15.*
Argyll Ferries: *<argyllferries.co.uk>, Greenock to Dunoon (passenger only).*

over the fences and ascend the steady and rather monotonous northern slopes of Beinn Mhòr to gain the rocky upper corrie and the small summit plateau crowned with a trig point (**13.5km; 1050m; 5h**). Return to the bealach and Bernice and the track back to Benmore (**24km; 1060m; 7h 30min**). It is possible to bike to the track high point above Bernice saving about 1h 50min on the day.

If the Benmore to Bernice approach has been made on foot, this allows a very fine return route to be had. From the summit of Beinn Mhòr follow the fenceline south-east then south to Capull Cloiche (577m), then cross the plateau south-east towards Creachan Mòr (571m). About halfway across, a diversion can be made to the north-east to take in the prominent Graham Top of Clach Bheinn (add 55min). From Creachan Mòr an increasingly narrow and rocky ridge with stunning views south to Holy Loch and the Firth of Clyde, leads over Creachan Beag and down to 482m A' Chruach.

From the summit follow old fence posts straight down to a gate and stile. Turn right to gain a track which is followed steadily downhill to the fence surrounding Benmore Garden and a junction with the outward Loch Eck track. A right turn leads back to the car park (**22km; 1190m; 7h 20min**).

The full 10km ridge above Loch Eck offers a fantastic north-south expedition from Glenbranter to Benmore, taking in Beinn Bheag and Beinn Mhòr en route. The pre-placement of a mountain bike at Benmore significantly assists the return along the track on Loch Eck's western shore.

Start from Glenbranter Forestry Commission car park (NS110978) off the A815 at the head of Loch Eck. Follow the road down and round in front of the Forestry Commission office and toilets, and continue south to a junction. Turn left over the river to Glenshellich, then left again, (white waymarks), to pass below the farm on a gravel track. Continue round Loch Eck to a point just after a track junction on the right, where there is a wide break in the trees, with a burn and rocky watercourse (NS127960). Ascend this, cross an upper track and continue up the burn's left side to a bouldery corrie and the col between Cruach Bhuidhe and Pt.568m.

Ascend to the trig point on Pt.568m, then down the rocky south face to a marshy col from where the summit of Beinn Bheag is easily gained (**6.5km; 740m; 2h 45min**). From here the route to Bheinn Mhòr and south over A' Chruach to Benmore is as described above (**18.5km; 1410m; 6h 50min**). From Benmore return the 15km along the west side of Loch Eck to Glenbranter (**33.5km; 1450m; 9h 10min**). Use of a bike, preplaced at Benmore Garden car park, can reduce this by around 1h 50min.

A forestry break on the western flanks of Beinn Mhòr, south-west of the summit could be utilised to gain the track and the ascent route up Creag Tharsuinn (see following page) to construct a round of all three Grahams from Glenbranter.

Looking north over the Bealach nan Sac to Creag Tharsuinn (Tom Prentice)

***Creag Tharsuinn**; 643m; (G184); L56; NS088913; transverse hill*

N ew forest tracks (not shown on maps) and felling have improved access in the upper Garrachra Glen, making the approach from Glen Massan the route of choice for Creag Tharsuinn. The ascent and descent involve firebreaks, where good route finding pays dividends.

The signposted road up Glen Massan is followed to its end at a small car park. Continue on the track past Glenmassan to a small loch and cross the bridge over the river to a track junction. Turn right and continue to a fork; the return route comes in from the left here. Follow the right track past the house and loch at Garrachara to a felled area where a new track goes left to the river.

The route follows the grassy gully of the Allt Nan Sac opposite and is worth noting from here, as trees restrict visibility in the lower section. Ford the river, a bridge may be constructed in the future, go right to the Allt nan Sac and follow it north. Care is needed as the trees close-up ahead and the firebreak pushes you left onto an off-route tributary rising to crags. Ascend ahead, easily through the trees on a short forested ridge (dividing the tributary and the Allt Nan Sac) to reach the wide and grassy upper gully.

Ascend steep grass on either side of the burn to a fence and continue north-east to the Bealach nan Sac, from where the south-west ridge leads over assorted rocky knolls to the summit (**7km; 580m; 2h 30min**). While the summit is usually marked by a few stones, the highest knoll is hard to determine if they are missing.

Return to the bealach and continue south-west to the cairn on Meall Dubh, then over Pt.578m to skirt a lochan and gain the trig point on Càrn Bàn (**10km; 690m; 3h 20min**). Descend east from the summit to the well-defined Allt na Cubhaige and follow its right (south) bank to the forest edge. Continue in the same line to cross over the burn and easily follow animal paths through the forest to a track. Turn right to the junction near Garrachara and follow the outward route back to the start (15km; 690m; 4h 40min). Biking to the fork before Garrachara saves 50min on the day. New forestry tracks and continued felling may alter the ascent and descent in the future.

An approach can also be made from the north, starting from the Glenbranter Forestry Commission car park (NS110978) off the A815 at the head of Loch Eck. Follow the road round in front of the Forestry Commission office and toilets and on past the turning to Glenshellish Farm and houses. The road turns to a track, crosses the Allt Robuic and forks. Take the right-hand fork uphill, keeping left where it bends sharply right, to enter Glen Shellish.

After about 800m an obvious wide firebreak containing the Alltan nan Deart is reached on the right (NS103956). Ascend to the left of the burn, rough at the start, then easier through broadleaf woodland to the wide ridge south of Sròn Crìche. Heather, tussocky grass and boggy sections lead to Creag Mholach, from where a grassier ridge leads over A' Chroidheachd and assorted knolls to the summit (**7.5km; 650m; 2h 45min**). See earlier for summit details. Descend by the same route (15km; 700m; 4h 35min).

The western approach from Garvie Farm on the A886, utilises the Cowal Way. Parking is very restricted at the start, otherwise it would be the easiest, if possibly the least interesting, route. Follow the track through the farm and east beside the Garvie Burn then north-east through forestry to a clearing at Tom a' Chromain (NS074915). From here a gate leads to open hillside and the Bealach nan Sac, to join the Glen Massan route described earlier (**7km; 610m; 2h 35min**). Descend by the same route (14km; 610m; 4h 15min).

The craggy summit of Stob na Boine Druim-fhinn from the east (Tom Prentice)

Stob na Boine Druim-fhinn; 658m; (G163); L56; NN168025; *stub of the white-backed cow*
Beinn Lochain; 703m; (G97); L56; NN160006; *mountain above the lochan*

Five Grahams and two Corbetts surround the village of Lochgoilhead at the northern end of the Cowal peninsula. Stob na Boine Druim-fhinn and Beinn Lochain are the most southerly of the five and along with the Corbett Beinn Bheula and the Graham Tops of Beinn Tharsuinn, Beinn Lochain East Top and Mullach Coire a' Chuir, they present an impressively mountainous escarpment on the west side of the head of Loch Goil, overlooking the village.

Stob na Boine Druim-fhinn and Beinn Lochain are easily climbed together, although the round can be extended to include Beinn Bheula. A bigger round can also be made including the northern Graham Cruach nam Mult and Mullach Coire a' Chuir. This route is described in the Lochgoilhead Hills panel on p87.

Park just off the road in a dirt layby on the west side of Loch Goil (NN189006), where a lochside track goes left to a boat yard and the main road starts to ascend. The layby is almost opposite the south end of the Drymsynie chalets. It should be noted

that there are a number of new forestry tracks on this route, not yet shown on OS maps.

Follow the main road about 180m uphill and turn right towards the Drimsynie Estate Office (named Corrow on OS maps). Go through the farmyard to a gate and a track which heads left then back right and climbs to a track junction directly below what was once a firebreak in the felled hillside above. Go up the 'firebreak' on a clear animal path passing through gates and over a forestry track then through more gates beyond to gain the open hillside below a small bluff.

Skirt this on either side to the broad ridge above and ascend this to its top where an obvious, deep cleft splits the cliffs. Ascend the grassy cleft beside a burn to gain the undulating upper ridge which leads to a final steep ascent past a short rock gendarme to the finely defined summit and trig point (**4km; 660m; 2h**).

Retrace your steps to the undulating upper ridge and descend south-south-east to the col below Beinn Tharsuinn. About 710m due west of here, on the edge of the

forest in the glen below, lies the wreckage of a B-29 US Army Air Force Superfortress which clipped the top of Beinn Tharsuinn on 17th January 1949 and crashed with the loss of all 20 crew. The site is at NS161022 and easily visited as a diversion en route to Beinn Tharsuinn. To do this, descend due west above the south side of the burn. The extensive wreckage lies at the forest edge, headed by a stone memorial to the crew. From the site, steady slopes of tussocky grassy lead south-east to the summit of Beinn Tharsuinn. This diversion adds 20min to the route, plus any time spent at the site.

The direct route ascends Beinn Tharsuinn's northern slopes from the col to gain a rocky ridge with fine views down to the village and over Loch Goil, to reach the 619m summit on top of an isolated knoll (**5.5km; 780m; 2h 35min**).

Continue down south to the col, cross a fence and make a steady ascent south then west to the cairned summit of Beinn Lochain (**7km; 970m; 3h 20min**) and fine views south over Curra Lochain to the big eastern corries of Beinn Bheula. Immediately east of the summit is a small knoll. From the col between it and the summit descend surprisingly steep, grassy slopes towards the east end of Curra Lochain to meet a path (the Cowal Way) and follow it over a stile to stepping stones at the east end of the loch. If the water level makes these difficult, there is also a handrail crossing about 100m downstream. Cross over onto a rough path on the south side of the burn.

From here it is possible to descend back to the start, or to include Beinn Bheula in the ascent. To continue the descent, follow the path to the Sruth Bàn waterfall and zigzag down grassy terraces marked by occasional white posts, then continue ahead through the firebreak to gain a forestry track. Turn right and descend, ignoring tracks off to the right, to houses at Lettermay and the main road which is followed back to the lochside (12.5km; 970m; 4h 45min).

To continue over Beinn Bheula, cross a fence and ascend the craggy north-east ridge to a higher fence. Cross over and continue up through crags to a grassy ridge leading to the summit trig point on Caisteal Dubh (**10km; 1420m; 4h 55min**). The quickest and shortest descent is back the same way to the Sruth Bàn water-

Superfortress undercarriage and Stob na Boine Druim-fhinn (Tom Prentice)

fall and the track to Lettermay as described above (16km; 1420m; 6h 30min). However, a very fine round can be had by returning via the rocky summit of the Sub 2000ft Marilyn of Cruach nam Miseag (606m); one of the most impressive mountains in the area when viewed from below.

Continue south over Creag Sgoilte and Ceann Garbh passing the wreckage of a fighter plane which crashed in 1940, to the marshy An t-Sreag col. From here descend north-east towards Lochan nan

Cnàimh and traverse round its west side. Ascend north-north-east over Pt.560, then south-east over Pt.571m to the summit of Cruach nam Miseag (**14.5km; 1790m; 6h 40min**).

Return west over Pt.571, then north-west past a small lochan, to the southern edge of recent felling. Follow a path down beside the forest edge to a track which leads to a lower one. Turn right and descend to a junction, then right onto the track to Lettermay (**19.5km; 1820m; 8h**).

See following pages for map

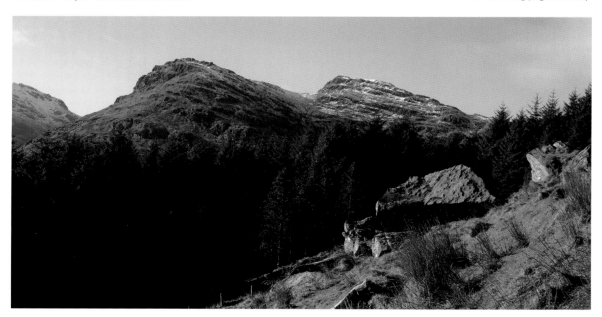

Beinn Lochain, right, and its East Top from the flanks of Stob na Boine Druim-fhinn (Tom Prentice)

Approaching Cruach nam Mult from the east along the ridge from Stob Liath (Tom Prentice)

Cruach nam Mult; *611m; (G221); L56; NN168055; heap of the wethers (sheep)*

When climbed from near the high point on the road through Hell's Glen, the quickest and most popular approach, 'heap of the sheep' seems an appropriate name for Cruach nam Mult. These rather dull western flanks are in complete contrast to the impressively steep and rocky north face which forms the south side of this deep-set glen, and the eastern end which terminates in the rocky stub of Stob Liath.

However, the advantage of this western approach, is that Cruach nam Mult and the Graham Stob an Eas on the north side of the glen can be climbed on the same day from the same parking spot.

Park at NN168074 just north of the high point on the B839, where tracks head east and west into the forest. Follow the western track to where it ends, then ascend straight up through forestry on a path to the left of a burn, to a high point. Now ascend diagonally right through the trees on an ill-defined path near a ramshackle fence (shown on the OS 1:25k map), to cross a deep-cut burn and exit the forestry at NN159060.

Ascend south-west initially beside the fence over the col between Cruach nan Capull and Cruach nam Mult, then east up the western flanks following wooden posts to gain the summit (**3.5km; 390m; 1h 25min**). There are two knolls of a similar height, although OS maps indicate the highest is that to the south-east. The prudent will bag both. Return the same way (**7km; 390m; 2h 15min**).

A more interesting but longer circuit climbs the hill from the south-east. From the same parking spot, descend the verge of the road through the quiet and scenic Hell's Glen passing alternative parking at NN179062 and beside the Moses Well at NN185056, to the bend below Monevechadan. Cut this by diverting through the trees to the bridge over the River Goil and a Forestry Commission track sign-posted Drimsynie.

Follow the track south then west up Gleann Canachadan to where it bends sharp left. Turn right at the bend and follow a path into the forest to a log bridge. Cross the burn and continue to a wooden gate and the open glen. Ascend left of the forestry to the top of Stob Liath (503m), which offers excellent views south over Loch Goil. Some prominent grassy knolls are now traversed west alongside a fence to the rocky eastern flanks of Cruach nam Mult, which are climbed via a wide grassy gully on the left (**8km; 650m; 2h 50min**).

Descend to the parking at the high point in Hell's Glen by reversing the popular ascent route described above, taking care to find the top of the path through the forest at NN159060 (**11.5km; 3h 40min**). Cruach nan Mult can also be combined with Stob na Boine Druim-finn and Beinn Lochain as described in the Lochgoilhead Hills panel opposite.

Lochgoilhead Hills

Of the five Grahams which surround Lochgoilhead, the three to the west of the village make a fine round with spectacular views. Some 7km of the route is on forestry tracks, although most of it is downhill.

Start at the dirt layby on the west side of Loch Goil (NN189006) and continue as for Stob na Boine Druim-fhinn, described on p84. Pass through Drimsynie Estate Office (Corrow) and ascend the 'firebreak' to the forestry track.

Turn right and follow the track north for 4km, mostly downhill but with a few short ascents. After a hairpin bend, the track descends into Gleann Canachadan, turns sharply right and crosses the glen's burn. Leave the track at the bend before the burn and follow a path into the forest to a log bridge. Cross the burn and continue to a wooden gate and the open glen.

Ascend left of the forestry to the top of Stob Liath (503m). Traverse west over prominent grassy knolls to the eastern flanks of Cruach nam Mult and climb them via a wide, grassy gully on the left (8km; 850m; 3h 10min). Descend south-west towards the forest edge in the col at the head of Gleann Canachadan, then ascend the northern flanks of 639m Mullach Coire a' Chuir to a grassy ridge, which leads south-east above the craggy north face to the summit (11km; 1090m; 4h 20min).

A south-westerly descent soon gains the next col, followed by a steeper ascent south-east to Stob na Boine Druim-fhinn (12.5km; 1260m; 5h). From here the route over Beinn Tharsuinn to Beinn Lochain (15.5km; 1570m; 6h 20min) is as described under Stob na Boine Druim-fhinn and Beinn Lochain on p84. From Curra Lochain, descend past the Struth Bàn waterfall to meet the track to Lettermay (21km; 1570m; 7h 45min).

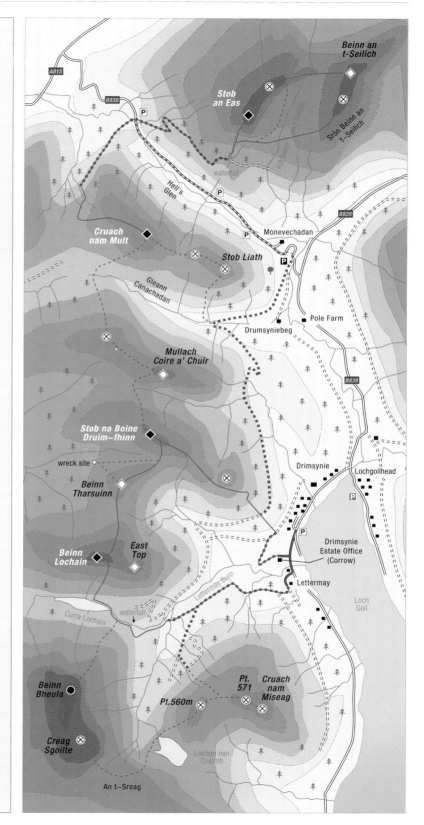

Stob an Eas; *732m; (G47); L56; NN185073; stub of the waterfall*

Stob an Eas is the most northerly of the Lochgoilhead Grahams and presents an unexpectedly impressive profile from many directions. One fine view is from its companion Graham Cruach nam Mult on the south side of Hell's Glen, from where it appears as a steep rocky pyramid. The two hills are often combined in a single day from the same parking spot on the B839 through the glen.

Park at NN168074 just north of the high point on the B839, where tracks head east and west into the forest. Parking is possible on either side of the road. Ascend the eastern track round two bends, to where the main track ends and a rougher track continues, contouring east round the lower hillside of Stob an Eas then ascending more steeply to reach a burn in a recessed gully and a clearing in the conifers (NN182067).

Leave the track and ascend the left-hand side of the burn until it is possible to cross over, then follow the right-hand side to gain and climb the increasingly steep southern nose of Stob an Eas, weaving in-between small cliffs of mica-schist to reach the summit trig point (**3km; 510m; 1h 30min**) and spectacular views.

Although a return can be made the same way (**6km; 510m; 2h 20min**), it is more enjoyable and perhaps less daunting to include the Graham Top of 719m Beinn an t-Seilich in the circuit. Follow the knobbly ridge north-east towards Glen Kinglas and more fine views, then descend east towards the col before Beinn an t-Seilich. Walkers desiring a quick return should turn south here and traverse below Stob an Eas's rocky east face back to the approach route and a return by the line of ascent (**8km; 510m; 2h 55min**).

Continuing the round, cross the col and climb Beinn an t-Seilich's western slopes to the summit cairn (**5km; 650m; 2h 15min**), from where the pleasant ridge of Sròn Beinn an t-Seilich leads south above the long and rocky east face, until a descent is made south-west into the corrie. Cross the Allt Beinn an t-Seilich and traverse west back to the approach route and a return by the line of ascent (**10km; 670m; 3h 30min**).

See previous page for map

Cnoc Còinnich; *761m; (G2); L56; NN233007; mossy knoll*

Missing Corbett status by a single metre, Cnoc Còinnich, the most easterly of the five Grahams surrounding Lochgoilhead, takes the joint accolade of highest Graham, alongside Beinn Tallaidh on Mull and Sgùrr a' Chaorainn on Ardgour.

It can be approached from east or west and both offer the opportunity to extend the route into a fine traverse of the Ardgoil peninsula if desired. A quick up and down ascent from the west allows it to be combined with one of the other swiftly climbed Grahams near Lochgoilhead.

The western approach starts from the large public car park on the east shore of Loch Goil at NN200013. From the north end of the car park cross diagonally left over the road and turn right onto a tarmac lane. Follow it past public toilets and the Scout Centre, continuing ahead onto a path which swings right to a track junction. Take the right-hand fork which ascends north then east beside forestry into picturesque Donich Glen, to a bridge over the Allt Airigh na Creige (NN213017). Just after this turn right onto a foot-

The impressive rocky pyramid of Stob an Eas (Tom Prentice)

path signposted Donich Glen, Coilessan Hill Path and follow this (the line of the Cowal Way) to a wide forest firebreak. Ascend this to the right of the burn, boggy in places and with occasional white posts, to cross a stile and gain the open hillside and an ill-defined grassy path which veers up and left following posts towards the col between The Brack and Cnoc Còinnich.

As this path starts to level out leave it for the flanks of Cnoc Còinnich and climb the broad ridge passing a small lochan to the summit cairn, perched on a crag, overlooking the steep east face (**4.5km; 760m; 1h 15min**). Return the same way (9km; 760m; 3h 30min).

A longer and more satisfying hillwalk with stunning views down Loch Long to the Firth of Clyde can be had by following the high ground south along the crest of the Ardgoil peninsula, with a return to Lochgoilhead on the cycle path. Descend the formidably steep southern nose of Cnoc Còinnich and follow the knobbly ridge south-west then south over the 655m high point to the trig point on Beinn Reithe (**7.5km; 890m; 4h 20min**).

The rocky ridge beyond is best tackled on the Loch Goil side, followed by a descent towards The

Cnoc Còinnich from the south-west with snow-topped Ben Donich behind (Tom Prentice)

Saddle (521m). Outflank this above forestry to the west (or climb it direct), to reach the track and cycle path (only marked on the OS 1:25k map) which is followed without deviation, north to Lochgoilhead (15km; 920m; 6h). A similar route is also possible after an ascent of Cnoc Còinnich from Coilessan to the east (see below), by following the cycle path south from this point to Corran Lochan, then north above Loch Long to the Coilessan Car Park. However, this return is longer and less attractive.

The eastern approach up Coilessan Glen starts from the forestry road along the west side of Loch Long, accessed from the Visitor Centre off the A83 at Ardgarten (NN269037), west of Arrochar. Follow the signposts to where the road ends at a car park (NN258011) below Coilessan Glen.

Continue south through a locked gate and over the burn flowing from the glen. Turn right at the first junction following the Coilessan Glen Road signpost and ascend north-west through forestry with views to the

Corbett, The Brack. Remain on the track past two junctions to a felled area at the very head of the glen where the track bends sharply to the east and contours below The Brack.

Ignoring the track straight ahead, descend left to a footpath beside the burn in the foot of the glen, signposted Lochgoilhead Hill. Cross two footbridges and ascend to the open hillside. Climb towards the col on an indistinct path with occasional white posts (the Cowal Way), then head off left picking the least boggy route to the north ridge, which leads quickly to the summit (**4.5km; 660m; 2h 5min**). Return by the same route (9km; 660m; 3h 20min).

Cnoc Còinnich can also be combined with The Brack, by an up and down route from the col via the south ridge to the summit, adding 4km; 330m; 1h 40min to the day. For anyone starting from Lochgoilhead the route can be extended further by descending west to the Bealach Dubh-lic, followed by the east ridge of the Corbett Ben Donich. Descend south then south-west to a track and waymarked path leading down to the B839, followed by tracks south past Inveronick back to Lochgoilhead (16km; 1550m; 6h 45min).

Beinn a' Mhanaich, left, and Cruach an t-Sìdhean from the flanks of Beinn Chaorach (Tom Prentice)

Beinn Chaorach; 713m; (G74); L56; NS287923; *mountain of the sheep*
Beinn a' Mhanaich; 709m; (G86); L56; NS269946; *mountain of the monk*

G len Fruin offers the easiest access to Beinn Chaorach and Beinn a' Mhanaich, the most southerly of the group of eight Grahams that make up the Luss Hills; see the information panel on p93.

The glen is best accessed by following the A82 past Balloch to the roundabout at Arden. Turn onto the A818 to Helensburgh, follow it to the next roundabout and take the second left signposted Glen Fruin. Follow this minor road north-west through the glen to park on the verge of a large layby at NS274900, about 250m north of Auchengaich and below a gated road; the old access road to Auchengaich Reservoir.

A second and newer road, the A817, contours the glen above its floor. This road was built for military

Beinn Chaorach, right, and Beinn a' Mhanaich (Tom Prentice)

vehicles serving naval bases on Loch Long and the Gare Loch and no parking, overtaking or stopping is allowed. However, it is possible to park at the start of the Auchengaich Reservoir access road where it is cut by the A817, but this can only be accessed from the west. Access from the east would involve a very dangerous turning on a blind summit and crossing over double white lines.

From the layby go through a gate, ascend a section of the old reservoir access road to the A817, cross over with care as visibility is poor and continue up the continuation access road to a stile and sign indicating a footpath to Glen Luss.

Ascend the hillside on the right, marshy to start, following a line through the bracken, then diagonally north-east towards the col between Auchengaich Hill and Beinn Tharsuinn. Paths and an atv track lead to the top of Beinn Tharsuinn, marked with a small cairn. Follow the fence to a marshy col, avoided to the left, and ascend to the summit of Beinn Chaorach, marked with a cairn on the left-hand side of the fence and a trig point on the right (**3.5km; 610m; 1h 50min**).

Descend the broad ridge in a north-westerly direction over the knoll of Pt.667m, then more steeply left of the fence towards Beinn a' Mhanaich, to the bealach between Glen Fruin and Glen Luss and a stile. Do not cross over, but continue beside the fence, which turns north-east, to arrive at the foot of a shallow rocky gully on the south-east face of Beinn a' Mhanaich. Climb the right flank of this to the col south of the summit, from where it is easily gained (**7km; 980m; 3h 30min**).

Return to the col, cross a gate in the fence and descend south along the fine, well-positioned ridge, to pass over Maol an Fheidh (591m). Continue down The Strone, marred slightly by old shooting range signs, then descend steeply south-east towards Auchengaich Reservoir. Cross over the dam to gain the access road and follow it back to the start (**13km; 990m; 5h**).

Doune Hill from the Beinn Lochain – Beinn Eich col to the south (Tom Prentice)

Mid Hill; 657m; (G168); L56; NS321962; *mid hill*
Doune Hill; 734m; (G39); L56; NS290971; *hill above Doune farm. Doune from Gaelic 'dùn', hillfort*
Cruach an t-Sìdhein; 684m; (G123); L56; NS275965; *heap of the fairy knoll*
Beinn Eich; 703m; (G96); L56; NS302946; *mountain of horses*

Mid Hill, Doune Hill and Beinn Eich form three sides of Glen Mollachan off upper Glen Luss and offer a horseshoe round of high quality, with a diversion west en route to pick-up Cruach an t-Sìdhein.

The easiest parking for these central Luss Hills is the pay & display car park in the centre of Luss (free out of season). Limited parking is also possible on the minor road up Glen Luss, a short distance on from the turning off the A82. There is no parking as such at the end of Glen Luss and while it might be possible to squeeze a car off the road in passing places or in the turning area at the end of the public road, this may well prove more trouble than it is worth.

Exit the car park, turn left and follow the road to the first turning on the right. Go up this past Luss

Mid Hill and Ben Lomond from Beinn Eich (Tom Prentice)

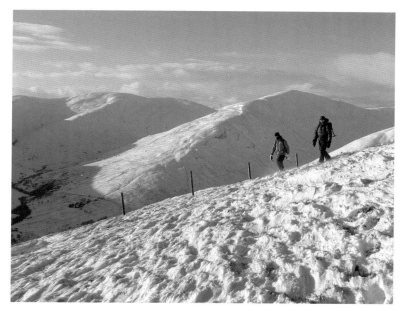

Beinn Eich, right, and Beinn Chaorach from Mid Hill (Tom Prentice)

and continue up the track above with increasingly good views over Loch Lomond and its islands. After a small section of woodland and a mobile phone mast, the track becomes more of a path and leads through bracken to the top of Pt.285m. Beyond this the path becomes marshy, but improves again as a fence is joined and followed via a stile to the top of 642m Beinn Dubh.

A broad expanse of open ridge now separates Beinn Dubh from Mid Hill, confusingly also named Beinn Dubh in Fiona Graham's original list. Continue north-west on the path until it deteriorates in an area of peat hags, then emerge from the other side to gain a cairn (NS322964), marked as the summit on OS 1:50k maps. About 145m to the south-west is a second cairn, with some quartz among the stones, which the OS 1:25k map correctly identifies as the summit (**5.5km; 690m; 2h 20min**).

Descend the broad summit area south-west for about 330m, then turn

Primary School, from where a tarmac path ascends to the wooden bridge over the A82. Cross over and past a house, then straight ahead onto a

gravel path. Go through a gate and turn right, then follow the fence to a stile and cross over.

Ascend to a metal gate with a stile

Luss Hills

Collectively known as the Luss Hills, the high ground between Loch Long and Loch Lomond contains eight Grahams; the highest concentration in such a small area, anywhere in the country. They are well proportioned hills, separated, by significant drops and deep glens, with outstanding views from the Southern Highlands to Arran and the Paps of Jura.

Glen Douglas splits the two northern hills from the main massif, which is partially sub-divided into a central and southern section by Glen Luss, the glen running west from the village of Luss on the shore of Loch Lomond.

*The hills lend themselves to a number of different approaches and are described in three main walks. However, it is also possible to link the six central and southern Grahams into a single high-level, high stamina circuit of exceptional quality. From the parking in Luss, ascend Mid Hill as described on this page (**5.5km; 690m; 2h 20min**) and continue to the summit of Doune Hill (**10km; 1270m; 4h 30min**). Continue south and skirt rounded Beinn Lochain to the east, to gain and climb Beinn Eich's fine west ridge to the summit (**13km; 1430m; 5h 30min**). Reverse the ridge and contour north-west below Beinn Lochain, before descending to the col below Cruach an t-Sìdean, from where a short climb gains the summit (**16.5km; 1600m; 6h 35min**).*

*A steep descent is made south-west then south to the forested col below Beinn a' Mhanaich. Follow the forestry fence round the west side of Beinn a' Mhanaich and once clear of the frontal crags, veer south-east up the hillside to meet another fence rising from below, which passes over the col south of the top. Leave the fence east to gain the summit (**19km; 1980m; 8h 15min**)*

*Descend straight down the east face, keeping left of a fence and wooded gully to the burn in the col below Beinn Chaorach. Cross over and head south-east to the north ridge of Beinn Chaorach and follow it beside a fence to the summit trig point (**22.5km; 2350m; 9h 55min**). From here descend south-east beside a fence to the top of Beinn Tharsuinn. Continue east beside the fence to Pt.693m, then north-east to the top of Creag an Leinibh (**26km; 2550m; 11h**).*

*Route finding at the start and finish of the next section requires a little concentration. Continue south-east beside the fence for about 165m, then turn sharp north and descend the steep north-east slope to the broad ridge of Coille-eughain Hill and continue to The Paps. From here descend well to the left of a larch plantation and the main mass of bracken. Head straight down to pass right of a small clump of birch trees in a burn above the main treeline to reach a track at NS344931. Follow this rightwards through rough pasture towards Auchengavin Farm. Before a barn, a diversion from the track takes you north to a stile and across pasture towards the farmhouse and round a hedge back to the track, which leads to the A82. Walk north to the Glen Luss road and turn left then right to gain the wooden bridge over the A82 back to Luss (**32km; 2570m; 12h 40min**).*

west to gain the west ridge (slightly hidden from above), which leads past crags, boulders and three old birch trees to the flat, bog myrtle covered col below Doune Hill. A relentless 470m ascent follows, keeping right of the tree-filled burn, initially on a grassy animal path to gain a shallow upper corrie and the summit of the domed East Peak, a Graham Top. Descend west to a small lochan at the bealach, then up to the trig point on Doune Hill (**10km; 1270m; 4h 30min**).

Gentler gound now leads south-west and south towards rounded Beinn Lochain. Skirt the top of this to the west and descend to the col below Cruach an t-Sìdhein, from where a short ascent gains the summit (**12km; 1440m; 5h 15min**).

Return to the col, ascend a little way then contour east below Beinn Lochain to gain the south ridge connecting it with Beinn Eich. A short ascent up a fine grassy crest gains the shapely summit (**15.5km; 1630m; 6h 25min**).

Descend more or less directly down the south-east ridge heading for the Edentaggart farm in Glen Luss below to a fence and stile over a wall to the right. Cross over and continue descending east to a stile over another wall, which gains a path skirting the farm to the north to arrive at the access track. Follow this back down Glen Luss to the road (**22km; 1680m; 8h 15min**).

This overall time can be reduced by about 50min using a bicycle to Glen-mollochan farm and ascending Mid Hill by the well-used path up the south-east ridge above Glen Striddle, thereby missing out the ascent over Beinn Dubh from Luss. The Glen Luss road is steep at the start but makes for a speedy descent.

These hills are also easily divided into shorter routes. Mid Hill can be approached over Beinn Dubh followed by the path down the south-east ridge to Glenmollochan and the road back to Luss (**11km; 720m; 3h 50min**). Doune Hill, Cruach an t-Sìdein and Beinn Eich can be climbed as a circuit via Glen Mollachan (**21km; 1240m; 7h 15min**). Use of a bike would ease this walk by about 50min as well.

See previous pages for map

Cruach an t-Sìdein from the Beinn Lochain – Beinn Eich col to the south (Tom Prentice)

Tullich Hill and Invergroin from the approach up Glen Douglas (Tom Prentice)

Tullich Hill; *632m; (G196); L56; NN293006; hill above Tullich farm. From Gaelic 'tulach', hillock*
Beinn Bhreac; *681m; (G127); L56; NN321000; speckled mountain*

Glen Douglas runs between Loch Lomond and Loch Long, separating the northern Luss Hills from the rest of the group and the road through the glen provides easy access for this pleasant circuit from Invergroin. Tullich Hill gives fine views north across Loch Long to The Cobbler and the high peaks of Arrochar, while Ben Reoch (661m) and Beinn Bhreac drop steeply to Loch Lomond on their eastern sides and present open vistas up and down the loch and across to Ben Lomond.

While the central and southern Luss Hills are predominantly rounded and grassy, with sheep frequently found on the summits, these northern hills display craggier mica-schist terrain, similar to that which characterises much of the landscape of the Southern Highlands.

The route starts from a parking area at NS310987 in Glen Douglas, directly below the conifer plantation before the farm and houses at Invergroin. From here continue up the road

to Invergroin and cross the bridge over the burn.

Just beyond this, go through the second gate on the right and ascend directly to an opening in the fence

above. Continue in this same line to another fence with a gate and pass through to open hillside. As height is gained the warren of military bunkers ▶

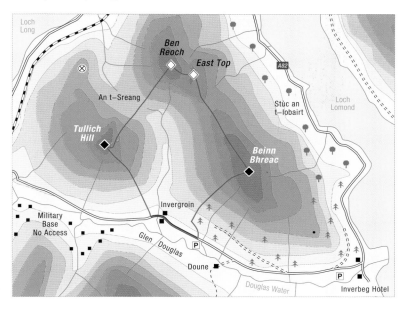

below Doune Hill on the south side of Glen Douglas come into view and the silence is often broken by tannoy announcements.

The broad south-eastern ridge of Tullich Hill becomes better defined and leads to the summit area, which has a number of high points separated by a small lochan. The actual summit is the westernmost of these points, marked by a cairn of quartz and mica-schist rocks (**3km; 530m; 1h 30min**).

A line of steep crags guard the southern side of the north-east ridge leading to the An t-Sreang col below Ben Reoch. To avoid these crags, descend east from the summit to gain lochans below and east of the ridge and continue north-east to the col below. From here a steep ascent in the vicinity of a line of old fence-posts leads to the cairned summit of Ben Reoch (**5km; 830m; 2h 40min**).

Drop down south then east over the rocky East Top and down to the col below Beinn Bhreac. A steady ascent up the broad rock strewn ridge leads to the summit, marked by a prominent trig point on a small crag (**8km; 1020m; 3h 40min**). The east face of Beinn Bhreac immediately below

Beinn Bhreac and Loch Lomond from Ben Reoch (Tom Prentice)

the summit is riven by crevasses from extensive rock-slides, common among many mica-schist mountains in the area. On the shore of Loch Lomond at the very base of the face is Stùc an t-Iobairt, where Robert I (The Bruce) is said to have rested in 1306 after defeat at Dalrigh south of Tyndrum.

Head west then south-west from the summit to gain the western top corner of the conifer plantation and follow this then the wall just beyond it to reach the road in Glen Douglas and follow it back to the parking area (**10.5km; 1020m; 4h 30min**).

Tullich Hill, left, above Arrochar on Loch Long (Tom Prentice)

Beinn Damhain from Meall an Fhùdair (Tom Prentice)

Beinn Damhain; *684m; (G124); L50, 56; NN282173; mountain of stags*

Lying well back from the main road through Glen Falloch, it is hard to get more than a fleeting glimpse of Beinn Damhain. Even the approach doesn't give much away and the hill's fine proportions and surprisingly rocky summit are only fully appreciated when viewed from the north across the Làirig Arnan.

The hill is easily accessed from lower Glen Falloch and provides an enjoyable up and down route, which can be extended into a circuit by including the Corbett Meall an Fhùdair and Troisgeach to the north.

Park at the base of a track on the north side of the A82, opposite Glen Falloch farm, at the foot of Glen Falloch (NN319197). Parking is limited, so maximise space for others and do not block access. Go over the locked gate and ascend over the railway to another gate. A steady ascent in a southerly direction leads to zigzags which can be clipped by ascending beside the burn to regain the track below electricity pylons. Turn left at the junction and skirt below Troisgeach until the track descends left to cross the Allt Arnan at a bridge over a rocky gorge below a hydro dam.

Remain on the track to where it ends, then follow sheep paths up the left bank of the main burn draining from Lochan Beinn Damhain on the mountain's eastern shoulder. At the top, where the ground levels out, stepping stones can be used to cross the burn. If they cannot be found, then the burn can be crossed at the head of the lochan, although this may necessitate wet feet if in spate.

Gain the heathery and rocky eastern ridge and follow it over successive humps to the surprisingly rocky and boulder strewn summit cone, topped by a medium sized cairn (**6km; 670m; 2h 25min**). Beinn Damhain's solitary position and well-defined summit means it holds its own among the surrounding hills and offers some fine views. Return the same way (**12km; 680m; 3h 55min**).

To continue to Meall an Fhùdair, descend from the summit to the marshy watershed, to pass immediately left of the large lochan. Ascend north-west up the slopes on the other side to the 764m summit (**8.5km; 1050m; 3h 50min**).

Now traverse the summit ridge east and north-east towards Meall nan Caora, then south-east across a peaty plateau to 733m Troisgeach (**10.5km; 1130m; 4h 25min**). Descend eastwards down the broad ridge to reach the track near the pylons and follow it back to the start (**14.5km; 1130m; 5h 40min**).

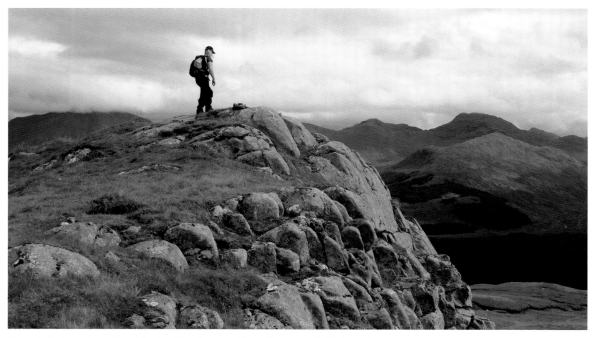

Cruach Ardrain from the dolerite dyke forming Fiarach's summit (Rab Anderson)

Fiarach; *652m; (G173); L50; NN344261; slanting hill*

Fiarach lies at the southern end of the Ben Lui horseshoe of three Munros and one Corbett, which enclose the River Cononish south-west of Tyndrum. It offers particularly fine views east to the Crianlarich Munros at the head of Glen Falloch.

Its companion Graham Meall Odhar (see opposite) lies at the northern end of the horseshoe and it is possible to climb both hills in a day from Dalrigh, especially if a bicycle is used. Fiarach is a broad, elongated hill topped with a distinctive castle-like summit, set well back from the frontal face which overlooks the A82 at Dalrigh. The summit is unusual, being the highest point on a dolerite dyke which erosion has left standing proud of the surrounding moorland, like a high wall in the middle of nowhere.

An ascent of Fiarach is easily made from the large car park at Dalrigh (NN344291), using the track up Gleann Auchreoch. From the bottom of the car park gain the old road and follow it south-east. Cross the bridge over the River Fillan, turn right onto a track and after 1km pass over the railway. Follow the track up Gleann Auchreoch, passing some fine stands of Scots pines to reach a gate at the edge of the conifer plantation.

Turn left and follow a fence uphill to gain a broad ridge. Continue

beside the fence and past Lochan Fiarach directly to the summit (**5km; 470m; 1h 55min**). Before descending, it is worth following the broad ridge south-west for a short way for a view of Fiarach's surprising dolerite 'wall'. Return by the same way (**10km; 470m; 3h 10min**).

Anyone wanting to link Fiarach and Meall Odhar into a single hillwalking circuit without having to return first to Dalrigh, can climb the intervening Munro Beinn Dubhchraig (978m). This mountain's south ridge is easily gained from the southern end of Fiarach and leads directly to the summit; an ascent of about 480m.

A descent is then made north-west to the lochan on the shoulder, then north along the ridge to the fenceline marked on the OS 1:25k. Follow this north-west, then break off north to the footbridge over the River Cononish, just south of Cononish (NN304283); about 8.5km from Fiarach. Gain the access track in the glen then ascend and descend Meall Odhar as described opposite, returning to Dalrigh by the West Highland Way; (approx 25km total).

Meall Odhar; 656m; (G171); L50; NN298298; dun-coloured hill

Meall Odhar lies at the northern end of the horseshoe which has Fiarach (see opposite) at its southern end. As an up and down ascent from near Cononish, Meall Odhar doesn't offer the hillwalker much to chew on, but combined into a circuit with the minor hills to its east and a visit to the old lead mines above Tyndrum, it offers a very pleasant outing.

From one of the large car parks in Tyndrum follow the A82 north, cross over the bridge, turn left opposite the mini-market onto the West Highland Way (WHW) and descend the road past a row of cottages to a wide path leading to Tyndrum Lower Station. Go right over the level crossing and take

the track on the left through the forest to reach the access track from Dalrigh in the Cononish glen.

Continue towards Cononish farm for about 1km to the second large area of rough pasture in the forestry covering the north side of the glen below Meall Odhar. Go through a gate and ascend to the obvious firebreak in the conifers. Cross over the fence and follow the firebreak to the open heathery hillside and ascend to the summit cairn (**5.5km; 460m; 2h 10min**).

Pass north over the summit, then head north-east to the rocky knoll of Drochaid an Droma. From here continue round to Sròn nan Colan (590m) and descend east over knolls

to a fence surrounding the old lead mine workings. Some of the workings are unfenced and all are unstable so keep your distance. From here, zigzag west on a good path through the mine debris littering the hillside to a scree cone and conifers. The scree becomes grassy then bare again, after which an ill-defined grassy path leads right and down through the trees to a cattle creep carrying the burn under the railway. If the level of the burn makes access difficult, the path and grassy track on the south side of the railway lead south-east to the lower station. Pass under the railway and follow the prepared path to the WHW and turn left back to Tyndrum (**10km; 540m; 3h 25min**).

Anyone climbing Meall Odhar and Fiarach in the same day (on foot or using a bike) should access the Cononish road direct from the car park at Dalrigh (NN344291) on the A82. Although the distance is the same as from Tyndrum, the circuit as described above from Dalrigh involves an extra 2km along the WHW from Tyndrum Lower Station back to the car park.

It is also possible to link Meall Odhar to the Corbett Beinn Chuirn via the col between the two. Follow the old boundary fence posts through a break in the forestry, go over a deer fence, and climb 410m up Beinn Chuirn's east face to the summit.

Meall Odhar from Gleann Auchreoch to the east (Tom Prentice)

Meall nan Gabhar; *744m; (G21); L50; NN235240; hill of the goats*

Beinn Bhalgairean; *636m; (G189); L50; NN202241; mountain of the fox*

Meall nan Gabhar from Beinn Bhalgairean (Tom Prentice)

Were it not for Meall nan Gabhar's impressively steep north face, these two mountains would be lost among the giants of the Ben Lui massif, which tower above the A85 on the south side of Beinn Lochy. Set back from the road and in full, unrestricted view, Meall nan Gabhar questions the mountain knowledge of passing hillwalkers and delivers a clear 'climb me' challenge. Something the retiring and less well-defined summit of Beinn Bhalgairean can not do.

Both hills can be climbed together from the access track to Succoth Lodge, signposted Succoth, which is located off the A85 at NN193275, about 350m west of the turning to Glen Orchy and just east of the access track to the houses at Corryghoil. Park in a layby at the start of the track. It may also be possible to park further up the track at the bridge over the Eas a' Ghaill, saving about 1.8km on the day.

It should be noted that there has been extensive felling below both mountains with the construction of tracks for logging lorries. Further felling is certain and may significantly alter the landscape and both restrict and improve access in the future.

Follow the track to a four-way junction at a bridge over the Eas a' Ghaill river. Two routes are possible from here; one up the north/east side of the Eas a' Ghaill which is the main route described and the other up the south/west side (described at the end) which is more suitable for those using bikes, or happy with a total of 10km forest track walking.

The main route follows the old drovers' road from Dalmally to Inverarnan on Loch Lomond, via Succoth Lodge and while it can be wet in places and obstructed by fallen trees – all easily passable – it gives softer and more enjoyable walking. Turn left over the bridge, signposted Succoth, then keep right alongside the river, passing Railway Cottages and under the railway to a T-junction at Succoth. Turn right between two houses to a gated grassier track down on the right.

Follow this track as it ascends beside the river, firstly through beautiful broadleaf woodland then conifers, felled in places, to emerge at a clearing below electricity pylons. Ascend intermittent atv tracks below the pylon line for 400m to an upper central section. This offers a surprisingly straightforward and grassy ascent to the col between Meall nan Gabhar's two summits. The OS 1:10k map indicates the south-easterly of these is 744m and the summit.

Turn right and ascend to the north-east top for the view, then return to the col and climb the south-east top (**7km; 700m; 2h 45min**). Continue south-east to the summit of Meall nan Tighearn (739m), then descend in a westerly direction close to the Eas a' Mhadaidh, heading for a gate at NN216239 in the deer fence which encloses the forestry surrounding Beinn Bhalgairean. The fence is not high and easily climbed if necessary.

Go through the gate and follow the fence north-east beside conifers then felling to reach the main forestry track. Turn left and continue to a junction. This is where the alternative forest track route up the south/west side of the Eas a' Ghaill arrives from below.

Turn left here and ascend to NN219247, where a narrow gravel track goes off left into felling. This track becomes grassier through the remaining conifers and rises to the open hillside and an atv track. Follow this, then more directly over tussocky grass and heather to a deer fence and gate at NN209245, from where the gentle eastern flanks lead to an old cairn on the most westerly of two hillocks (**13km; 1045m; 4h 50min**). Ben Cruachan dominates the view to the

north-west, with the Grahams of Beinn Donachain and Beinn na Sròine to the north and north-east.

Retrace the route to the junction on the main track. To return via Succoth turn right and follow the track down to the pylon clearing and the outward route (21km; 1045m; 7h). Alternatively, turn left and descend the forest track on the west side of the Eas a' Ghaill to the bridge and parking, in the same overall time and distance.

For the alternative route up the south/west side of the Eas a' Gaill, which involves a greater distance on forest tracks, don't cross the bridge over the Eas a' Ghaill, but continue straight ahead and ascend to the track junction below Beinn Bhalgairean. Ascend Beinn Bhalgairean (**7km; 590m; 2h 30min**) as already described, then Meall nan Gabhar (**12km; 985m; 4h 25min**) via the fence and the west face, before returning over Meall nan Tighearn. Return to the track and retrace the ascent route to the start in the same overall time as the Succoth route (21km; 1045m; 7h).

For mountain bikers the forest track on the west side of the Eas a' Ghaill offers a relentless uphill route, but the gradients are never excessive and the surface is generally good. The return is exhilaratingly fast, downhill almost the whole way to the parking and can save at least an hour on the day.

forestry track. Cross over and continue on another grassy atv track up the clearing to a deer fence and gate at the forest edge. From here, continue up the corrie past the Ben Lui National Nature Reserve sign and two pylons, to below the east face of Meall nan Gabhar, which looks steeper and bigger than it is.

Cross south over the burn and ascend the face left of the craggier

Beinn Bhalgairean and distant Ben Cruachan from Meall nan Gabhar (Tom Prentice)

SECTION 1b
Loch Lomond to Loch Tay

Cruinn a' Bheinn and Ben Lomond (Andrew Fraser)

Cruinn a' Bheinn; *632m; (G194); L56; NN365051; roundness of the mountain*

A number of fine Grahams flank the shores of Loch Lomond, their deep glens and craggy sides scoured by repeated periods of glaciation into classic mountain profiles. Unfortunately the glaciers gave Cruinn a' Bheinn fewer favours, grinding it into a bit of a rounded lump, compared with lofty and majestic Ben Lomond next door.

While the views from the summit are good, the hill's lowly height and set back position from the lochshore, means they aren't as grand as those from the Grahams perched on Loch Lomond's western shore.

However, what Cruinn a' Bheinn lacks in character it more than makes up for in the beauty of its approach. The route along the West Highland Way south from Inversnaid passes through glorious oak woodland, while the track above Cailness offers truly spectacular views across Loch Lomond to the surrounding mountains.

Park at the Inversnaid Hotel, follow the West Highland Way (WHW) signs south round the front of the hotel and cross the bridge over the Inversnaid

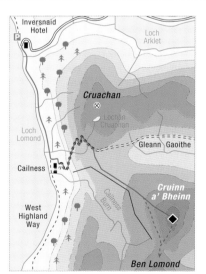

falls. The WHW is now followed without deviation through the lochside woodland and out into open grassland to arrive at the red and white painted cottage of Cailness.

Before reaching the cottage, cut up the bank beside a bushy drainage channel to reach the fence above then go along this and pass through a

gap where it meets the fence around the cottage. This gains a track which leads steeply up the hillside in a series of zigzags. Almost at its highest point, before it breaks over into broad Gleann Gaoithe, and with Cruinn a' Bheinn now visible to the south-east, leave the track to follow a fence down on the right across the moorland and when it swings away continue uphill by the line of an old fence to a final short, steep slope leading to the relatively flat summit area. A small cairn at the south-western end of the high ground marks the top (**7.5km; 630m; 2h 40min**). Return by the same route (**15km; 640m; 4h 30min**).

An ascent of Ben Lomond's unfrequented north ridge is easily made from here by descending south-west to the Bealach Cruinn a' Bheinn, then climbing the ridge to join the well-worn 'Ptarmigan' path beyond Pt.768m and following it up the rocky north-west ridge to the summit. Return to the bealach and follow the fence back, adding (6km; 520m; 2h 40min) to the day.

> **Ben Venue**; 729m; (G53); L57;
> NN474063; small, or pointed
> mountain

High on the south, huge Benvenue
Down to the lake in masses threw
Crags, knolls, and mounds,
confusedly hurled, The fragments
of an earlier world;

Published in 1810, Walter Scott's epic poem *Lady of the Lake* heralds a change in the Lowland perception of the Highlands, from an area of malevolence to be feared and avoided, to an area of romantic scenic beauty to be embraced and experienced.

Scott mentions a number of Trossachs mountains, but none as many times as Ben Venue. *Lady of the Lake* attracted the tourists and later the hillwalkers to Ben Venue, making it one of the country's best-loved small mountains, a position it retains to this day.

There are two principal approaches, from Loch Achray to the east or Ledard on Loch Ard to the south. Loch Achray lies at the heart of The Trossachs and has always been the most popular approach. However, much of the route is through forest which is being steadily felled with the path closures, tracks, and debris that entails. The approach from Ledard offers a more satisfying hillwalk, combining fine oak and birch wood-

land at the start with a traverse through dramatic mountain scenery to meet the Loch Achray route south-west of the summit.

The Loch Achray route can be started from three locations; the Ben Venue pay & display car park (NN506069), a pull-off at the start of the private road to Loch Katrine Dam (NN500068) and a layby on Loch Achray (NN506064). The path from the Ben Venue car park passes the parking on the Loch Katrine Dam road. The layby on Loch Achray allows a slightly shorter approach via the Loch Achray Hotel, about 200m to the

north-west, and joins the Ben Venue car park route at NN494060.

From the Ben Venue car park, paths at the left and right corners form a loop so follow either to where they join (the left is slightly shorter) then descend with views ahead to Ben Venue to meet the Loch Katrine Dam access road where there is parking for a few cars. Turn left and follow the road for about 560m, then take a path which goes off left to a foot-bridge over the Achray Water.

On the other side, ascend to a track and turn right, signposted Ben Venue. Follow the track for about 340m to a waymarked path on the left, with two large boulders at its base. A steep ascent through conifers is followed by a steep descent to a track; the route from Loch Achray Hotel.

The alternative approach via Loch Achray Hotel starts from the layby on Loch Achray. Walk north along the road then up the access road to the back of the hotel and a gated track sign-posted Ben Venue, which ascends into the forest above the Achray Water. Turn left at a track junction, sign-posted Ben Venue and continue to a second track junction. Veer right here, the mountain is straight ahead, to meet the car park route descending from the conifers on the right.

Both routes now continue as a prepared path leading to a forest

Ben Venue summit above Loch Katrine (Tom Prentice)

Ben Venue and Loch Achray from the east (Tom Prentice)

track. Turn left and follow this for about 150m to a path on the right, marked by a cairn and beside a burn. Ascend this rough, mountain path through felling to reach a higher track, where a left then right turn regains the path. Further felled areas are passed on the ascent of Gleann Riabhach and the path can be waterlogged in places.

Exit the last of the forestry to the open hillside and cross a section of boardwalk. Continue north up the corrie on an obvious but rough and often boggy path, with views up towards the summit, the left-hand of Ben Venue's two highpoints. Ascend right of the Spùt Bàn waterfall and continue north-west for 600m to reach a col marked by a prominent cairn.

Ascend the eroded path to NN473063, where it traverses a small top above a col directly below the main peak. The path divides here, the right-hand branch dropping to the col, then traversing right below the main peak towards the lower East Top with its trig point. Follow the left-hand path to the far side of the col and ascend the rocky west ridge to the summit cairn on top of the rocky high point

(**6.5km; 670m; 2h 35min**). Continue south-east beside an old fenceline to meet the path left earlier, which leads to the East Top (727m). From here descend south to a prominent knoll, then continue south-west down grassy slopes to regain the Gleann Riabhach path, which is followed back to the start (**12km; 730m; 4h**).

The southern route starts from a large pull-off (NN459023) on the B829 west of Aberfoyle, at the foot of the access road to Ledard Farm, on the shore of Loch Ard. Follow the access road, signposted to Ben Venue, to a gate on the left. Go through, cross a bridge over the Ledard Burn and continue round Ledard waterfall to a path on its left side which ascends through oak woodland. Pass over a section of boardwalk and through a gate in a deer fence, protecting new broadleaf planting.

Higher in the woodland the path divides at a marker post (NN495034). Turn sharp left uphill, the path soon levels out, and continue to open hillside. Higher up the path crosses the Ledard Burn at a rocky section where care is needed if the burn is in spate.

Go over a stile in the deer fence beyond and continue up the glen to the col between Creag a' Bhealaich and Beinn Bhreac. The Graham Tops of Beinn Bhreac (700m), Beinn Chochan (703m) and Stob an Lochain (684m) can be climbed from the col, although they add little aesthetically to the route and give rough going over wet and heathery terrain.

Cross the stile at the col and traverse north-east below Creag a' Bhealaich to the prominent cairn on the route from Gleann Riabhach described earlier. Ascend the eroded path to NN473063, where it traverses a small top above a col directly below the main peak. The path divides here, the right-hand branch dropping to the col, then traversing right below the main peak towards the lower East Top with its trig point. Follow the left-hand path to the far side of the col and ascend the rocky west ridge to the summit cairn on top of the rocky high point (**5km; 690m; 2h 15min**).

Continue to the East Top (727m), then descend on the main path back to the prominent cairn. From there, return to the start by the line of ascent (**10km; 720m; 3h 40min**).

> **Meall Mòr; 747m; (G17); L50, 56; NN383151; big hill**

Located at the western end of the high ground separating Loch Katrine from lochs Doine and Voil, Meall Mòr offers the hillwalker two routes with very different characters. Bikes can be used on both routes and will shorten the on foot return timings given by about 1h 30min.

Although the northern approach from Inverlochlarig allows Meall Mòr to be combined with the Graham Stob Breac, a more interesting and satisfying round can be had from Loch Katrine to the south. The only downsides are that new planting restricts access to the steep southern slopes and summer bracken can make for heavy going.

The route starts at Stronachlachar on Loch Katrine, gained by car from the B829 from Aberfoyle, or via the steamer Sir Walter Scott <www.lochkatrine.com> from Trossachs Pier to Stronachlachar (restricted winter service). The route can also be approached from the Trossachs Pier car park via a 16km bike ride along the private road on

Meall Mòr above Loch Katrine and Glengyle house (Tom Prentice)

the north side of Loch Katrine, with a return via steamer if desired.

From the Stronachlachar car park and cafe, follow the road 5km to the track up Glen Gyle, about 300m north-west of The Dhu. The track leads below pylon wires to the Glengyle Water which is crossed on a sleeper bridge. Continue alongside a fence and after 200m cross a burn, turn right and follow it up the steep hillside to reach a fence. Cross this at a wooden section on the far right near the burn and continue to above a line of crags, where the angle eases.

Cross right over the burn and head north-east to the summit. This lies some distance back and is the right-

hand of two similar knolls, east of a lochan and south of the fence posts (**8.5km; 630m; 3h**). The view north to the Munro giants Beinn Chabhair, An Caisteal, Beinn a' Chroin, Cruach Ardrain, Stob Binnein and Ben More is spectacular.

The ridge is now followed south-east then north-east beside the fence posts and over the East Top and various knolls, to the much more attractive Graham Top of Stob an Duibhe overlooking the unnamed loch below Stob a' Choin. Descend south-east from here to the Bealach na Cloiche, followed by a steady ascent to An Garadh (**12km; 850m; 4h 10min**).

The summit of Meall Mòr and Ben Lomond (Tom Prentice)

Sgiath a' Chàise; 645m; (G181); L57; NN583169; *wing-shaped hill of the cheese*

Crowning the high ground dividing Strathyre and Glen Ample, Sgiath a' Chàise is a long grassy ridge surrounded by forestry and topped by a number of craggy summits. The smallest and most impressive of these is Creag a' Gheata, overlooking Loch Lubnaig and the A84.

The hill is easily climbed via the right of way from Loch Lubnaig to Loch Earn, which ascends the glen north of Ardchullarie More to the watershed, then descends Glen Ample to Edinample. It is a short though pleasant outing with fine views north to the Ben Lawers range and could be combined with an ascent of the Corbett Beinn Each on the east side of the glen.

Start from a layby on the north side of the A84 just west of Ardchullarie More. Follow the access road towards the house then left onto a signposted footpath which ascends through woodland beside the Ardchullarie ▶

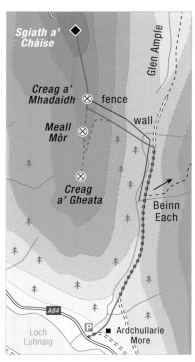

From there, descend south-south-west towards the burn in the corrie to reach the upper limit of a fence enclosing the lower part the hillside and a gate at NN399136. Go through and follow the fence and atv track to another gate, then straight down to a third gate to reach the road east of the white railing bridge over the burn. Turn right and follow the road past Glengyle back to Stronachlachar (**21km; 850m; 6h 30min**).

The northern ascent starts from the car park before Inverlochlarig (NN446185) and involves a 7.5km approach south-west beside the River Larig to where the track ends at NN384164 and the river forks. Cross the river, easy when the water is low, and make a steep ascent direct to the summit (**9km; 620m; 3h**). The highest point is marked by a small cairn and is the furthest of two knolls, east of a small lochan and south of a line of fence posts. Return the same way (**18km; 620m; 5h 15min**).

It is possible to continue east over Stob an Duibhe and the Corbett Stob a' Choin to Stob Breac (see p111). But this will involve a lot of ascent and descent and if a bike has been used for the approach, Stob Breac can more easily be climbed in a single day with Meall Mòr, by returning first to Inverlochlarig.

Sgiath a' Chàise, right, and Creag a' Mhadaidh above Glen Ample, from the flanks of Beinn Each (Tom Prentice)

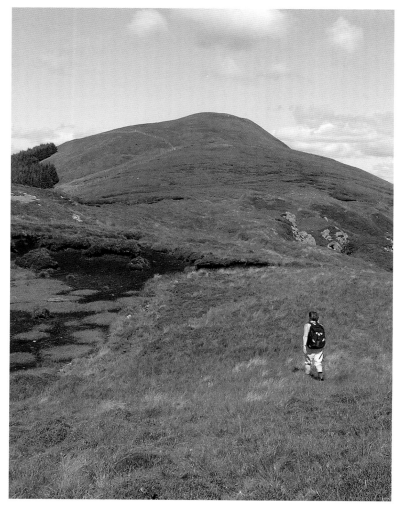

> **Creag Mhòr;** *658m; (G164); L57;*
> *NN510185; big cliff*

Creag Mhòr lies at the north-eastern end of the high ground separating Lochs Doine and Voil from Loch Katrine and is the lowest of the four Grahams in the area.

Its northern and eastern flanks are forested complicating access from Balquhidder, but the hill is easily ascended from Ballimore in Glen Buckie to the south and offers a delightful route over a knobbly, grassy ridge with fine views across the Braes of Balquhidder to the Graham The Stob and the Munro giants Ben More and Stob Binnein.

However, this ascent is short and quick and while this presents an opportunity to bag another Graham in the vicinity on the same day, such as The Stob, the route over Creag Mhòr can also be extended to the nearby Corbett Beinn Stacach (previously known as Stob Fear-tomhais) to produce a fine round of the Fathan Glinne; the route described here.

The summit of Sgiath a' Chàise from the south (Tom Prentice)

Burn to a forestry track. Turn left, follow the track out of the trees and up the glen. As height is gained the craggy flanks of Creag a' Gheata give way to Meall Mòr and the pointed top of Creag a' Mhadaidh, with the grassy dome of Sgiath a' Chaise beyond. Near the watershed at NN590150, a signpost is reached indicating the path up Beinn Each on the east side of the glen; the inclusion of this adds 3.5km, 480m, 1h 45min to the route.

About 600m beyond this at NN590156 and just short of the watershed, a track goes off left towards the wall marking the lower boundary of the conifers. Follow the track through a gap in the wall, swing left onto a grassy track and gain the hillside beyond.

Climb the heathery hillside right of the trees to gain the crest of the ridge just south of the pointed top of Creag a' Mhadaidh (557m). From here follow the broad grassy ridge across a shallow col cut by peat hags to gain an old fenceline which leads to the unmarked high point (**4km; 520m; 1h 45min**). Return by the route of ascent (**8km; 530m; 2h 45min**).

For anyone not in a hurry to descend, the route can be extended over Creag a' Mhadaidh and Meall Mòr to Creag a' Gheata for fine views south over Loch Lubnaig to Benvane and Ben Ledi. Unfortunately, there is no easy way through the forestry below, so a return must be made back past Meall Mòr; an added 2.5km, 100m, 50min to the route.

From Balquhidder drive south up Glen Buckie to where the public road ends at a cattle grid and bridge over the river. Park on the left just before the access road to Ballimore farm. Walk back along the road, turn left onto a track just before a bungalow and ascend to a gate in the high deer fence on the left. Up and right of this is another gate in a stock fence. Go through this gate and ascend diagonally up and right, heading for the corner of the conifer plantation, where a gap in the fence gives access to the open hillside.

Ascend the broad ridge with increasingly fine views to gain the hummocky summit ridge, marked by small, rocky escarpments of upturned mica-schist. The summit lies on one of these and is marked by a small cairn (**2.5km; 480m; 1h 20min**). Immediately north-north-west across Loch Voil is The Stob, a hill whose summit is as hard to locate from a distance as it is close up! To the east, three distinct lines of hills separate Glen Buckie, Strathyre and Glen Ample. The closest hill is knobbly Beinn an t-

Sìdhein. The middle is a long grassy ridge with forested lower regions, the Graham Sgiath a' Chàise, while the furthest is the impressive craggy buttresses of Beinn Each, Stùc a' Chroin and Ben Vorlich.

Descend the ridge west, avoiding or taking in the last top to the south, towards the Bealach Driseach. From here it is possible to return to Ballimore by following animal paths south then south-east beside the Allt

Fathan Glinne to a cattle barn. Cross the bridge over the burn and traverse south towards a small hut with a corrugated iron roof, beyond which there is a footbridge over the Allt a' Ghlinne Dhuibh at NN508156. On the other side follow the river east to a junction with the tributary joining from the south. Cross this and the fence beyond and ascend to a path; the right of way between Glen Buckie and Glen Finglas. Turn left and follow the boggy and occasionally ill-defined path north then east to the Ballimore road (**9.5km; 500m; 3h**).

If continuing to Beinn Stacach from the Bealach Driseach, continue south-west and climb grassy slopes on the south-west side of Pt.587m to gain a broad ridge. Climb this south-west alongside an old fence towards Ceann na Baintighearna. About 500m before the summit, the fence swings south and broad slopes lead to the trig point on Beinn Stacach (**8km; 900m; 3h 20min**). A small pile of stones just to the east marks the highest point.

Descend south-east then east to gain the long north-east ridge and follow it over the distinctive pointed top of Pt.684m. Continue on the ridge until grassy slopes can be descended east to reach the footbridge over the Allt a' Ghlinne Dhuibh at NN508156, just south of the small hut with a corrugated iron roof. Cross the bridge and gain the right of way path back to Ballimore as described above (**15km; 950m; 5h**).

Creag Mhòr from Glen Buckie to the south (Tom Prentice)

The Stob; 753m; (G10); L51; NN491231; the stub

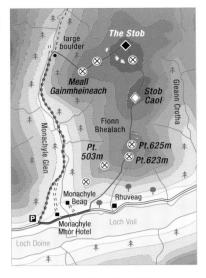

An illusive summit from all directions, near and far, The Stob marks the highest point on the ridge between the Monachyle Glen and Gleann Crotha above the Braes of Balquhidder.

Viewing the hill from a distance, the eye is drawn to the more prominent southern peak, the Graham Top of Stob Caol; 734m and a mere 19m lower. The actual summit lies further north, a rocky stub on a ridge of mica-schist. It rises only 20m above the surrounding moorland and is difficult to identify, making The Stob a navigational challenge in poor visibility. The summit area also carries the name Meall na Frean.

Park at the start of the track up Monachyle Glen, about 350m west of the turning to the Monachyle Mhòr Hotel. Follow the track for 3.5km up the glen, first on the west side of the Monachyle Burn, then on the east, to where it ends at a footbridge over the burn (NN475230). Do not cross over but continue on the path on the east side of the burn, past a large boulder

to a firebreak.

Follow the firebreak to where the trees end and continue steeply up the hillside, heading rightwards towards crags on the skyline to gain a deer fence. Follow this up and left to just left of the crags, where there are various gaps in the fence as it passes over a small rocky knoll at NN480227.

Continue ascending, either taking in the top of Meall Gainmheineach, or passing to its north then go over Pt.666m and on to Pt.687m beyond to gain the edge of the summit plateau. The summit lies some 750m to the north-east, marked by a cairn on a raised rocky ridge crossed by an old fence (**5.5km; 620m; 2h 25min**).

From the summit go south over a small knoll, then leave the fence, descend to a col and ascend to the top of Stob Caol. Continue south across the Fionn Bhealach and over the slight rise of Pt.625m to Pt.623m overlooking Loch Voil. Leave the ridge at this point, descending south over open slopes (named Coire Bheathag on the OS 1:25k map) to reach a

broad grassy gully with a burn.

Descend this avoiding the bracken to a fence enclosing the broadleaf woodland below. Animal tracks lead west beside the fence to a wooden gate beside a wall at NN481199. Cross over, descend the left side of the wall to a gap, go through, and continue down to a ladder stile and the road. Follow the road right to the start (**10.5km; 730m; 4h**).

The broad summit of The Stob, with the more prominent top of Stob Caol immediately to its right (Tom Prentice)

Stob Breac from the flanks of Stob Binnein (Tom Prentice)

Stob Breac; *688m; (G122); L57; NN447166; speckled stub*

As the name states, Stob Breac is a bit of a stub, but it is a fine viewpoint and offers a number of routes.

All start from the car park before Inverlochlarig (NN446185). Exit right (south) from the car park onto an old tarmac road signposted Blaircreich Estate and keep left through a gate to cross a bridge over the Inverlochlarig Burn, then a bridge over the River Larig signposted to Blaircreich farm.

Go past a bungalow, then turn left at the next junction and through a gate in the deer fence, or over the stile, and zigzag up a grassy track to a junction. Firebreaks on both sides of the mountain offer ascent lines, but those on the west are steeper and harder to locate. A frontal ascent involves a deer fence and new planting and is not recommended.

Turn left (east) and traverse the hill to the first good firebreak on the east side (NN455174) which contains the Allt a' Choire Bhain. Ascend beside this, the forest appears to close higher up but doesn't, to a narrow section requiring care beside a small waterfall, to exit the trees to open hillside. Continue beside the burn up the obvious rift, then ascend right (west) to the summit, marked by a cairn (**5km; 560m; 2h**). Return the same way

(**10km; 560m; 3h 25min**).

A more interesting walk can be had by heading south along Stob Breac's elevated ridge. This leads over two distinctive tops and assorted knolls to An Stuchd (**7km; 650m; 2h 35min**) which has fine views south to Loch

Katrine and the double topped summit of the Graham Ben Venue.

A return is now possible down tracks on the west side of Stob Breac or over the Corbett Stob a' Choin. For the track route, descend south-west to a fence and follow it beside a burn to a firebreak in the trees. Where the burn joins the Allt Sgionie turn right and follow a path beside that burn to a track back to the outward route and the car park (**12.5km; 650m; 4h**).

For Stob a' Choin, continue beside the fence to a stile at NN442146, cross over and descend to the Allt Sgionie. From here ascend north-west initially over grassy and hummocky ground, then more steeply to Pt.736m and a little further north to Pt.836m, marked by a small cairn atop a small crag. Continue north-west on the ridge over Meall Reamhar to reach the summit of Stob a' Choin (**11km; 1230m; 4h 35min**).

Carry on to the North Top and down the north ridge for about 560m to near the 630m contour, then east and north-east across the burn draining from the Bealach Coire an Laoigh to a footbridge over the River Lairg at NN427175 from where the track is followed to Inverlochlarig and the road (**15.5km; 1230m; 6h**).

Stùc na Càbaig, left, and Beinn Dearg (Tom Prentice)

Beinn Dearg; *706m; (G87); L57; NN696197; red mountain*

While the hills on the south side of Glen Artney lie in the Lowlands (see Uamh Bheag in Section 0c), two Grahams on the north side are in the Highlands, the Highland Boundary Fault running the length of the glen. These hills can be combined into a single round, but this involves climbing over a deer fence, something which will not suit everyone. Thankfully Beinn Dearg and Mòr Bheinn also make enjoyable routes when climbed separately and are described in that way.

It should be noted that an unratified survey shows the Graham Top of Stùc na Càbaig to be 708m in height, the high point on the ridge and the Graham, rather than 706m Beinn Dearg beyond. However, both hills are climbed on this round.

From the car park below Glen Artney church walk north-east back up the road to a track on the left and follow it down past Dalchruin to a bridge. Cross over the Water of Ruchill keeping right at the first junction, then left shortly after and pass through a gate to reach Dalclathick. Follow the now grassy track past

ruins and a plantation on the left to a stile in a wall giving access to the open hillside. Continue ascending alongside a fence enclosing a broadleaf plantation on the south side of the Allt Coire a' Choire to reach a gate.

Ascend almost due west and climb the broad bulk of the Graham Top Sròn na Maoile (618m), initially rough then rocky. The worst of the peat hags are turned to the north to gain a gentler, broad ridge and the ill-defined summit. Descend to the start of a more prominent knobbly ridge and follow this over Sròn nam Broighleag (679m), to the Graham Top of Stùc na Càbaig (**6.5km; 630m; 2h 30min**).

Continue round the steep-sided corrie and ascend to Pt.680m, beyond which the ridge leads over assorted small tops to the summit of Beinn Dearg, marked by a small cairn (**8km; 750m; 3h**). To the east, the Graham Mòr Bheinn and the Graham Top Ben Halton (621m) face Beinn Dearg across the Allt Glas. From the summit it is possible to return directly to the start by descending the south ridge to complete the round, or to

descend the rocky north-east ridge and include Mòr Bheinn and Ben Halton.

To return directly to the start, descend east then south, keeping to the right-hand (due south) of the two

Mòr Bheinn, left, and Ben Halton from Beinn Dearg (Rab Anderson)

ridges which fall from the summit, to gain the lower reaches of Coire Innein. Continue down to gain a vague atv track with the occasional sleeper bridge, aiming for the Àth na Mèine ford across the Allt Coire Choire at NN707175. This lies above a small but impressive jammed boulder forming a natural arch above a waterfall on the burn.

Cross over and follow the atv track to the corner of the fence enclosing the broadleaf plantation on the south side of the Allt Coire Choire and the gate crossed on the ascent. Retrace the ascent route by the fence to the stile in the wall and back to Dalclathick and the start (14km; 800m; 4h 30min).

To include Mòr Bheinn, descend due north from the summit for about 300m to avoid the steep north-east face, then north-east to gain the north-east ridge. Weave down grass between the rocky knolls on the ridge until slopes lead eastwards to marshy ground and the deer fence in the glen. Cross this at about NN707204 and ascend beside the old fence enclosing the forestry to gain the col between Ben Halton and Mòr Bheinn. From here animal tracks lead north up to the rocky summit of Mòr Bheinn with its trig point (**11km; 1080m; 4h 30min**). Return as described for Mòr Bheinn, opposite, taking in the Graham Top of Ben Halton (621m) if desired (18km; 1230m; 6h 30min).

Mòr Bheinn; 640m; (G186); L51, 52, 57; NN716211; big mountain

Mòr Bheinn and its neighbour the Graham Top of Ben Halton (621m) make a pleasant route by themselves, or they can be linked with Beinn Dearg opposite, providing you are prepared to scale the deer fence in the glen between them.

From the car park below Glen Artney church walk north-east back up the road to a track on the left and follow it down past Dalchruin to a bridge. Cross over the Water of Ruchill and keep right at the junctions to cross a second smaller bridge.

Beyond this, turn left and ascend a grassy track to gain sheep pens beyond which an atv track winds its way up through rough pasture to a wall. Go over this to a vehicle track and follow it left to a gate in the deer fence crossing it. Pass through, turn right and ascend the hillside on an atv track marked with wooden posts

to a deer fence.

Cross the ladder stile and continue over boggy ground, keeping straight ahead where the atv veers right, and ascend the pathless heathery ridge to gain an elevated plateau of peat encircled lochans and knolls, between Pt.615m and the Graham Top of Ben Halton (621m). Make a short detour north-east to the summit of Ben Halton before returning and descending north-west to the col below Mòr Bheinn, from where animal tracks lead up the south ridge to the rocky summit and trig point (**7km; 620m; 2h 35min**).

To the north-west, the Graham Creag Ruadh can be identified above St Fillans at the eastern end of Loch Earn, with the Graham Creag Each further to its west. Return by the same route (13.5km; 750m; 4h 25min).

East across Glen Ogle to Meall Buidhe (Tom Prentice)

Meall Buidhe; 719m; (G67); L51; NN576275; yellow hill

Meall Buidhe, together with its adjacent neighbour, Beinn Leabhainn, provides a good short route with fine views. It makes an ideal ascent for a summer's evening or a quick hit when passing up or down the A85.

Start from the car park at the picnic area on the east side of the road at the head of Glen Ogle (NN559285); the Làirig Cheile. For a number of months in the year there is a good mobile cafe here. Follow a track which heads east through a gate into a forestry plantation. After passing beneath an electricity pylon line the track zigzags easily uphill through the forest out onto the open hillside, then climbs steadily around some crags to end at an incongruous communications aerial.

Leaving the aerial behind, the way ahead is south-east, aiming for a shallow col between the two hilltops. The going is tougher, through heather and across boggy ground that is path-less save for the odd sheep track. Firmer ground is soon reached and this leads easily to the flat summit of Meall Buidhe (**3.5km; 430m; 1h 30min**). There is a splendid view south down Glen Ogle over the head of Loch Earn to Ben Vorlich and Stùc a' Chroin. On her way to Lochearn-head in 1842, on one of her frequent Scottish visits, Queen Victoria remarked in her diary of Glen Ogle's resemblance to the Khyber Pass!

Carrying on, descend north across a shallow col and climb to the top of the neighbouring and only slightly lower Beinn Leabhainn (709m) which is about 900m away. It is worth continuing north then south-west to take in the two northern highpoints. The view from here extends down the length of Loch Tay. Killin lies below, at the head of the loch, with Meall Tarmachan behind and the Ben Lawers group to the side. To the west along Glen Dochart lie Ben More and Stob Binnein.

The return is made by dropping steeply westwards through heather to regain the track, which is followed back to the start (**7.5km; 500m; 2h 40min**).

Creag Gharbh; 637m; (G187); L51; NN632327; rough cliff

Located on the south side of Loch Tay, Creag Gharbh is a pleasant double-topped hill with a fine outlook across the loch to the Breadalbane Hills of the Meall Tarmachan and Ben Lawers groups. Start from Ardeonaig some 7 miles (11km) along the south Loch Tay road to the east of Killin. The Ardeonaig Hotel has a convenient car park and it should be possible to park here with permission.

At the post box opposite the hotel, walk uphill on the Braes of Ardeonaig road and follow this past the Abernethy Trust's Outdoor Centre. This is the route of the Rob Roy Way long distance footpath. Beinn Ghlas and Ben Lawers dominate the view across the fields here. In a short distance the road becomes a track and leads past the farm, then through gates onto more open hillside.

Cross a burn and now on a path, head for a gate in a wall at the edge of a small plantation. Continue up the side of the burn in front of another small plantation passing the ruins of old sheilings and climb up onto a track traversing the hillside. This track runs alongside a pipeline carrying water to Loch Lednock Reservoir, which lies over the hills to

the south-east.

Walk south-westwards along the track, the pipeline soon disappears underground, then loop around the flanks of the hill and follow the track uphill to a communications aerial. Head across heathery ground and make the short ascent to the top of Meall Odhar (628m). The slightly higher summit of Creag Gharbh with its trig point lies on another knoll 900m to the north-west, reached across the somewhat boggy intervening ground (**7.5km; 570m; 2h 40min**). The view

from here of the Ben Lawers and Tarmachan Hills is very fine indeed.

Descend the south-east shoulder back towards Ardeonaig, as far the knoll of Sròn na Crìche (562m) next to the knoll of Stùc Mhòr, then drop down east and follow first a fence then a wall back towards the small plantation passed on the ascent. A short distance before the gate, go through a gap in the wall and cut across to join the upward route, which leads back to the hotel car park (**13km; 590m; 4h**).

Creag Gharbh, far right, from Killin at the west end of Loch Tay (Tom Prentice)

Creag Each from the track in Glen Tarken (Rab Anderson)

Creag Each; *672m; (G143); L51; NN652263; horse cliff*
Creag Ruadh; *712m; (G77); L51; NN674292; red cliff*

Close to St Fillans on the sunny side of Loch Earn, these two hills are separated by the flat and boggy Glen Tarken but conveniently accessed by tracks. Start opposite the Loch Earn Sailing Club at Woodhouse, from one of two lay-bys on the A85, where a track (NN669247) leading up into Glen Tarken begins just west of a barn.

Follow the track which zigzags up through the trees past the old steadings of Wester Glentarken to swing round and ascend into the glen where Creag Each becomes visible on the left. Go through a gate in a wall by some sheep pens and after crossing the main burn (NN664261) which drains from beneath the top of the hill, leave the track just before it forks.

Climb the hillside to the right of the burn, aiming for an obvious cairn on the skyline to the east of the summit. The slopes to the left of the burn can

Clach Mhòr Na h-Airigh Lèithe, or the Glen Tarken Stone with the summit of Creag Ruadh on the right (Rab Anderson)

also be climbed to gain the south shoulder of the hill. The top itself is defended by small crags, easily rounded (**3.5km; 580m; 1h 45min**). To the north over the Graham of Creag Gharbh the Ben Lawers range dominates, while west beyond the Graham of Meall Buidhe lie Ben More and Stob Binnein. Ben Vorlich lies to the south over Loch Earn and to the east over Glen Tarken and Creag Ruadh is Ben Chonzie.

Descend by the north ridge, over heather and grass, passing some large boulders to reach an obvious loop in the upper track which is joined by the lower track. This is just beyond an impressive huge boulder known as Clach Mhòr Na h-Airigh Lèithe, or the Glen Tarken Stone. From this descent a gorge can be seen cutting into the hillside on the opposite side of the glen and the

Creag Ruadh from Creag Each (Ken Crocket)

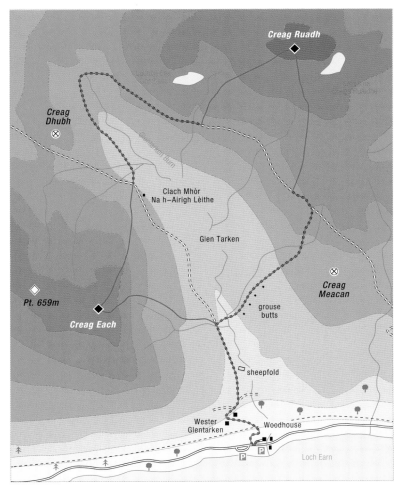

edge of this provides the route up onto Creag Ruadh. The gorge is formed by the Allt Eas Domhain and has waterfalls. Although it is possible to cut directly across the glen to the gorge this is wet and boggy, so follow the track easily around the head of Glen Tarken to reach it.

Leave the track just to the east of the gorge and climb the hillside over grass and heather passing to the east of a small lochan, Loch Eas Domhain. The summit slopes are guarded by numerous outcrops and a delightful maze formed by them leads eventually to the rocky top (**9km; 910m; 3h 30min**). From here, south-east over St Fillans beyond the Graham Mòr Bheinn, the Ochils and the Lomond Hills complete the view.

To avoid a steep crag on the descent, initially go east to a col where easy grassy slopes lead down. Head for the outflow from Lochan Creige Ruaidhe and pick up a faint path parallel to the burn which leads down to the track in Glen Tarken again. Follow the track for 800m or so then take the right branch and descend to the floor of the glen and cross the Glentarken Burn via stepping stones. The track of the outward route is joined just above and this leads downhill back to the start (**15.5km; 930m; 5h 20min**).

SHEE OF ARDTALNAIG; Pointed hill (above) Ardtalnaig
Ciste Buidhe a' Claidheimh; *759m; (G5); L51, 52; NN729351; correctly Ciste Bhuidhe a' Chlaidheimh – the yellow chest of the sword, after the impressive rock-cleft north-east of the summit*

Despite being flanked on both sides by higher and more extensive summits, this hill more than holds its own, thanks to its prominent profile when viewed from Loch Tay to the north and Glen Almond to the south-east.

Shee of Ardtalnaig relates directly to the whole hill and its profile, while the actual summit is named Ciste Buidhe a' Claidheimh. It offers an enjoyable short walk on its own, but it can also be linked with the two flanking Corbetts, most easily with Creagan na Beinne to the north.

Park at Milton of Ardtalnaig on the west side of the road just south of the bridge over the Ardtalnaig Burn (NN702393). Walk south up the hill, turn left just before the phone box and follow the road past the tennis courts (possible parking) and on for about 2km to Claggan farm.

Go rightwards through the farmyard to a track and cross a burn, beyond which the track divides. Take the right-hand track to a gate then leave the track and climb the frontal face to an atv track on the crest of the ridge. It is also possible to continue up the main track into Gleann a' Chloidh, from where it zigzags up to the ridge. Peat hags are a feature of this ridge

and while they pose no problems in summer, the track does miss some of them and might offer pleasanter going if the weather is poor or conditions are very wet underfoot.

Follow the ridge through the hags scattered with blocks of bleached mica-schist, silver sand and mountain hares. The worst of this ground is easily avoided by sticking to the east edge overlooking Gleann a' Chilleine. At the foot of the final steepening to the summit lies the impressive cleft of Bual a' Claidheimh, created by a

rock slip. These features are common in mica-schist rock throughout the Southern Highlands, some of the most impressive being on the Corbett Ben Donich near Arrochar. A small pile of stones marks the summit (**5.5km; 630m; 2h 15min**).

A descent can be made by the same route, or by a steep descent south to pick up a track which swings round into Gleann a' Chilleine, then leads north-west, back to Claggan and the start (**13.5km; 640m; 4h**).

Alternatively, the route can be extended over Creagan na Beinne (888m) by descending to the track in Gleann a' Chilleine and following it south to the moraine mounds by the cottage at Dunan. Gain the south ridge of Creagan na Beinne (named Dunan Hill) and follow it to the summit (**10km; 1100m; 4h 15min**).

Descend north beside the fenceline over boggy ground and pass over the hump of Pt.658, to a fence at the col below Beinn Bhreac (716m). A grassy track starts here and descends west into Corrie Cruinneachan to pasture and an exit onto the road at a gate with white gateposts, just north of the bridge over the Ardtalnaig Burn (**18km; 1140m; 6h 15min**).

Shee of Ardtalnaig and Creagan na Beinne, left (Tom Prentice)

The rounded summit of Beinn na Gainimh and rocky Creag Grianain from the head of Coire Grianain (Tom Prentice)

Beinn na Gainimh; 730m; (G51); L52; NN837344; mountain of sand

---

Beinn na Gainimh is the westernmost of four Grahams which occupy the high ground on either side of the road through the Sma' Glen and Glen Cochil, between Crieff and Aberfeldy, the line of one of General Wade's military roads.

Some 2.5 miles (4km) along the minor road that runs between Amulree and Kenmore on Loch Tay, there is verge parking next to the wall about 150m north-west of the entrance to Glenquaich Lodge. Walk back down the road until opposite the entrance to Glenquaich Lodge, then take a track that leads around the side of Croftmill cottage and past the end of a plantation, out onto the hill. Continue up the glen for 800m and after passing through a gate in a wall, break off left away from the track. Cross the burn, gain the shoulder of Meall Mòr and climb steeply to the left of a small rock outcrop to gain easier ground leading to its 704m summit (**3km; 420m; 1h 25min**).

Now follow a somewhat unsightly electrified double fence, down and around the head of Coire Grianain, then ascend quite steeply to the summit of Creag Grianain (683m), an unusually shapely and rocky summit for these parts. Still following the fence, drop to a col, then ascend

steeply up the side of the upper edge of a landslip and where the ground flattens cross through the fence. Although the current is not permanently on, it is possible to step through between the wires without touching them. The summit of Beinn na Gainimh is a large expanse of flat ground and a cairn in the middle appears to indicate the actual top (**5km; 620m; 2h 15min**). The bigger Beinn Chonzie and Auchnafree Hill lie

to the south-west on the other side of Glen Almond, whilst the three neighbouring Grahams, Meall Reamhar and Meall nan Caorach are to the east with Meal Dearg to the north-east across Loch Freuchie.

Return to the col, then make a zigzag descent to reach the floor of Glen Lochan, east of Lochan Uaine. At some point in the geological past there appears to have been a massive landslip here and the steep slope that falls away into Glen Lochan is riven with hollows and minor rock outcrops, requiring some care.

Cross the outflow from Lochan Uaine to gain the track (the route of the Rob Roy Way) and follow it past Lochan a' Mhuilinn back to the start (**9.5km; 620m; 3h 30min**).

Another route starts at the Newton Bridge car park in the Sma' Glen. Follow the track west along Glen Almond to NN852318, then ascend north-west on another track to gain the shoulder and climb this to Sròn Bealaidh and Beinn na Gainimh (**7.5km; 510m; 2h 30min**). Traverse round over Creag Grianian to Meall Mòr then descend south-east over Geal Charn and Am Bodach to the trig point on Meall Reamhar (667m), from where a steep descent leads back to Newton Bridge (**15km; 860m; 5h**).

Meall nan Caorach, left, and Meall Reamhar from Creag Liath (Rab Anderson)

***Meall Reamhar**; 620m; (G206); L52; NN922332 ; fat, broad, mountain*
***Meall nan Caorach**; 623m; (G201); L52; NN928338 ; sheep mountain*

Lying to the north-east of the Sma' Glen, this pair of Grahams lie on the line of the Highland Boundary Fault and are the highest points in the triangle of hills between Crieff, Dunkeld and Perth. A track leads from the starting point to the col between the two summits, though the ridges either side of this track make a much more pleasant route possible, providing a circuit through an extensive area of heather and grass moorland.

Park at Amulree Village Hall and carefully walk south along the A822 for 800m then take the track which leads to the farmhouse at Girron. Continue on the track and about 1km further on, at any convenient spot, before the track swings left uphill leave the track to cross a small burn and head uphill for the north-west ridge of Meall Reamhar. Once on the heathery ridge a drystane dyke then fence leads south-east along the gently undulating ridge, over a minor top, gradually curving east to the summit of Meall Reamhar (**5km; 350m; 1h 45min**). Be aware of some old discarded fencing at one or two spots. There is a fine view west to Glen Almond and the Graham Beinn na Gainimh.

Follow the fence north-east and make a steep 160m drop to the col between Meall Reamhar and Meall nan Caorach then climb steeply back up the other side to the summit of the latter which has a cairn and trig point (**6km; 510m; 2h 25min**). Loch Freuchie in Glen Quaich is prominent to the north-west, with the Càrn Mairg group and Schiehallion beyond. A bit further right is the Graham Meall Dearg and to its right the distinctive pointed top of the Corbett Farragon Hill.

From Meall nan Caorach head north along the ridge to Creag Ghorm, gradually bending north-west. Just past the summit of Creag Ghorm a cairn is passed with a white stone of pure quartzite. At the first dip after the cairn turn down west and descend easy grass slopes to gain an atv track which leads to the main track at the top of a steep section at the 400m contour (NN917349). This track then leads back past Girron to the main road and Amulree (**11km; 540m; 3h 45min**).

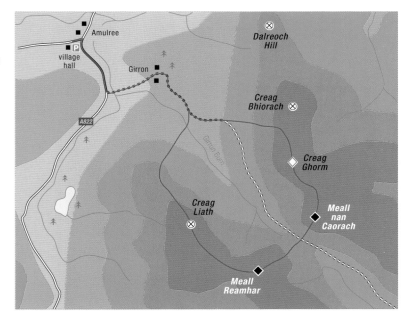

Meall Dearg; 690m; (G117); L52; NN886414; red hill

Meall Dearg is the highest of a number of small tops that make up the high ground between Glen Quaich and Glen Cochill south of Aberfeldy. It is best climbed by a route that starts at an elevation of 400m on the A826 to the south of Loch na Craige, where there is a parking area at the entrance to the Calliacher Wind Farm. The Griffin Forest car park lies 100m up the road to the north.

Go through a side gate and follow the main track through the forestry plantation, passing forks off to the right then the left, and swing westwards uphill to exit the forest by a gate. The wind turbines lie ahead with Loch Hoil in front and the peak of Schiehallion behind. Take the track on the left and climb south, passing a track off left, to reach its high point. Leave the track and climb onto Pt.637m, an unnamed Graham Top. A short descent then rough going along the crest leads above Loch Fender, nestling in the hollow between four hilltops. Creag an Loch, another Graham Top, is easily gained after a short climb (**6.5km; 300m; 2h**). A track crosses some of the ground from the south side of Pt.637m but it lies off

the crest and misses the views across the loch.

Descend north-east to Loch Fender, cross the outflow then ascend to the trig point on Meall Dearg (**7.5km; 410m; 2h 30min**); a fine vantage point. Drop north-west towards the unnamed 640m central top and either climb this, or traverse its east side across a burn. Descend north beside another burn, crossing the track that traverses the hillside to reach the fence around the forest at a break. Either step through a gap or climb the fence and follow the right side of the break down and round to a side track then the main track which leads back (**10.5km; 410m; 3h 30min**). Alternatively, regain Pt.637m from the 640m top and return via the approach route (**14.5km; 480m; 4h 15min**).

Another route starts from Amulree to the south, parking at the former hotel. Cross the old bridge over the River Braan then go right and turn off left to follow the road then track northwards past the farm. This leads to a track in Glen Fender, gained by a stile at NN908384. Follow the track up the glen and take the second track off right to gain the top of Beinn Liath

then ascend the undulating peaty ridge to Meall Dearg (**7km; 470m; 2h 20min**). Drop to Loch Fender and climb Creag an Loch then descend south over Pt.608m to pick up a track which leads downhill beside the Kinloch Burn to join the track in Glen Quaich, which leads back to Amulree (**14.5km; 600m; 4h 20min**).

Descending from Creag an Loch towards Loch Fender and Meall Dearg (Rab Anderson)

SECTION 2-3
Loch Tay to Loch Linnhe

Meall a' Mhuic, viewed from the south over Glen Lyon (Rab Anderson)

Meall a' Mhuic; 745m; (G18); L42, 51; NN579508; hill of the pig

Meall a' Mhuic's location in Glen Lyon, one of the finest glens in the Southern Highlands, and the views it offers makes it a worthwhile short outing. It sits sandwiched between two Corbetts, Beinn Dearg to the east and Cam Chreag to the west and all three hills can be climbed together. For the round of all three hills, good tracks at the start and finish are helpful but steep feature-less slopes between Meall a' Mhuic and Beinn Dearg are not, so although the link is there it is perhaps not the most pleasant. The westward link over Meall nam Maigheach to Cam Chreag is better. These extended outings are not described.

Start from the public car park on the Meggernie Estate at Innerwick (NN587475), behind which the summit of Meall a' Mhuic can be seen. Walk east along the road and cross the bridge over the burn then, just past the war memorial opposite the pretty white church, go left onto an estate track which heads north into the wooded glen between the hills. This is the Kirk Road, an old route used by people travelling from Loch Rannoch to the church in Glen Lyon.

After 500m, where the track rises away from the burn above a planta-tion, break off left to follow an old track beneath the plantation. This rejoins a branch of the track on the other side of the plantation where it descends to the junction of three burns. Take the track which crosses the right-hand burn by a bridge and ascend the hillside. It is a somewhat

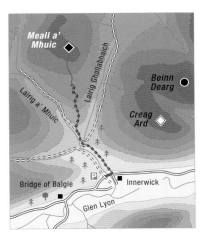

unsightly track but after 500m or so it is quit for an older grassy track which breaks off right; don't take the newer scar that traverses round the spur to the right, although from the start of this a section of old track runs parallel to the main track and can be followed to NN581488 where the old track swings uphill. The old track leads pleasantly up the broad crest of the hill before petering out on easy-angled heathery terrain. This is crossed to reach the summit cairn (**4km; 540m; 1h 45min**) where there are fine views north over afforested slopes to Loch Rannoch and the mountains beyond, as well as west to Glen Coe.

Although it is possible to vary the descent, unless one is planning to extend the outing to include one of the neighbouring hills, it is definitely better to return the same way. As well as avoiding the steep heathery slopes on either side, this has the advantage of allowing one to fully appreciate the splendid view south over Glen Lyon to the Ben Lawers massif and the hills to its west (**8km; 540m; 2h 45min**).

A' CHRUACH; The heap
Stob na Cruaiche; 739m; (G34);
L41; NN363571; stub of the
heap

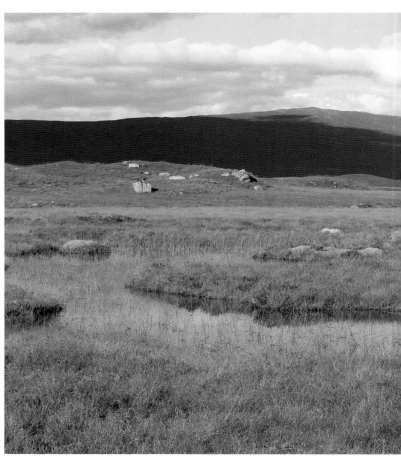

S tob na Cruaiche is the named
summit of A' Chruach which sits
on the edge of Rannoch Moor
between Loch Laidon and Blackwater
Reservoir. Due to the fact that it rises
from the 300m contour, the hill
presents a dull looking squat ridgeline to those who pass on the road
across Rannoch Moor. It is a reasonably high Graham though, however its
principal feature is that being
surrounded by mountains it is a fabulous viewpoint, which fully repays the
effort involved in getting to it. The
best route is the one that traverses
much of the length of the hill from
east to west, thereby making the
most of the hills situation and the
views it affords.

Start from the car park at Rannoch
Station (NN423578) at the end of a
lengthy but scenic drive along Loch
Rannoch, the only road in. Given
there is a station here, it is an ascent
that can be made by train, thereby
saving time on the drive round. There
is a tea room open from March until
November, as well as a hotel.

Walk south past a cottage then
take the track down to the railway,
going through a gate and crossing
this by a level crossing. The track
leads north-west towards the forested

Stob na Cruaiche across Rannoch Moor to the south (Rab Anderson)

hillside across the head of Dubh
Lochan at the end of Loch Laidon. To
the north-east over the viaduct is
Beinn Pharlagain with the pointed top

of Sgòr Gaibhre behind and the long
ridge of Càrn Dearg to the left.

Go along the edge of the forest for
100m or so to a locked gate

(NN418579) in the deer fence where another track heads off into the forest. To the left of the gate the barbed wire has been removed and access to the track is simplified. Follow the track uphill to emerge from the trees and continue up the hillside. At the highpoint (NN412585), where the main track goes down right, go to the end of the left-hand track then continue up the broad crest of the ridge following a vague atv track. Head towards an obvious boulder to gain the hill's 580m eastern top, Meall Liath na Doire. Schiehallion stands proud to the east whilst Chno Dearg and Stob Coire Sgriodain are prominent to the north. The summit of Stob na Cruaiche is visible beyond another top, although it appears much further away than the map suggests. Drop down, dodging in and around peat hags, then climb to the subsidiary top of Meall a' Bhùirich (638m).

Descend a short way, again dodging in and out of small peat hags, then climb onto the shoulder of Stob na Cruaiche and pick up an atv track which leads to the summit trig point (**7.5km; 540m; 2h 35min**). South across Rannoch Moor are the Bridge of Orchy hills, then the Blackmount hills and Meall a' Bhùirdh before the

hills of Glen Coe. To the north-west across Blackwater reservoir are the Mamores then Ben Nevis and Aonach Beag, whilst closer to the north the vast bulk of one of the higher Corbetts, Leum Uilleim, blocks out much of the Grey Corries.

A return via the route of ascent (15km; 640m; 4h 25min) maintains the views, although an option is to descend the atv track back off the summit and out onto a little spur at NN377567, until the forest and Loch Laidon can be seen. Follow the atv track on a diagonal descent across the hill to enter the forest at NN391569 then cross the Allt a' Bhùirich and go down its north side to reach the forest track which leads back to Rannoch Station (14km; 550m 4h 5min). A slightly longer route back by 1.5km, which gains the track quicker, descends south from the little spur to cross the burn draining the hillside to reach a gate in the deer fence at NN380556. An atv track then descends south-east onto the track leading into the forest.

A bike can be used on the track through the forest to the atv track at NN385555 and it is also possible to bike in from the Kingshouse Hotel past Black Corries Lodge.

Approaching the summit trig point of Stob na Cruaiche (Jim Teesdale)

Beinn na Sròine; 636m; (G190); L50; NN233289; mountain of the nose

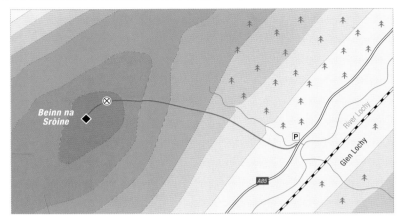

Although surrounded by higher and grander mountains, the curve of Glen Lochy allows Beinn na Sròine to dominate much of the view when travelling west down the glen. The summit marks the high point of the western end of the long ridge separating Glen Lochy from Glen Orchy and is rather better defined than Beinn Udlaidh and Beinn Bhreac-liath, the two Corbetts at the eastern end.

With a starting altitude near the 200m contour, Beinn na Sròine is a direct and quick ascent from the A85, offering a pleasant diversion for anyone en route to or from other destinations, such as Oban and an Inner Hebridean ferry.

Start almost directly below the summit, at a small parking area on the A85 (NN246287), where a burn descends beside the conifer plantation flanking the eastern side of the hill. Care is needed when leaving the parking area as the traffic visibility westwards is poor.

Follow the burn to a fence, go through and gain the high ground left of the burn. Ascend steadily leftwards into the middle of the grassy face to where the angle eases. The face is not as steep as it looks from below. Continue left below some small areas of scree to a final steepening leading to the eastern summit, marked by a rough cairn. A further 200m or so gains the cylindrical concrete trig point on the summit (**1.5km; 435m; 1h 5min**).

Across Glen Lochy, the pointed profile of Ben Lui fills the view, but there are also fine views west to Ben Cruachan and north to the peaks of Glen Etive and Glen Coe. A number of Grahams can also be identified including Beinn Bhalgairean and Meall nan Gabhar, south-west across Glen Lochy and Beinn Donachain to the north-west across Glen Orchy.

Like the summit of nearby Beinn Udlaidh, the top of Beinn na Sròine is marred by concrete foundations and cable supports for an aerial, removed at some point in the past, but still marked on some OS maps. The best descent is via the line of ascent, which can be varied as desired (**3km; 435m; 1h 40min**).

Beinn na Sròine above the River Lochy (Tom Prentice)

Beinn Donachain and Ben Eunaich, right, from the east (Ken Crocket)

Beinn Donachain; *650m; (G176); L50; NN198316; bad or evil mountain*

Lying between Glen Strae and Glen Orchy, this hill is most conveniently climbed from the latter. Start towards the lower end of Glen Orchy where there is a suspension bridge (NN232305) over the River Orchy at the Catnish picnic area. Cross the bridge and go left along a path by the river through lovely woodland.

Beyond a forestry plantation go through a gate in a deer fence (there is also a walkers' gate to the left), cross a burn and gain the rough track which can be seen rising up the hillside. This leads uphill to the left then turns sharply back up right through a gate to exit the fenced area and pass beneath a prominent crag, Creag Ghlas. Between this and another crag, Creagan Glas, cross a burn then break off left and climb steeply up the grassy slope next to an old fence. The slope briefly eases level with forestry on the right and the ridge becomes more outlined above.

Leave the fence and go up left onto the ridge and climb this to gain the high ground which leads pleasantly around to the north of Heart Loch and the double top of Cruach nan Nighean (584m). There are beautiful outcroppings of clean, schistose rocks here, which become lighter coloured with height.

The views are superb. The bulk of Beinn Mhic Mhonaidh fills the view to the north, with the Graham Meall Tairbh and its neighbour Ben Inverveigh to the right. Further north, the Ben Alder massif is viewed over the wilderness of the Rannoch Moor with Beinn Dorain and Beinn an Dothaidh to the right. Looking up Glen Orchy the cliffs of Beinn Udlaidh are visible while to the south-east over the top of the neighbouring Graham, Beinn na Sroine, the summit of Ben Lui looks as fine as any Alpine peak.

Cross the col from Cruach nan Nighean and head past a small lochan towards the summit of Beinn Donachain to climb a deer fence by an integral ladder on the right (in 2013 part of the fence was down). Once up the final steep rise onto the large summit area the first top gained has a small cairn and is probably the highest point, there is another a little to the south (**5.5km; 625m; 2h 15min**). About 180m to the west yet another cairn beckons, however this is lower. The view now includes the Cruachan Ridge and Ben Eunaich to the west with the Graham Meall Garbh to the north-west over Glen Strae. The best descent is to return to the deer fence then cut across the corrie down the side of Heart Loch and make a descending traverse onto the ridge of the ascent route. This is followed back to the old fence then down to the track (**11km; 625m; 3h 45min**).

Another route starts at the Eas Urchaidh Falls car park and utilises a forestry track which follows the Allt Broighleachan and loops round to end at Lochan Coire Thoraidh from where Cruach nan Nighean is gained. (**7.5km; 650m, 2h 45min**); (**15km; 650m, 4h 25min**).

Meall Tairbh and Lochan Coir' Orain from Ben Inverveigh, with Ben Cruachan in the distance (Tom Prentice)

Meall Tairbh; *665m; (G154); L50; NN250375; hill of the bull*

Situated at the south-west end of Loch Tulla above the Inveroran Hotel, Meall Tairbh is usually combined with Ben Inverveigh, its lower but more shapely neighbour.

Park off the road where the West Highland Way (WHW) meets the road (NN275414) to the east of the Inveroran Hotel. Follow this route south-east onto the shoulder of Ben Inverveigh, as far as the highpoint at Màm Carraigh where the WHW descends to Glen Orchy. Break off southwards and follow a grassy track up the initial part of this long ridge onto Pt.546m where Meall Tairbh comes into view. Beyond another rise the rest of the ridge provides pleasant high-level grassy walking with scatterings of large flat rocks, leading past a tiny lochan and eventually on to the 639m summit of Ben Inverveigh (**4.5km, 470m; 1h 50min**). There are fine views in all directions, including, to the south, the unusual dyke which cuts across the north ridge of Beinn Udlaidh.

Ben Inverveigh only just falls short of Graham status, the drop to the col between it and Meall Tairbh being c144m. When descending south-west off Ben Inverveigh to gain this col it is best to keep to the ridge for as long as possible since the slopes on the west

are heather covered and awkward. The col is an amazing collection of glacial drumlins, including an unusual grass-covered pyramid. These are glacially dumped hillocks, what geologists sometimes refer to as a 'basket-of-eggs topography'. The small Lochan Coir' Orain is easily lost to view in this jumble. Ahead, a brief but steep climb up heathery slopes leads onto the broad ridge, then the summit of Meall Tairbh (**7km; 640m; 2h 50min**).

The descent down the north ridge

of Meall Tairbh is along a broad ridge, transected by numerous boggy hollows and burns. In compensation the views ahead are excellent, with the Starav group, the Blackmount, and the upper parts of the Bridge of Orchy hills. As the slope steepens the vegetation becomes lush and boggy. Towards the bottom break slightly right to avoid much boggier ground by aiming for the hotel, a forestry plantation and eventually the Allt Orain draining from the glen between the hills (**12km; 640m, 4h**).

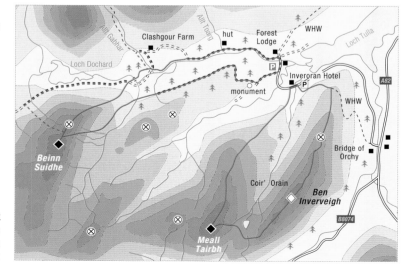

Beinn Suidhe; 676m; (G139); L50; NN211400; mountain of the seat or shelf

S tarting from the Victoria Bridge car park at the west end of Loch Tulla (NN270419), Beinn Suidhe is best approached along the north bank of the Abhainn Shira. Take the path north onto the road leading over Victoria Bridge to Forest Lodge then follow the track west along the river, passing the tiny hut used by Glasgow University Mountaineering Club; once the local school! Beyond, the riverside path gives rutted, soft going with lovely views to the hill and leads eventually to the confluence of the Allt Gabhar and the Abhainn Shira. A bridge here has been washed away but the Allt Gabhar is usually low enough to be forded. Cross over the Allt Gabhar then over the stile in the deer fence enclosing the forestry, from where a path leads through a break in the trees to a bridge over the Abhainn Shira (NN232418).

If the Allt Gabhar is high, head north to a small footbridge over the Allt Gabhar (NN233426) to the west of Clashgour. On the other side, avoid the firebreak in the forestry which leads to a dangerously boggy area

and follow the west bank back down to pick up the path leading to the bridge over the Abhainn Shira.

Beinn Suidhe rises steeply ahead and is climbed initially via the knoll of Tom Liath and the rocky rise beyond to reach a brief easing on the shoulder. The final steep slope is climbed by a zigzag line up grassy ramps on the north-east face which avoids any difficulties and leads abruptly onto the north end of the main ridge. Cross the northern top (636m), then drop to a col and climb through rocky ground to gain the summit 800m further on (**7.5km; 510m, 2h 30min**). It is an excellent viewpoint, not only for the surrounding Munros, but also for several neighbouring Grahams, including the remote Beinn nan Lus and Meall Garbh to the south-west, and the neighbouring Meall Tairbh to the south-east.

Return north to the col between the summit and the northern top then descend steeply eastwards through a gap in the rocky terrain to reach the moor below. From here a contouring line leads through the shallow Beal-

lach an Tailleir (NN227409). Either return via the bridge over the Abhainn Shira and the approach route, or cross the Allt Sùil na Curra and go through a gate in the deer fence. A path then leads through a forestry break to reach a track.

This track leads back to the car park but there are a number of gates to be climbed. In the second forestry plantation, stay with the track where it doglegs up right, avoiding a tempting break on the left, and emerge from the forest with the Druimliart Memorial on the right. This is at the ruins of the house where the bard Duncan Ban MacIntyre was born in 1724; best known for his poem *In Praise of Ben Doran*, which there is a lovely view of from here. The track descends to the car park (**15km; 510m; 4h 20min**).

An alternative is to descend the uncomplicated slope north-west from the col to gain the Glen Kinglass track and follow this back past idyllic Loch Dochard and the splendid amphitheatre this sits in; an extra 2km but worthwhile.

Beinn Suidhe from the north bank of the Abhainn Shira (Tom Prentice)

Meall Garbh from the Làirig Dhoireann (Ken Crocket)

Meall Garbh; *701m; (G102); L50; NN168367; rough mountain*

Meall Garbh is a fine and remote hill between Glen Kinglass and Glen Strae. It could be approached via Loch Etive and Glen Kinglass as for Beinn nan Lus, which it sits opposite and can be combined with, though this might entail an overnight stay for all but the very fit. The route described is the shortest and approaches via Glen Strae, up whose west side it is possible to drive for about 800m. There are several parking spots, one being at the north end of a marshy pond (NN149301), a few hundred metres before the first gate.

Walk up the glen to a second gate where the Allt Dhoirrean flows under the road at a fine pool then take the atv track up the west bank of the burn, through a gate and so onto the hill. Glen Strae and Glen Kinglass are connected by the Làirig Dhoireann, which is followed by the initial section of this route. Continuing up the track, the cliffs of Beinn Eunaich gradually impose on the left, with the dark, forbidding cleft of the Black Shoot prominent. This was a favourite target of the Victorian mountaineers.

Either continue to follow the track, or make your own way over the drumlin strewn and gully incised slopes to reach the col where the

Làirig Dhoireann crosses over. The source of the burn is a small lochan at the col where several cairns and a perfectly positioned shelter mark the edge overlooking Coire Dhoireann to the north. Meall Garbh is now visible for the first time, peeking over the

west shoulder of Meall Beithe.

From the col make a slightly rising traverse to the north-east, across Beinn Lurachan, to gain the col south of Meall Beithe, from where this 693m top is easily gained. Meall Garbh is now fully visible, as is its neighbouring Graham, Beinn nan Lus further west. Descend north-north-east to the col and make the short, steady ascent of Meall Garbh (**8km; 890m; 3h 20min**). The summit is a delight of rocky outcrops and small lochans, with glacial erratic blocks of granite perched on metamorphics. The outlook in every direction is superb.

Retrace your steps to the col and skirting the east slopes of Meall Beithe gain the ridge of Beinn Lurachan (719m). This narrows as it approaches the summit and affords interesting views over to Ben Lui in particular. The squat bulk of Beinn Mhic Mhonaidh and Beinn Donachain, a Graham, are well viewed on the other side of Glen Strae. The descent of the south-west ridge is a continuous knee-grinder leading to the banks of the Allt Dhoirrean. Follow this down past several enticing pools to regain the track and so back to the starting point (**15.5km; 1160m; 5h 45min**).

Beinn nan Lus; 709m; (G85); L50; NN130375; *mountain of the herbs*

This is a remote Graham lying on the north side of Glen Kinglass, the glen which runs eastwards from Loch Etive to provide a through route to Victoria Bridge and Loch Tulla. The hill is best accessed from near Taynuilt by mountain biking in using the track along the east side of Loch Etive, a 40km round trip. The hill itself is relatively short and could be combined with Meall Garbh, the Graham facing it across Glen Kinglass, but this might involve an overnight stay for all but the fittest. The access track is a roller coaster with the odd rough section and some may find themselves having to occasionally push the bike up the steeper bits. However, the effort is eased by the stunning views of Loch Etive and the surrounding mountains.

Start at Inverawe Country Park where there is a large car park and picnic site (NN021317). Take the road back for about 500m and turn off left for the track up Loch Etive. The first section is uphill through pine wood before dropping down to cross the

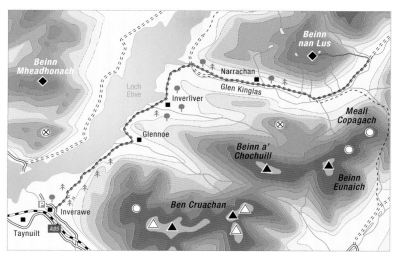

River Noe by a bridge. After another uphill section the track leads downhill to a bridge over the River Liver then up and around Inverliver Bay before climbing over and back down to a third bridge over the River Kinglass. Turn right here and take the track up Glen Kinglass. At this point one might wish one knew a friendly boatman,

but the pedalling up the glen is straightforward and scenic. On the left, Narrachan Bothy is passed which some have used as a rough lodging for a night. About 1km before Glenkinglass Lodge, the Allt Hallater flows into the River Kinglass and bikes are left here (**20km; 2h 40min**).

On foot now, follow the east shoulder of Beinn nan Lus, steep at first then easing, to pass a tiny Lochan about 400m before the top (**2.5km; 1h 45min**). On the ascent there are fine views north to Beinn Starav and Beinn nan Aighenan, with Glas Bheinn Mhor tucked behind the latter. The summit itself, with its granite outcrops, is a grand vantage point and views open up west over Loch Etive to Beinn Sgulaird and Creach Bheinn, then the Grahams Màm Hael, Beinn Mòlurgainn and Beinn Mheadhonach.

South lie Beinn Eunaich and Beinn a' Chochuill then the Cruachan range. Spinning round towards Glenkinglass Lodge, Beinn Suidhe, another Graham, dominates the upper part of the glen. Heroic walks have been done which take in the three Grahams; Meall Garbh, Beinn Suidhe, and Beinn nan Lus, but this definitely requires an overnight stay and perhaps an approach from the Loch Tulla side. Retrace the ascent route (5km; 2h 45min on foot) then bike back to Inverawe Country Park (40km; 5h by bike).

Beinn nan Lus and Beinn Mheadhonach, left, from Meall Garbh (Ken Crocket)

Beinn Mòlurgainn from the ascent to Beinn Bhreac (Rab Anderson)

Màm Hael; *726m; (G57); L50; NN008408; 'màm' Gaelic breast. Also area between breasts, or cleavage. Name probably relates to pass, east of the peak. Hael problematic as no words begin H in Gaelic: the burn running north from the pass is Abhainn Teithil (pronounced approx tay-heel), but meaning obscure*

Beinn Mòlurgainn; *690m; (G118); L50; NN019400; mountain of the bare hill of the long ridge*

Beinn Mheadhonach; *715m; (G73); L50; NN019369; middle mountain*

Sitting between Loch Creran and Loch Etive, these hills form the base of a chain of hills which gradually increases in height northwards to Bidean nam Bian above Glen Coe. This is one of a few walks where three Grahams can be conveniently linked into a suitable round, however the terrain is complex and good hill skills are required. The views are superb, especially to Ben Cruachan on the opposite side of Loch Etive.

Start in Gleann Salach at NM985367, on the B845 to Barcaldine, at the foot of Beinn Bhreac's long south ridge. This is almost at the top of the hill where there is a passing place on the west side of the road that can accommodate a car parked off the road; there is a better place on the east side of the road 50m downhill.

Just above the passing place, follow a track through a gate for a very short way then head up Beinn Bhreac's long and broad south ridge. Soon, this hill and the three Grahams come into view, as does Ben Cruachan revealing itself behind Beinn Mheadhonach. Cross a flat section halfway up then head up and right for a gate (NM994391) in a deer fence that cuts across the hillside. Continue up rockier ground to the large cairn on the 708m top of Beinn Bhreac (**4km; 570m; 1h 50min**).

Head north along the rugged summit with fine views to Mull, Ardgour and the Ballachulish hills then swing round and drop east to a col. Across Gleann Dubh to the north is the Eas Garbh chasm on the

Màm Hael from the ascent to Beinn Bhreac (Rab Anderson)

Corbett Creach Bheinn. Cross an old wall and climb to the top of Màm Hael past numerous tiny lochans. The hill is unnamed on OS maps and has been called Beinn Bhreac by some. However, the map clearly indicates this name refers to the hill to the south-west. It is more logical to use a different name from the map and Màm Hael just to the east has been chosen (**6km; 680m; 2h 30min**).

Descend east along a narrowing ridge and make a slight rise to a cairn before turning and dropping south to a col. An easy 150m ascent gains the right-hand of two knolls that is the summit of Beinn Mòlurgainn (**8km; 830m; 3h 10min**).

Drop steeply off this narrow hilltop and at the bottom cross a deer fence to reach the col. Tiresome mossy ground on the other side leads to the top of Meall Dearg; OS 1:25k and 1:50k maps show different knolls as being the 578m top.

Beinn Mheadhonach from the east (Rab Anderson)

The onwards terrain is complex and best covered by pretty much staying on the high ground. Descend south-west then climb onto another knoll (548m) with a prominent boulder on its top; a small lochan lies below. Go down south and pass a smaller 528m knoll on its west side to ascend a third knoll (550m) at NN023380. Drop south-east off this knoll to a shallow col, aiming for the next in this chain of knolls (497m) but cut around beneath its top then descend to the Bealach Carra below Meall Biorach with Lochan Bealach Carra to the west.

Cross a fence and from the high-point of the bealach climb the left-hand rocky skyline ridge, which is perhaps preferable to the slope on the right. A stiff climb gains the 710m east top of Beinn Mheadhonach, after which a rocky cleft is crossed to gain the main summit (**12km; 1270m; 4h 50min**).

Descend west across another similar but not so steep cleft and continue to Pt.619m. There is now a choice of descents. Either go down to the north-west and cross the river (possibly difficult in spate) to reach some old sheilings then follow a path that traverses the side of the slope above the River Esragan to get back to the start. Alternatively, descend the south-west ridge to a col, go through a gate in the fence and climb onto the final 387m top. Drop steeply down the other side and follow a burn to three fields below; there is a gate out of the middle field at NM990355. Follow the road north back to the start (**17km; 1430m; 6h 30min**).

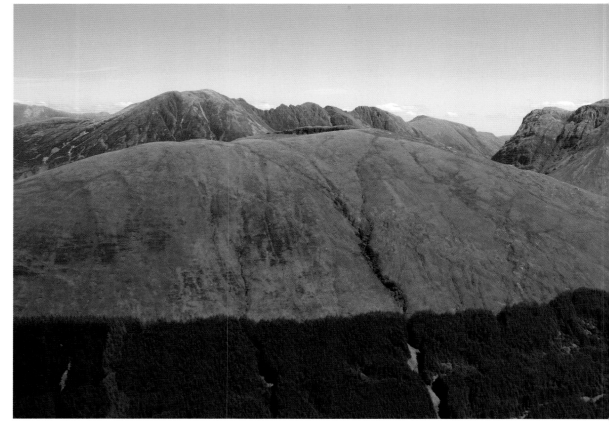

Meall Mòr, topped by the Aonach Eagach and Bidean nam Bian (Rab Anderson)

Sgòrr a' Choise; *663m; (G159); L41; NN084551; peak of the foot or leg (shape)*
Meall Mòr; *676m; (G141); L41; NN106559; big hill*

This is an excellent walk taking in a fine pair of Grahams with stunning views of Glen Coe and its surrounding peaks. Start from the car park at the Tourist Information office on the edge of Ballachulish (NN083585), just off the main A82.

Walk into the village, cross the road and go up Loanfern past the Co-op then the playing fields to cross the pedestrian bridge over the River Laroch. Turn left and go up a narrow road signposted as the Public Footpath to Glen Creran, passing the primary school. When the road ends continue through gates into the open along firstly a track, then a footpath. The day's first objective, the shapely peak of Sgòrr a' Choise, lies ahead and is gained by following the path beneath it into Gleann an Fhiodh with the Munro Top of Sgòrr Bhàn on the

right. Cross a number of burns and continue almost to a large cairn at NN069548. Break off the main path which continues into Glen Duror and cross the River Laroch by stepping stones.

The map shows a path hereabouts, heading diagonally up the slope to the Màm Uchdaich, then over to Glen Creran. However, if it's there it's difficult to find and perhaps the simplest option is to make a direct assault up the steep, heathery slope to gain the long south-west ridge of Sgòrr a' Choise. Easy going then leads along this above the top edge of a forest, on a hill path following a line of old fence posts. Ahead, is the summit cone of Sgòrr a' Choise, flanked on the left by Sgòrr na Cìche (Pap of Glencoe) and on the right by Bidean nam Bian. A splendid narrowing rocky ridge leads

to a delightful and airy summit (**6.5km; 660m; 2h 35min**). Meall Mòr now lies ahead with the jagged ridge of the Aonach Eagach rising behind it.

Descend the steep south-east ridge, go through a walkers' gap in a deer fence at NN089548, then swing around over the top of Meall a' Bhuige and descend the grassy slope to gain the col at the foot of Meall Mòr. A long ascent ensues up the broad and grassy south ridge to gain the high ground where a traverse leads north-east to the summit cairn, perched above a small slabby crag (**9.5km; 1000m; 4h**). Sgòrr na h-Ulaidh is prominent to the south and to the north the hooded bulk of Ben Nevis rises above the Mamores. It is worth walking down and out a bit for the wonderful view east along Glen Coe.

Retrace your steps along the top,

parking area at a bend on the A82 (NN120564) at the entrance to Glen Coe. Walk carefully along this fast stretch of road (especially the verge-less bridge) then go along the track to Gleann-leac-na-muidhe. Skirt the cottages and the house by the sign-posted path on the left to rejoin the track beyond and continue to where it ends. Ford the Allt na Mùidhe and strike west up the side of the burn. Go over Meall a' Bhuige then through the gap in the deer fence and climb

the steep south-east ridge to gain the top of Sgòrr a' Choise (**5.5km; 640m; 2h 20min**). Retrace your steps to Meall a' Bhuige then drop to the col and climb Meall Mòr (**8.5km; 980m; 3h 45min**). From the top the option exists of descending steeply to the road with Glen Coe spread out at your feet (**10.5km; 980m; 4h 30min**). It is perhaps less punishing although longer to return via the south ridge and the approach route through the glen.

then swing around and descend the north-west ridge heading for the aerial on Am Meall to the north. There is a gate in the deer fence slightly to the left. Cross an area that has been clear felled to gain a forest track at the col then go right and break off on another track which leads uphill to the communications aerial on Am Meall. Cross the fence by a ladder stile and follow the fence downhill alongside the edge of the forestry plantation, crossing another stile. There are fine views back to Sgòrr a' Choise whilst ahead lies the Ballachulish Bridge with the hills of Ardgour beyond. On the other side of Loch Leven is the long ridgeline of the Graham Tom Meadhoin. Towards the bottom, pick up a path which swings west around the top of the old slate quarry through a gate, then down to the quarry entrance just out in front of the car park (**14km; 1070m; 5h 15min**).

An alternative route starts from a

Sgòrr a' Choise from the col with Meall Mòr (Rab Anderson)

Sgòrr na Cìche from Am Meall (Rab Anderson)

Sgòrr na Cìche (Pap of Glencoe); *742m; (G28); L41; NN125594; peak of the breast*

Despite its bigger neighbours, this distinctive little peak stands proud above Glencoe village. It is generally climbed by simply going up and down its south-west flank, however a better route is by the circuit described here, which ascends the west shoulder then descends by the south-west flank.

Park in the village and walk towards the Pap. Cross the Bridge of Coe and take the road off left to Glencoe Lochan. Where the road bends left after 100m, continue ahead on a footpath, through the trees to the right of the burn, then swing left across the burn to gain a forestry track. Go straight over, up some steps, and continue on the path to the left of the burn to reach another forestry track. Cross over this and follow the path through an old gate in a fence then up a clearing with a low overhead line. Ignore a

route off right, which leads to the end of a track, and at the highpoint, about 50m past the second double pole on the overhead line, break off right to climb a narrow route through the trees. Exit the forestry by stepping over a fence to gain the open hillside then climb the shoulder above. If this shortcut is missed, continue downhill

on the path to go through a gate then break off right and follow the forest edge uphill to meet the shortcut at the fence. Higher up, traces of path begin as the summit dome is approached and the ground steepens and becomes rockier. The path leads through a rock band to gain the splendid summit with its stunning views (**3.5km; 730m; 2h**).

The surest descent is to head north-east towards Kinlochleven, on the path off the back, for 50m or so. The path drops down then swings round south beneath the craggy summit crown to cut diagonally down across the slope then descend more easily to the col at NN127591. There are others ways but they involve a little scrambling and route finding. It is a popular peak so take care not to dislodge rocks and be wary of others who might. Sgòrr nam Fiannaidh, the Munro at the end of the Aonach Eagach, can be gained from here.The peaty hillside below has been scarred by the passage of countless feet and although a number of paths lead down, it is best to keep to the main path to contain any erosion. Ignore a path on the right before the col and descend the main path from the col to the left-hand burn. Another direct path down the side of the burn should also be ignored in preference for the main path. This swings away left downhill from the burn then cuts back right to zigzag down the side of its gully before crossing it.

Traverse the hillside on the path to cross a burn by a bridge and follow a track down to the road which leads back to the village (**7.5km; 730m; 3h 15min**).

Sgòrr na Cìche from the west across Loch Leven (Jim Teesdale)

Sgòrr na Cìche from the south-west (Grahame Nicoll)

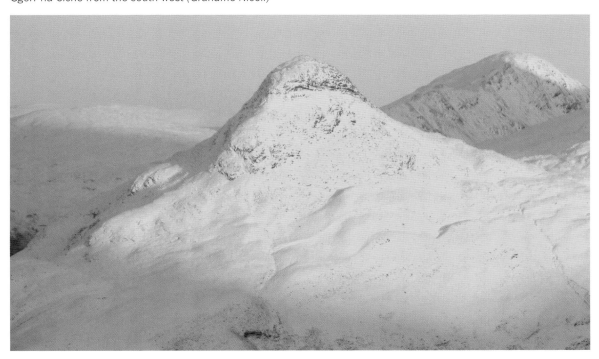

SECTION 4
Loch Linnhe to Loch Ericht

Tom Meadhoin and Loch Leven from the south (Rab Anderson)

Beinn na Gucaig; *616m; (G213); L41; NN062653; mountain of the little bell (probably bluebells)*
Tom Meadhoin; *621m; (G204); L41; NN087621; middle knoll*

These two fairly low Grahams throw down long ridges to the south-west, either side of Gleann Righ, which reach the sea at Inchree and Onich on the point between Loch Leven and Loch Linnhe. These ridges enable a scenic but lengthy circuit to be made of both hills, although the drop and re-ascent in between is not for the faint hearted! Start from the Glenrigh forestry car park at NN030634, accessed off the A82 via Inchree.

Exit the car park in the south-east corner to follow the 'Waterfalls' trail which climbs up the side of the splendid Abhainn Righ Falls to emerge onto a forest track. The south-west ridge begins here and atv tracks climb the hillside above onto this. However, it is perhaps better to walk along the track to the right for 400m, round the base of the ridge, following the An Drochaid circular trail and 50m before this turns off right to cross the river, break off left. Pass between two posts on an old track which soon disappears then continue up the edge of the forest behind a knoll onto the crest of the hill. The atv track is joined above, where the more defined ridge provides a splendid route to the South-West Top (575m). Drop off the back and head slightly right to go through a gate in the deer fence then climb to the top of Beinn na Gucaig (**5.5km; 590m; 2h 10min**).

Descend south-east to the fence then swing gradually east beside this ▶

and plunge down steeping slopes to gain the sanctuary of the floor of the glen; a 470m drop. Pause for breath then climb the other side to the left of the forest, directly to the top of Doire Bàn (566m); a sub 2000ft Marilyn. It is a 420m re-ascent followed by a 161m drop south to a col where a final weak kneed ascent of 216m leads up the ridge to Tom Meadhoin (**11.5km; 1230m; 4h 50min**).

Continue westwards onto Creag Bhreac (615m) then descend the Leac Mhòr ridge to the top edge of the forestry and climb onto the knoll of Tom Iain (NN061617). It is possible to stay on the high ground and cross to the trig point on Beinn an Aonaich Mhòir then continue on to Sìthean an Aonaich Mhòir (297m) before descending north-west to the bridge at NN035626 then back to the car park via the waterfalls (**19km; 1440m; 6h 50min**). However, the terrain is difficult at times and perhaps the better route is to cut north from midway between Tom Iain and Beinn an Aonaich Mhòir and cross the fence by a stile at NN059621. Descend to a forest track, follow it left over a burn, then descend beside the burn and the forest, crossing back over the burn at the bottom to the cottage at Sallachail. Cross the footbridge over the Abhainn Righ then follow the track through the glen and back down the side of the waterfalls (**20.5km; 1330m; 7h 5min**).

Tom Meadhoin is easily climbed (**3.5km; 610m, 1h 50min**) using the right of way that begins 100m to the west of a small parking area at NN097604 at the side of Loch Leven. This gains the col that links it to the Corbett Màm na Gualainn, which can also be included (**6.5km; 940m; 3h 5min**), (**10km; 940m; 4h 15min**).

Beinn na Gucaig can be climbed from Lundavra south of Fort William where there is good parking by the bridge at NN096665. Climb north-west up Sròn Garbh then south-west to Beinn na Gucaig (**4km; 500m; 1h 45min**). Tom Meadhoin can also be included (**9.5km; 1050m; 4h**), descending as above but avoiding the top of Doire Bàn, then taking this in on the return to descend its north ridge (**14.5km; 1210m; 5h 30min**).

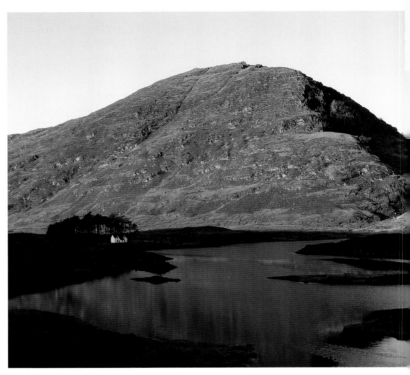

Creag Ghuanach and Creaguaineach Lodge beside Loch Treig (Noel Williams)

Creag Ghuanach; *621m; (G203); L41; NN299690; unsteady or nodding cliff*
Beinn na Cloiche; *646m; (G179); L41; NN284648; mountain of the stone*

Approaches on foot to this pair of hills, which lie in fairly remote country between Blackwater Reservoir and Loch Treig, are likely to involve a night in one of several possible bothies, perhaps Loch Chiarain bothy (NN289634) being the most convenient. However, they can also be tackled in a single day by taking the train to Corrour and it is this option which is described.

Catch an early train to Corrour, either from the north (Fort William & Tulloch) or south (Glasgow & Crianlarich) <www.scotrail.co.uk>, 0845 601 5929, (watch seasonal variations, restricted Sunday service and request stopping!). For the southbound return there are two evening trains and for the northbound return there is a mid-afternoon, then a late evening train. Plan well, take warm clothing for the wait and check <www.corrour-station-house-restaurant.co.uk>.

The start of the outing from Corrour Station is something of a problem because the path on the west side of the railway is exceptionally boggy for the first kilometre. A better option, which is double the length, follows a track towards Loch Ossian then turns left towards Loch Treig. The track crosses a bridge over the Allt Lùib Ruairidh and immediately goes under the railway. Both routes join here and the track descends quite steeply to Loch Treig then continues round the end of the loch where there are fine views of Creag Ghuanach, the first

objective. The track ends at a dilapidated bridge over the Abhainn Rath leading to Creaguaineach Lodge. It is possible to bike the 8.5km to here.

The eastern end of Creag Ghuanach has some awkward craggy ground. So the best option is to cross the bridge, turn left and follow the path on the north bank of the Abhainn Rath upstream for about 600m to a prominent bend in the river. Turn right here and head for a grassy depression in the middle of the south-east face which splits higher up into two narrow gullies. The aim is to eventually gain the right-hand fork. Ascend the hillside to a broad central area with much bracken in the summer. Traverse rightwards near a tree and eventually slant back leftwards to gain the right-hand grassy gully which is then followed without difficulty. Weave a way up through minor crags to gain the crest of the hill. There are superb panoramic views from here, which include the Easains and Grey Corries to the north. Just to the west of a second small lochan, a tiny cairn on a rocky protuberance marks the summit (**10.5km; 410m; 3h 5min**).

The second objective, Beinn na Cloiche, lies 4.5km away to the south-south-west. When water conditions are low a direct line can be taken. Head easily down the south-west ridge from the summit and continue directly down the steeper hillside in the direction of Staoineag bothy. There are some poor stepping stones in the river immediately west of the bothy and crossing here will normally entail getting wet feet. Otherwise a

lengthy detour has to be made to recross the Abhainn Rath near Creaguaineach Lodge.

From the bothy, ascend the hillside in a southerly direction initially passing some stone ruins. When the angle eases slightly slant rightwards at first then contour along the hillside. Cross the burn from Loch na Staoineig then ascend the long but easy north-east ridge of the mountain. Head leftwards over a slight depression to reach the highest point which lies just east of a small lochan (**15km; 780m; 4h 55min**). The views are not as spectacular as from the first summit and it feels more desolate. Glas Bheinn lies to the west with Leum Ullieim to the east, both Corbetts.

Go south past the summit for about 150m then descend the eastern face before heading north-eastwards to the broad bealach south of Loch na Staoineig. The natural continuation from here is to head for Meall a' Bhainne, a Graham Top which fails by only a few metres to get separate Graham status. Ascend the south-western flank of the hill without difficulty and continue up the broad plateau to the summit from where there are fine views northwards to Loch Treig (**18km; 930m; 5h 55min**).

Descend the north-eastern ridge easily at first, but partway down it is best to slant leftwards to find the easiest way. Eventually gain a poor path in Gleann Iolairean and take this down to Loch Treig. Follow the track used in the approach for 7.5km, back to Corrour Station (**28.5km; 1110m; 8h 45min**).

Beinn na Cloiche (Noel Williams)

Cnap Cruinn; *742m; (G27); L41; NN302774; round knob*

Broad and sprawling, Cnap Cruinn lies on the south side of Glen Spean somewhat isolated from its neighbours. There are two approaches.

For the first, leave the A86 by a single track road leading to Fersit. Cross the railway then the River Spean and after 1.7km park with care where a forest track forks off to the right at Inverlair (NN339798); space is limited.

Ascend the track, initially in the open with good views back to the Graham Creag Dhubh on the north side of Glen Spean, then through the forest to where it runs beside the Allt Laire. At the point the track swings right, the east flank of Cnap Cruinn is visible straight ahead. Continue between plantations where the track coincides with the position of the former 'puggy line', the narrow gauge railway used in the construction of the tunnel for the Lochaber hydro-electric scheme. A mountain bike could be used on this 4km of track.

Leave the track soon after it exits the plantation and head over rough ground directly for the summit. Climb quite steeply to reach a sizeable cairn then continue southwards for a further 130m to the true summit, marked by a small cairn on a rocky rib (**6km; 540m; 2h 15min**). There are fine views of Sgùrr Innse, Cruach Innse

Cnap Cruinn from the Inverlair approach (George Archibald)

and the Grey Corries to the south-west, as well as the Munros, Stob a' Choire Mheadhoin and Stob Coire Easain, to the south.

Rather than return the same way, descend north-west to a broad bealach where Buachaille Etive Mòr comes into view framed between Sgùrr Innse and Cruch Innse and continue over a minor top to reach Beinn Chlianaig (724m), a Graham Top, (**7.5km; 600m; 2h 40min**). To the

north past Creag Dhubh, the Parallel Roads indicating the water level marks of ancient glacial lakes can be seen in the lower reaches of Glen Roy, together with two Grahams, the Leana Mhòrs, which sit opposite each other on either side of the glen.

Return to a dip below the summit, then slant leftwards (east) across a burn and descend the hillside beyond to cross the Allt Boidheach and make a beeline for the forest track used in the approach. Return by this to the start (**14km; 600m; 4h 25min**).

A good alternative starts at the Cille Choirill church car park (NN306812), as used for the ascent of Creag Dhubh on p177 and enables both hills to be climbed in the same day. Walk down to the main road, go carefully straight over and cross the railway by a bridge, then swing right to gain the Monessie Gorge suspension footbridge at NN299811. Go through the farm at Monessie and climb the hillside onto the spur which leads to the low point between the tops then the summit (**5km; 610m; 2h 10min**). Traverse over to Beinn Chlianaig then descend back to Monessie (**10.5km; 720m; 3h 40min**).

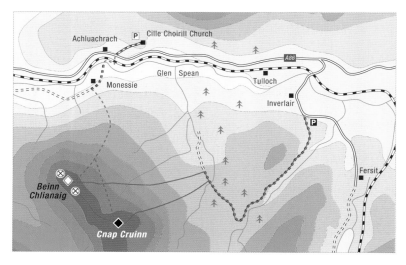

Binnein Shios; *667m; (G150); L34, 42; NN492857; easterly pointed top*
Binnein Shuas; *747m; (G16); L34, 42; NN463826; westerly pointed top*

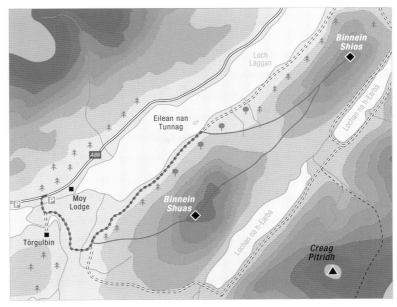

A very good outing can be made by combining these two fine hills on the south side of Loch Laggan, opposite Creag Meagaidh. Start between Loch Laggan and Laggan Dam Reservoir to the west, from a popular layby (NN433830) on the A86. This is on the east side of the concrete bridge over the River Spean. There is another layby 200m to the west.

Follow a track over the bridge and soon after take the left fork which leads to a high fence and gate. Continue on the east side of the Abhainn Ghuilbinn then climb more steeply eastwards to where the track divides after 1.9km. Take the left-hand track, which descends slightly and continue along the south side of Loch Laggan. There are fine exposures of pink and white pegmatite cutting the schist on the uphill side of the track. Follow the lochside for about 2km until just short of a tiny island in the loch called Eilean nan Tunnag.

Leave the track and head up eastwards through pleasant open woodland. Clamber through an old wire fence to gain the open hillside and head leftwards for the south-western end of Binnein Shios. Climb steadily up the grassy hillside for some distance and eventually rocky outcrops appear on the crest. From here there are good views southwards of the two long lochs which bear the same name, Lochan na h-Earba, and west across Loch Laggan to mighty Creag Meagaidh.

▶

Binnein Shios and Ardverikie House from across Loch Laggan (Grahame Nicoll)

Binnein Shuas and Lochan na h-Earba from Binnein Shios (Noel Williams)

The angle eases and a long gentle climb eventually leads to the highest point which lies at the far end of the summit ridge (**9km; 450m; 2h 45min**). Beyond this, the northern slopes drop much more steeply to forestry and Ardverikie on Loch Laggan.

To reach Binnein Shuas, however, do an about turn and return south-west along the crest for about 1km and descend the end of the ridge slightly leftwards to reach the broad saddle between the two peaks.

The north-eastern end of Binnein Shuas is quite complex and has several steep crags, so it is important to try and identify the best way up this ground in advance. There is a broad gully well over to the left but the most direct way is to stay on the crest of the broad grassy ridge from the saddle and slant slightly right higher up. After this follow a leftward slanting diagonal weakness up steep grassy ground with boulders and continue more easily in a broad runnel. The upper part of the mountain is somewhat confusing, especially in poor visibility. Slant slightly left to reach the upper tier and scramble up easy rocks to reach the highest point (**13.5km; 810m; 4h 30min**).

The views from the summit are very fine. Out of sight below is a rock face that is popular with rock climbers. Across the loch to the south-east is Creag Pitridh, with Geal Charn behind, whilst to the south is the great mass of Beinn a' Chlachair with its high central corrie. From the summit go down the south-west ridge and follow the base of a long left-facing rock wall. Once past this, the track used in the approach can be seen. Descend the grassy hillside and head straight for the left end of a conifer plantation. The ground here is tussocky and somewhat boggy. The junction on the track is reached soon after. Return by the track to the start (**18km; 810m; 5h 45min**).

With the use of a mountain bike it is easy enough to climb these hills individually, biking to NN453809 to climb Binnein Shuas and return. Then biking to NN488842 and doing the same with Binnein Shios. This enables the lovely Lochan na h-Earba lochans to be explored and allows the cliffs of Binnein Shuas to be viewed, as well as avoiding the steep northern end of that hill.

Binnein Shuas, left and Binnein Shios above Lochan na h-Earba (Jim Teesdale)

Meall nan Eagan through the Dirc Mhòr (Rab Anderson)

> *Meall nan Eagan; 658m; (G165); L42; NN596874; mountain of the notches*

Meall nan Eagan is a small but fine peak to the north of The Fara whose top remains largely hidden from view and although it can be glimpsed from various points on the road it is not easy to identify. The best approach follows the Allt an t-Sluic to the east of the hill.

Start from a parking area at the Crubenmore junction on the road north out of Dalwhinnie. This is at a bend just past the distillery, after the road crosses the railway. Walk up the road behind the distillery for 900m, passing a gated track into the forest, to reach a track towards the top of the brae signposted 'Old Drover's Route to Feagour'. Follow this to a track on the left which climbs onto the northern ridge of The Fara (a Corbett) and is the return route for walkers including that hill in the round.

Continue above the Allt an t-Sluic to the keeper's house, with its inevitable barking dogs, go down left and where the track ends go uphill, as directed by a waymark, onto another track. This leads pleasantly through the glen, crossing the burn a couple of times; if the water is high, continue on the original side. The track stops at a fenced plantation where the glen opens out and the hill is visible straight ahead. Ford the burn once more, then cross the flat floor of the glen and climb the heathery flank of the hill onto the east ridge. The ridge leads to a fine summit; steeply in places past rock outcrops and following a line of rusty fence posts (**5.5km; 310m; 1h 45min**).

Loch Caoldair with Creag Dubh beyond lie to the north-east, a view now spoiled by the Beauly to Denny pylon line that spans the glen. To the south the bulk of The Fara is close but cut off by two impressive rocky gashes slicing through the hillside. These are the Dirc Bheag and the Dirc Mhòr, particularly fine examples of glacial meltwater channels. The shortest route returns the same way (**11km, 310m, 3h 10min**).

However, a splendid extension explores the 'Dircs' and The Fara. Descend south-west to a col then traverse a deer track into the Dirc Bheag. Carefully go through the boulder-field to reach secluded Lochan Doire-uaine and beyond some crags climb steeply to the top of Creag nan Adhaircean. Traverse the rim of the Dirc Mhòr then cross the top of this and follow a line of fence posts to the 911m summit of the Fara (**11.5km; 810m; 3h 45min**). Descend the north-east ridge to gain a track and follow this to rejoin the approach route (**17.5km; 830m; 5h 15min**).

Meall nan Eagan can also be approached via Loch Caoldair to the north, although this is slightly longer and rougher going, as well as crossing beneath the pylon line. A track, then a path lead to the loch, thereafter deep heather, bog myrtle and deer fences have to be crossed to reach the hill's east ridge (**6.5km; 340m; 2h**), (**13km, 340m; 3h 40min**).

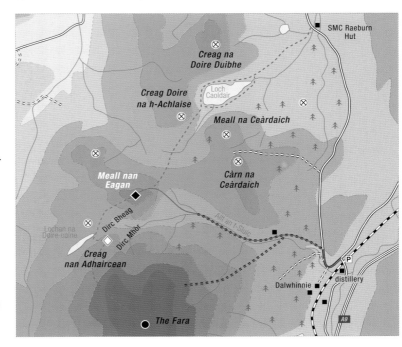

SECTION 5-6-7
Loch Ericht to Glen Esk

The 'undistinguished' Creag a' Mhadaidh above Loch Errochty (Rab Anderson)

> **Creag a' Mhadaidh;** *612m; (G217); L42; NN634650; cliff of the fox (dog)*

Creag a' Mhadaidh lies in the remote and unfrequented ground between Drumochter and Rannoch. It is a rather undistinguished hill and the word 'creag' is misleading as the hill is no more than a high point in an area of rolling heathery moorland. Approaches to the hill can be made from Dalnaspidal on the A9 to the north, from Loch Rannoch to the south, or via Loch Errochty to the east. The Loch Rannoch approach is the shorter and is the one described. Given that all of the approaches are on tracks then bikes could be used to shorten the timings, especially from Dalnaspidal where there is less uphill involved.

A right of way begins 2.5km west of Kinloch Rannoch at Annat (signposted to Dalnaspidal) and makes for a pleasant approach. About 100m west of the start of this track, between the road and the loch, is the Gibbet Tree. The last man to be hung here, in 1754, was a cattle thief. There is off road parking in a clearing next to the tree and in a pull-off 100m beyond this.

Walk up the track to Annat Farm and continue alongside an old stone wall until a sharp turn right leads into an old lane between high stone walls. There is a fine view of Schiehallion from here. A short while later the track turns left, still between walls, then emerges onto the open hillside. Before long the track forks and the ruins of Old Annat can be seen ahead. Either fork leads over the Annat Burn and up to a forest. The track traverses below the forest before emerging onto a high open moor.

A little further on there is a junction with another track that comes up from Craiganour Lodge and Aulich. This is an alternative way up or down from this point. The track climbs gradually, passing a small dam where water is diverted to Loch Errochty, to gain the wide col between Gualann Sheileach and Creag a' Mhadaidh. Leave the track, cross the boggy col and ascend an easy heathery slope to the summit (**9km; 400m; 2h 40min**). The cairn is substantial for such an unfrequented hill. The view of Schiehallion is now obscured by Càrn Fiaclach but the view east over Loch Errochty to Beinn a' Ghlo is splendid.

Although the Corbett Beinn Mholach lies to the west and the Corbett Beinn a' Chuallaich to the south-east, adding either into a walk with Creag a' Mhadaidh would make for a long day. Most walkers will be content to return by the approach route (**18km; 400m; 4h 40min**).

The ascent from Trinafour (parking at NN725649, or at NN725644) can be made via a pleasant circuit around Loch Errochty (**22km; 360m; 5h 30min**).

Creag Ruadh, left, and Meall Chuaich from Glen Truim to the west (Rab Anderson)

Creag Ruadh; *658m; (G166); L42; NN685882; red cliff*

Creag Ruadh is an elongated hill overlooking the A9 between Dalwhinnie and Newtonmore. It appears as an insignificant heathery slope partially obscuring its grander neighbour, the Munro Meall Chuaich.

It is a hill that is probably best climbed on its own, albeit that the fit might consider adding it after an ascent of Meall Chuaich. However, for the Graham bagger it makes a convenient route to do on the way up or down the road, or in combination with

one of the other single Grahams nearby. Although it could be climbed in less than an hour starting from Layby 96A, the closest point on the A9, the better route starts from Cuaich. This is the normal starting point for Meall Chuaich and makes use of the track leading to Loch Cuaich.

Park at Layby 94 on the east side of the A9, or in Layby 93 on the west side of the road, some 3km northeast of the Dalwhinnie turn-off and just south of the turning to Cuaich.

Traffic moves fast here, so great care and attention are advised.

Almost opposite the entrance to Cuaich there is a gated track. Go through the gate and straight on to join the main track running alongside a concrete aqueduct. This was constructed in the 1950s and carries water from the Allt Cuaich and other nearby burns to Loch Ericht.

After about 20min the track crosses the aqueduct to reach Cuaich Power Station. Although the dam is easily crossed, a gate and two fences have to be negotiated. Perhaps better is to go through the gate to the side of the aqueduct crossing, to ford the usually small burn then go through the gate in the fence beyond to ascend the hillside past a line of shooting butts.

The going is rough but easier if you take advantage of the strips of muir burn. Before long the ground levels off and a sizable cairn and stone shelter are reached at the summit (**4km, 310m, 1h 25min**). The best views are to the north over Badenoch where Creag Dubh is prominent. Return the same way (**8km; 310m; 2h 20min**).

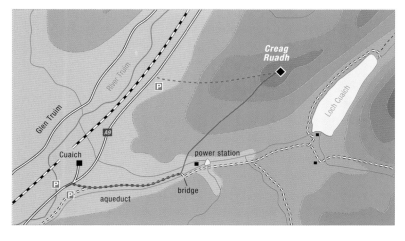

Blath Bhalg; *641m; (G185); L43; NO019611; pleasant bulge*

Pleasant bulge seems an appropriate description for this hill, which offers a very pleasant excursion for a short day, perhaps while en route up or down the A9.

The hill is easily accessed from the A924 north of Pitlochry. From the highest point of the road before it descends into Glen Brerachan, park on the right at a track leading to a pominent aerial marked on OS maps.

Follow the track past the aerial to gain a grassy track leading towards Dalnacarn Craig, the first hill on the route. The track is boggy in places, although these areas are easily avoided, and is followed to below the hill, from where a short ascent beside wooden posts gains the broad top and a small cairn, well seen from below.

It is worth pausing here to take in the view. Ben Vrackie to the northwest does not present it's best aspect from here, but behind and slightly further east the high peaks forming the long ridge of Beinn a' Ghlo are better appreciated.

Assorted animal paths lead over the broad Dalnacarn Craig as the main Blath Bhalg ridge, rather hidden from the road, opens up ahead and a fence is reached. Follow a small path beside the fence over the long, knobbly ridge with a few small rock steps, to cross points 637m and 639m and reach the summit cairn (**3.5km; 270m; 1h 15min**). The junction of a few fences in the cairn's vicinity involve a bit of jigging from one side to the other, but this is easily done.

The view from the summit is extensive for such a small hill. Beinn a' Ghlo remains prominent to the north and west, but the north-east is now dominated by the high hills of the West Mounth and Glas Maol above Glen Shee.

From the summit it is tempting to descend north to a track leading to the A924 at Dalnacarn, but this would involve walking back up the road to the parking place and hardly seems worth the effort for such a small hill. Better perhaps to return by the outward route, enjoying the view west to Schiehallion and south over Loch Broom and Strath Tay (**7km; 310m; 2h 15min**).

The long, knobbly ridge leading to the summit of Blath Bhalg (Rab Anderson)

Duchray Hill from Mount Blair (Ken Crocket)

> **Duchray Hill**; 702m; (G100); L43; NO161672; dark corrie, probably, from Gaelic 'dubh coire'. Also known as Mealna Letter, 'meall na leitir', hill of the broad slope
>
> **Mount Blair**; 744m; (G20); L43; NO167629; hill-mass (above) the plain, from Gaelic 'monadh blair'

These two Grahams are easily combined into a pleasant circuit when ascended from the B951, which connects Glen Shee with Glen Isla, starting at a height of about 360m. Park off the road on the right opposite a strip of forestry, just beyond the highpoint of this road as it starts to descend to Glen Isla

Walk downhill crossing over the Duchray Burn and about 50m beyond the entrance to the farm at Balloch go through a gate into the field on the left. Climb uphill to pass through a gate in a wall, then cross over a track and continue up onto the grassy ridge of Càrn an Fhidleir (518m). Continue north to ascend the south-east spur of Duchray Hill then swing left alongside a drystane dyke to gain the top,

Ancient and modern on the summit of Mount Blair (Rab Anderson)

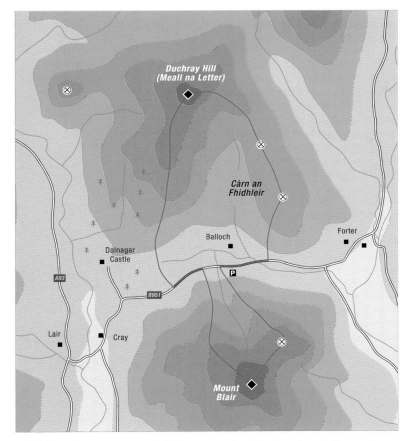

Forest prominent. Another Graham, Badandun Hill, can be seen across Glen Isla to the east.

Returning south, follow the dyke downhill back to the B951, passing through a marshy section at the lowest point just before regaining the road. Mount Blair is predominant, with its disfiguring communication tower an unwelcome if functional eyesore. Walk 200m east and start the ascent of Mount Blair at a gate, following a grassy track uphill to a second gate then the top (**9.5km; 780m; 3h 25min**).

There is a large prehistoric cairn, supplemented by the tower and a badly damaged circular viewpoint, which helpfully points to hills visible from here in good conditions. Mount Blair obviously has, despite its despoilments, a strong following in the neighbourhood, and it certainly stands out independently of any other hill.

Rather than return the same way, a better route heads north-east following a path to point 653m above Creag na Cuigail. Descend from here via the north-west ridge passing through two gates at the bottom to regain the road next to the starting point. If it can be found, there is a rough atv track which eases the heathery descent (**12km; 790m; 4h 20min**).

which lies a few metres west of the dyke (**4km; 380m; 1h 35min**). There are particularly fine views to the north with the hills of the Caenlochan

Mount Blair from Duchray Hill (Rab Anderson)

> **Badandun Hill**; 740m; (G31); L44; NO207678; mapped as Baldendeen (1794). Probably Gaelic 'bad an dùn' or 'duine', tuft or spot, of the hill-fort, or of the man

This fine little hill lies tucked away from general view towards the head of lovely Glen Isla, opposite Duchray Hill. It can be accessed from the A93 through Glen Shee to the west by taking the minor road between Cray and Meikle Forter, then driving up the glen almost to the end of the road. Start just beyond the public telephone box at Delnamar, at the far side of a small forestry plantation where there is space to park around the entrance to the track to the Keeper's Cottage at Fergus. Walk up this track and cross the River Isla to reach Fergus then take the uphill track through the trees onto the open hillside.

Badandun Hill lies to the right but the track stays left, climbing up the Fergus Burn almost to the top of Craig Lair (711m). The track to Badandun forks right just below the top of this hill however it is worthwhile making the short detour onto its summit via the left-hand track then crossing through heather to the cairn on its top. The views north to the Glen Shee hills, Caenlochan Glen then the Munros of Mayar and Dreish are splendid. Drop off the top through some small rock outcrops to regain the track and follow this onto Badandun Hill. Where the main track starts to descend, take to a rough track which climbs the shoulder to the trig point on the summit; another excellent and panoramic viewpoint (**6km; 530m; 2h 15min**).

A direct descent to the track up the Fergus Burn shortens the walk. However, a better route descends south on a rough track which cuts through some peat hags then drops south-west towards Glen Isla before cutting across onto the track taken by the Cateran Way; a circular long distance footpath that starts in Blairgowrie, passing through Spittal of Glenshee, Forter, Kirkton of Glenisla and Alyth. Reach the road at Bridge of Forter then take the track which leads pleasantly along the east side of the River Isla back to Fergus (**14km; 590m; 4h 15min**).

Badandun Hill from Duchray Hill to the west (Ken Crocket)

Cat Law from the north across Glen Uig (Grahame Nicoll)

Cat Law; *671m; (G145); L44; NO318610; probably (wild) cat hill. However Gaelic 'cath', battle, is possible from long-held belief that the battle of Mons Graupius was fought nearby*

Corwharn; *611m; (G222); L44; NO288651; pointed hill of the springs 'Corr an fhuarain'*

The round of Glen Uig taking in Cat Law and Corwharn makes for a very satisfying day. They are the highest tops of the hills south of Glen Prosen and Cat Law in particular is a fine hill commanding a superb outlook over Strathmore. Glen Uig cuts deeply into these hills westwards from the entrance to Glen Prosen and the walk described makes a complete circuit of this short glen. There are fences along all the ridges hereabouts and many hill tracks, making for easy walking.

It should be noted that an unratified survey has measured Corwharn at 609.1m, which would mean it is not high enough to be a Graham. Those wishing to omit it from this route can return the same way from the summit

of Cat Law, or descend north-west to pick up the track which descends to the road end at Wester Lednathie.

From Kirriemuir take the minor road to Lednathie. Just before Easter Lednathie farm there is a stone

bridge (NO341628). The walk starts on the south side of this bridge where there is a gated track entrance with a sign. There is limited verge parking by the wall 100m to the north of the

▶

bridge and around a track entrance 100m further on; the hillside verge to the south of the start is another option. Walk back to the bridge, go through the gate, then step over the burn and go through another older gate to follow the track uphill beside the burn, then across the hillside to a forestry plantation. The track continues up onto the shoulder of Peat Shank following the line of a fence. Turn west at the T-junction of fences on the broad ridge leading out to Long Goat and after 1km the summit of Cat Law is reached (**3.5km; 470m; 1h 35min**).

The top is flat and the OS show the high point to lie just 100m north of the trig point. On a clear day, the view to the south is extensive, with even the Pentland Hills visible behind and just to the left of East Lomond. Away to the west are Ben Lawers and Schiehallion whilst to the north little Corwharn is almost indistinguishable against the bulk of Dreish and Mayar.

Descend north-west alongside the fence, swinging right across the track that comes up from Wester Lednathie to take the track that heads north past Monthrey then up onto Cormaud. From here continue west, then break off the track which starts to descend to the glen below and

head north beside the fence to Tarapetmile. Careful navigation will be required in mist due to the broad ridges and confusing network of fences and tracks, many of which are not marked on the map. Now descend a heathery slope quite steeply onto the track through the watershed between Glen Uig and Glen Quharity. This has a remote feel although it is only a few kilometres to the public road in each direction. Climb the track on the opposite side directly up the flank of Cairn Corse and swing round by the fence to Corwharn where a tall cairn marks the top (**9.5km; 760m; 3h 30min**). Mountain hares are abundant around here.

To return to Lednathie continue on the high ground eastwards, then south-eastwards following the fence over Hill of Adenaich, then Finlet and Broom Hill. This is all on wide tracks, to finish down the track marked on the OS 1:50k map. Follow the road downhill back to Easter Lednathie (**16.5km; 830m; 5h**). From the col to the east of Corwharn it is easy to descend into Glen Uig via a track which runs down the Shank of Cromlet, the south-east shoulder of Hill of Adenaich; avoid Wester Lednathie Farm by the high track.

Hill of Wirren; 678m; (G134); L44; NO522739; hill of springs from Gaelic 'fhuaran'. Mapped Worren (1755) and Warren Hill (1794)

This broad sprawling hill lies 15km north-west of Brechin and throws out ridges, or 'shanks', in all directions. It lies on the Highland Line which possibly explains why there are no less than four aircraft wrecks on its slopes. The hill can be climbed from Glen Esk to the north and east, Glen Lethnot to the west or Strathmore to the south. It is therefore a good hill to traverse if transport arrangements allow. Starting at Bridgend, to the west of Edzell, the southern approach is described and offers the easiest route, following a track to within a few hundred metres of the summit.

Parking is possible out in front of Lethnot Primary School at Bridgend. Follow the track which climbs the hillside to the left of the school onto the brow of the ridge. Continue past the cottage of Dikehead then fork right onto a track that leads past a small man-made lochan to another fork just beyond a fence. Take the left-hand branch which climbs up the side of

Corwharn (Grahame Nicoll)

Hill of Wirren, left, and East Wirren from the south (Grahame Nicoll)

Craig of Finnoch onto the ridge, the Shank of Ledmanie. Pleasant walking through a patchwork of burnt heather and grouse butts leads up the easy-angled ridge.

Not far below the plateau the track forks. Go left here on the now fading track which traverses beneath the peaty plateau. On the left where it levels out, are the remains of a Consolidated Liberator which crashed in October 1944; miraculously two of the nine crew survived.

Beyond a fence that traverses the hillside, continue beside the uphill fence that this joins, then a little higher cross a stile over this fence, just below another fence that joins it. The summit trig point lies a further 200m uphill to the left of the fence (**6km; 550m; 2h 15min**). The views are of the rolling hills of The Mounth, however it is the view south to the lowlands that is best and East Wirren is a much better viewpoint.

Cross back over the fence via the stile, then follow the fence just above this as it traverses south-east through peat hags before swinging east. Join a grassy track then go through a gate in the fence and continue to the top of East Wirren and the second trig

point of the day (**8km; 570m; 2h 45min**). On a clear day the view stretches to the Pentland Hills, closer is the Montrose Basin whilst only 7km away are the twin bumps of the Brown and the White Caterthun with their Iron Age forts.

The descent is straightforward, following the track through a gate and south down the crest of the ridge. At the col before Craig Narb turn right at

a small hut onto another track (not shown on the map) which descends back into the valley of the Burn of Drumcairn. Cross the burn and continue to rejoin the upward route (**14km; 570m; 4h**).

The summit can be gained in less than an hour by a shorter up and back route from Glen Lethnot, via Auchowrie and the track up the hill beyond this.

Hill of Wirren from the south (Rab Anderson)

Hunt Hill and Craig Maskeldie, left (Rab Anderson)

Hunt Hill; 705m; (G92); L44; NO380805; hunt(ing) hill

Glen Esk runs north-westwards from Edzell and splits into Glen Mark and Glen Lee at Invermark. In turn, Glen Lee splits at the Waters of Lee and Unich. Hunt Hill stands prominently between these two Waters which drain the high plateau behind. The walk to and over Hunt Hill gives a very fine outing.

Start at the large car park at the end of the public road in Glen Esk; also the normal starting point for Mount Keen. Follow the road past the church and the track off right to Mount Keen and Ballater, taking the sign-posted route to Milton of Clova. Cross the bridge over the Water of Mark and pass a cottage, then Invermark Castle.

This dates from around 1526 and was important in defending the vital pass between Glen Esk and Deeside. It's worth stopping to see if you can find the door! Continue along the track through birch woodland alongside the Water of Lee then pass out in front of Invermark Lodge and the

old graveyard at Kirkton to reach the black waters of Loch Lee.

Further on, the dark crags of Craig Maskeldie dominate the glen and soon the steep face of Hunt Hill comes into view. Keep going on the

main track to the end of the flat floor of the glen until it starts to rise and a footbridge can be seen; don't go to the rusty hut. Cross the bridge over the cascading Water of Lee to head towards the Falls of Unich and the

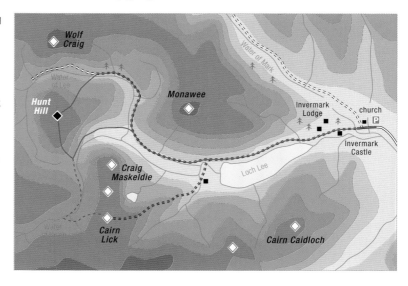

narrow glen beyond. The falls look diminutive from a distance but are more impressive close up and can have a large volume of water crashing over them.

The path now rises into the narrow rocky glen to provide a quite delightful route alongside the tumbling river. On emerging suddenly onto the plateau turn sharp right, or continue first a short distance to view the Falls of Damff, then traverse deep heather to a wide col. A steep pull now leads up to shorter cropped heather and the summit. This is marked by a small quartz cairn (**9km; 460m; 2h 50min**). The views are extensive over a vast area of barren high ground. Mount Keen is obvious to the north whilst Lochnagar is prominent away to the west.

The best and quickest descent is to head north-east down gradually steepening slopes to the Water of Lee. This can be crossed by a rickety, steel girder bridge at NO388815, about 200m upstream of a forest, to gain the track on the other side. The lower part of the forest has been

The Falls of Unich (Rab Anderson)

felled, exposing a tiny but well-frequented bothy. The track curves pleasantly downhill through the glen with the fine sight of Craig Maskeldie filling the view ahead. Join the upward route where it left the track earlier on the walk and follow this

back (**18km; 460m; 5h**).

An alternative route which is not that much longer than the route described here, is to ascend the track up the Shank of Inchgrundle from the head of Loch Lee onto Cairn Lick and hence to the Falls of Damff.

Hunt Hill from the top of the route through Unich gorge (Grahame Nicoll)

SECTION 8
Deeside to Speyside

Creag Bhalg from the Linn road (Fran Pothecary)

Creag Bhalg; 668m; (G148); L43; NO091912; bulge cliff

A modest hill situated on the edge of the Cairngorms extensive massif, Creag Bhalg presents two faces as you approach by road to the Linn of Dee from Braemar. The eastern face dropping to the Linn of Quoich is craggy and tree covered while open heather and pine clad southern and western slopes rise more gently above Mar Lodge and the valley of the upper Dee.

The main route starts from Linn of Dee, from a National Trust for Scotland Pay and Display car park with toilet facilities. A signed path out of the car park to the north leads to the track to Derry Lodge along the west side of the Lui Water. Alternatively, a short walk along the road to the east and across the bridge over the Lui Water then gives access to a pleasant stroll along the east bank of the river. This alternative route is a beautiful start to the walk and there is plenty of interest in the fast flowing lower reaches of the Lui where there is evidence of old dams and sluices.

Both routes meet at the bridge further up the Lui at NO063914 and take the track that leads back south-east toward Claybokie and Mar Lodge. About 500m from the bridge, branch off left on a track (shown as a footpath on the OS 1:50k map) which becomes increasingly overgrown as it rises through the open woodland of the Doire Bhraghad. The track is joined by another from the left and continues until it hits a deer fence with stile at NO084908. A few metres short of the fence and stile, take an indistinct atv track which heads north past a lone dead pine onto the broad summit.

A low stone shelter affords a dramatic panorama of the heart of the southern Cairngorms, ranging from Cairn Toul and Ben Macdui, the remote corries of Sputan Dearg, Derry Cairngorm, the tors of Beinn Mheadhoin and over to the vast bulk of Beinn a' Bhuird and Ben Avon. Of the two cairns the rightmost is the true summit (**5km; 300m; 1h 40min**).

Continue east on a small path over the lower 657m top to where the ridge begins to narrow and drop to the south-east. A fence blocks the route at the rightmost of two wooden masts (NO108908) and is crossed by a stile to follow a path with a wooden handrail south-west for 200m to the end of an old track. The track takes a delightful gently descending, sometimes undulating traverse, offering beautiful views over Mar Lodge and its grounds, and the Dee valley. Cross over two tracks, those branched off earlier on the walk, to emerge onto the road 500m to the west of Claybokie. A pleasant walk of just under 2km along the road leads back to the start (**11.5km; 320m; 3h 15min**).

An alternative route from Linn of Quoich gives the opportunity to take in the Clais Fhearnaig, a meltwater channel cut through between Glen Lui and Glen Quoich. The route leaves the parking area at the road end and heads up Glen Quoich on a track, branching west into the Clais Fhearnaig after 5km. From the Clais, the two north-western tops of Creag Bhalg can be gained, though 'tops' is maybe a slightly disingenuous description, situated as they are on a flat featureless expanse of moorland! From the main top (**9.5km; 340m; 2h 40min**) gain the east top and follow the south-east ridge back to the Linn of Quoich, with some quite steep ground through the trees (**12.5km; 360m; 3h 30min**).

Geallaig Hill from the B976 to the north-west (Rab Anderson)

Geallaig Hill; *743m; (G24); L37, 44; (NO297981); white one, probably from Gaelic 'geal', white. Mapped Mountains of Gallag (1725)*

Commanding a fine position between the straths of the River Dee and the River Gairn, Geallaig Hill is a large and bulky Graham. With its open, featureless higher slopes, it appears to hold few secrets for the walker but its lower slopes were once heavily farmed and supported a far greater population than today.

The obvious and quickest ascent up Geallaig Hill is from Glen Gairn, starting at a height of 360m from Braenaloin, a small farm on the B976, and following a track all the way to the summit (**3km; 380m; 1h 20min**); (**6km; 380m; 2h**). There is rough off-road parking opposite the farm at the base of the track. A higher start, though taking a longer route, could be made from another track at 480m on the B976 to the south, and this could be combined into a circular route, albeit involving a section of road walking between the start and finish points.

However, if time and a second car, or driver, or strategically placed bike allow, the most interesting walk involves a traverse of the mountain from west to east, beginning at Crathie in Deeside and ending at the small farm on Gairnside. A large pay & display car park for the benefit of those visiting Balmoral Castle is sited on the A93 and makes as good a start point as any. Cross the main road and follow the small road up to Crathie Kirk. Just past the Kirk, take a left at the old quarry and head up onto the ridge of Creag a' Chlamhain. There is no path but the ridge guides you up through open birch and pine woodland, mossy boulders and steeper craggy ground.

The ridge opens out into heather

moorland and evidence of muirburn points to the importance of the area for grouse. On top of The Maim at 601m, the circular track of the northern route is picked up and is easily followed to the flat summit of Geallaig Hill, dominated by a trig point atop a large drystane circle (**5.5km; 470m; 2h**).

As with many of these intermediate hills, the view to the higher hills offers a different perspective on their traditional vistas. From Geallaig to the south over the Dee are the lower hills of Lochnagar, flanked by the Abergeldie triumvirate of Creag nam Bàn where 'French Katie' was burned for witchcraft; Creag Ghiubhais topped by twisted pines and the long light green spine of the Coyles of Muick. To the north-west the eye is drawn over the ruined farmhouses of upper Glen Gairn to the rolling featureless hills of the eastern Cairngorms and the complex bulk of Ben Avon itself.

Either return the same way (**11km; 480m; 3h 15min**) or descend to the road at Braenaloin (**8.5km; 470m; 2h 40min**). An alternative is to follow the ridge to the east over Creag na Creiche and Cairn Dearg, down to Bridge of Gairn or Torbeg.

Section 8 – Deeside to Speyside

Mona Gowan; 749m; (G14); L37; NJ335058; hill-mass (or moss) of the smith from Gaelic 'monadh' (or moine) 'gobhann'

Mona Gowan is one of the foothills of the Cairngorms and gives a high-level but easy and scenic walk. At the highest point of the A939 between the River Don and the River Gairn, a long layby at NJ303052 provides parking. From the centre of the layby, a well-defined but narrow path starts up stone steps and goes steeply to a cairn overlooking the road. Adders are common here and there is a warning sign about them on the road below, so the chances of a sighting are good; they slither away unless touched.

Walk easily across short heather and past ancient peat cuttings to a track which leads to Scraulac (741m). Cairnagour Hill (744m) lies in front of Mona Gowan and fills the view, though there are distant views of Ben Avon, Lochnagar and Mount Keen. Continue smoothly to Cairnagour Hill, then more roughly down and back up to the slightly higher Mona Gowa (**3.5km; 300m; 1h 20min**). A fence connects these hills; the path lies just out from it on the way down but close to it on the way up. The summit has a huge cairn, erected in 1887 for the Golden Jubilee of Queen Victoria.

For the return, a descent into Glen Fenzie is a possibility but the walk back over the tops, heading towards the high Cairngorms and the setting sun, is the better option and more direct (**7km; 400m; 2h 15min**).

Beyond Mona Gowan, the Corbett Morven beckons and the walk can be extended over the Slacks of Glencarvie and Mullachdubh to this (**9km; 660m; 3h 10min**). Returning the same way is quickest, cutting across the slopes of Mullachdubh (**18km;** **1010m; 5h 50min**).

Another option for either hill, or both, is to start from the parking area further south on the A939 at NJ313027 and utilise the improved though unsightly tracks that run past the ruin at Glenfenzie. Either go direct to Mona Gowan, or take in Scraulac and Cairnagour Hill (**5.5km; 460m; 2h**). From the summit of Morven (**11km; 820m; 3h 50min**), atv tracks then estate tracks lead past Morven Lodge back to the start (**19.5km; 920m; 6h**).

Mona Gowan and Morven from Cairnagour Hill to the west (Jim Teesdale)

> **Pressendye**; 619m; (G207); L37; NJ490089; Copse of the fire, probably, from Gaelic 'preas an daigh'

Pressendye lies at the east end of a long ridge which forms the watershed between the rivers Don and Dee in the Cromar district, north of Dinnet and Aboyne. This is quite an extensive upland ridge with a great atmosphere and the view from the summit not only covers the lower hills towards Aberdeen, like Bennachie and Hill of Fare but also the hills to the south, a line increasing in height from Kerloch to Clachnaben, Mount Battock, Mount Keen and finally Lochnagar. There are many routes of ascent, each with a different style, and three are described here.

The simplest route, being all on tracks, is north-east of Tarland, from The Petts farm, as signposted on the road but named on the OS 1:50k map as Pett (NJ498065). There is room to park at the side of the B9119 at the start of the road to the farm. Walk to the farm and go up the continuation track. The maze of tracks is complex and inaccurate on the map but there are waymark posts placed by the MacRobert Trust and the Upper Deeside Access Trust. Ignore a left fork to Petts North and continue to another left fork and a black waymark post at the edge of the forestry plantation. This is marked Alternative Route; the standard route from Tarland joins further on.

Go up this left fork until the track descends left, then take a rising right fork on a more overgrown track (waymark) to meet a good track above. Follow this upper track, (marked on the map), bending west around Pittenderich, past where the blue and red waymarked routes join at NJ493077. Continue to where the track passes through a fence and take the blue waymarked left fork to the summit, composed of a large cairn and trig point (**5km; 420m; 1h 50min**). On the return it is worth taking in Pittenderich, a few minutes walk along the red waymarked route (10km; 420m; 3h).

A slightly shorter but less popular route is by one of the traditional Scot-

Pressendye from Pittenderich (Rab Anderson)

tish Hill Tracks. Park 100m east of Boig (NJ472076), walk to the farm and up a track signposted to 'Cushnie via Humphrey's Well'. Walk up this muddy track beside a forest, then where it turns right, go straight on across open grazing to meet a track where it enters the forest. Follow this track for 400m, then turn left up an overgrown track with bracken in the summer (marked as a footpath on the OS 1:50k map) and follow it to the ridge crest. Briefly join a new track which leads to a large mast, but leave it along a less distinct track which follows a fence along the crest to the summit (**3.5km; 360m; 1h 25min**); (7km; 360m; 2h 15min).

Both these routes are quite short. For a good high-level walk approaching from the north, park to the north-west at NJ424110 (spot height 333m) and follow an old drove road to Lazy Well. Go east along the open crest over Green Hill and Broom Hill to Pressendye (**8km; 400m; 2h 30min**). Return towards Broom Hill but pass it on the north by a track and head down to a memorial above Mill of Culfork. Descend fields to the road and a 2.5km walk back along roads to the car (16km; 400m; 4h 20min).

The Buck; 721m; (G63); L37; NJ412233; from Gaelic 'boc', a male deer. Known locally as The Buck o' the Cabrach after the hamlet to the north-west

Set on the edge of the high moorland which leads north and east from the Cairngorms, The Buck offers fine views across the farmland of rural Aberdeenshire to the coast. It is a shapely hill which attracts attention from large distances around, even seen as a distant cone from the high Cairngorms, and its ascent provides a short but remarkably rough walk without the sizeable path one might expect of such a prominent and popular landmark.

Start at NJ421251 at a height of 420m on the B9002, a minor branch off the A941 Rhynie to Dufftown road, where there is limited parking (further parking 500m to the east). This is just north of a boundary which consists of a fence leading to the top of the hill. Step over the fence behind the parking spot and cross a grassy area. On reaching heather, there is a path on the left, some 10m from a burn. This follows the right edge of reeds in the burn bed to more heather. Head left on intermittent bits of path to the boundary fence and cross to its left side to reach Dry Know. Carry on beside the fence on anything but dry ground until the path becomes more distinct once the going becomes steeper (**2km; 300m; 1h**).

An interesting but less direct start can be made by parking at NJ420254 and going over the rocky outcrops and juniper summit of Meikle Cairn. From here there is a lovely view of the route to the summit

of The Buck, but then it is even rougher and wetter to reach the boundary fence.

The summit is a slight tor with a trig point and a great view over the colourful fields of Aberdeenshire. The higher hills of Mount Keen, Lochnagar, Ben Avon and Ben Macdui are clearly visible but rather too distant to be spectacular. The four surrounding Grahams; Cook's Cairn, Pressendye, Ladylea Hill and Mona Gowan can also be identified.

Open moorland with a mosaic of peat hags leads south-west to Glen Buchat from where a remote alternative route is possible for those with some determination. In the rocks beneath the trig point there is an incised motif of three intertwined fish, which is recorded as an ancient monument. Whilst thought not to be Pictish or Medieval it is of unknown origin.

Returning down the fence (4km; 1h

30min) may be too short and dull. A nicer option is to head south along the boundary and disused fence, with a small path leading almost to the col before Kebbuck Knowe. Where the path peters out, head east across a gentle soft slope which misses most of the peat hags to reach Scad Hill with its prehistoric-looking peat mounds. Some grouse butts are soon reached, then a track heading east which is followed a short way. Force yourself to leave the track and find better going than expected to reach Clayhooter Hill, which is what you'll get if you trip in the mud!

Continue on down taking the more direct route across an atv track to reach another track (marked as a path on the OS 1:50k map) at the point where it crosses a burn just west of a tiny lochan. Cutting the corner here is hard work. The track leads back to the road (**8km; 320m; 2h 20min**).

The Buck from the B9002 to the north-east (Andy Nisbet)

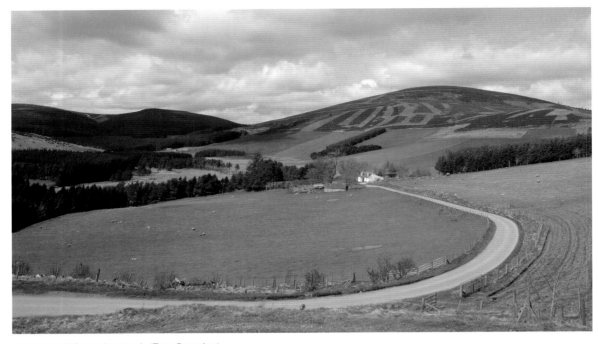

Ladylea Hill from the south (Tom Prentice)

Ladylea Hill; *610m; (G224); L37; NJ343168; grey hill-slope, probably, from Gaelic 'leathad liath'*

Lying on the Candacraig Estate to the north of Strathdon, Ladylea Hill tops the high ground between Glen Buchat and Glen Nochty, both offshoots from the main River Don valley. As the lowest Graham and with a fairly high starting point, it can be climbed quickly. It should be noted, however, that while the hill is included in this guidebook, an unratified survey has measured Ladylea at 609.1m, which would mean it is not high enough to be a Graham.

Local folklore has it that the hill's name comes from a lea on its lower Glen Buchat slopes, where a beautiful lady Cameron watched a fight between a young Forbes, so enamored of the young lady that he resolved to win her or die, and Mowat, a Deeside Chief who had massacred her clan of Camerons. Anyone who wanted her hand in marriage had to avenge her family by killing the Mowats; they chose a personal duel rather than a full scale clan battle. Forbes won, but it was a close call.

The upper hillside has been planted using indigenous tree species as part of a native pinewood scheme and is surrounded by a deer fence with limited access gates. Keeping to these gates and the rough tracks through the planted areas is the only suitable means of accessing the summit.

There are two routes of ascent. The first and more scenic is from the south, starting from good parking at the edge of a large cleared area opposite the entrance to Invernettie (NJ342153). Walk up the track following the Nettie Burn past the farm, go through a gate in the deer

fence and continue up the valley to some trees and a small hut. Cross the burn then take the right-hand track which heads up the east side of the slope before swinging up towards the cairned summit, gained across the heather (**2.5km; 290m; 1h**).

The hill is too low for an extensive view but Ben Avon can be seen together with the neighbouring Grahams, Mona Gowan, Pressendye and The Buck. Return by the route of ascent (**5km; 290m; 1h 35min**) or follow the deer fence round onto Clashenteple Hill then descend south and pick up a track leading back to the burn and Invernettie.

The second route ascends the north side and starts further up the road at a parking area beside an old quarry (NJ336177). Follow the track through the forest, right then back left to a high point. Leave the main track for an earth track on the right which leads to a gate in the deer fence and open hillside. Continue on the atv track through plantings before breaking off right to the top (**2.5km; 200m; 55min**). Return by the same route (**5km; 200m; 1h 30min**).

*Cnap Chaochan Aitinn; 715m;
(G72); L36; NJ145099; knob of
the juniper stream*

The relative remoteness of this hill is offset by the ease of access to it, circumscribed as it is by vehicle hill tracks. In fact, the ascent of the hill could be taken in on a complete mountain bike journey circuit, the only walking section a mere 50m to the jumble of quartzite stones, a small wind turbine and telecommunications mast which grace the summit. An ascent by mountain bike would knock two to three hours off the time for the straightforward out and back route.

Whether an ascent is made on bike or by foot, the starting place is the car park at NJ165176 below Queen Victoria's viewpoint, about 1km outside Tomintoul. The private road to Inchrory and on through the Bealach Dearg to Deeside is rough and partially surfaced, maybe as a deterrent to drivers hoping to drive into the heart of this area.

Glen Avon is a magical place by reason of the fact that it lies on the boundary between the granites of the Cairngorms and the softer calcareous rocks to the west, so the landscape is really quite different – almost reminiscent of the Yorkshire Dales with limestone grassland and grey shattered outcrops. It is worth keeping an eye out for the brown mosses and yellow saxifrages that characterise the stony wet flushes along the road.

The route takes the track on the east side of the River Avon. After going through the main gates onto the Inchrory estate at Birchfield, 3.5km from the start, cross the river by a hump-backed bridge then branch off uphill to the south-west beside a small burn to pass the renovated cottage at Wester Gaulrig.

This was, and is, a heavily grazed area, and the birches lining the stream are themselves in effect a 'population of old age pensioners'. Once out of the field system, the vehicle track offers an unmistakeable scar to follow on the hillside and rises steadily past the imperceptible

Approaching Cnap Chaochan Aitinn (Rab Anderson)

summit of Cairn an' t-Sleibhe (589m) then swings south-east towards Geal Charn.

Before the track crosses the Little Allt Bheithachan, take a branch to the south-west (not shown on the current OS 1:50k map) which goes over the shoulder above the col between the summit of the hill and Càrn na Ruabraich. This continues down into Glen Loin in a series of steep and

stony switchbacks, but before it does, the top of Cnap Chaochan Aitinn is easily reached after a few hundred metres on another track (**9.5km; 380m; 2h 50min**). The best views are to the south across Big Garvoun to the northern corries of Ben Avon and Beinn a' Bhuird, as well as south-west across the Loch Avon basin to Ben Macdui and the main Cairngorm massif. Bikers may decide to make an exhilarating descent south into steep sided Glen Loin and back down Glen Avon for a fine circuit, however there is still a considerable distance to travel (**30km; 400m; 5h, by bike**). The on foot timing is for a return by the same route (**19km; 380m; 5h**).

A return can be made via the tops of Càrn na Ruabraich and Càrn Ruabriach to provide a circular route on foot; if using bikes these should be left at the burn crossing at NJ148135. From the summit, head north-west to the first top and descend northwards to climb to the second top above the Water of Ailnack. Unfortunately the convex slopes afford no views into this dramatic gorge. The somewhat heathery trudge is enlivened on the last section by a line of beautifully constructed and maintained Victorian grouse butts, lined with stone, disguised by heather and still draining freely (**21km; 530m; 5h 40min**).

The ruin at Suie with Cook's Cairn beyond (Jim Teesdale)

Cook's Cairn; 755m; (G9); L37; NJ302278; 1850s OS Name Book says Clinton's and Knox's Cairns, on the same hill mark the spots where Lord Clinton, and Knox, future Lord Cavendish, 'shot their first deer'. Likely that Cook, an aristocratic friend, did likewise here. Roy mapped Corryhabbie Hill as Cook's Carn

Situated in the Ladder Hills, which lie north and east of the Lecht and the infamous Cockbridge to Tomintoul road, this is one of the more remote of the eastern Grahams. Despite a 10km approach, the going is fast on various tracks all the way to the top. Although there are a number of possible approaches, the easiest is perhaps from Glenlivet.

Glenlivet is the discreet end of the Cairngorms National Park, ideal for quiet walking away from the glamour and crowds of Aviemore. This area is more famous for distilleries than hills, with around 20 of them within 16km, considerably more than the number of Grahams. A mountain bike is helpful for this hill and although it saves about an hour on the day it is worth noting that the cycling is quite rough. However cycling may be more entertaining than walking along tracks, particularly as the route is quite slippery when wet. Times given are on foot. Much of the ground on the approach forms part of The Crown Estate lands with walkers and bikers welcomed. For more information about low level walks and mountain bike routes, see <www.glenlivetestate.co.uk>. There is an Information Centre at Tomintoul.

For the start of the walk to Cook's Cairn, turn off the B9008 just north of Tomnavoulin where there is a small sign for Tombae but no indication that this is also the direction for several of the Glenlivet walks. Drive to the end of the tarmac and the Allanreid car park (NJ237249). The walk starts alongside the River Livet, on the continuation track signposted to Achdregnie and takes the old drove route to Cabrach known as The Steplar. Where the farm road track goes uphill, go down almost to a bridge across the river but keep to the east side and follow the grassy river bank. Although cyclists may worry about going off-road here, this is part of Glenlivet Estate's Cycle Trail 5. Walkers may also be surprised at the lack of path, but it is a right of way and marked as a path on the map; Walk 3 on the Estate's walking

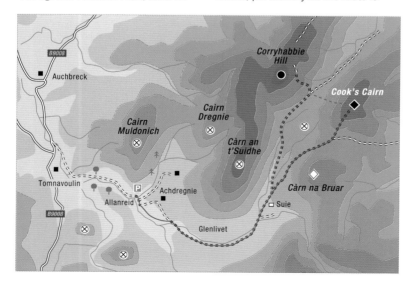

trail network. Go through a section of forest on a rough track then follow the base of fields to meet the farm track coming down from above. Follow the track to the river and cross via a footbridge, then continue along the south side of the river for 3km, sometimes rough, to reach a ford across the Kymah Burn.

Cautious cyclists will leave their bikes here and it may be possible to cross with dry feet. If not, there is a footbridge 300m upstream to the right. Beyond the ford the track forks with the more obvious right branch going to the ruined cottage at Knochkan. Take the fainter left branch up to Suie, now a grand old ruin. Walk past Suie, then an outhouse to reach another fork in the track. This is as far as most people will be able to bike.

Take the right fork and head up to a col between Càrn na Bruar and Cook's Cairn. Here vehicle tracks lead off left and pass some 50m east of the summit of Cook's Cairn, which has a small but well-built cairn. However remote these moorland hills, someone always seems to reach them by vehicle, and sure enough one or two tracks go there (**10km; 480m; 3h**). The view west is dominated by the nearby Corbett, Corryhabbie Hill, with Ben Rinnes just poking out beside it. East is mostly moorland but the nearby Graham The Buck is prominent. To the south-west are the Cairngorms, with Ben Avon the closest. Return by the same route (**20km; 480m; 5h 20min**).

The ambitious could descend west to a col then climb Corriehabbie Hill by an all too obvious snaking track which passes close to its summit (**13.5km; 760m; 4h 20min**) followed by a return via Suie (**25km; 760m; 7h**). For those on foot a return via Càrn an t-Suidhe, or the track down Cairn Dregnie is an option.

A shorter route comes in from Aldivalloch (NJ361264) to the east, via Dead Wife's Hillock (**7km; 540m; 2h 30min**); (**14km; 680m; 4h 20min**). This is perhaps more convenient for those on that side of the hills since it could be combined with an ascent of The Buck which is nearby, or Ladylea Hill.

HILLS OF CROMDALE
Càrn a' Ghille Chearr; *710m; (G82); L36; NJ139298; hill of the unlucky (or awkward) boy*
Creagan a' Chaise; *722m; (G60); L36; NJ104241; little crag of the cheese*

The Hills of Cromdale form a long ridge wedged between the River Spey and the River Avon before they join just to the north. The hills are quite prominent from a number of directions and their length makes them appear higher than they really are, especially when covered in snow. Since the summits of the two Grahams lie some 7km apart with a central col at 531m, they make one of the best high-level walks in the eastern highlands. However, be warned, for the traverse is no stroll, especially the soft going across the central col where only the hoofed, the winged and the hardy can cross with ease!

The hills can be climbed from either the east (Avon) or the west (Spey) side. Although there isn't much difference, the route from the east gives a slightly better circuit for climbing both Grahams on the same walk, as well as having better parking.

For the route from the east, start from the public car park at Ballcorach (NJ155265) next to the bridge over the River Avon. The route takes a track which is a signposted Right of Way over the hills to Cromdale. This leads north to the farmstead at Knock where another track is followed up the hillside crossing the Knock Burn a couple of times. When the track ends towards the top, a fading atv track then vague sheep-tracks lead to the ridgeline route. The ground is heathery but managed for grouse, so there are usually large burnt areas for easier walking. Note how blaeberry and cowberry grow first ahead of the heather, hence the reason it's burnt. The rare orange-tailed bilberry bumblebee (Bombus Monticola) likes the sunny slopes and flowers in the morning, whilst cloudberry is much in evidence along the ridge.

Turn north and climb over Càrn Eachie via an atv track then a path to reach the flat summit of Càrn a' Ghille Chearr with its trig point (**6km; 490m; 2h 10min**). On the left there are ▶

Càrn a' Ghille Chearr (Andy Nisbet)

Càrn a' Ghille Chearr, left, and Ben Rinnes, right, from the ascent to Creagan a' Chaise (Rab Anderson)

views over the Paul's Hill Wind Farm to the Moray Firth with the hills of the North-west beyond. On the other hand Ben Rinnes looks splendid with Corryhabbie Hill to its south. A cairn on a lower top just to the east is worth visiting for this view. The remains of a crashed wartime Armstrong Whitley lie just south of the summit.

Return south-west along the crest towards a distant looking Creagan a' Chaise with Ben Avon, Beinn a' Bhuird and the rest of the Cairngorms spread out ahead. The going is mostly easy except for the soft central col. Pass the end of a fence on the first top beyond the col to reach a large pointed cairn on the next. This is the Coronation Cairn, erected by the people of Cromdale on the site of the bonfire for King Edward VII's 1902 coronation. Continue on to Creagan a' Chaise with increasingly good views of the main Cairngorm massif. Unfortunately atv's have scarred this section. On the summit

there is another trig point and a magnificently constructed cairn-castle, which celebrates the 1887 Golden Jubilee of Queen Victoria (**13.5km; 720m; 4h 20min**). There is a visitor book here which can be signed. To descend head towards Carlag, the north-east top, then drop down the east ridge to meet a track which reaches the road at Milton. A pleasant walk of 2.5km leads along the road back to the start (**20km; 720m; 6h**).

The approach from the west is likely to be via Cromdale itself. This was the original settlement in Strath-spey, being at least a thousand years old and only bypassed when a new bridge was built across the Spey in 1754. Park at Wester Rynabeallich (spelt Rynaballoch on the map). Walk 150m south-west along the road to pick up a track, then head across rough ground to meet a new and prominent track snaking above. Go to its original top then take the line of the old and barely detectable path,

east then south-east, to gain the crest of the ridge. First go to Càrn a' Ghille Chearr (**6km; 450m; 2h 5min**) then traverse the summit ridge to Creagan a' Chaise (**13.5km; 680m; 4h 10min**).

Return to the Coronation Cairn and descend a path down the spur to Clach nam Piobair (Piper's Stone) where a fatally wounded piper played for the Jacobites at the battle of Cromdale in 1690. The Jacobites were defeated, with 400 killed out of 800, and this battle marked the effective end of the Jacobite uprising. Continue down the track and if keen on Scotland's national flower, then cut across open ground to the start, otherwise follow the track to the road (**19km; 680m; 5h 40min**).

To climb the hills individually from the east, go up and down the ascent route for Càrn a Ghille Chearr and up and down the descent route for Creagan a' Chaise. To climb Creagan a' Chaise from the west, go to the top of the snaking track, then continue south up a rougher track and a line of grouse butts to gain the small top north of the Coronation Cairn; return via the Piper's Stone. To climb Càrn a' Ghille Chearr from the west, park at NJ111298, signposted to the Cromdale Hills, then go through a field to cross the Allt na Criche and follow its left side for about 1km before gaining the ridge of Càrn na h-Iolaire which leads to Càrn Eachie on the summit ridge.

Creagan a' Chaise (Andy Nisbet)

SECTION 9
Speyside to the Great Glen

Càrn Glas-choire from the south-east (Andy Nisbet)

Càrn Glas-choire; *659m; (G161); L35, 36; NH891291; hill of the green corrie*

Càrn Glas-choire lies in the heart of the Dava Moor, an expanse of mostly heather moorland north-east of Slochd Summit on the A9, which is really an extension of the Monadh Liath. This is grouse country, with Cawdor Estate and this hill to the south-west and Lochindorb Estate to the north-east of the B9007, a minor but fast road which crosses the moor from near Carrbridge over towards Nairn and Forres.

The ascent of this hill is a great walk if east coast moorland interests you. The peak bagger may regard it as flat and featureless but this is a rarely visited hill, so the high moorland is largely unspoilt, the peat is untrampled and only animal prints are seen on the soft ground. Tracks go close to the summit and a bicycle can be used to make an easier outing; times given are for walking.

A track leaves the B9007 at NH929261, sign to Auchterteang and a Cawdor Estate sign which is a warning for the grouse season. There is possible parking 300m to the south where there is room at a track

entrance into a forest on the east side of the road but forestry operations could affect this. There is also space for a few cars on the east side of the road at the end of the forestry plantation, 800m north of the walk start.

Follow the track beyond the keeper's house and kennels at Auchterteang, gently uphill staying with the main track as it contours round past a green hut, then take the uphill branch to a fork at NH906283 where bikes can be left. The left fork extends over the col to the east of the summit and enables a more direct approach but this would make a dull route and is better left for the return journey.

More interesting is to branch right and head uphill past Creag na h-Iolaire along a track which loops past a small hut to Càrn Mheadhoin and beyond, much further than marked on the map. Reach the boundary watershed and at the high point of the track leave it to follow the boundary west. There are expansive views over the lower moors of Nairn-shire with Lochindorb as the centrepiece. From here to the summit

is about 3km of high moorland with occasional peat hags.

Two steep little cnaps break up the flat moor and cloudberries grow on their slopes. Between them, stream channels up to 2m deep, just reach down to a mixture of granite, schist and quartzite rocks in their bases and show the depth of the peat. There are also thick branches of bog wood, a surprising altitude for Scots Pines of that size and the curved branches show how they must have battled against the wind. The number of hares here is notable.

This traverse along the watershed between the rivers Spey and the Find-horn gives great views, from the high Cairngorms to the Moray Firth coast and beyond to the Graham Morven in the far north. The summit has a trig point, the saviour of nervous naviga-tors and there are some small walls offering marginal shelter (**8.5km; 400m; 2h 35min**). It's exposed here and on a windy day it may be better to have a stop lower down.

To the east of the summit the left fork of the ascent track extends further than marked on the map, crossing a branch of the burn and continuing over the plateau. Descend east-north-east across the head of the burn to pick up the track and follow this to join the upward route which leads back (**15km; 400m; 4h**).

Over to the west there is extensive forest, but this is largely young forest managed for regeneration of native species. Protected by deer fencing and hare culling, it is amazing how quickly the pines have grown.

The southern flanks of Càrn nan Tri-tighearnan from above Daless on the approach (Andy Nisbet)

Càrn nan Tri-tighearnan; *615m; (G214); L27; NH823390; hill of the three landowners*

This east coast moorland hill is remarkably flat and open, with distant views to match. Despite its lack of dramatic slopes it provides a good short outing, although the flat ground does give some soft going cut by peat hags.

Approach via the B9007 Carrbridge to Nairn and Forres road, turning off west to Dulsie where there is a fine bridge across a gorge on the River Findhorn and a viewpoint. On the north side of the bridge take a small road westwards along the north bank of the river. This tiny road almost makes a tunnel through beautiful birch woods with glimpses of the river in its clean-cut valley.

Beyond Drynachan Lodge, the road deteriorates and has a thick stripe of grass down the middle but is drivable with care to its end at a ford across the Allt Breac opposite Daless Farm where there is ample parking.

Cross the Allt Breac and take the track uphill behind Daless to a fine platform overlooking the River Findhorn. Continue past three rough tracks off right, which should be ignored since these lead to cages of partridges, then take the clear track off right at NH852384. This leads over the crest then drops down across the Allt Breac to join another track just above. Follow the track steeply uphill to its end just below the plateau then make a short climb to gain the flat ground and walk out to the trig point on top of Càrn an Uillt Bhric (599m) which lies over to the

right. The view north across the Moray Firth to Morven and the other Grahams of the far north-east is fine, whilst to the south the nearest hill is another flat moorland Graham, Càrn Glas-choire, which is too low to block out the Cairngorm massif beyond.

An unusually flat plateau links this top with the main summit, although the going is not as bad as appearances suggest. The central section has many peat hags but as the ground is horizontal, they run in all directions so sometimes it is easy to climb into one and follow its stony base. Careful linking means the 1.5km crossing is not too tough and a second trig point is reached on the higher summit (**4.5km; 400m; 1h 45min**).

The view to the west has now opened and a myriad of distant hills can be argued over. Ben Wyvis, Sgùrr a' Mhuilinn and the Strathfarrar hills are there but which is Mam Sodhail in Glen Affric and are those the Glen Shiel hills and is that really Ben Nevis in the distance?

A good return descends south-east on the other side of the Allt Breac, crossing a deep side branch, to reach a gentle ridge which leads to a series of grouse butts and finally a better track which soon joins the route of approach (**9km; 400m; 2h 45min**).

Càrn na h-Easgainn; 618m; (G211); L27; NH744320; hill of the eel

Càrn na h-Easgainn overlooks Strathdearn on the opposite side of the A9 from Càrn na Tri-tighearnan. It is a useful hill with a track all the way to the summit, which means it can be quickly climbed when passing, or combined with another nearby Graham.

Turn south off the A9 at NH768340 onto a road signposted to Lynebeg. The tarmac ends opposite the houses where there is parking; it might be possible to drive to Lynemore and a little further.

Follow the track, which is not on current maps, to a junction 5m short of the trig point. The high point is some 50m to the south-east (**3.5km; 310m; 1h 20min**). There is a shooting bothy by the summit and the 40 wind turbines of the Farr Wind Farm lie on the other side. Despite these intrusions there are some fine views. Return the same way (**7km; 310m; 2h 5min**).

A longer option, perhaps for those who want to cycle, starts in layby 162

(NH787321), on the west side of the A9. Follow a track under the railway then up beside the Allt a' Chùil to NH765313 where a track branches off right. Follow this to where the ground levels near the crest and continue north-east to the summit. A cycle loop is possible by descending to Lynebeg and returning along Sustrans Cycle Route 7 which runs through layby 162 via the B9154 parallel to the A9.

Càrn na h-Easgainn from the north-east across Strathdearn (Andy Nisbet)

Creag Liath from just north of Glenballoch (Rab Anderson)

Creag Liath; *743m; (G26); L35; NH663007; grey cliff*

Occupying a central position in the Monadh Liath mountains, Creag Liath is climbed by a short looped walk. It can be combined with nearby Creag Dubh, although this provides a nicer walk on its own from the south. It could also be added-in with an ascent of the Munro, Càrn Dearg and the other two Munros here, since the route to, or from Càrn Dearg passes through the c550m col to the north of Creag Liath.

In the centre of Newtonmore, turn northwards up Glen Road to reach Glen Banchor, which was heavily populated until the residents were cleared for sheep in the early 1800s. The landowner wasn't totally ruthless however for they were re-housed in newly built Newtonmore.

After 2km of grazed open ground, a parking area is reached just before the road drops to a gated bridge over the Allt a' Chaorainn, from where it becomes a track. Follow the track to a bridge leading to the ruinous buildings at Glenballoch. The quickest ascent would be to head for the top from here, but the terrain is generally rough and pleasanter in descent.

Turn right and follow a grassy then stony track up the glen beside the Allt Fionndrigh to where the track ends.

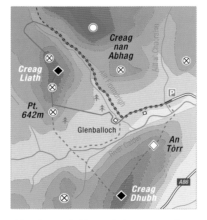

50m beyond this, go left at a small cairn onto a path leading down to a bridge at NH660019 (shown on the OS 1:25k, but not the 1:50k map).

The path leads up a boggy gully to a col where atv tracks turn right. A left turn leads towards the hill's northern ridge. The ground is soft initially but soon a small path develops as the heather shortens on the crest of the ridge. The going is now pleasantly easy over a small top and final rise to the cairned summit (**6.5km; 450m; 2h 15min**).

The top is like an emperor's seat, facing an amphitheatre of Monadh Liath mountains to the north. To the

east are the Glen Feshie Cairngorms and to the south-west, the upper reaches of the River Spey, while lying beyond are Ben Alder and Creag Meagaidh, better seen from the lower southerly top.

Turn south-west to gain the southern summit and continue down the south ridge towards the prominent final top of Pt.642m. From the col before this, follow grass and heather slopes south-east, heading for the far corner of the plantation beside the Allt Fionndrigh. Follow the south side of the forest to the burn, from where an atv track leads to Glenballoch and the main track back to the start (**11km; 460m; 3h 25min**)

Inclusion of Creag Dubh depends on the level of the River Calder, as there are no bridges, despite one being shown on the OS 1:50k map. From Pt.642m, continue down the south ridge to reach the river. This will need to be waded but it is generally shallow when water levels are low. A fairly direct line leads to the top of Creag Dubh (**11km; 870m; 4h**).

The return leads down the north-east ridge, followed by a more crucial wade across the now wider river, although this is still easy when low (**14.5km; 880m; 5h**).

Creag Dubh; 756m; (G8); L35; NN678972; black cliff

A ttractive and unusually shapely for the area, Creag Dubh overlooks upper Strathspey and offers a fine ridge walk to a popular summit.

Park at NN673958 on the A86 south-west of Newtonmore and opposite Lochain Ulvie where there is room for about six cars. This is also the car park for Creag Dubh, the famous rock climbing cliff which lies directly above. Walk west along the road for 400m to a gate on the right, opposite and just before the gatehouse to Creagdhubh Lodge. Go through the gate and follow a grassy track into woodland for a short way to reach a gate in a fence.

Leave the track and go through the gate then cross a burn and climb uphill beside this, through woodland beneath the left end of the line of cliffs. Emerge into the open then climb a steep grassy slope to swing round north-east above the cliffs on a rough path which becomes more distinct as height is gained.

This point can be reached from

Auchmore a little further west where a rough track starts at a gate (NN664947) 200m west of a small pull-off opposite the house. The track can also be gained by a traverse along a gated forest track with parking which starts at NN656947.

Once on the main path, simply follow the fine crest. There is a small

top first, then a drop to a stile, then up more steeply, almost scrambling. The crest narrows and there is another small top with gentle scrambling up to the summit of this miniature mountain. The east of the two cairns is probably the highest (**3.5km; 520m; 1h 40min**). There are lovely views to the Cairngorms, especially Braeriach and the Glen Feshie hills, with Cairn Toul and Sgòr an Lochain Uaine just showing. The villages of Newtonmore and Kingussie show up well in the sun, as do the Monadh Liath and Creag Liath – see opposite for the combination of that hill with Creag Dubh.

A return can be made straight down to Creag Ruadh, avoiding all the cliffs to reach the road 1.5km from the car. The further north-east you head along the summit ridge before descending, the longer you enjoy the view but the longer the walk back to the car. However, the best return is to simply descend the approach route (**7km; 530m; 2h 40min**).

Creag Dubh from the south (Andy Nisbet)

Creag Ruadh from the north-east across the Spey Dam Reservoir (Andy Nisbet)

Creag Ruadh; *622m; (G202); L35; NN558913; red cliff*

Situated on the ridge between the A86 Newtonmore to Spean Bridge road and the upper River Spey above Laggan village, this hill offers inspirational summit views.

The best route is from the north. From Laggan village on the A86, take the Garva Bridge and Corrieyairack Pass road and park just before Sherrabeg (NN571930); ample space on the grass. Walk towards Sherrabeg, cross the bridge over the burn in front of the cottage and go through a gate. Head up through sheep-cropped grass, with lots of bog asphodel and eyebright in summer, to a point which is shown on the map as a narrow gap between the two types of forest.

Go through a gate in a deer fence here then break out right onto a shallow ridge. Continue up this lovely ridge over various craggy bumps with hints of footpath to reach a cairn almost overlooking the high Loch na Lairige. Cross a deer fence on the left and follow old metal fence posts across nice short heather to the summit (**2.5km; 350m; 1h 20min**).

The finest view is that down Loch Laggan to the Grey Corries. Creag Meagaidh lies to the right and Binnein Shuas to the left with Ben

Alder not far behind. To the north lie the Monadh Liath and east the Cairngorms. Return the same way (**5km; 350m; 2h**).

A fine circuit can be made by crossing south-east to Pt.560m, then heading north-east over the fence to the knoll of Pt.565m. Here a waymarked path leads to a junction and interpretative board for the Dùn-da-lamh Pictish fort on the knoll to the north. A walk around this fort is

recommended; return to the path junction. A direct route to the road can be contrived from here but this involves thrashing through forest, crossing a fence and descending steep, boggy ground.

Instead, leisurely descend the path south onto a forest track then turn north and follow this beneath the steep slopes below the fort. Turn left at the road and walk back to Sherrabeg (**10.5km; 560m; 3h 20min**).

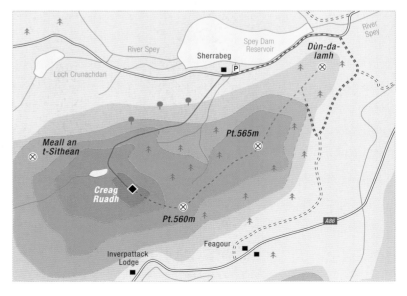

Creag Dhubh; 658m; (G167); L34, 41; NN322824; black cliff

A somewhat rounded and rather dull looking hill, Creag Dhubh has an easy western flank which can be ascended quickly and without difficulty from Glen Spean. On the ascent it offers views of the two Glen Roy Grahams to the north, as well as Aonach Mòr and the Grey Corries to the south-east. Another Graham, Cnap Cruinn (see p142), sits on the opposite side of Glen Spean and since one of the routes to this uses the same car park, it can be conveniently climbed as a second hill, accessed across the River Spean by the Monessie Gorge footbridge.

About 450m to the east of the Glenspean Lodge Hotel a narrow tarmac road rises to a car park at NN306812, just before a tiny church called Cille Choirill (Cairell's Church). If travelling from the east this turning comes up quickly after a bend, so care is needed here. The church was renovated in 1932 and is thought to have been built originally in the 15th century and named in honour of Saint Cairell, an Irish missionary who preached Christianity in the area around 600AD. There is a well-kept graveyard beside the church where many generations of Highlanders are buried. It has a commanding view eastwards up Glen Spean and is popular with tourists.

From the car park head north-west away from the church and ascend a heathery slope, which has much tussock grass higher up. As the angle eases head northwards to the corner of a wire fence (NN304818) which corresponds with the level of a Parallel Road at 261m. This feature can be traced for long distances around the hillsides on both sides of Glen Spean and marks the level of a huge body of water created some 12,000 years ago, when the western end of Glen Spean was blocked by glacial ice. The water escaped into the Spey Valley by spilling over a col through the Feagour channel, at the foot of the Graham Creag Ruadh (see opposite), about 4km to the east of Kinloch Laggan at the eastern end of Loch Laggan.

Step over the fence with care then head directly uphill on heathery ground and after a climb of 120m pick up a rough atv track. Turn right and follow this track steadily uphill and when it fades turn rightwards and ascend slightly steeper ground without difficulty. The summit area is slightly more interesting than expected and small outcrops of rock appear. A short distance beyond the cylindrical trig pillar there is a fairly large summit cairn with views east to the Creag Meagaidh range (**3km; 460m; 1h 25min**). Return by the same route (**6km; 460m; 2h 15min**).

Creag Dhubh and Cille Choirill (Rab Anderson)

Lèana Mhòr West from the north-east (Noel Williams)

Great Glen to the Meall na Teanga group and up Glen Roy are good and the summit plateau of Lèana Mhòr east (see opposite) is conspicuous on the other side of the glen.

To descend, head north-east then go down a broad ridge on the other side of the corrie. Cross the burn where it joins the main burn draining from between the hills (**4km; 500m; 2h**).

To include Beinn Iaruinn, descend north to a col then climb the long but steady whaleback of a slope to a final short walk around the rim of a corrie to reach the 803m summit (**5km; 800m; 2h 30min**). The best descent, which also maintains the fine views, is to return to the col, then follow a deer track down and across Lèana Mhòr before dropping towards the start. Cross the burn coming from Lèana Mhòr where it joins the main burn draining from between the hills (**8.5km; 810m; 3h 30min**).

Lèana Mhòr (west); 684m; (G125); L34, 41; NN284878; big meadow

Glen Roy contains two Grahams named Lèana Mhòr which face each other on either side of the glen. This is the one on the west side of the glen and it gives an easier ascent than its partner. The outing can easily be extended to include the Corbett, Beinn Iaruinn.

Leave the A86 in Roybridge and follow a single track road up Glen Roy to a viewpoint and interpretation board from where the Parallel Roads for which the glen is famous become apparent. These features represent different levels of ice-dammed lakes which were formed around 12,000 years ago when a glacier spread up into the mouth of the glen.

A further 3km up the glen, at a bend in the road, is a bridge over the burn draining from the hill and the col to its north. There is good parking on the verge beyond the bridge. The route is well seen from here, taking the steep shoulder to the left of the narrow Coire an t-Seilich on the north-east face.

Walk over the bridge then climb the steep bank on the left to walk alongside a fence before heading up the

hillside to climb the shoulder. Cross all three of the Parallel Roads which strike across the slope; there are good views of the matching Parallel Roads on the other side of the glen. Continue up the steeper ridge to a wide flattening then cross a slight dip and climb the slope above, curving gradually north to reach the broad summit (**2km; 500m; 1h 15min**). There is a small cairn on otherwise featureless ground. The views across the

Lèana Mhòr (east); 676m; (G140); L34, 41; NN317879; big meadow

A pproached from further up Glen Roy, this hill is harder to ascend than its namesake on the opposite side. It can only be reached conveniently by crossing the River Roy by a bridge a short distance before the end of the road up the glen. There is no longer a bridge across the river to Cranachan on the south side of the hill. In low water conditions it is possible to wade across to Brunachan Bothy on the north side of the hill.

As well as being more interesting, it is a natural combination to climb the hill as part of a round with Càrn Dearg, a Corbett to the north-east.

There is limited parking on the verge opposite a bridge and green shed at NN330909, about 500m before the end of the public road up Glen Roy; take care not to block access. In addition, there is good off road parking 200m downstream, as well as 500m upstream where the public road ends.

Cross the bridge and head south a short distance, then cross the Allt na Reinich and continue up a broad ridge. The aim now is to slant rightwards up the hillside to the level of the third and highest of the Glen Roy Parallel Roads, which runs around the hillside at the 350m contour. The feature is not always obvious on the ground, but it should be possible to judge height from the equivalent Parallel Road on the opposite side of the glen. Contour in a south-westerly direction and gradually turn leftwards into the deep indent created by the Allt Brunachain.

If you find the correct level you should see a fork where the water from Coire Dubh joins the Allt Feith Bhrunachain. Cross this left-hand fork and ascend the ground between the two burns. Continue climbing southwards on the steep eastern bank of the Allt Feith Bhrunachain. After about 500m, cross the burn and head directly up the hillside, then climb a deer fence and continue up heathery ground to gain the crest of the north-north-east ridge.

An alternative, if coming up from Brunachan, or having traversed the lower 261m Parallel Road from the bridge then crossed the Allt Bhrunachain (if the burns are not running high) just below this, gains a gate in the deer fence at NN320894, then a rough atv track which climbs onto the crest of the ridge. The crest leads to what is an extensive plateau, where a small pile of stones marks the summit (**4km; 460m; 1h 35min**).

Head south-east off the summit then descend more steeply east to the floor of the glen. Cross a fence then a burn to ascend either side of a prominent straight gully and continue at a gentler angle. Pass to the right of a small lochan at Pt.745m and after 1km reach the pleasant 834m summit of Càrn Dearg (**7.5km; 790m; 3h**). There are unusual views of the north side of Creag Meagaidh.

Descend easily in a north-easterly direction to a saddle, then either gain the North Top, or avoid it by slanting down to another dip at about 645m. Trend leftwards, maintaining height for another 500m then descend the hillside on the north side of the Allt na Reinich directly to the bridge (**11km; 790m; 4h 5min**).

Lèana Mhòr East, right, with Càrn Dearg behind (Rab Anderson)

SECTION 10a
Loch Linnhe to Glenfinnan

Beinn Mheadhoin viewed from the north across Coire Bàn (Noel Williams)

Beinn Mheadhoin; 739m; (G33); L49; NM799514; middle mountain

On the east side of Morvern, close to Loch Linnhe, there is a fine ring of hills facing the tiny community of Kingairloch, of which Beinn Mheadhoin is the highest. It is a hill that can be climbed most simply by its east-north-east ridge from the Old Mill in the floor of the glen (**6km; 740m; 2h 35min**); (**12km; 740m; 4h 15min**). However, the full circuit of the hills makes a much finer expedition.

From the Corran ferry take the A861 towards Strontian and after 10km turn south onto the B8043 for Kingairloch. Follow this single track road for almost 13km, then take a left fork down to Kinglairloch itself and park by the shore just past the Boathouse Restaurant at the head of Loch a' Choire. Walk along the road past the grounds of Kingairloch House then turn left and cross a bridge over the Abhainn na Coinnich, downstream of a power station.

The first aim is to reach the eastern shoulder of Sgùrr Shalachain, called Sròn Seann. Ascend north-westwards on a forest track. Ignore tracks off left and continue up the track until it starts to level off, then

turn left and head up the open hillside. At a height of 200m start to follow the left flank of the shoulder and cross a burn before eventually regaining the crest. Steep grassy ground leads to the broad summit of Sgùrr Shalachain (538m), which has three tops of similar height (**3.5km; 540m; 1h 40min**). Most of the hard work has now been done.

Continue easily along the broad, undulating ridge for a further 1.5km to the flat top of Meall na Grèine (609m) from where there are fine views across Coire Bàn to Beinn Mheadhoin. Descend to lochan-

peppered Bealach a' Choire Bhàin and climb more steeply to a subsidiary top 400m away from the summit. Descend to a broad dip with a shallow lochan and continue easily to the main summit (**7km; 830m; 3h**).

The quickest way back is to descend the east-north-east ridge, taking special care at a steep nose in the upper section (**13km; 830m; 4h 40min**). However, by heading south around Coire nan Each, over Pt.702m then down the ridge, it is possible to get impressive views into the 1km-wide Glensanda Superquarry. From Lochan Lag a' Mhàim at the end of the ridge, skirt the next small top on the north side and descend northwards along the ridge of Meall an Doire Dhuibh.

Just in front of the last cairned knoll, pick up a stalkers' path on the left which zigzags down to the west bank of the Allt na Carraige. From the buildings at South Corry, head northwest and cross the Abhainn na Fearna by a couple of footbridges. At North Corry pick up a track which soon joins the route used in approach (**15km; 940m; 5h 25min**).

Beinn na Cille; *652m; (G172); L49; NM854542; mountain of the church*

This hill is situated just north of Loch a' Choire and overlooks the small community of Kingairloch. It forms the most southerly summit of a circle of hills, including two Corbetts, which surrounds Glen Galmadale to its east. Although it can be ascended most directly from the roadside by its south flank, a track up Coire Ghardail to the west gives slightly easier-angled access and allows a pleasant circuit to be made of that corrie. The route includes the Corbett Fuar Bheinn but is not as demanding as the round of Glen Galmadale.

Parking along the B8043 above Kingairloch is limited. There is space for a car on the north side of the road immediately west of the bridge over the Abhainn Ghardail (NM829541). Otherwise, park with care in a passing place further to the west. The Coire Ghardail track leaves the north side of the road a few metres west of the bridge.

Climb steadily up the track into the corrie and follow it for just over 1km. Turn right at a junction and descend slightly to the Abhainn Ghardail where there is an intake for a small hydro scheme. Cross the burn and head directly up the hillside in an easterly direction. It is hard-going on the lower slopes where there is much tussock grass but as the angle steepens the ground becomes easier. Higher up, where the angle starts to ease again, there is an outcrop of a distinctive, brown-coloured dyke.

Once on the crest turn right to reach the summit of Beinn na Cille (**3.5km; 580m; 1h 45min**). There are superb views east to the hills around Glen Galmadale, as well as Beinn Mheadhoin, the neighbouring Graham to the south-west. The whole island of Lismore is conspicuous further south in Loch Linnhe.

Return the same way for a short distance, then descend north to Bealach Coire Mhic Gugain. From here it is possible to truncate the outing by turning left to descend by the Allt a' Cheallaich (**7.5km; 580m; 2h 55min**). However, it makes a more satisfying day to climb northwards to the summit of Fuar Bheinn (766m) (**6km; 890m; 2h 50min**) and then descend its north-western ridge to Bealach a' Mhonmhuir. Continue over undulating ground along a broad ridge to Glas Bheinn (**9km; 990m; 3h 45min**), then descend diagonally across the hillside in a southerly direction to regain the track in the corrie floor (**12km; 990m; 4h 45min**).

Beinn na Cille can be climbed from the parking area at (NM866531) in Glen Galmadale, ascending steeply between the forestry plantation and the burn (**2.5km; 650m; 1h 40min**), (**5km 650m; 2h 40min**). Continuing over both Corbetts for the Glen Galmadale horseshoe gives a classic but more arduous round (**16km; 1500m; 6h 30min**).

Beinn na Cille, right, with the Corbetts Fuar Bheinn, left and Creach Bheinn, centre (Noel Williams)

Druim na Sgriodain, centre left, and shapely Sgùrr na h-Eanchainne from the Corran road (Tom Prentice)

Druim na Sgriodain; *734m; (G40); L40; NM978656; ridge of the scree*

Druim na Sgriodain sits above the Corran Narrows on the west side of Loch Linnhe, towards which it presents a fine south-east facing corrie. As well as offering an excellent varied walk, the trip also involves a ferry crossing as a foot passenger, adding something a little unusual to the day.

Park beside the Corran ferry slipway and take the ferry over to Corran in Ardgour, which gives time to survey the objective; a round of Coire Dubh taking in two summits. Sgùrr na h-Eanchainne is the shapely peak on the right which dominates the view and tends to overshadow its marginally higher neighbour, Druim na Sgriodain, which sits further back at the head of the corrie.

From the pier out in front of the Inn at Ardgour, walk north-west along the road for 2km, then go through a gate to Cille Mhaodain (the clan Maclean burial ground), beyond which another gate leads onto the open hillside. Steeply climb above the burial ground onto the rounded spur and continue over a knoll to a col. Swing round south and climb the ridge to reach the summit of Sgùrr na h-Eanchainne (730m) and its trig point (**5km; 730m; 2h 20min**); a tremendous viewpoint.

Drop off the top and head west past tiny Lochan a' Choire Dhuibh, around the head of the corrie, then make the short ascent to the summit of Druim na Sgriodain, which sits atop a small knoll beside some tiny lochans (**7km; 830m; 3h**).

Descend the long curving ridge which drops southward, and follow it as it swings east to where steep slopes fall away to the forest below. Drop north into the corrie and cross the burn just before it cascades over the lip to form Tubhailt Mhic 'ic Eòghainn (Maclean's Towel), a lovely waterslide. Follow the path down the north side of the waterslide and at the bottom head for an aerial, beyond which a track leads down through the forest to Ardgour House.

Cross the bridge over the river, then take the track south-east through the woods to reach the minor road at Clovullin. A short section along the main road leads back to Corran and perhaps a brief refreshment while the ferry is waited on (**13km; 830m; 4h 40min**).

Ascending the Druim an Iubhair towards Sgòrr Mhic Eacharna (Rab Anderson)

Sgòrr Mhic Eacharna; *650m; (G177); L40; NM928630; MacEachern's peak*
Beinn Bheag; *736m; (G38); L40; NM914635; little mountain*

Sgòrr Mhic Eacharna, Beinn Bheag and the Corbett Garbh Bheinn encircle Coire an Iubhair and offer a superb round through some of the rockiest and most dramatic mountain scenery in the area. Rough terrain with some steep descents and ascents requiring care and good navigation in poor visibility or wintery conditions, mean the route feels longer and more tiring than the time and distance might suggest. The round can also be extended to the north-west to include the Graham Sgùrr nan Cnamh (see the end of this description and p186).

Park off the A861 on a section of old road at the foot of Coire an Iubhair and follow the path up the corrie on the east side of the Abhainn Coire an Iubhair to join a track up the corrie. Cross straight over and ascend the hillside, passing west of Lochan Druim an Iubhair to gain Druim an Iubhair and follow this broad, rock scattered ridge over assorted small knolls.

Increasingly rocky and steeper terrain leads towards the top of Sgòrr Mhic Eacharna to meet an old fence-line which is followed to the cairned

summit (**4km; 640m; 2h**). Garbh Bheinn dominates the view to the west, with the cone of the Corbett Sgùrr Dhomhnuill prominent to the north-west. To the south, beyond Mull, are Grahams Beinn Shiantaidh and Beinn a' Chaolais, two of the four Paps of Jura.

Descend west, nearer to the fence-line at the start then more to its south, to gain the Bealach nan Aingidh, with Beinn Bheag towering above. From here a steep and surprisingly rocky ascent, initially close to the fenceline before it veers off west, leads to a small, craggy top followed by scree and boulders to the cairned summit (**6km; 910m; 3h**).

Beinn Bheag (Jim Teesdale)

Garbh-Bheinn; alternatively go right into the corrie, then up. Drop off the back and continue south up to the summit of Garbh Bheinn (**9km; 1310m; 4h 30min**).

From the summit follow the path due west to clear the sheer South Face crags before descending south to the bealach. Continue on the ridge in a more easterly direction over Pt.823m then south-east down Sròn a' Gharbh Choire Bhig. The path fades in places and there are some short rocky sections, making the descent feel long and quite hard going (**13.5km; 1380m; 6h 15min**).

If continuing on to Sgùrr nan Cnamh from the ridge west of Beinn Bheag, climb over Pt.682m to drop steeply west off the back and cross the intervening col just south of Loch nan Dearcag. Gain a grassy traverse-line and follow this across the north-east side of Drùim Min then cross gentle slabby ground and climb to Pt. 634m. Drop to a narrow col and climb steeply through a rocky band then on up to the summit of Sgùrr nan Cnamh. Return the same way and cut across to the Bealach Fèith 'n Amean; an additional (**4.5km; 220m; 1h 45min**) on the day.

A fine elevated ridge now leads west then south-west over the craggy West Top (Pt.696m) to a grassy col before Pt.682m, overlooking Lochan Coire an Iubhair on the Bealach Fèith 'n Amean below. A possible extension continues west from here to pick up Sgùrr nan Cnamh; described at the end.

Continuing to Garbh Bheinn, descend the steep grassy gully from the col to reach the eastern end of the lochan. A return can be made from here, east down Coire an Iubhair to pick up a rough path (**12.5km; 950m; 4h 45min**). To complete the round, ascend above the lochan by taking a grassy zigzag line up the mixed slope between the large rounded buttress of the North Face cliffs on the left and a grassy gully on the right. Above, the rocky ridge of Sròn Lag nan Gamhna can be climbed direct by easy but fine scrambling to gain the top of Fiaclan

Beinn Bheag and Garbh Bheinn, left, from Sgòrr Mhic Eacharna (Rab Anderson)

Sgùrr nan Cnamh; 701m; (G104); L40; NM886643; peak of the bones

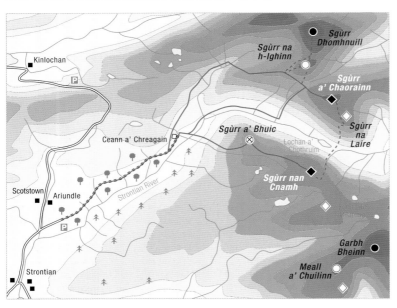

Sgùrr nan Cnamh is a solitary hill which rises from an extensive area of rough moorland south and east of the Strontian River. It is a north-westerly outlier of Garbh Bheinn and lies to the south of the big ridges around Sgùrr Dhomhnuill, from which it is separated by deep glens.

Approach from the Loch Sunart side, from the car park 2.5km north-east of Strontian, just inside the Ariundle Nature Reserve, at NM826633. Follow a forest track gently uphill through beautiful pine and oak woods for 3km to a fork. Take the right branch and gradually descend north-east for 1km to the ruined croft at Ceann a' Chreagain.

Cross the potentially large Strontian River and follow the Allt a' Bhuic east, taking the left-hand tributary higher up. Clamber over rough, slabby ground to gain the subsidiary summit of Sgùrr a' Bhuic (461m). Undulating ground gives slow going for 1km before the final steady uphill climb to Sgùrr nan Cnamh's summit (**7.5km; 730m; 3h**). Descend the same way (**15km; 750m; 5h**).

Sgùrr nan Cnamh can be combined with Sgùrr a' Chaorainn, in which case it is better to climb the latter hill first (see opposite for details of the link). If connecting transport can be arranged, a better extended excursion is to continue east from Sgùrr nan Cnamh to traverse over the Grahams of Beinn Bheag and Sgòrr Mhic Eacharna, descending to the car park at the foot of Coire an Iubhair at NM928597. This makes a fine walk, passing the remote Loch nan Dearcag and scaling the grand prow of the west top of Beinn Bheag.

Sgùrr nan Cnamh can also be easily taken-in after the Sgòrr Mhic Eacharna to Beinn Bheag traverse, returning to the bealach at the foot of Beinn Bheag; (see previous route for details of that link).

The craggy north-east face of Sgùrr nan Cnamh above Lochan a' Chothruim (Tom Prentice)

Sgùrr a' Chaorainn and Sgùrr Dhomhnuill from the south (Rab Anderson)

Sgùrr a' Chaorainn; 761m; (G3); L40; NM895662; peak of the rowan tree

Ardgour being an area of extremely rough terrain, it is no surprise that some of its Grahams give testing excursions; this is one of them. Sgùrr a' Chaorainn forms part of the high ridge on the north side of the Glen Gour to River Strontian divide, sitting between its Corbett neighbours, Beinn na h-Uamha, which is higher by just 1m, and Sgùrr Dhomhnuill, at 888m Ardgour's highest peak. Along with Mull's Beinn Talaidh and Lochgoilhead's Cnoc Coinnich, Sgùrr a' Chaorainn shares the distinction of being the highest Graham.

It is best climbed as part of a larger traverse of these hills and a fine route starts at Sallachan (NM978628), taking in Beinn na h-Uamha and Sgùrr a' Chaorainn, then either traverses to Strontian or returns to Sallachan via Glen Gour. Extending the traverse to include Sgùrr Dhomhnuill gives the best expedition although the finish at Strontian is some way from the start.

If Sgùrr a' Chaorainn is the main focus, then approach from the west.

Start from the car park 2.5km north-east of Strontian, inside the Ariundle Nature Reserve, at NM826633. Follow a forest track through beautiful natural woodlands for 3km to a fork. Take the left branch which after 1km becomes a path that ends at the old Bellsgrove lead mines by the Allt Fèith Dhomhnuill. Cross the burn at NM862667 and climb onto Druim Leac a' Sgiathain, the attractive west spur of Sgùrr na h-Ighinn. Follow this to c600m, just east of a lochan at NM879669.

A worthwhile diversion makes a rising traverse below Sgùrr na h-Ighinn's north-west face to take in Sgùrr Dhomhnuill. Sgùrr na h-Ighinn (766m) can then be included, or skirted on the east, before dropping steeply to the col with Sgùrr a' Chaorainn; adding (3km; 380m, 1h 25min) to the figures given for that hill.

The direct route to Sgùrr a' Chaorainn traverses east from just above this lochan, below a band of crags. Once past the crags, 100m is lost in

the descent past a knoll to reach the Bealach Mam a' Bhearna west of Sgùrr a' Chaorainn. The climb from here is straightforward, steep at first, then with a final blocky, almost gentle walk to the summit cairn (**9km; 850m; 3h 30min**).

To descend it is best to return to the Bealach Màm a' Bhearna and drop steeply into Strontian Glen. Traces of a path can be picked up, which lead to the ruin at Ceann a' Chreagain where a track climbs gradually south-west for 1km to return to the fork on the track 3km from the start (**17.5km; 870m; 5h 45min**).

It is possible to extend the traverse to include the neighbouring Graham, Sgùrr nan Cnamh, which lies 2km to the south. However, the hills are separated by a 500m drop and the difficult link is only for the strong and the determined. It may also give some interesting moments!

Descend south to the col with Sgùrr na Làire (624m), which can be included. It can be avoided by a descending traverse south-east beneath its crags from the col, whilst staying above other crags below. After dropping about 100m, make a dogleg west then pick a way carefully down the steep and rocky hillside, especially if the slope is wet or frozen. Cross the top of the glen east of Lochan a' Chothruim to gain the craggy flanks of Sgùrr nan Cnamh.

Initially follow the burn which emanates from the central corrie below the summit, then bear south-east up a gully to arrive at a small col just above a spur at NM893643. Some 250m of scruffy slab and vegetation lie in wait, requiring care. Higher up, the angle relents. Reach a minor top, from where there is a short but steep rocky climb to the summit (**13km; 1410m; 5h 35min**). The way off Sgùrr nan Cnamh is over Sgùrr a' Bhuic and past Ceann a' Chreagain by reversing the route described for the ascent of Sgùrr nan Cnamh (**20.5km; 1460m; 7h 40min**).

Easier than this link is the inclusion of Sgùrr nan Cnamh in the Sgòrr Mhic Eacharna to Beinn Bheag traverse (see p184), leaving Sgùrr a' Chaorainn to be climbed with its neighbouring Corbetts.

Stob Mhic Bheathain and Pt.706m, right, from the approach up Cona Glen (Noel Williams)

Stob Mhic Bheathain; 721m; (G64); L40; NM914713; MacBeth's peak

Situated on the south side of Cona Glen, in the northern part of Ardgour, there is a hidden range of hills, which stretches almost from Loch Linnhe to Loch Shiel. Stob Mhic Bheathain lies on the western half of this range, more than 11km as the crow flies from the road at Inverscaddle Bay on Loch Linnhe.

Although it is little frequented, Cona Glen is one of the most delightful glens in the area. A rough vehicular track runs along the north side of the Cona River for most of its length. The only drawback in using this as an approach, is that there are no convenient bridges in the upper half of the glen, so any ascent from the north will entail fording the Cona River.

The quickest approach is by mountain bike which allows a rapid return down the glen at the end of the day. However, if on foot, a more varied option is to approach by Cona Glen and return by Glen Scaddle, on the south side of the range. It is this route which is described.

Park just off the A861 at Inverscaddle (NN022686), by the start of a tarmac estate road. Follow the estate road through pleasant woodland past several buildings, turning left at a junction to continue on a rough track. After a few hundred metres the track re-enters natural oak woodland and runs beside the Cona River. Continue past several more open areas with conspicuous

The summit from Pt.706m to the west (Noel Williams)

further east.

If returning to Cona Glen it is best to make a clockwise circuit of Coire Liath Mòr, wading the river from the base of the hillock just above the rapids and climbing the rocky ridge directly to the summit to descend Sròn a' Choire Lèith Mhòir.

For those continuing on foot, head in an easterly direction, passing to the south of Lochan nan Stob. Go round the head of a gully (NM929708), then descend 350m to a building called Tighnacomaire. Follow an undulating track along Glen Scaddle for some 11km back to the start (**29km; 830m; 8h 20min**). A high-level return along Druim Leathad nam Fias is also possible.

Stob Mhic Bheathain can also be approached via Callop to the north, from the car park at NM924792. A track goes as far as a dam at NM918770 (used on the approach to the Grahams, Meall nan Damh and Glas Bheinn, see following route) where a path continues through the hills to drop into the head of Cona Glen (**10km; 910m; 3h 45min**); (**20km; 1000m; 6h 30min**).

lazy beds; a legacy of when the glen was extensively cultivated. Eventually, the track begins to undulate and there are distant views of Stob Mhic Bheathain in the upper glen. Shortly after, pass a locked bothy on the uphill side of the track called Corrlarach.

Just after some fine Scots pine trees the track rises past Tom na h-Eilde (194m), an isolated hillock. There are some spectacular rapids in the Cona River nearby. When the

track levels off, continue for a few hundred metres before looking for a suitable place to wade the river (NM930726).

The most straightforward option is to ascend the crest of Sròn a' Choire Lèith Mhòir, the ridge to the west of the summit, to gain Pt.706m. From here continue east beside the remains of a wire fence over some fine rock slabs onto the summit (**14km; 760m; 4h 15min**). There is a very slightly lower top 200m

Looking east along the rocky summit ridge towards Ben Nevis and the Mamores (Noel Williams)

Meall nan Damh from Sròn Meall nan Damh (Noel Williams)

Meall nan Damh; *723m; (G59); L40; NM919745; hill of the deer*
Glas Bheinn; *636m; (G191); L40; NM938758; green mountain*

These two hills are clearly seen from the roadside shortly after the A380 passes under the railway some 2.5km to the east of Glenfinnan. At the apex of a wide bend, turn off onto a track which leads over a bridge across the Callop River. Immediately on the right there is a car park (NM924792) and from here both hills can be conveniently combined into a single outing.

Head south on the track which passes a small power station then Callop Cottage and continue up the glen on the track which was constructed for the installation of a hydro-electric scheme. After just over 2km, note a side track on the left which descends steeply to a bridge in the floor of the glen; the return route. In another 250m, the Cona Glen path is signposted off up right. Ignore this and continue the short distance to the end of the track where there is a small dam in the burn (NM918770).

Cross the rocky bed of the burn just below the dam and clamber up the far bank. Ascend tussock grass to a fence around an extensive area of woodland then traverse below this to the right. Turn a corner and follow the fence uphill over a short steepening; this can be bypassed to the right by a steep slope above the burn. Continue to where the fence joins another fence and cross at the corner to gain the open hillside. Now climb south up the broad and rocky crest of Sròn Meall nam Damh, zigzagging at times on the steeper sections. It is a splendid ridge with fine views west to the Corbetts on the opposite side of

Meall nan Damh summit with Ben Nevis in the distance (Rab Anderson)

Glas Bheinn from Sròn Meall nan Damh (Rab Anderson)

the glen and east across Coire Fada towards the main summit and its north ridge with Glas Bheinn beyond.

Eventually reach the western summit (722m), which is only one metre lower than the main summit. There are now views south across Cona Glen to the remote Graham Stob Mhic Bheathain and the prominent Corbett of Sgùrr Dhomhnuill. The highest point of Meall nan Damh lies some 900m further east and is reached by an easy ridge which drops only 40m at its lowest point (**6.5km;** **770m; 2h 45min**). There is no cairn on the summit itself. However, on slightly lower ground about 120m further along there is a prominent cairn with a large up-ended rock flake. Bidean nam Bian is prominent to the south-east whilst to the east there is an unusual view of Ben Nevis.

Descend the ridge more steeply eastwards and at a slight flattening turn left and continue down, passing occasional lochans on increasingly rocky ground. Cross Glas Bhealach, the low point on the ridge, and ascend the broad south-west ridge of Glas Bheinn without difficulty to the summit plateau with its sprinkling of tiny lochans. There is a trig point on the first top but the summit lies about 80m further to the north-west and is one metre higher (**9.5km; 920m; 3h 45min**).

Since the west face of Glas Bheinn is fairly steep, the best descent option is to head north-west from the summit and drop down for about 1km before turning more sharply westwards. A bridge is obvious below, part of the hydro scheme, and the aim is to eventually reach this or the head of the track which can be seen running north-west from it. To gain the track, either scale a fence and a pick up a faint path heading north-west from one of the small dams on the Allt na Teanga Duibh (NM925765), or take a longer route around the southern side of the fence and cross two burns before going through a gate and heading north.

Follow the track through a gate and continue through the forest. The track eventually becomes rather boggy and tree trunks have been laid across it. Exit the forest, go through another gate and descend to a bridge over the Allt na Cruaiche then ascend the other side more steeply to join the track used in the approach (**14.5km; 940m; 5h 20min**).

Croit Bheinn from the north-north-east (Jim Teesdale)

Croit Bheinn; 663m; (G158); L40; NM810773; *hump mountain*
Beinn Gàire; 666m; (G152); L40; NM781748; *laughter or noise mountain (probably from burns)*

Lying in a fairly remote part of Moidart, sandwiched between Loch Shiel on the east and Glen Moidart on the west, this pair of hills forms a broad mountain ridge. Consequently they are best climbed together.

From Lochailort on the Road to the Isles, take the A861 south to Glenuig. Continue over the hill to Loch Moidart and after a further 4km turn off at Ardmolich on a single track road up Glen Moidart. Cross the River Moidart at Brunery by a picturesque bridge and park at the end of the public road.

The road ahead leads to Glenmoidart House. Ignore this and go back along the road for 65m to take the track on the east side of the road which crosses over a slight shoulder and passes Loch nan Lochan. After a further 1.2km leave the track on the left and cross a footbridge over the River Moidart (NM754732). Head over rough ground in a north-westerly direction and join a track which leads up Glen Moidart.

Glen Moidart has an unfortunate claim to fame as one of the boggiest glens in Lochaber. In all but drought conditions the next 1km or so will be very wet underfoot, although eventually the going improves. In the upper part of the glen there is plentiful evidence that numerous people once lived there. Ruined buildings and shielings can be seen at three separate locations; Inchrory, Assary and Ulgary. The remains of the latter settlement are somewhat hidden behind a rock-bar which guards a very flat stretch of glen floor. On the south-facing slopes above Ulgary there are numerous lazy beds. Families were cleared from Moidart in the middle of the 19th century and many emigrated to Australia.

The glen now changes character and the river runs through a narrow gorge. It is best to avoid the gorge and ascend the steep slope on the left (north) side of the river to a broad shoulder at about 220m. This is the Bealach na Lice and it is the key to reaching the upper glen. From here descend very slightly at first, before gradually gaining height again to

Beinn Gàire from Glen Moidart (George Archibald)

contour along the hillside on the north side of the glen for some distance, staying well above the river. This upper section of glen is continuous with Glen Moidart but is given a separate name, Glen Gluitanen.

Continue contouring the hillside and eventually cross the burn in the floor of the glen at (NM798770), at a height of about 250m. Gradually head away from the burn and climb eastwards more steeply to eventually reach the delightful little summit of Croit Bheinn (**10.5km; 660m; 3h 55min**). There are spectacular views across Glen Aladale to the east and the whole Rois-bheinn to Druim Fiaclach ridge fills the skyline to the west.

The next objective, Beinn Gàire, is of very similar height but lies over 4km away. Descend in a south-westerly direction to the Bealach a' Choire Mhòir (c430m), then cross this rather complex col and go steeply up the other side to regain the crest of the

Croit Bheinn from the north-eastern flanks of Beinn Gàire (Noel Williams)

ridge. Climb over a minor summit and descend to a slight dip, shortly after which the ridge broadens out considerably. At this point there are many outcrops of rock with very conspicuous dark crystals of hornblende.

Continue ascending to another higher top and descend only very slightly to the shallow Bealach Gainmheach, with the summit still 1km away. Go round the north side of a lochan and continue ascending gently to yet another minor top then head south-west for 300m to reach the cairn on the summit of Beinn Gàire (**14.5km; 930m; 5h 25min**). The

summit plateau is quite extensive and peppered by several lochans. Though the views are not as dramatic as on Croit Bheinn, they are more extensive and Beinn Resipol stands out to the south.

Head over to the westernmost top which is 300m away then descend in a west-south-westerly direction to the southern end of a wide saddle. Traverse across the slope on the right and descend the ridge of Sròn Dubh an Eilich quite steeply, direct to Glenforslan in the floor of the glen. Pick up a rough track which leads back to the start (**20km; 950m; 7h 15min**).

SECTION 10b
Glenfinnan to Glen Shiel

The summit of Stob a' Ghrianain from the west (Noel Williams)

DRUIM FADA; long ridge
Stob a' Ghrianain; *744m; (G19); L41; NN087824; peak of the sunny spot*

North of Corpach and Loch Eil is the long and broad east-west ridge of Druim Fada, whose highest point is Stob a' Ghrianain. A traverse of this ridge makes a fine outing, although a shorter and very pleasant option is to make a circuit of Coire an Lightuinn at the eastern end of the ridge. The view across the Great Glen to Ben Nevis is superb. The best approach is by a signposted route to Stob a' Ghrianain through the forest from Glen Loy.

Turn off the B8004 between Corpach and Gairlochy into Glen Loy and follow the single-track road beside the River Loy. Look for the start of a forest track on the left, just before the road crosses to the north side of the river by a bridge. There is parking on the left at a gate into the forest.

Go through the gate and follow the track straight ahead. After about 400m another track joins from the left. Continue for 300m, where the track dips to cross a burn, and in a further 400m where the main track curves to the right, take a less used track off to the left. It is important

then to find the start of a rough atv track which heads off on the right after less than 100m. This leads pleasantly through the forest with a dilapidated stone wall on the right-hand side. The track is a boggy in places but climbs uphill to eventually emerge from the forest at a gate.

Walk on for about 200m and cross the burn in the floor of the glen by a hidden wooden bridge at NN112821. Climb straight up the hillside ahead by following a faint atv track up the line of a small burn to reach the ridge

which is then climbed. Higher up a couple of minor cols are crossed before the ground eventually begins to ease in angle.

Go along the top of Coire Odhar past the right-hand side of a lochan and make a slight detour to the right to visit a prominent cairn which overlooks Glen Loy. Turn left and head up to the tiny cairn which marks the highest point on the flat grassy summit (**5km; 680m; 2h 15min**).

Continue along the rim of Coire Dubh to a small pointed top on the other side of the ridge with fine views to the south. The slope beneath this is very steep, so to return go left and head east for 270m before descending the grassy hillside by the burn to where it drops into Coire an Lightuinn. Either descend more steeply into the corrie to follow the burn, or continue east along the ridge to Sròn Liath before descending north to the burn to rejoin the track used in the approach. Neither way is as easy as it looks (**11km; 700m; 3h 45min**).

From the summit, if time is not pressing, it is relatively simple and worthwhile to continue along the ridge, certainly to the far side of Coire Dubh for the view back, then westwards around Coire an Fhuidhir to the West Top (729m). The trig pillar at 716m lies some 700m beyond this (**9km; 770m; 3h 20min**). The Grahams, Aodann Chlèireig and Meall Onfhaidh sit on the other side of Gleann Sùileag to the west. Return along the ridge towards the summit then cut down the grassy hillside south-eastwards to join the descent described above (**17.5km; 800m; 5h 30min**).

Meall Onfhaidh from Aodann Chlèireig (Noel Williams)

> **Meall Onfhaidh**; *681m; (G128); L41; NN010840; hill of the storm*
> **Aodann Chlèireig**; *663m; (G157); L40; NM994825; clergyman's face*

These two hills are accessed from Fassfern, a tiny settlement on a loop of the old road along the north side of Loch Eil. Turn off the A830 at the signpost for Fassfern and after 800m reach a car park on the west side of the small bridge over the An t-Suileag. An anti-clockwise circuit of the two hills is described and those looking for a more demanding outing can easily include Meall a' Phubuill, the Corbett a little further to the north-east.

Cross the bridge over the An t-Suileag and follow a track (signposted Public Footpath to Glen Loy) up the east side of Gleann Suileag through lovely woodland. After 2km the track climbs rightwards away from the river then continues leftwards where another track joins, to eventually emerge from the main forestry plantation 3.5km from the start.

Continue on a rougher track through native woodland for just over 1km to cross a bridge over the An t-Sùileag and go through a gate;

Glensulaig bothy is situated 350m further upstream. The track now climbs quite steeply up the other side of the glen to reach a bridge across the Allt Fionn Doire. Break off left here and head westwards up the hillside, initially on a rough atv track. The angle gradually increases until the broad south-east ridge is gained and leads more easily to Meall Onfhaidh's summit cairn (**8km; 670m; 2h 55min**). The status of this cairn is somewhat uncertain as the ground about 85m to the north-east is marked as the summit on OS maps and certainly seems to be of similar height, if not higher. A visit to both points is recommended. To the north, there are fine views of the neighbouring Munro, Gulvain.

From the bridge over the Allt Fionn Doire, Meall a' Phubuill can be climbed with Meall Onfhaidh being gained via the Fèith an Easain col (9.5km; 1060m; 4h 10min); an additional 1h 15min on the day. The descent of Meall a' Phubuill's south-

west ridge is very steep and although some crags are easily avoided, it might be preferable to return by the ascent route to the bridge, certainly in winter.

To continue from Meall Onfhaidh, head westwards from the summit and descend the steep grassy hillside, gradually curving leftwards to reach the bealach below. Cross this and climb the broad northern shoulder of Aodann Chlèireig. At a height of about 500m, a ramp slants rightwards below a small rocky escarpment on the north side of the summit and leads without any difficulty onto the western shoulder of the mountain. Turn left and after about 200m reach the summit cairn which is situated on a rocky knoll (**11km; 990m; 4h 20min**). Two slightly lower knolls are situated within 200m of the main summit and might cause confusion in poor visibility, especially when approaching from the south. There are splendid panoramic views.

To return, follow the remains of a

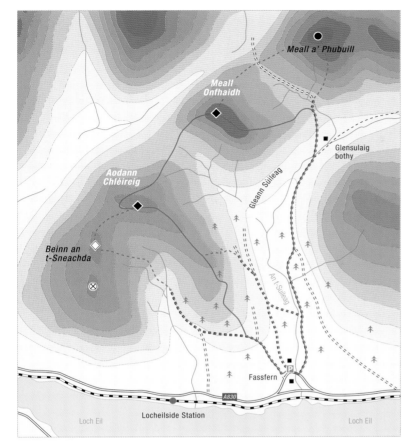

wire fence in a south-easterly direction until it veers off downhill and continue south-east down the broad ridge of Druim Beag. On the left side of the ridge, hidden from view, a gate in the fence around the forest at NN009811 offers a route onto the forest tracks which can be followed back. However, the felling of the trees here makes this not so attractive an option and it is probably better to stay on the ridge, crossing a stile over a deer fence to pick up a rough atv track. This leads downhill with fine views ahead to Ben Nevis, through breaks between younger trees onto a track. Turn left and continue downhill to be soon joined by another track from the left then pass between two ponds where a short link path accesses the car park (**16.5km; 990m; 5h 50min**).

The Graham Top Beinn an t-Sneachda (625m) lies to the south of Aodann Chlèireig and can be included, with a return being made via the track through the forest above the Abhainn Bheagaig, taking the left fork to Fassfern (**18km; 1040m; 6h 15min**).

Locheilside Station is close enough for these hills to be done by train from Fort William

Approaching the ramp below the summit of Aodann Chlèireig (Noel Williams)

Glas-chàrn; 633m; (G193); L40; NM846837; grey-green hill

Situated a few kilometres west of Glenfinnan, Glas-chàrn is the highest point on a broad ridge of rugged country sandwiched between Loch Beoraid and Loch Eilt. Although its ascent gives a relatively short outing the upper ground is fairly complex and in poor visibility may require good navigational skills.

Park in a layby on the south side of the A830 just west of a bridge over the Allt Fèith a' Chatha; there is also space on the east side of the bridge. The route starts 200m to the east of the bridge at a gated forest track on the north side of the road. Squeeze through the gate and follow the track uphill through the forest for about 400m. Continue for a further 400m and where the track swings right-wards go straight on to cross the Allt an Utha by a footbridge.

Follow the vestiges of a boggy path in a north-westerly direction on the east side of the Allt Fèith a' Chatha for about 1.2km then leave the path and follow the burn in a more west-erly direction. Cross a northern fork in the burn where there is a slabby rock pool. Stay on the north side of the main burn and shortly after this head directly up the hillside beyond. The ground is quite complex at times but a grid bearing of 282 degrees will lead directly to the summit (**4km; 520m; 1h 50min**). Another option is to continue to the col at NM865837 where an old fenceline can be followed across flat ground then up the side of the burn's right fork. The fence passes just beneath the top.

The summit is a fairly prominent rocky knoll with a tiny lochan just below it on its north-west side. A deep glen to the north contains Loch Beoraid, which can be glimpsed by making a short descent northwards. There are good views north-west to the more remote neighbouring Graham, Meith Bheinn.

Instead of returning the same way, a pleasant circuit can be made by visiting Sgùrr a' Mhuidhe, a promi-nent hill to the south-east with outstanding views. Descend in a

Below the rocky summit of Glas-chàrn (Noel Williams)

south-easterly direction and cross a broad section of plateau before drop-ping to a bealach at 454m. Continue over a broad rocky knoll to a slight dip with numerous small lochans then climb more steeply to the summit (**6km; 630m; 2h 35min**).

There are twin summits of similar height with the more northerly one having a spot height of 562m. To descend, head quite steeply down the east-south-east ridge which leads directly back to the start (**7.5km; 630m; 3h 15min**).

Including the Corbett Sgùrr an Utha, beyond Sìdhean Mòr to the east, gives a longer and more substantial route although this involves a 500m climb. Descend the fenceline to the col at NM865837 then break away from it and climb steeply up the hill-side to the right of the main burn past a huge boulder, keeping north of more complex ground.

Gain the col at the back of Sìdhean Mòr where the fenceline is rejoined then climb the splendid rocky ridge to the summit of Sgùrr an Utha (**8km; 1020; 3h 50min**). Traverse across to Fràoch-bheinn then descend south-west and cut across the side of Druim na Brein-choille to pick up the head of a track at NM881827 and follow this back (**13km; 1080m; 5h 30min**).

MÈITH BHEINN; fat, oily (as in boggy water) mountain
Sgùrr na Maothaich; 710m; (G83); L40; NM821872; peak of softness or moistness

This great sprawling hill is set in a fairly remote stretch of country between Loch Beoraid and Loch Morar. Its finest feature is the north-east ridge which can be approached via Oban bothy on the south side of Loch Morar, from where it is possible to combine it with the neighbouring Graham of An Stac. However, this is a longer expedition usually involving an overnight stay and Mèith Bheinn together with part of the north-east ridge can be included in a more convenient circuit starting from the A830 at the west end of Loch Eilt, about 1.5km (1mile) east of Lochailort.

Park in a layby (NM784832) on the south side of the road and walk east to the start of a track on the north side of the road. Head off at a right angle to the road on a path which leads to stepping stones under the railway. Continue by the east bank of the Arienskill Burn at first then head eastwards and slant up the hillside to follow the west side of the Allt na Criche. When the path splits keep right and eventually cross to the east bank of the burn. Head away from the burn where it starts to turn westwards and shortly after cross the remains of an iron fence. The path is difficult to follow from here on.

A rather boggy section is crossed at the watershed where there are distant views of Mèith Bheinn. Start to descend more steeply down the other side. One of Prince Charlie's Caves can be seen beneath a giant boulder on the right-hand side of the path. Continue descending through open woodland then look carefully for a crossing place over the Allt a' Chuirn Mhòir. It is important to find the correct level and then follow a ledge system rightwards (east) on the steep northern bank until it is possible to turn left (north) away from the burn. Contour across the slope for about 200m then descend the hillside and cross a couple of footbridges by a hydro-electric scheme at the western end of Loch Beoraid.

Follow a track to a junction and turn right, then a little way short of a boathouse, take a path on the left. After about 200m leave the path and start to ascend the hillside in a slight depression then climb quite steeply up the long south-west ridge. From the broad West Top (660m), descend some 30m to pass a lochan by its western end. Climb north-east to another minor top and shortly after-wards gain the true summit, named Sgùrr na Maothaich, marked by a cairn and trig point (**7km; 940m; 3h 15min**).

Although it is easier to return the same way it is more interesting to descend the rocky north-east ridge until it flattens out slightly at a height of 520m. Turn left off the ridge here and descend to a broad bealach before dropping into Slaite Coire. After 2.5km pick up a path which leads down to Meoble then follow a track southwards and cross a bridge over the river at NM799867. Ascend across the hillside on a faint path which soon becomes difficult to follow. The path rises to 310m before descending to join the path used on the outward journey (**17.5km; 1240m; 6h 40min**).

Sgùrr na Maothaich and the surrounding summits of Mèith Bheinn above Loch Beoraid (Noel Williams)

Mullach Coire nan Geur-oirean across Loch Arkaig (Rab Anderson)

Mullach Coire nan Geur-oirean; *727m; (G56); L41; NN049892; summit of the corrie of the sharp edge or boundary*

Sandwiched between Loch Arkaig and Glen Mallie is a long and broad ridge, the high point of which is the remote summit of this hill. At its western end the ridge links with the Munro of Gulvain. The best approach is from the eastern end of Loch Arkaig. A mountain bike can be used on 8.5km of rough track. Times given are on foot and use of a bike should reduce the overall time by about 2h.

Start from the car park by the Eas Chia-aig waterfall at the western end of the Mìle Dorcha (Dark Mìle), a deeply wooded and mossy glen. Head west along the road for 400m then turn off left and go round a locked gate to access a road that leads to Achnacarry. Cross a bridge over the River Arkaig where it flows out of

Loch Arkaig then turn off right to follow a rough undulating track through the forest for 3km.

After exiting the forest, continue westwards on the main track which runs south of the bothy at Inver Mallie and cross the River Mallie by a bridge. Follow the track up Glen Mallie with its Caledonian pine trees for 4km to some isolated trees on the hillside. About 100m beyond these, at the high point of the track (NN098876), an atv track climbs the hillside and is the return route. Bikes are best left here. Continue for another 1.5km to the end of the track by the ruin at Glenmallie then follow a rough track along the north bank of the River Mallie for a further 3km to the remains of a large shieling called

Ruighe Mòr.

Now climb the steep and grassy hillside on the west side of the burns draining from Coire nam Fuaran, the shallow corrie directly below the summit. A steady plod eventually leads to the broad crest of the ridge where a right turn gains a small cairn which marks the high point on the flat summit (**15km; 730m; 4h 35min**). A short diversion to the north gives the best view of the hills to the north of Loch Arkaig, including the Corbetts Sgùrr Mhurlagain and Fraoch Bheinn, with the distinctive chisel-like summit of the Munro of Sgùrr Mòr, behind. Then there are the three Grahams, Meall Blair, directly opposite, with Sgùrr Chòinnich then Glas Bheinn to the east.

Descend eastwards along the broad ridge of Druim na Giubhsaich, with views of the Nevis range to the south-east, framed between Beinn Bhan and the Graham Stob a' Ghri-anain. Eventually leave the crest and descend more steeply in the same general direction to pick up the atv track which leads back to the track used in approach (**29km; 750m; 8h**).

Glas Bheinn; 732m; (G46); L34; NN171918; green mountain

Overlooking the eastern end of Loch Arkaig, Glas Bheinn is the most easterly of the three Grahams on the north side of the loch. It is a compact hill, set apart from its higher neighbours by deep glens on three sides. Although it can be approached from Gleann Cia-aig to the east, the preferred option is the unnamed glen on its western side since this gives the most open views and has the simplest return route. A north to south traverse gives the best outing.

Approach via the road through the Mìle Dorcha (Dark Mile) to reach the eastern end of Loch Arkaig then continue along the north side of the loch for just over 2km to Achnasaul. Parking is limited but perhaps best in a long grassy passing place at NN151893, just beyond Marine Harvest and a track to the loch.

Take the grassy track which heads north up the east side of the Allt Dubh then away from it. There is a route of sorts though it is somewhat boggy to start with. Cross a side burn and soon pick up an atv track which eventually leads across another side

burn to a more definite track that continues up the glen. There are some fine Scots pines below the track on the banks of the Allt Dubh.

Follow the track almost to the head

of the glen where it peters out into a footpath then turn right and head up the heathery hillside for some distance. Eventually gain the crest of the hill at a slight flattening with fine views eastwards across Coire na Còsaig. Continue south up the crest to reach the cairn on the broad, flat summit (**5km; 680m; 2h 15min**). To the south there are distant views of Ben Nevis and the Grey Corries.

From the summit, head in a southerly direction at first before turning away to the right and descending much more steeply, directly down the south-western flank to regain the track used in the approach (**9km; 680m; 3h 25min**).

It is possible to link this hill with the two Corbetts to the north for an excellent round. On Geal Charn, a grassy atv track runs up the burn from NN164927 which can be used in ascent, or descent, depending on whether Glas Bheinn is tackled first or last. The link with Meall na h-Eilde is made by the prominent steep spur of Pt.681m. Either way, Glas Bheinn stands proud by a not inconsiderable 292m (**17km; 1360m; 6h 45min**).

Glas Bheinn from the south (Rab Anderson)

Sgùrr Chòinnich; 749m; (G13); L34; NN127949; peak of the moss

The middle and highest of the Grahams on the north side of Loch Arkaig, Sgùrr Chòinnich has a rather dull and sprawling south-western flank but more interesting northern and eastern sides. The best outing is to gain the north-east ridge via Coire Mhuic to the south.

Drive along the north side of Loch Arkaig for just over 6km to a car park at NN121912 on the north side of the road before the bridge over the Allt Mhuic. The start of the walk goes through Forestry Commission Scotland's Allt Mhuic Butterfly Reserve; one of the best places in Britain to see a rare chequered skipper.

Head directly uphill from the car park and follow a pleasant path through the reserve to a forest track. Cross over the track and continue up the pathless hillside to a wire fence. Clamber over the fence and ascend heathery ground for some distance. Continue by traversing the steep slope overlooking the Allt Mhuic. This is quite hard going initially but when the angle of the burn starts to ease-off slightly, drop down to reach its eastern bank and follow this a short distance, before crossing the burn. Continue up the corrie, gradually rising away from the bed of the burn,

heading towards the watershed at Lochan an Fhithich between Sgùrr Chòinnich and Càrn Dubh.

Start to slant leftwards up the hillside towards the north-east ridge and follow the remains of an iron fence up onto the crest, then turn left to ascend this, still following occasional fence posts. At a short level section of ridge, cross over to the right and ascend some steeper ground which soon eases. The fence posts lead directly to the summit cairn (**5km; 700m; 2h 20min**). There are views across Glen Garry to the north, east to the Corbett Geal Charn and Graham Glas Bheinn and west to Meall Blàir.

Continue along the summit ridge a short way, then turn leftwards and head due south. Descend the monotonous southern flank for almost 3km to a boundary fence and after a further 400m regain the forest track. Look for a gate on the south side of the track which gives access to the return leg of the trail through the Butterfly Reserve. The road is reached a little to the west of the car park (**9.5km; 700m; 3h 40min**).

It is possible to link this hill with Meall Blàir to the west (see following page). From the summit, follow the fenceline west to a lochan at

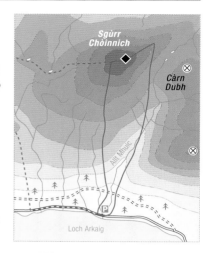

NN110947, then north-west to another at NN105950 before heading across the watershed. Climb to the lochan-studded top of Meall Lochan nan Dubh Lochan, then past Lochan na Beinn Bàine to the top of Meall Blàir (**10.5km; 950m; 4h**). Return downhill past the lochan, continuing south-east to pick up an atv track which leads to a cluster of lochans at NN093936 then carries on in the same direction before dropping south. Cross a forestry track at NN100917 and gain the road below, 2km west of the start (**17.5km; 950m; 5h 50min**).

Sgùrr Chòinnich from the east (Noel Williams)

Meall Blàir and elevated Loch Blàir from the Graham, Mullach Coire nan Geur-oirean (Noel Williams)

Meall Blàir; *656m; (G170); L33; NN077950; hill of the plain*

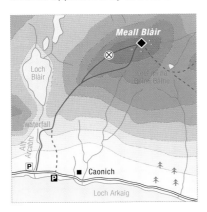

Meall Blàir is the most westerly of the three Grahams on the north side of Loch Arkaig and although it is generally climbed as a stand alone hill it can be linked with Sgùrr Chòinnich (see previous page). It has a more complex summit area than the other two Grahams and scenic Loch Blàir lies to the west of it. The obvious approach is by its southern slope where an atv track can be followed for much of the way.

Drive along the rollercoaster road on the north side of Loch Arkaig for some 13km. There are two possible starting places which join about 1km up the route. Either park in a small passing place opposite where an atv track leaves the road at NN057923 or continue along the road for 400m and park more easily in some natural woodland immediately beside the Allt Arcabhi (NN053923).

The first start up the atv track can be boggy in places, so the second option may be preferable. Ascend a faint path by the east bank of the Allt Arcabhi as far as a small waterfall before slanting slightly rightwards away from the burn to join the atv track at a height of about 270m. Follow the track without any difficulty until Loch Blàir eventually comes into view on the left. Continue more easily at first then ascend slightly steeper ground, with occasional marker posts, for some distance. Pass to the right of two minor tops to reach the cairn and trig point marking the main summit (**4km; 600m; 1h 55min**).

The summit area is peppered with numerous tiny lochans and there are extensive views in all directions. Glen Kingie lies to the north with the Munro Gairich and a number of major hills at its western end. The Corbett Sgùrr Mhurlagain lies across Loch Blàir to the west, whilst to the east is Sgùrr Chòinnich with Glas Bheinn to its side and to the south another Graham, Mullach Coire nan Geur-oirean, which sits straight across Loch Arkaig.

On the return take in the various minor tops to the west of the main summit and from the last of these (646m) take a direct line down the south-west flank. Rejoin the atv track after 1.4km and return by the route of ascent (**8km; 630m; 3h 5min**).

Glenpean bothy and An Stac at the head of Glen Pean (Jim Teesdale)

An Stac; *718m; (G69); L40; NM866889; the steep rocky hill*

This very remote hill overlooks the eastern end of Loch Morar. Any approach from the south would be long and entail a lot of ascent, descent and re-ascent. The described route along Glen Pean to the east of the hill, although long, is scenic and involves only a minor amount of height loss. A mountain bike can be used to advantage on the initial 5km of track through the forest.

An Stac can be approached most easily by boat along Loch Morar to Oban bothy (NM863901) at its foot, however, this is expensive (<*vivmorar @aol.com*>; 01687 462388).

For the Glen Pean approach, drive along the undulating single-track road on the north side of Loch Arkaig to a good parking area where the tarmac ends. Follow the continuation track and take the left-hand fork downhill past Strathan to cross the River Dessarry by a bridge. Shortly after this enter a large forestry plantation, pass a track off right and head into Glen Pean. The track rises gently before descending through a felled

area and where it ends a rough track then a path lead to Glenpean bothy, visible ahead.

Beyond the bothy, continue through the wonderful glen, following a fairly

wet path and atv track for 2km on the north side of the River Pean to suddenly reach Lochan Leum an t-Sagairt. The route along the north side is too difficult, so go downstream

Looking down Glen Pean to An Stac (Noel Williams)

around a knoll and ford the river then ascend a path which traverses the steep hillside above the south side. Once beyond the lochan descend to the floor of the glen again.

In a further 2km the glen narrows and has been filled by rockfall from a crag rising above it. Bypass this completely by a rough path crossing the steep slope on the left, or find a way through it and boulder-hop alongside the hidden reed-covered Lochan Dubh then clamber between some gigantic boulders. The floor of the glen here has been filled by an enormous landslide originating from the impressive crag strewn hillside of Meall nan Each to the north and is similar in character to the famous Coire Gabhail landslide in Glen Coe.

Either way, climb the slope above the landslide formed watershed on the south side of the glen to intersect a stalkers' path which comes up from Gleann an Obhain Bhig and Loch Morar to the west. This well-engineered path climbs onto the Munro Sgùrr nan Coireachan and initially runs between the two burns that drain the hillside, then crosses the left-hand burn before crossing

back over again higher up. Ascend the path to the 350m contour then leave it and cross the right-hand burn, the Allt an Toll Gainmhich, at the point it swings right into another valley. Climb up right onto a delightful slabby ridge, which leads to the minor summit of Cnoc Gorm (527m). At one point there are some impressive vertical clefts on the crest where the ground has started to slip away.

Descend slightly then climb the broad continuation ridge and weave a way up slightly steeper ground to arrive at the fine rocky summit of An Stac (**14km**; **860m**; **5h**). There are superb views of Loch Morar with Rum behind. The neighbouring Graham of Meith Bheinn lies some 5km to the south-west.

On the return it is perhaps better to follow the right bank of the Allt an Toll Gainmhich and where this swings north, cross the next burn and the stalkers' path to continue heading east to a shallow bealach at NM892891. Descend diagonally across the hillside to the floor of Glen Pean then follow the approach route back (**27.5km**; **1020m**; **8h 50min**).

An Stac from the west (Noel Williams)

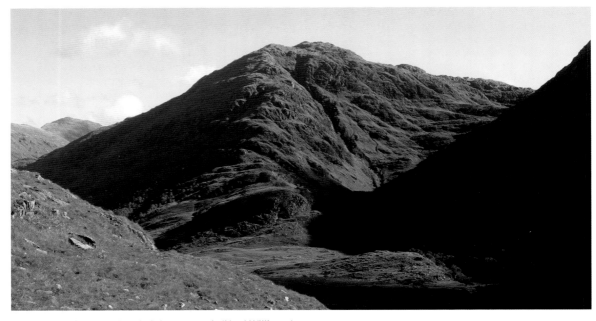

Slat Bheinn from the Barrisdale approach (Noel Williams)

Slat Bheinn; *700m; (G106); L33; NG910027; erect mountain*
Meall nan Eun; *667m; (G151); L33; NG903052; hill of the birds*

Superbly situated in the north-eastern corner of the remote and rugged Knoydart peninsula, these two Grahams are best climbed together. Sitting opposite each other, either side of deep Glen Barrisdale, their ascent gives a demanding route, best achieved by an early start on a summer's day. Another option is to walk-in and spend the night at Barrisdale where there is bothy, camping and self-catering accommodation.

The ascent of Slat Bheinn as described entails twice fording the River Barrisdale which may well be a problem in spate conditions.

The best approach is from the road end at Kinloch Hourn, gained after a lengthy but scenic 35km drive along the single track road which branches off the A87 to the north of Invergarry. There are two car parks on the left side of the road. The closest one to the farm at Kinloch Hourn is for overnight visitors and has to be paid for in advance at the farmhouse. The day visitor car park is a little further on and has an honesty box. There is a useful seasonal cafe at the farmhouse.

Follow the tarmac road for about 750m to where it ends at a turning area. From here, a good though in places rough path provides an undulating but scenic route alongside the fjord-like sea loch of Loch Hourn. Initially stay beside the loch then head inland on the path to cross the Allt Coire Mhicrail by a footbridge. Pass above the building at Skiary, climbing to just over 100m before dropping back down to near sea-level. Head up and over a second shoulder at about 110m then descend to the shore again just after Runival. After a further scenic section beside Loch Hourn climb to a third and final high point of 90m before eventually descending to a track on the east side of beautiful Barrisdale Bay. Follow the track south for almost 2km, past Barisdale Lodge, to the bothy at NG872042, just before a bridge over the River Barrisdale (**11km; 350m; 3h**).

Climbing Slat Bheinn first, continue on the east side of the River Barrisdale and follow a faint path southwards away from the bothy. This soon develops into a more prominent track and gradually rises to a shoulder before turning eastwards into Glen Barrisdale. Continue along the track for a further 1km with good views of the western ridge of Slat Bheinn straight ahead. In normal conditions it is possible to cross the River Barrisdale with dry feet by hopping across rock outcrops in the riverbed at NG893032.

Skirt the steep buttress near the bottom of the west ridge on the left-hand side before climbing more steeply to gain a slight flattening on the crest of the ridge. Follow the ridge to another slight flattening with good views of the south flank of An Caisteal on the north side of Glen Barrisdale. From here the ridge steepens significantly and at times it is necessary to zigzag to avoid rock buttresses, before the angle eventually eases. There are good views of the second objective, Meall nan Eun, on the north side of Glen Barrisdale at this point. Finally, turn rightwards and head south across a slight dip for about 100m to reach the summit itself (**16km; 1080m; 5h 20m**). The

Druim Chòsaidh ridge dominates the view to the south and Beinn Sgritheall stands out to the north-west.

The next objective is to descend to the floor of Glen Barrisdale to gain its most northerly point at NG913043, then ascend the opposite flank in a north-westerly direction. Head north-north-east at first then, either turn right and descend the eastern ridge to gain the path in the floor of the glen, or take a more adventurous route northwards which, although shorter, involves some careful route finding to avoid bands of steep rocky ground.

Ford the river and ascend diagonally leftwards beside a burn for some distance to a shoulder overlooking Lochan Coire Chaolais Bhig. Turn slightly right here and head up through very rocky ground to the main summit of Meall nan Eun (**20km; 1600m; 7h 25m**). This is only 1m higher than the West Top, some 450m to the west, which can be included first if desired. There is a prominent lochan on the north-east side of the summit.

To descend, head in an easterly direction for just over 1km to the bealach below Sgùrr Sgiath Airigh, then turn left and descend a broad corrie which gradually steepens in

angle. Slant down rightwards more steeply heading as directly as possible for the shoulder west of Skiary. Rejoin the coastal path and follow this back to Kinloch Hourn (**26km; 1650m; 9h 10m**).

Another option for these hills is to reverse the route described above all the way to Slat Bheinn, then return up the slope and over the bealach between Meall nan Eun and Sgùrr Sgiath Airigh. To do so, ascend Meall nan Eun via its East Top, climbing from the 100m high point of the Kinloch Hourn to Barrisdale path on the first of the rises after passing Skiary (**6km; 720m; 2h 30min**). Head south from the summit for 300m or so then descend south-east to the floor of the glen before crossing the river to climb the north ridge of Slat Bheinn (**10km; 1280m 4h 40min**). Return down the north ridge and climb the slope above to gain the bealach then descend to rejoin the approach route (**18km; 1650m; 7h 40min**). On initial inspection this route would appear to involve more ascent than the other but interestingly, due to the undulations of the Barrisdale approach, it does not. This route also opens up the possibility of including the Corbett, Sgùrr nan Eugallt in the round.

Meall nan Eun from Slat Bheinn (Noel Williams)

The eastern ridge of Beinn a' Chapuill (Noel Williams)

Beinn a' Chapuill; *759m; (G4); L33; NG835148; mountain of the horse*

Three Grahams lie along the north side of Loch Hourn. They are approached by turning off the A87 at Shiel Bridge, at the end of the long north ridge of Biod an Fhitich, the final Graham in this Section. A single track road leads over Bealach Ratagain and makes the long descent to the village of Glenelg which sits directly across the water from the three easternmost Grahams on Skye.

The road then continues southwards past the turning up Gleann Beag to Beinn a' Chapuill, and on round the coast for a further 15.5km (9.5miles) to reach the Munro Beinn Sgritheall overlooking Loch Hourn, beyond which lies the tiny village of Arnisdale from where the Grahams Beinn Clachach and Druim Fada are approached.

Beinn a' Chapuill is first seen in the distance from the road over Bealach Ratagain en-route to Glenelg. It can be combined with its higher neighbour Beinn Sgritheall but is described here on its own, as a traverse taking in its long and very fine eastern ridge.

The single-track road up Gleann Beag leads past the remains of two impressive brochs, Dùn Telve and Dùn Troddan. Parking is limited in the upper part of the glen but since the walk returns along the final bit of this road there are several places where it is possible to pull off onto the grass verge. The tarmac eventually ends at Balvraid Farm.

Walk along a muddy track from the

farm then continue up the glen on a better surface. Continue for another 1km then pass under pylon power lines. After another 300m or so look carefully on the south side of the track for a small suspension bridge over the Abhain a' Ghlinne Bhig (NG866158). Go over the bridge and shortly after cross a fence by a stile. Head south-west back under the power lines and ascend to the crest of the eastern ridge.

Follow this pleasant easy ridge for just over 3km all the way to the summit, marked as Pt.759 on the OS 1:25k map, but unmarked on the 1:50k map (**6km; 730m; 2h 35min**). There are fine views of Beinn Sgritheall directly to the south.

The undulating summit plateau is complex and extends westwards for another 1km. There is a lochan just west of the summit and others between the various small tops dotted about the plateau, all of which are all slightly lower than the summit. From the summit head west-south-west to Creag Bealach na h-Oidhche (775m), then north skirting Pt.757m to its west, to reach the edge of the steep north face overlooking Gleann Beag.

From here continue west-north-west round the corrie edge to Pt.742 which sits above the western end of the north face. This is the top actually named Beinn a' Chapuill on OS maps, despite being one of the lowest points on the plateau. There are fine views westwards to Skye, with the Grahams Beinn na Caillich, Sgùrr na Còinnich and Ben Aslak clear across the water. Beyond these the rounded granite Grahams of Beinn na Caillich and both Beinn Dearg Mhòrs are prominent in the distance, backed by the jagged peaks of the Cuillin.

The north side of the hill is steep and although a way can be found down the northernmost buttress, it is not easy. The best option therefore is to go west from Pt.742m and descend a depression with a small burn. Towards the bottom start heading in a more northerly direction to gain the Allt Eas Mòr Chul an Dùin and follow that down, to a gate at the left edge of the forestry.

Descend beside the forest to a stile and go through deciduous woodland to pasture beside the Abhainn a' Ghlinne Bhig below. Follow this right-wards until an opening in the forestry gives access to a forest track. After 1km, turn left where the track divides and cross the bridge (NG836170) over the river to reach the road in Gleann Beag, which leads back to the start (**12km; 760m; 4h 20min**).

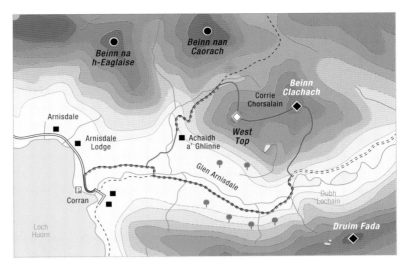

Beinn Clachach; 643m; (G183); L33; NG885109; stony mountain

Located on the north side of Glen Arnisdale, this hill sits between Druim Fada, the neighbouring Graham on the south side of the glen, and two Corbetts. Although it can be climbed with Druim Fada the drop between the pair is considerable, so it is generally climbed on its own. For those seeking an extended outing it is perhaps more conveniently climbed with the Corbett to the north, or even both. The approach to all of these hills starts to the south of Arnisdale, from a car park at the road end just before Corran.

Beinn Clachach is a double-topped hill whose actual summit is an unnamed top on the east side of Coire Luachrach, 1km east-north-east of the hilltop named Beinn Clachach on OS maps. The hill can be climbed utilising the track which rises into Coire Chorsalain to the north but it is more interesting to make a traverse from the south. The initial part of the route is the same as for Druim Fada.

A path on the south side of the River Arnisdale is poor so it is perhaps best to walk back along the road for 400m and turn right onto a track which leads eastwards up Glen Arnisdale. In ▶

The West Top of Beinn Clachach from Corran (Noel Williams)

The summit of Beinn Clachach, right, from Druim Fada (Noel Williams)

the distance a conspicuous dip called Bealach an Fheadain can be seen in profile on the south ridge of Beinn Clachach. After about 1.5km cross a bridge over the river and continue for a further 2.5km, dropping north to cross the River Arnisdale by a bridge just before Dubh Lochain. Shortly before this the Druim Fada route heads up to the right.

The temptation is to immediately head up the south ridge of Beinn Clachach. However, the north side of

Bealach an Fheadain is a tricky vegetated scramble, so the best option is to continue along the track for a further 400m to where it runs beside Dubh Lochain then head north-north-west up the hillside towards a broad heathery gully. Ascend the gully without difficulty to gain the grassy crest of the ridge at NG883098.

Continue up the broad ridge and soon get good views of a large lochan on the left. Eventually head north-east along an easier section of ridge

to a minor top of just over 600m. Turn to the north-west here and soon after descend a grassy break rightwards to avoid a steep crag then cross a dip before climbing again towards the main summit. Go around a couple of lochans, the second is partly filled with reeds, to reach the cairn marking the highest point (**7km; 680m; 2h 40min**). There are fine views of the Corbett, Beinn nan Caorach to the north-west. Leave the summit at first to the south-west then weave down to a broad bealach before following an easy ridge to the neighbouring West Top (618m), to which the OS have assigned the hill name (**8km; 740m; 3h**).

The north-west flank of Beinn Clachach is rather steep so descend initially in a north-north-east direction for about 300m before turning leftwards and dropping to the path in the floor of Coire Chorsalain. There are fine views of an impressive rock slope failure on the south-east flank of the Corbett Beinn Bhuidhe. The path leads to a track which drops past a waterfall before zigzagging down to Achadh a' Ghlinne to regain the track in Glen Arnisdale (**13km; 740m; 4h 30min**).

Approaching the summit of Beinn Chachach (Noel Williams)

Druim Fada; 713m; (G76); L33; NG894083; long ridge

Druim Fada is the second of the Grahams approached from the car park at the road end just before Corran. It is the high point on a long undulating ridge running along the south side of Glen Arnisdale. The ridge forms the northern side of the Loch Hourn narrows, a familiar sight to those walking-in to Knoydart from Kinloch Hourn. It can be climbed with Beinn Clachach (see opposite) but the drop between them is significant and it is more pleasant to climb them separately. The initial part of the route is common with Beinn Clachach.

The path on the south side of the River Arnisdale is poor so it is perhaps best to head back along the road for 400m and turn right onto a track heading east into Glen Arnisdale. Follow this for 1.5km to cross a bridge over the river. After a further 2km the track starts to climb more steeply and eventually there are good views of the small waterfall where the water drains from Dubh Lochain.

Leave the track on the right at NG884090, shortly before it starts to head northwards, and slant across a small burn, the Eigin Allt. Continue rising leftwards across the hillside by a grassy break through the crags and so gain the crest of the mountain's north-west ridge.

Follow this pleasant ridge with fine views to the north. At one point it is possible to scramble up some delightful easy slabs. Continue for some distance eventually heading slightly leftwards to the first summit. The highest point is a knoll 130m further east (**6km; 710m; 2h 30min**).

The best option is to return along the fine undulating crest of Druim Fada over Sgùrr Mòr (627m). There is some interesting route finding at times and on the penultimate top (614m) there is a fragmented trig pillar (**8.5km; 810m; 3h 15min**). Eventually start to head northwards and descend on the east side of the Allt Blàr an Eich before crossing it and descending to the track used on the approach (**13km; 840m; 4h 35min**).

Druim Fada can be climbed from Kinloch Hourn via the Cadha Mòr track and the stalkers' path up the east ridge to Lochan Charn nan Caorach. A bad step on the far side of Carn na Caorach is best avoided from about 50m above the lochan by traversing a deer track down and across a shelf below the crags on the south side. Continue over Pt.647m to the summit (**8km; 850m; 3h 15min**); (**16km; 970m; 5h 30min**).

East across Loch Hourn to Glen Arnisdale and Druim Fada (Noel Williams)

Biod an Fhithich; *644m; (G182); L33; NG950147; point of the raven*

Although dwarfed by the impressive mountains that tower around it, Biod an Fhithich in Glen Shiel is a fine little hill which gives a lovely walk to a grand viewpoint. It has a distinctive pointed summit, well seen from the road as it descends through the glen past the old bridge and the 1719 battle site where government troops defeated a force of Jacobites and Spanish troops. The long north ridge and pointed summit are also clear in the background of the classic picture postcard view of Eilean Donan Castle looking up the glen.

This long, narrow ridge runs north from Shiel Bridge for 4.5km to the summit and although it provides the superior route, the peak is generally climbed from further up the glen where a convenient stalkers' path climbs Meallan Odhar to the Bealach na Craoibhe between it and Biod an Fhithich. This is the route to the Forcan Ridge and The Saddle and Biod an Fhithich is often climbed as a quick addition from that route.

Lying a distance of only 600m to the side of the path to The Saddle, it

The long A' Mhuing ridge of Biod an Fhithich from Glen Shiel (Noel Williams)

Biod an Fhithich, centre left, and Eilean Donan Castle (Rab Anderson)

On the Glen Sheil side the slope plunges 600m to the road giving a great sense of exposure. It is a fabulous summit and whilst there are no distant views, the view up and down Glen Shiel with the wall of mountains formed by the Five Sisters of Kintail across the glen, together with the Forcan Ridge and The Saddle opposite, is magnificent (**6km; 610m; 2h 30min**).

A longer route, more befitting of this hill and its splendid surroundings can be had by climbing the length of the long north ridge from Shiel Bridge. This narrow, knobbly ridge is called A' Mhuing, the English translation *mane of the horse* being particularly appropriate.

Start from the campsite car park (check with the petrol station first) and take the path alongside the Allt Undalain for 600m or so and before

reaching the fence break off left up a spur onto the ridge. Although the ridge is narrow and the drop-offs on either side become increasingly bigger and steeper, the crest is grassy and leads without any difficulty over Pt.533m and the narrow gap beyond up to the exposed summit (**4.5km; 710m; 2h 10min**).

Drop north off the back to gain Bealach na Craoibhe and the stalkers' path coming up from Glen Shiel. The obvious onward extension is to continue up the Forcan Ridge onto The Saddle but the route described here simply descends west into Coire Caol to pick up a path that leads above the burn to Gob na Roinne where three burns meet. Cross over and follow the path on the other side along the foot of Sgùrr Mhic Bharraich back to the start (**10.5km; 710m; 3h 40min**).

can be a straightforward there and back diversion taking as little as 35min; an easy ascent for a Graham. However, it is a fine hill in its own right and proves useful for when time is short, or when one is passing through Glen Shiel en route to or from another destination such as Skye.

A gate in the fence at NG968143 marks the start of a stalkers' path which climbs Meallan Odhar to the Bealach na Craoibhe. There is a large layby 150m or so to the north of this on the east side of the road. A path starts opposite the layby and follows the fence, thereby avoiding the walk along this fast stretch of road. It is a busy spot and there is further parking in a layby some 500m to the south of the start.

Follow the well-engineered path to the bealach then break off onto a small path, faint in places, which leads to the summit (**3km; 610m; 1h 40min**).

SECTION 11
Glen Shiel to Loch Mullardoch

Càrnan Cruithneachd from Iron Lodge at the head of Glen Elchaig (Jim Teesdale)

Càrnan Cruithneachd; 729m; (G54); L25, 33; NG994258; hill of the Picts

C àrnan Cruithneachd is a magnificent peak and a hill of extreme contrast. From the south its rolling moorland barely makes an impression, but to the north its slopes plunge dramatically into Glen Elchaig, a vertical drop of 650m in a distance of just 1km.

There are two main routes of ascent; one from Glen Elchaig to the north and the other from Strath Croe at the head of Loch Duich to the south. Both routes have their merits but the northern route approaches the hill via the splendid deep gorge of the Falls of Glomach and allows the majestic northern aspect of the hill to be fully appreciated.

The Glen Elchaig route has two start points depending on whether one approaches on foot, or by cycle. The cycle route along the north side of the glen starts from a car park at Killilan (NG940303) where a tarmac estate road leaves the public road at a right-angled turn at the head of Loch Long. The walking route starts at the end of the public road 2km further on, at a car park at Camus-luinie (NG948283) where a footpath on the south side of the glen leads to

▶

Càrnan Cruithneachd and the River Elchaig (Rab Anderson)

south-east into the bowl in the centre of the gorge. The path of the upwards route leads back to the track in Glen Elchaig (**10.5km; 700m 4h**).

Total cycle approach (**18km; 100m; 1h 30min** by bike, plus **10.5km; 700m; 4h** on foot). Total walking approach (**24.5km, 800m 7h 20min**).

The southern approach starts at the public car park at Morvich and follows the Falls of Glomach sign-posted route, first to the end of the road then across the bridge past Inchnacro and alongside the river. Cross the bridge at NG982223 and go up the forest track on the Falls of Glomach route but at NG983230 take the left fork. Ascend some zigzags then turn right onto a path to emerge from the forest at NG983240. Either leave the path after 1km and make a steady grassy ascent to gain the top, or (better) continue until close to the col then pick a line up the rocky outcrops on the west ridge, which give excellent but avoidable scrambling (**7.5km;**

a bridge over the river to join the cycle route on the north side. Both routes then lead through the glen beneath the steep slopes of Càrnan Cruithneachd to NH009271 where the Falls of Glomach path starts (**9km; 100m, 45min** by bike); (**7km; 100m, 1h 40min** on foot).

Follow the path across the bridge over the main river, then the bridge crossing the Allt a' Ghlomaich as it pours out of the mouth of the gorge ahead, and continue uphill into the gorge. After the first section is passed the gorge widens into a bowl; the return route descends into this. The upper fall lies above and the path climbs a rib then traverses up and across to the top of the fall; with care a small path can be descended to view the fall. Continue on the path to Morvich which turns to the south-west and climbs to the Bealch na Sroine. Leave the path and tramp north across bog and heather over the minor top of Suie Dhu (615m) towards Càrnan Cruithneachd. The final steep slope is climbed by a ramp which cuts up from right to left to gain the narrow pointed summit (**6km; 690m; 2h 45min**). It is a stunning view-point with the cairn perched in an exposed and lofty position.

To descend, return down the ramp then cut across to the north of Suie

Dhu to gain the north-east ridge which is followed to a slight rise at its end. Descend a steep but easy slope

Sgùrr nan Ceathreamhnan from Càrnan Cruithneachd (Rab Anderson)

720m; 2h 50min).

Descend south-east from the summit, over the grassy minor top of Suie Dhu, then head southwards to gain the path through the Bealach na Sroine. This is followed to a bridge at NG985238 where the forest track leads back to the start (**16km; 750m; 5h**). A 2km detour can be made to the north-east to view the Falls of Glomach and its deep gorge.

A rewarding return from the Bealach na Sroine can be made over the Munro, A' Ghlas-bheinn (918m). Either ascend its north ridge by Meall Dubh and Creag na Saobhie, or climb steeply for about 120m from the path, then cut across in front of these tops by a traverse above a small waterfall. The climb to the summit of A' Ghlas-bheinn is steep but uneventful (**12km; 1200m; 4h 45min**). Return by the west ridge, which steepens just above the bridge and forest track at NG985238 (**19km; 1200m; 6h 45min**). A return by the Bealach an Sgairne to the south adds just over 1km.

Càrn Mhic an Toisich from Càrn na Caorach (Rab Anderson)

Càrn Mhic an Toisich; *678m; (G135); L34; NH310185; MacIntosh's hill*
Meall a' Chràthaich; *679m; (G130); L26, 34; NH360220; hill of shaking*

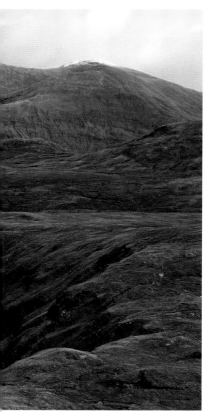

Standing just north of the Great Glen, on a clear day these two unassuming foothills of the Western Highlands give unparalleled mountain panoramas from their summits. Access is relatively straightforward, but once the road is left behind, both have a satisfying air of remoteness.

Start at the cluster of houses at Bhlàraidh in Glen Moriston, where a forestry and hydro track leaves the A887 immediately east of a bridge; verge parking either side of the road at the west end of a crash barrier over the bridge. Care is required as the traffic is very fast at this point. There are pros and cons to using a bike. The track has several steep sections, giving a hard climb but a fast descent. Times given are on foot.

Either way, after 1.5km take the left fork, passing Bhlàraidh Reservoir and continue almost to Loch Liath. Climbing Càrn Mhic an Toisich first, leave the track at a fork (NH337194) just before the Liath dam and climb a slight ridge leading roughly west. Suddenly all the forestry and hydro intrusions are left behind, and a great wall of mountains starts to come into view, beginning with the Strathfarrar and Glen Affric hills.

Underfoot, the going is typical rough moorland so there is little energy to be saved by avoiding the intermediate top of Càrn na Caorach, especially as the magnificent view continues to open out as height is gained. The summit cairn of Càrn Mhic an Toisich is capped with a luxuriant green cushion of vegetation, revealing a wonderful panorama extending from Ben Nevis and the Mamores in the south around to Ben Wyvis in the north. Be prepared to sit back and try to recognise many familiar hills, or simply be inspired. Unfortunately the line of pylons carrying the Beauly to Denny power line runs across the foreground, so pleasure may not be perfect (**9km; 660m; 3h 10min**).

To climb Meall a' Chràthaich, return to the junction below the Liath dam and follow the right fork north to the end of the track at the hydro dam at the south end of Loch ma Stac. The climb north-east from here is rougher and more boggy, with the ▶

Meall a' Chràthaich and Loch Liath from Càrn na Caorach (Rab Anderson)

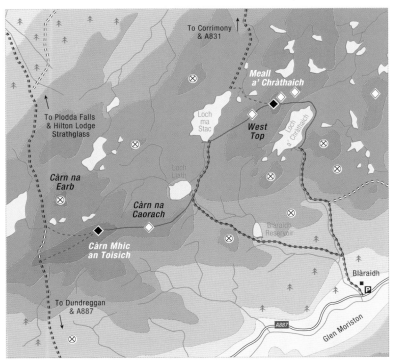

enticing views behind and out of sight, though an occasional glimpse over the right shoulder will reveal the distinctive profile of Ben Nevis. The summit is also hidden until the West Top (632m) is gained or skirted, and the line of a derelict and rusty wire fence points the way. The summit trig point of Meall a' Chràthaich shares the magnificent panorama of its neighbour, with the added bonus of overlooking a scattering of remote lochs to the east, and glimpses of the more extensive waters of Loch Ness and the Moray Firth (**16km; 1030m; 5h 20min**).

Without a bike to return to, it is possible to make a more interesting circuit by descending north-east then east to go around the far side of Loch a' Chràthaich to join the track leading up to yet another dam, eventually rejoining the route of ascent at the junction above Bhlàraidh (**24km; 1030m; 7h 15min**).

Càrn Mhic an Toisich can be

climbed on its own from Glen Moriston to the south or Strathglass to the north, utilising a track over the high ground in between; this is a right of way and the route used by Bonnie Prince Charlie in 1746.

Start at NH313138 in Glen Moriston where there is a pull-off opposite a signpost and gate. A path leads through woodland onto the track (known as Eve's Road), which starts 300m to the east at Dundreggan. Unfortunately the track follows the route of the new Beauly to Denny super pylons, no chance of getting lost here! The track crosses the south-west shoulder of Càrn Mhic an Toisich at NH290177 at a height of 550m and from there it is just over 2km to the summit (**7.5km; 560m; 2h 40min**); (**15km; 560m; 4h 20min**).

The track runs through to the Strathglass road at Hilton Lodge (NH285244) where it can be gained from, or by cutting though the woods from the Plodda Falls car park at NH280238 (**8km, 480m; 2h 35min**); (**16km; 480m; 4h 25min**).

Meall a' Chràthaich can be climbed on its own from the north via Corrimony where there is chambered cairn signposted off the A831 through Glen Urquhart. Dating from the third millennium BC, this ancient tomb is worth a visit. There is ample parking at NH384303 and a few spaces closer to where the track starts about 1km further on at a bridge (NH375302). A path cuts the corner following the west bank of the River Enrick for 500m to join the track again. Much of the route passes through an attractive RSPB nature reserve.

Just beyond Loch Comhnard take the left fork (NH360272). Bikes are not recommended beyond here. A substantial, but rather dilapidated bridge crosses the Abhainn na Ruighe Duibhe just upstream of the ford. The summit is in view from here and it may be worth cutting across to climb to it before reaching Loch ma Stac. However, the curious will want to take a closer look at the unusual semi-derelict three storey tower-like lodge perched on a tiny island just offshore. (**10km; 540m; 3hrs 10min**); (**20km; 540m; 5h 30min**).

> *Meall Fuar-mhonaidh; 699m; (G107); L26, 34; NH457222; hill of the cold hill-mass*
> *Glas-bheinn Mhòr; 651m; (G175); L26; NH436231; big green hill*

Rising steeply half way along the west shore of Loch Ness, Meall Fuar-mhonaidh is one of the dominating features of the loch's landscape. Its lofty dome is an obvious sight from Inverness and it is a popular local walk. Due to the lush vegetation of its steep flanks, it is not normally climbed from the loch and the ascent is usually made by a well-worn path from the north-east. Combined with its modest western neighbour, Glas-bheinn Mhòr, it gives an enjoyable circuit.

Turn off the A82 Inverness to Fort William road at Borlum Bridge (NH513291) on the southern outskirts of Drumnadrochit and take the minor road to Bunloit for 6km, to a small car park at Grotaig.

Walk along the road for 100m then branch off on a signposted path which leads past fields then gains height through a birch forest. Emerge onto open moorland and continue up to a stile at NH477238. The well-used but rather soft path follows the ridge south-west, rising steadily, before rearing up steeply for the final climb onto the summit dome. The high point is at the furthest cairn (**4.5km; 510m; 1h 50min**). The view up and down Loch Ness is superb and there is a tremendous panorama of the Affric, Cannich and Strathfarrar hills out west.

Most walkers return the same way. However, those after the second Graham now need to continue on pathless rough ground. Steep and craggy slopes lie west of Meall Fuar-mhonaidh, so it is best to descend to the south end of Loch nam Breac Dearga by dropping south-west for 1km to a grassy flattening at NH450215. Cut back north from here and descend steeply to gain the loch ▶

then cross its outflow. A steady ascent, passing west of the small Loch Ruighe an t-Seilich, gains the cairned high point just south of the trig point on Glas-bheinn Mhòr (**8km; 680m; 3h**). The summit view, whilst fine, is less open than its neighbour's.

The best return descends around the east side of Loch Ruighe an t-Seilich, then crosses moorland to gain the north end of Loch nam Breac Dearga. Climb around the back (south) side of the knoll above then traverse east-north-east following animal tracks to regain the path of ascent 1km above the stile. Return by this to the start (**14km; 700m; 4h 30min**).

An alternative is the pleasant but lengthy Dhivach Lodge route, starting from the Divach Falls car park at NH494278, suitable for either or both hills. A track and a path lead to Loch Dubh to the north-east of Glas-bheinn Bheag. Continue towards Loch nam Breac Dearga then climb onto Glas-bheinn Mhòr (**9km; 500m; 2h 50min**). Reverse the previous route to Meall Fuar-mhonaidh via the south

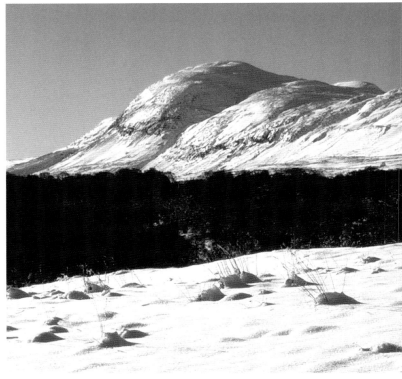

Meall Fuar-mhonaidh from above the car park at Grotaig (Jim Teesdale)

Glas-bheinn Mhòr from Meall Fuar-mhonaidh (Rab Anderson)

Càrn a' Chaochain; *706m; (G88); L34; NH235177; hill of the little streams*

Càrn a' Chaochain is the furthest west of the chain of five Grahams which occupy the tract of rolling hills which begins midway up Loch Ness and runs westwards between Glen Morriston and Glen Affric.

To its south-west the ground rises to Sgùrr nan Conbhairean and the other two Munros, one either side of it, which dominate the view with their wild east facing corries. Slightly closer to the west is the complex bulk of the Corbett, Aonach Shasuinn, whilst to the north and north-west lie the Munros of Glen Affric. To the south Ben Nevis rises above everything.

Therein lies the attraction of this hill, for although pretty nondescript in itself, it does provide a splendid vantage point from which to view the hills that surround it. The much smaller Graham, Beinn a' Mheadhoin (the last hill in this section), lies on the other side of Loch Beinn a' Mheadhoin in Glen Affric just to the north and since both hills are approached via Strathglass the pair could easily be climbed in a day, especially since the drive between

them is not far. However, for those not in a hurry, both of these hills provide enjoyable if short outings on their own.

Càrn a' Chaochain is best approached from Cougie to its north since routes from the south are rather long and tedious. Cougie is 16km south-west of Cannich in Strathglass and it is possible to drive to it along a forest track, passing first Hilton Lodge and then Plodda Falls where the tarmac ends and there is a sign Pony Trekking Cougie. The surface of the track can suffer due to forestry operations so it is worth checking its condition first. An alternative would be to leave the car in the Plodda Falls car park and bike the track rather than drive it.

Cougie is a pleasant spot situated in an area of woodland which is being targeted for natural regeneration of native species by Forestry Commission Scotland. Already substantial stands of mixed Scots pine and birch are thriving. Park at a junction beside some sheds (NH242209) and take ▶

end of Loch nam Breac Dearga (**12.5km; 770m; 4h 10min**) then regain the approach route to the north of the loch (**20km; 770m; 6h**). A quick mountain bike route to Glas-bheinn Mhòr can be made by a track along Glen Coiltie, to the north of Dhivach Lodge.

Another route starts next to Loch Ness Youth Hostel at Alltsigh (NH457190) where there is parking off the main road at the start of a forest track. The track leads left past a house then right up the south side of the Allt Saigh. Immediately north of a bridge at NH437192 a track goes west then north to join another track at NH434209. This terminates at a cut-off dam at NH438216 from where it is just over 2km to the top of Meall Fuar-mhonaidh (**8.5km; 680m; 3h**).

A link can be made with Glas-bheinn Mhòr by descending north-east then steeply north and north-west by a burn to the north end of Loch nam Breac Dearga (**11.5km; 840m; 4h**). Descend south-east then south to the track (**19km; 840m; 5h 50min**).

West to the sprawling corries of Aonach Shasuinn (Meryl Marshall)

Looking north-east to the trig point, left, from near the summit of Càrn a' Chaochain (Meryl Marshall)

the track on the south side of the river westwards for a few hundred metres. At a small cairn, a rough track strikes up the hill following the Allt na Fearna and continues through a gate onto the open moorland then onward to reach the Bealach Fèith na Gamhna at a height of 531m. From the bealach, climb steadily up the north-east spur of the hill, passing several small tops. The easiest ground is found in a direct line, firstly towards Loch Càrn a' Chaochain and then westwards to a trig point on the northern top (704m). From there the true top, 2m higher, lies some 400m to the south-south-west, with a short drop and re-ascent. There is a small cairn (**4.5km; 460m; 1h 45min**).

Rather than returning the same way, an option which gives a circular route is to descend the north-west spur over rough terrain and continue north towards the small rise of Meallan na Duibhre then the top edge of the forestry plantation lower down. Cross a deer fence and make for the furthest west branch of an un-named burn which offers a line of weakness leading to the forest track, south of the Allt Riabhach. Walk north-east along this for about 250m to a junction where both tracks lead back to the start either side of the Allt Riabhach. Much of the forest has been felled here, so going left and crossing a bridge to take the track on the north side through pine woods is perhaps better (**9km; 460m; 2h 45min**).

Beinn a' Mheadhoin; 613m; (G215); L25; NH218255; mountain at the middle

This small hill sits next to the loch named after it in beautiful Glen Affric and is somewhat overshadowed by the considerably bigger Munros to its north and west. It is sometimes climbed as an afterthought by those doing the shorter Toll Creagach and Tom a' Chòinich Munro round but is generally either climbed on its own, or with one of the other nearby Grahams with a short drive in between.

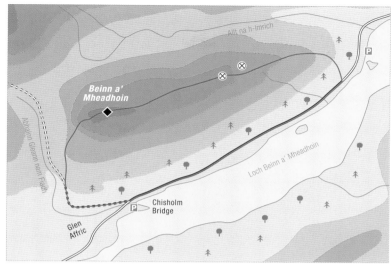

Although a pleasant outing at any time of day, it makes a lovely evening walk and a fine place from which to appreciate Glen Affric, especially so in autumnal colours.

The walk starts from the car park at Chisholm Bridge about three quarters of the way along Loch Beinn a' Mheadhoin. Cross the road and follow the track above the Abhainn Gleann nam Fiadh, which is the approach to the Munros. However, after 1km break off right just past the last trees to find a vague atv track and climb to the rocky summit of Beinn a' Mheadhoin (**2.5km; 380m; 1h 10min**). Whilst this may be a small hill, it is a grand summit with an even grander view.

Rather than return the same way (**5km; 380m; 1h 45min**), and if not dashing off for another hill, a lovely walk can be had by descending east along the ridge onto a small knoll. Drop down in front of another knoll to the north-east and cross a deer fence by a stile at NH232259. Continue east close to the shoulder of the hill to enter woodland and drop down south-east on a rough path to emerge onto the road at NH242258 by a large pine, about 500m south of the Loch Beinn a' Mheadhoin car park. A pleasant 3km stroll along the road leads back to Chisholm Bridge (**8km; 380m; 2h 30min**).

Beinn a' Mheadhoin from Glen Affric (Rab Anderson)

SECTION 12
Loch Mullardoch to Glen Carron

Approaching Càrn na Breabaig, centre foreground, along Glen Elchaig (Rab Anderson)

Càrn na Breabaig; 679m; (G132); L25; NH066301; hill of the little brae 'braigh beag' or hill of the little separate hill 'breab beag'

Hidden away at the head of Glen Elchaig, this hill is overshadowed by its larger neighbours and as a result is not often climbed. It stands astride the main east-west watershed and has commanding views down Glen Elchaig and along lonely Loch Mullardoch. The best approach is to bike to the head of Glen Elchaig from where the peak is but a short ascent. It can easily be combined with an ascent of the Munro, An Socach, or the remote Graham, An Cruachan (see p229).

The cycle route starts from a car park at Killilan (NG940303) where a tarmac estate road leaves the public road. The walking route starts at the end of the public road 2km further on, at a car park at Camus-luinie (NG948283) where a footpath leads to a bridge over the river to join the cycle route. Both routes then lead beneath the Graham of Carnan Cruithneachd (p215) and the Falls of Glomach; the latter being worth a detour, time and energy allowing (**13km; 130m, 1h 30min** by bike); (**11km; 130m, 2h 40min** on foot).

Leave the glen at a rather neglected-looking Iron Lodge and follow the zigzag track uphill before breaking off up the south-west ridge

of the mountain. The ascent is mainly grassy and passes a lochan near the summit (**3.5km; 560m; 1h 45min** from Iron Lodge); (**7km; 560m; 2h 40min**) plus (**26km; 130m 2h 30min** by bike) or (**22km; 130m, 5h 20min** on foot).

If continuing to the Graham of An Cruachan, there are two routes. One descends north-east to Loch Mhoicean onto the track going north-east down the glen, before climbing

to the broad bealach of Màm Ruisgte south of the summit (**7km; 360m; 2h 20min** from Càrn na Breabaig). Alternatively climb Meall Shuas to the east then contour north across the west slope of An Socach (steep at first) to Màm Ruisgte; more pleasant if the weather is good (**7.5km; 520m; 2h 40min** from Càrn na Breabaig). Return to Iron Lodge via the track past Loch Mhoicean.

Càrn Gorm; 677m; (G138); L26; NH328355; *blue hill*

Càrn Gorm is rather overlooked by most hillwalkers on their way to the bigger peaks to the west. However, it occupies a handy niche of wild land, ideal for a short day from the village of Cannich. The shortest approach to the summit is from Glen Cannich to the south although the preferred route is from Glen Strathfarrar to the north. This is longer but more aesthetic, climbing through attractive Scots pine woodland and offering the potential for a good circuit of the whole massif, from Sgòrr na Ruadhraich in the west round to Càrn a' Mhuilt in the north.

Drive up Glen Strathfarrar to park in a lay-by at NH329396, roughly 7.7km from the gatehouse. For access information to the glen see opposite. It is possible to park in the car park at Inchmore and use a bike, thereby not being reliant on the gate times.

Walk back east along road for about 100m to a small path leading off right down to a footbridge across the River Farrar at NH330397; the

Pollcherian Bridge. Follow a path (indistinct in places) through the pine forest to the right of the Allt Coire nam Bràthan. At NH326384 there is a clearing with a deer fence and stile. Do not cross the stile but rather follow the fence to the left (south-west) parallel to the burn, emerging from the trees onto flatter, boggy ground. After another 1.5km or so cross the burn and climb to the top of Sgòrr na Ruadhraich. Continue eastwards over heather and grass to a well-made cairn at the summit of Càrn Gorm (**6.5km; 690m, 2h 40min**).

Although a direct descent can be made to the north to pick up a path and rejoin the approach route, a more pleasant return continues along the ridge north-eastwards. This leads over the east top to Càrn a' Mhuilt then to the path at NH342374 in front of Càrn nam Barran. This is followed west then north-west beside the burn back to the trees where the approach route is joined after fording

the Allt Coire nam Brathan (13.5km; 770m; 4h 20min). This route could be linked to the Corbett of Sgòrr na Diollaid (5km; 430m; 1h 50min from Càrn Gorm), although this circuit is

Càrn Gorm from the flanks of Sgòrr na Ruadhraich (Rab Anderson)

Vehicular access to the road up Glen Strathfarrar is restricted all year round (Noel Williams)

perhaps better done from Glen Cannich.

The ascent from Glen Cannich is made from Craskie, 4.5km from Cannich. It is a shorter approach and more easily combined with Sgòrr na Diollaid. Parking is limited and perhaps best at a small pull-off about 100m west of the track to Craskie. Cross the causeway and follow the track to Craskie house, skirting round the west side of the garden to the bridge crossing the burn. Aim directly uphill on the west side of the wooded ravine onto the open hill, passing a tall cairn on the way to reach Pt.638m; rough going in places. Descend to the lochan and so to the summit (**4km; 620m; 2hr**). Return via Sgòrr na Ruadhraich (**8.5km; 720m; 3h 20min**).

To climb Sgòrr na Diollaid, head west, over or round Sgòrr na Ruadhraich, then pass to the north of the small Loch Càrn na Toiteill and climb to the rocky summit (**5km; 430m; 1h 50min** from Càrn Gorm). Return towards the small lochan then go over, or round Càrn na Toiteill and descend to Crask (**9km; 450m; 3h** from Càrn Gorm).

Càrn Gorm can also be climbed direct from Cannich; useful for those without transport. Start up the edge of the forestry 500m north-east of the village on the A831 to Beauly.

Strathfarrar Access

The road up Glen Strathfarrar is private. There is a locked gate at its start (NH394406), at Inchmore near Struy Bridge. Vehicular access is restricted but access on foot and by bike is unaffected. There is a parking area on the left at Inchmore. For current access information check the Mountaineering Council of Scotland (MCofS) website, <www.mcofs.org.uk/strathfarrar-access.asp>

Summer Access: This is controlled by a gate-keeper. At the time of writing access is available from about Easter to 31 Oct, from 9am until dusk (Apr 6pm; May 7pm; Jun, 8pm; Jul 8pm; Aug 8pm; Sept 7pm; Oct 6pm). The glen is closed to vehicles all day Tues and until 1.30pm on Wed.

Winter Access: The gate is locked and there is no gatekeeper. Access is only available by telephone arrangement with the MCofS (01738 493942). At the time of writing this is 1 Nov to late Mar. The following information is required; date of visit, car registration; occupant's names and a telephone contact number. A combination number for a lock on the gate will be issued. This number is changed regularly, so call the MCofS every time a visit is planned. Each trip under the winter arrangements has to be notified to the MCofS – there is no need to notify the MCofS of summer access. Do not leave calls until the morning of the visit. The best times to call are between 10.30am and 3pm.

Access Rights: These apply to the glen using non-motorised vehicles at all times of day or night and include wild camping (away from road and buildings). These rights apply to responsible behaviour under the Scottish Outdoor Access Code and includes using the Hillphones service to check possible restrictions during the stalking season. These rights do not extend to vehicles and overnight parking is not permitted in the glen. Anyone wishing to stay overnight should walk in, bike in or arrange to be dropped off and the vehicle driven out of the glen.

Notes: A maximum of 25 vehicles are permitted in the glen on a given day. Last vehicle access is one hour before closing time. Vehicles can be taken to the Loch Monar Dam, across it and 3km further to the Uisge Misgeach power station at NH183381.

The road through the glen (twisty, potholed single track with passing places) is some 25km long and it takes about 40min to drive its length. Plan this into your walk itinerary!

Beinn na Muice from the Loch Monar dam (Meryl Marshall)

Beinn na Muice; *695m; (G112); L25; NH 218402; mountain of the pig*

This fine little rocky peak is situated above the Monar Dam at the head of Glen Strathfarrar. It lies at the centre of a large tract of country which holds some of Scotland's remotest Munros. Beinn na Muice is in fact an extension of the Strathfarrar Munros and can easily be included with the westernmost of these, or indeed at the end of the full traverse of four Munros and two Munro Tops where the southward running ridge leads to it from Sgùrr na Fearstaig to provide a fitting finale (**4km; 290m; 1h 30min** from Sgùrr na Fearstaig). It can also be combined with Càrn Gorm, the other short Strathfarrar Graham. However, it does offer a good short day in its own right.

Drive up Glen Strathfarrar and 2.5km east of the Monar Dam park at NH224392 at the foot of the track which follows the west bank of the Allt Toll a' Mhuic. Climb the track and after 1.3km, at the Eas na Muice waterfall, leave it and ascend the steep east spur of Beinn na Muice. A grassy gully provides easier going and

although it has a couple of short, steep sections these can easily be bypassed on the south side. The final 500m of ascent is along a pleasant gently rising ridge with several rocky knolls. The summit itself has a small cairn (**2.5km; 540m; 1h 30min**). There are outstanding views of Maoile Lunndaidh and its neighbours to the west, the Mullardoch hills to the south-west and the Strathfarrar hills

to the north-east.

Complete the traverse by going westwards along the broad rocky ridge for a further 500m. The views across Loch Monar are impressive. The quickest descent is via the south-west spur to the 330m bealach with Meall an Tairbh (which can be ascended) then go south-east down a small glen to the road which is followed back (**6.5km; 540m; 2h 35min**).

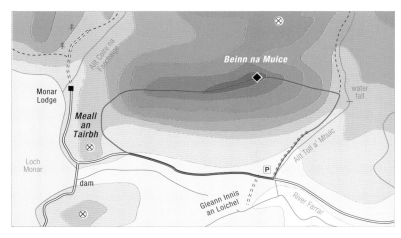

An Cruachan; 705m; (G90); L25; NH093358; the little heap

An Cruachan is one of the most remote Grahams. It has a lonely feel with superb views, rarely climbed except by dedicated hill-goers. Its central location gives a choice of possible routes. The fastest approach is probably from Glen Strathfarrar in the east. Start from the end of the road at the parking area at the Uisge Misgeach power station (NH183381). Walk west along a track then take the good path which continues south-west, uphill by the cascading burn, to peter out at NH137365 just short of the Clach an Daimh bealach. From there it is 4.5km to the summit of An Cruachan, westwards over the col and across an open expanse of rough country – not for the faint-hearted! There are occasional peat hags, some with remnant stumps of ancient trees. Whilst a little off route, a small bridge across the Allt Riabhachain at NH117371 could be useful if the burns are in spate, although there are no bridges across the other burns.

Ascend the grassy east slopes of the hill to the col below the summit cone then turn south-west up the

ridge which is pleasant underfoot (**10km; 630m; 3h 30min**). The summit has a conical cairn, surprisingly well built for such a remote spot. Return the same way (**20km; 740m; 5h 50min**). In good weather, lovers of solitude who have come this far might wish to continue to the outlying top of Beinn Bheag to the north-east (**2km; 100m; 45min** from An Cruachan), bearing in mind the added time and the Strathfarrar gate closing time. See Strathfarrar Access

information on p227.

The other main route to An Cruachan is from Glen Elchaig to the south-west, starting at Killilan at the head of Loch Long. Although longer than the eastern approach, it is an easy bike ride to Iron Lodge. The Graham Càrn na Breabaig can easily be included in this route; see the start of this Section for approach details and times to Iron Lodge.

From Iron Lodge, a footpath follows the Allt na Doire Ghairbh and continues past Loch Mhoicean. About 3km after the loch, break off up the slopes to the Màm Ruisgte bealach, south of An Cruachan. A short, steep pull leads to the summit (**9km; 700m; 3h 10min** from Iron Lodge); (**18km; 780m; 5h 35min**). Including Càrn na Breabaig in this route only adds a total of **1km, 240m** and **45min** by returning to the north end of Loch Mhoicean then climbing to the summit. Traversing up and across An Socach to Meall Shuas then dropping down to climb Càrn na Breabaig adds **1.5km, 260m** and **55min**.

Another approach is from Attadale on Loch Carron to the west, via tracks past Bendronaig Lodge. Bikes can be used to NH044393 by Loch Calavie between Beinn Dronaig and Lurg Mhòr (**16km; 500m; 2h**); harder biking but a quick return. This route has the disadvantage of a potentially tricky river crossing just past Loch Calavie (**6.5km; 550m; 2h 25min** from the bike); (**13km; 650m 4h 15min**).

An Cruachan from An Riabhachan (Rab Anderson)

***Càrn na Còinnich**; 673m; (G142); L26; NH324510; hill of the moss;*
***Meall nan Damh** (twin); 673m; L26; NH353522*

Càrn na Còinnich is an unusual Graham in being the highest point of a rolling plateau of peaks, three others of which are within 2m of the height of the main summit. Indeed, Meall nan Damh is also accorded 673m on the OS 1:25k map, so there may be merit in climbing this. However, an unratified survey has measured Meall nan Damh at 670.1m and confirmed Càrn na Coinnich as the summit at 673.4m.

Start from the small car park at Milton Mill (NH304552) on the north side of the Strathconon road, 500m past the school in the village of Milton. Go west for 100m, cross the bridge over the River Meig and walk through the Dalbreac Lodge estate buildings. Swing left then after 100m take the track leading uphill to a fork at a burn. The left fork is the return route, giving an easier but less interesting line of ascent (**6km; 560m; 2h 15min**). Instead, go right and follow the track until it enters forestry at NH302539.

Strike south up heathery slopes to the right of the burn, cross a flat area, then either pass to the left of Creag a' Choire Riabhaich to gain the ridge, or climb steeply onto the ridge to its right. The ridge gives a pleasant and scenic route to the top of Meall Doire Fheara (671m); a good viewpoint from which to survey the Corbetts of Meallan nan Uan and Sgùrr a' Mhuilinn across the trench of Strathconon.

Continue south on easy terrain, crossing through the gap between Loch an Daimh Ghlais and Loch Gruamach, then follow a mossy ridge to the stark summit trig point of Càrn na Còinnich (**6km; 630m; 2h 30min**). The view is extensive but less interesting than that from Meall Doire Fheara. To return, descend the mossy shoulder gently northwards for 500m to avoid some crags, then drop east and climb to a track. This is followed steeply down into Strathconon, going left at the fork (**12km; 630m; 4h**).

For the enhanced outing, gain the track then cross over and traverse round the south side of a knoll past a sometimes lily-bedecked lochan to climb Càrn Uilleim (651m). Drop north-east, passing the outflow of Loch na Caillich, then make a rising traverse to reach point 637m. Descend to a col and climb by an old fenceline to the summit of Meall nan Damh (673m), (**10km; 900m; 3h 50min**).

To return, follow the fenceline along the tops to Meall a' Bhogair Mòr (672m) then descend west for 500m onto the track which leads back via the left fork. (**17.5km; 1000h; 5h 50min**).

An alternative starting point is from a gated track entrance at Bridgend at NH323549 from where the track is followed west for just over 1km to a track which connects to the one used in the descent route described above.

Càrn na Còinnich from Meall Doire Fheara (Rab Anderson)

Meall na Faochaig; *681m; (G129); L25; NH257525; hill of the shell, or spiral*

Meall na Faochaig from above Inverchoran (Rab Anderson)

Ghlas. On a clear day the outline of the hills of Torridon and the Fannaichs form a tremendous panoramic backdrop to the vast spaces of moorland lying to the north-west. Most descend by the same route (7km; 560m; 2h 35min), especially if also climbing Beinn Mheadhoin.

Alternatively, extend the route by following Meall na Faochaig's north-west ridge past scenic Lochan na Croraig and over some peat hags to the heathery top of Cnap na Feola (579m) before dropping to the east end of Loch Beannacharain by the shoulder of Meall Dubh and the Allt a' Chàrnaich (16km; 650m; 5h). The steep south-east ridge of the hill provides a shorter circuit, down the side of Creag na Sàile to reach the road 400m from the start.

M eall na Faochaig is situated on the north side of the River Meig where it bends north-east after exiting Loch Beannacharain at the far end of Strathconon. It is an accessible and relatively undemanding hill which has been helpfully equipped with a stalkers' path to make the ascent even easier. Beinn Mheadhoin, the third of the Strathconon Grahams, sits on the opposite side of the glen above Inverchoran (see p232).

Parking is common to both hills, at the start of the track to Inverchoran (NH261508) and also down by the bridge. Walk west along the road for 300m and use the stalkers' path to gain height by a big dogleg up the hillside to where it terminates at a col. It is worth making a detour to visit Creag Iucharaidh (388m) for the striking views down and across the glen.

Return to the end of the path then climb the shallow south spur of Meall na Faochaig. This leads to the main ridge and a fenceline which is followed eastwards for 500m or so towards the summit cairn (**3.5km; 560m; 1h 40min**). There is a very fine view across the deep forested trench of Gleann Mèinich to Meallan nan Uan and the rocky crags of Creag

Beinn Mheadhoin and Bac an Eich, far right, from the east (Jim Teesdale)

Beinn Mheadhoin; *665m; (G153); L25; NH258477; middle mountain*

Lying on the south side of upper Strathconon above Inverchoran farm, Beinn Mheadhoin appears as a rolling area of hillside with no obvious summit to draw the eye. This is deceptive, although the hill's finest characteristics are reserved to the few who cross over into remote Glen Orrin to enjoy its southern features which include the craggy flanks of Creag a' Ghlastail.

Park as for Meall na Faochaig (see p231), at the start of the track to Inverchoran (NH260508), or down by the bridge. Follow the track over the bridge and circumnavigate Inverchoran farm by gates to its west.

Cross a bridge and follow the Gleann Chorainn track for 300m, then take the left fork which leads steeply up and round to the east of Creagan a' Chaorainn. There are good views north looking back over Strathconon to Meall na Faochaig and Meallan nan Uan.

About 100m after fording a burn, a stalkers' path leaves the track at NH267487 (not shown on the OS 1:50k map). Follow this path west-south-west onto a spur until it peters out at around NH263484 then continue up the spur and heathery slopes to the summit (**4km; 520m; 1h 45min**).

The upper part of the hill has a number of undulations and false tops which may confuse the unwary in poor visibility. The summit cairn is on an outcrop and gives fine views west to Bac an Eich and south across Glen Orrin to the North Glen Strathfarrar ridge.

Most return the same way (**8km; 520m, 2h 45min**) although a pleasant extension takes in the West Top (627m) whose summit sits amongst a number of craggy knolls. From here, descend north-east past the end of a tiny lochan then climb onto the triple topped summit of Creagan a' Chaorainn (552m). Either descend steeply

east back onto the track used on the ascent, or descend north towards Inverchoran a short way before heading right to pick up the track (**9km; 640m; 3h 15min**).

A longer option goes down the knolly south-west ridge via the West Top to reach the col at Torran Ceann Liath from where the Corbett of Bac an Eich (849m) can be climbed by its southern slopes (**9.5km; 990m; 3h 50min**). Either return to the col and go down the path through Gleann Chorainn or descend the ridge south-east then east to join this path further on (**15km; 990m; 5h 15min**).

Rather than climb Bac an Eich, an easier option from the col at Torran Ceann Liath is to return down Gleann Chorainn to Inverchoran, or drop south to Loch na Caoidhe and walk east along the Glen Orrin path to reach the end of the track used in the ascent.

See preceeding page for map

Creag Dhubh Mhòr; 612m; (G218); L25; NG982404; big black cliff

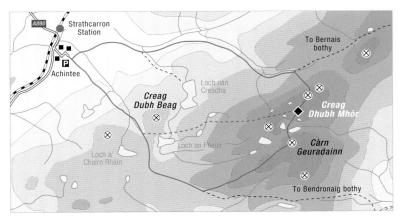

Creag Dhubh Mhòr marks the high point of a large tract of relatively unfrequented hill country between Strathcarron and the glen to the east which contains the bothies at Bendronaig and Bearnais. The hills are generally heathery and grassy but Creag Dhubh Mhòr is the culmination of a complex area of craggy knolls and lochans, bounded on its north-west side by a steep face. Traversing it provides an interesting and challenging exercise in route finding, particularly in poor visibility. On a clear day the views to the north and west are particularly rewarding.

Several excellent hill paths serve the area and a clockwise traverse of the hill makes good use of these. Start at Achintee (NG942417) where there is limited parking (beside the substation is a possibility). Achintee is 400m to the south of Strathcarron station and the timing of the trains is convenient if travelling from the east.

Follow the signposts through Achintee and past the electricity sub-station and 50m beyond a gate take the small path on the left signposted to Bearnais bothy. Cross a stile then a small burn and join the original path coming up the north side of this burn.

After 2km take the left fork across a burn and continue for 3km. Leave the path at NG982412 and head for a broad grassy gully in the crags on the right. This provides relatively easy going to a col just 600m to the north-east of the summit. Thereafter a further 100m of ascent, initially steep and then over a false top, gains the summit (**5.5km; 600m; 2h 10min**).

The shortest and the safest descent if the visibility is poor and route finding abilities are in doubt is west-south-west passing two small lochans and then westward to Loch an Fheòir to join the path from Bendronaig to Achintee (10.5km; 600m; 3h 30min).

However, continuing over Càrn Geuradainn (594m), 800m to the south-south-west of Creag Dhubh Mhòr, gives a more complete day. From the summit take a south-westerly line aiming between two lochans for a col at NG979400. It is then a short ascent to the trig point on Càrn Geuradainn. The south-west ridge gives an easy and interesting descent; avoid the steeper lower section by heading westward to gain the Bendronaig path (12km; 670m; 4h).

Looking north across Coire Odhar to the summit of Creag Dubh Mhòr (Meryl Marshall)

SECTION 13
Glen Carron to Loch Maree

Beinn na Feusaige from Coille Bhreac (Rab Anderson)

Càrn Breac; *678m; (G136); L25; NH045530; speckled hill*
Beinn na Feusaige; *627m; (G198); L25; NH090542; mountain of the beard*

Càrn Breac and Beinn na Feusaige form a substantial and heathery retaining wall along the north side of the upper reaches of Glen Carron. The starting point for the ascent of both hills is to the south-west of Achnasheen, on the A890 to Lochcarron, where a loop of the old road leaves the main road at NH091530 at the west end of Loch Sgamhain. There is limited parking to the side of a locked gate here, as well as to the side of the access road to Loan on the opposite side of the road.

The most worthwhile route makes a clockwise circuit of the hills around the Allt Coire Crubaidh. Cross the gate and walk along the old road, then go over the bridge and immediately go through a gate in the deer fence into an area of regenerating woodland. Ascend rough ground through this and exit the enclosure by the gate at NH080528, which can be seen from the start, just south of the corner of the older plantation. Ascend tussocky slopes onto Coille Bhreac. The terrain becomes easier as height is gained and fine views of Moruisg and Sgùrr nan Ceannaichean open up to the south.

Continue along the top of Coille Bhàn then swing round past the head of the narrow Coire Dubh-riabhach to gain the upper slopes of Càrn Breac ▶

Trig point and shelter on the summit of Càrn Breac (Rab Anderson)

where a rising traverse leads northwards to the summit (**6km; 530m; 2h 15min**). This final section crosses featureless slopes, where navigation could be challenging in poor visibility.

Càrn Breac's stone trig point and surrounding shelter provide an excellent grandstand from which to appreciate the superb panorama. To the west is the triple-peaked Beinn Liath Mhòr, with Sgòrr Ruadh rising behind and Fuar Tholl to the side, then the Torridon hills, Beinn Eighe and Liathach, which are seen across Loch Coulin. North is the Graham Beinn a' Mhùinidh with Slioch behind, then the Letterewe and Fisherfield hills with the Grahams, Beinn Bheag and Groban easily picked out. Not so readily identifiable are the Grahams Meall a' Chaorainn and Beinn nan Ramh lying in front of the Fannaichs and to the side of Fionn Bheinn. To the east are the Strathconan peaks then south, Moruisg, Sgùrr nan Ceannaichean and yet more hills.

Head north-east, gradually descending the long crest, then swing east and climb easily over Meallan Mhic Iamhair (499m) to reach the outflow of Lochan Meallan Mhic Iamhair. Beinn na Feusaige rises above and is gained by a steady 230m climb beside an old fence. Just below the summit area are the remains of a Martin B-26 Marauder which crashed in June 1943.

The top is located at the west end of the flat summit area, to the south-west of a small lochan (**11.5km; 830m; 4h**). The OS 1:25k and 1:50k maps show a lower 625m height some 300m further east. The view is less fine that that from Càrn Breac.

To return, descend west for 1km, then veer south-west and drop steeply down a narrow, heathery buttress between two burns, to the west of a plantation, to a gain the end of a track which is followed back to the road (**14.5km; 830m; 5h**).

Càrn Breac can be approached by the track and path on the north bank of the Allt Coire Crubaidh. The path forks at the midway point at NH063538 by some old shielings and the right fork climbs steeply to run out on the north-east slopes, leaving easy walking to the summit. The rest of the route is as previously described. There is little difference in distance and time between the routes.

Càrn Breac from Meallan Mhic Iamhair (Rab Anderson)

The summit of Sgùrr a' Gharaidh from the east (Jim Teesdale)

Sgùrr a' Gharaidh; *732m; (G45); L24, 25; NG884443; peak of the cave or den*

With its outlying subsidiaries, Sgùrr a' Gharaidh is an extensive hill which couples a fine location with some rugged and exciting scenery. The hill's fine northern features are not obvious until after the A896 leaves Kishorn and heads towards Shieldaig.

The best starting point is from Loch an Loin; parking at a passing place at NG852447, or 20m down the track to the loch. Walk along the track past the keeper's cottage and turn right after 1km to enter an enclosed section of regenerating birch wood. The track deteriorates to a rough atv track which traverses through Coille Dhubh and stops at a small bridge over the Allt a' Ghiubhais at NG882455. The map suggests that this point can be reached by the Bealach a' Ghlas-chnoic path, but on the ground whilst the path is good initially it fades, so the track is the better option.

Cross the burn and follow the line of the path under the rocky flanks of Sgùrr a' Gharaidh. After 1km, re-cross the burn at NG893450 and follow a tributary south-south-east to a grassy flattening just west of a lochan at NG896447. Climb a scree shoot directly above to reach the upper slopes at NG896443. Locating this

scree shoot requires precise navigation in mist or in descent and suitable equipment in winter.

Having reached the upper slopes, made up of a confusing area of knolls, lochans, burns and gentle moorland, it is worth taking in Glas Bheinn. To do so, head south-south-east past a lochan to reach the trig point (711m) which gives a fine view down to Loch Carron then return north to the actual top of Glas Bheinn (729m). Continue north-west past another lochan onto the top of Creag na h-Iolaire, then descend south-west.

Now follow the ridge west for 1km, past a series of lochans and steeply climb Sgùrr a' Gharaidh's summit

cone, passing another lochan (**9km; 860m; 3h 30min**). There is a fine view south-west over Loch Carron to Skye, north-east to the Coulin hills, and westwards into the jaws of Beinn Bhàn's corries.

The quickest descent heads west for 2.2km to Cnoc nam Broc at NG863437, the initial descent being rough and rocky. From there, drop down easy slopes to the Loch an Loin track and back to the road (**13km; 860m; 4h 25min**). For those wishing to climb Sgùrr a' Gharaidh quickly, this descent serves as the way up, although this misses out the hill's finest features (**4km; 680m; 2h**); (**8km; 700m; 3h 10min**).

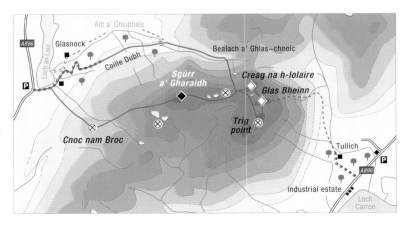

Beinn a' Chlachain; 626m; (G199); L24; NG724490; mountain of the clachan (church hamlet)

Like the nearby village of Applecross, from which it is separated by Applecross Bay, Beinn a' Chlachain is a secluded secret, only discovered by those prepared to pass the more obvious delights of Beinn Bhàn and Sgùrr a' Chaorachain. It is also a journey to get there starting from sea level at Loch Kishorn, crossing over the Bealach na Bà pass, at 620m the highest in Britain, then dropping back down to the sea again at Applecross.

Since the hill itself provides a relatively short outing it is worth taking the day to explore the Applecross Peninsula and savour the scenery. Applecross itself has a fascinating history and much can be learned about this at the Heritage Centre at Clachan.

Most of Beinn a' Chlachain is tussocky and undulating with long slopes, sprinkled with lochans, that run north-west down to the sea. However, on its south-east side the slopes drop steeply by terraced sandstone tiers into Srath Maol Chaluim and this is the where the hill is best approached from.

Start at the north end of Applecross Bay, from the beach parking area opposite the Heritage Centre car park. Walk along the road for 300m then take the road and track up cultivated Srath Maol Chaluim for 3km. This runs alongside the River Applecross and passes the Venture Trust buildings at Hartfield. Leave the track at the east corner of a forestry plantation (NG731477) and head uphill to gain the western edge of Coire Glas, a fine recess which bites deep into the side of the mountain. The angle, though steep, is never excessive and relents at around 530m. Easy walking then leads past a scenic small lochan to the summit trig point and its stone enclosure (5km; 630m; 2h 10min). An alternative is to go up the right side of Coire Glas to climb Meall an Doireachain, then traverse to the top.

There are fantastic views across the Inner Sound to Rona and Raasay then across the Sound of Rassay to Skye. There are glimpses through to Torridon as well. The descent can be by the same route (10km; 630m, 3h 30min), particularly if the approach has been facilitated by mountain bike.

However, it is better to make the most of the hill by walking down its long south-west ridge towards Applecross Bay, reaching Pt.402m after about 2.5km. Continue down the ridge past a large cairn then make a short and steep descent onto the coast path to Sand which leads to a parking area and alternative start point on the road just beyond Cruarg. A brief walk leads back along the road to the start (10km; 650m; 3h 30min).

Beinn a' Chlachain from the Bealach na Bà road (Tom Prentice)

Liathach from the summit of Beinn na h-Eaglaise (Rab Anderson)

Beinn na h-Eaglaise; *736m; (G37); L24, 25; NG908523; mountain of the church*

What it lacks in height, Beinn na h-Eaglaise more than makes up for with the superb views it provides of its better known neighbours, from its central Torridonian position.

Start from the large car park at The Torridon Inn (NG889541), signposted 'Beinn Damh Hill Track' from the A896 Torridon to Shieldaig road. The initial part of this route is the same as for Beinn Damh. Walk west along the road through the rear courtyard to a bridge over the Allt Coire Roill. Cross over then turn left onto a signposted path leading through woodland to reach the main road.

On the other side, go up a stalkers' path that disappears into the rhododendrons. The path climbs uphill above a gorge with waterfalls, through beautiful natural pine forest to emerge onto the more open, Caledonian pine and boulder-strewn hillside. Take the left fork at NG884533 and when this reaches the river, head upstream a little to make the crossing. To regain the path on the far side, go downstream for 50m.

Follow the path for another 600m onto the flanks of Beinn na h-Eaglaise then leave it and gain the

ridge above. This becomes better defined as height is gained, although it is rough and offers short sections of easy scrambling on sandstone. The views to Beinn Damh and behind over Upper Loch Torridon to Beinn Alligin are excellent. The angle eases off towards the top (**4km; 710m; 2h 5min**). It is a superb viewpoint from which to appreciate the grandeur of the surrounding Torridonian scenery.

Descend rough, stony ground south-west to pass between a chain of lochans and climb onto the South Top (676m). Continue down, crossing a fine sandstone table, to reach the path by a small lochan at the Drochaid Coire Roill bealach. The quickest return is down the Coire Roill path (**10.5km; 750m; 3h 40min**).

An alternative from the summit, is to descend the south-south-east ridge to Loch an Eion to pick up the Glen Carron to Torridon path. This leads to the road at Annat, passing below Beinn na h-Eaglaise's craggy eastern flanks (**11.5km; 710m; 3h 50min**).

From the Drochaid Coire Roill an excellent hill extension climbs to the 903m summit of Beinn Damh via its east ridge (**7km; 1180m; 3h 35min**) and traverses the length of that peak northwards before returning to the path then to the car park (**14km; 1430m; 5h 45min**).

An Ruadh-mheallan from the south (Jim Teesdale)

An Ruadh-mheallan; 671m; (G144); L19, 24; NG836614; the little red hill

Located on the doorstep of one of the country's grandest mountain arenas and usually overlooked by the hillwalker, An Ruadh-mheallan is a subtle hill worthy of exploration. A generally grassy peak with a steep sandstone summit cone, it rises north of the Diabaig road to the west of Beinn Alligin.

The approach starts from the aptly named Bealach na Gaoithe (pass of the wind) at the highpoint of the twisty single track road between Torridon and Diabaig. There is a layby at NG824592 (2 - 3 cars) with a bench overlooking Loch Diabaigas Airde, just before the road starts the descent to Diabaig. There is also parking at the viewpoint 500m downhill to the south.

Head north, then cross a mixed landscape of heather, knolls and lochans to pass west of Loch nan Tri-eileanan. Continue north-east on gently rising rough ground, then climb more steeply north to a small lochan at NG834611. The final climb up the summit cone is steeper still, with some avoidable scrambling, leading to large sandstone platforms (**3km; 430m; 1h 20min**). The view is tremen-

dous, stretching across the Minch and the Sound of Raasay to Skye with the Western Isles beyond. There is also a good perspective of the Coulin

hills and Beinn Damh. Beinn Alligin blocks the view east, from this side a grassy monolith, although the Graham Beinn a' Chearcaill is visible beyond this.

To descend, continue by the east shoulder for 500m, and on gaining a flattish spur, turn south-east and drop into An Reidh-choire. Descend its north-west side to a burn junction and shieling at NG838602. Climb briefly south-west to pass south of Loch nan Tri-eileanan and then continue south-west to regain the road (7km; 470m; 2h 30min).

For those willing to sort out the logistics, a great extension from the summit is to head east then north-east to Meall na h-Odhar-aghaidh (537m) and then east and north-east to Creag a' Chinn Duibh (675m), (**6km; 670m; 2h 30min**).

This provides fine views of the Toll nam Biast cliffs on the north side of Beinn Alligin, as well as Beinn Dearg and Liathach. Head east-south-east amidst dramatic scenery, passing between the Horns of Alligin and Beinn Dearg by the Bealach a' Chomhla. Descend by the Horns of Alligin path to the Coire Mhic Nobuil car park (13km; 670m; 4h).

Beinn a' Chearcaill; 725m; (G58); L19; NG930637; mountain of the circle

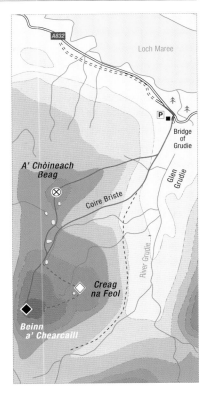

Beinn a' Chearcaill will often be observed from the main Torridon summits as a low, well-defended peak with an intriguingly flat summit. The usual approach is from the A832 Kinlochewe to Gairloch road by Loch Maree, from which side the hill is overshadowed by Beinn Eighe. The northern slopes are gentle and featureless so the walk is best saved for a good day which also allows the quality of the views and the unusual summit to be fully appreciated.

Start from a pull-off on the old road at NG962680. This is 500m west of Bridge of Grudie, the bridge over the river at the mouth of Glen Grudie. Walk south-east along the road to the white cottage then follow a good stalkers' path up Glen Grudie for about 2km. Shortly before the path dips into Coire Briste, a less distinct path branches off right at NG953661 (cairn). Follow this as it makes a gradual rising traverse up the back of the corrie to disappear near the outflow of a teardrop-shaped lochan at NG936653.

The top of the hill lies 1.8km south, reached by a gentle climb up rough heathery slopes liberally covered in large blocks (**6km; 700m; 2h 30min**). It is easy enough to detour east on the final ascent to include the outlying top of Creag na Feol (641m) as a slightly longer but varied route. The striking summit area is composed of a vast sandstone platform, reminiscent of a small airstrip, dotted with boulders.

Jagged Torridonian peaks rise on all southern aspects. There is a fantastic view straight into the jaws of Coire Mhic Fhearchair on Beinn Eighe, whilst Beinn an Eòin rises like a prow to the west.

Return northwards, passing just west of the teardrop-shaped lochan, and rise slightly to A' Chòineach Beag (558m). This gives a great view of Loch Maree and across to Slioch's impressive south-west face. Head east-north-east for 1km to a spur, then trend north-east, dropping gradually back to the Glen Grudie path (**12km; 740m; 4h**).

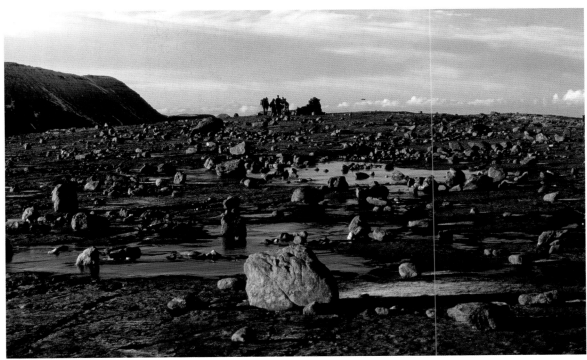

The striking summit of Beinn a' Chearcaill (Jim Teesdale)

SECTION 14
Loch Maree to Loch Broom

Meall a' Chaorainn, left, and Fionn Bheinn from across Loch a' Chroisg (Jim Teesdale)

Meall a' Chaorainn; 705m; (G93); L19, 20, 25; NH136604; hill of the rowan tree

Meall a' Chaorainn is an outlier of the Munro Fionn Bheinn, to which it is connected by a high col. It is a remarkably inconspicuous hill from below but offers a good and easily accessed viewpoint. Start from the railway station parking area in Achnasheen. This is another hill that can be done by train.

Walk to the telephone box on the main road then go up the road to its left, over the bridge and take the first track right, through a gate following signs to the hill. The track runs over the burn to the Achnasheen Water Treatment Works where a path by the burn leads to a gate. Above this, cross back to the west bank of the Allt Achadh na Sine (the path on the east bank is boggy) and climb steadily uphill to where, not far above a small waterfall, the burn enters a level but contorted area of peat hags. After crossing this area in a westerly direction for 800m, a climb of some 180m leads to the small summit cairn (**4km; 560m; 1h 50min**). There is an extensive view towards Torridon, Slioch and the Fisherfield hills. It is an excellent balcony from which to try to name the many peaks spread out to the south.

Although a return can be made the same way (**8km; 560m; 3h**), it is worthwhile extending the day to include Fionn Bheinn. To do this, head north-north-east from Meall a' Chaorainn's summit for 200m, thereby avoiding its steeper eastern slope, then descend into the head of the unappealingly named Coire Bog. Fionn Bheinn (933m) is climbed by a steady grind up its southern slopes (**7km; 980m; 3h 20min**). Descend towards Creagan nan Laogh then regain the Allt Achadh na Sine and return to Achnasheen (**11.5km; 980m; 4h 40min**).

Another approach can be made from verge parking about halfway along Loch a' Chroisg (NH124588). A forest track leads into a plantation by the Allt Duchairidh. Follow this for 1.2km to emerge into patchier forestry and just after a burn crossing make a rough way northwards up the steep hillside just north of a fence. When the angle relents head for the north-west ridge of Meall a' Chaorainn, then its summit (**3.5km; 550m; 1h 40min**). A gentler approach, for those whose knees are no longer under manufacturer's warranty, follows the track to its end where a stalkers' path climbs up the Feadan Duchairidh, then trends north-east. Leave the path at its high point and follow the easy north-west ridge to the summit (**6km; 550m; 2h 15min**). Return by either route (**1h**, or **1h 30min**).

Beinn nan Ramh (see following page), to the north of Fionn Bheinn can be included from Loch a' Chroisg, or indeed from Achnasheen (perhaps even taking in Fionn Bheinn) utilising the stalkers' path which descends into Strath Chrombuill.

Map on following page

Beinn nan Ramh seen from the east across Loch Fannich (Jim Teesdale)

Beinn nan Ramh; *711m; (G78); L19, 20; NH139661; mountain of the oars (or trees)*

A fine and remote hill at the west end of Loch Fannich, Beinn nan Ramh takes the form of a lengthy east to west whaleback ridge and fully repays the effort involved in getting to it.

The best approach uses a track which starts at NH199599, between forestry plantations about 4km east of Achnasheen. The nearest suitable parking is a layby about 1km east of here at Dosmuckeran; although it is possible to squeeze off-road closer to the track. A high metal gate has to be scaled to access the track; especially awkward with a bike, the recommended mode of transport.

The track leads northwards over a low pass with fine views to the Fannaichs then drops to Loch Fannich before turning west to meet the Srath Chrombuill hydro pipeline. Beinn nan Ramh rises ahead. At NH175649, turn right onto a track (unmarked on the OS 1:50k map) which is followed for 800m to NH176655 where the steep east ridge of Beinn nan Ramh is climbed.

The ridge eases and great views open up on both sides and back down Loch Fannich as far as Ben Wyvis. The final 3km to the summit gives easy walking with one short narrow section. A small cairn marks the top (**13.5km; 650m; 4h 5min** on foot). There is a superb and open panoramic view of the Fannaichs, the Fisherfield hills, Beinn Eighe and across Srath Chrombuill to Fionn Bheinn. As Beinn nan Ramh does not easily combine with other hills, return

by the same route (**27km; 720m; 7h 20min** on foot).

Beinn nan Ramh can also be climbed by its south-west flanks, although this lacks the grandeur of the Loch Fannich approach. One route starts from Loch a' Chroisg, west of Achnasheen. Leave the road at NH124588 and follow a track through forestry up the Feadan Duchairidh. This turns into a stalkers' path which crosses the shoulder of Meall a' Chaorainn (see previous page) and drops to the hydro track in Srath Chrombuill. Leave the track,

cross the river and grind up broad slopes to the top (**9km; 840m; 3h 25min**); (**18km; 1130m; 6h 15min**). Meall a' Chaorainn can be taken in on the return, adding 1h to the trip.

Another option starts from the Incheril car park at Kinlochewe (NH037624). Walk or cycle up the track past the Heights of Kinlochewe to its end at Leckie. A stalkers' path continues north-east for 2km to end near a burn. The summit lies a further 3km east across featureless moorland (**12km; 700m; 3h 50min** on foot); (**24km, 730m; 6h 30min** on foot).

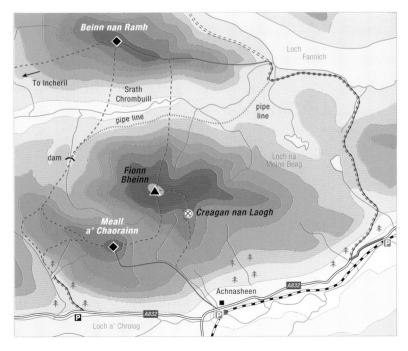

Beinn Bheag; 668m; (G147); L19, 20; NH085713; *little mountain*
Groban; 749m; (G12); L19, 20; NH099708; *little hill, swelling. (It may refer to the large boulder at the summit)*

Beinn Bheag and Groban are a rounded and remote pair of peaks located in the rolling area of lower hills between the Fannaichs and the Fisherfield hills and boast views to match their surroundings.

The least lengthy approach starts from 6km beyond the Braemore Junction on the A832 to Dundonnell where there is parking in a layby at NH162761, just north of the start of a track to Loch a' Bhraoin. This is the same starting place for the western Fannaich Munros and the eastern Fisherfield Munros. Follow the track down to the boathouse at the east end of the loch. The track has been extended along the north shore and although rough, it can be biked (definitely a mountain bike) as far as the cottage and splendid bothy (one that boasts a flushing toilet!) at Lochivraon at the west end of the loch; (1h 20min on foot; 45min by bike). The domes of Beinn Bheag and Groban rise to the south-west of here.

Beinn Bheag is best climbed first by following the rough track then footpath west for a further 1.7km from Lochivraon. At a path junction, cross

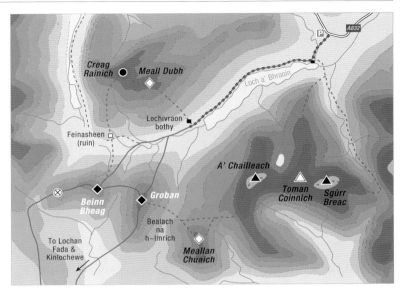

the burn at NH101729, as for the route to the Fisherfield hills, then leave the path and follow the west bank of the burn which leads towards the Bealach Gorm between the hills.

After some boggy ground, leave the burn and climb more steeply southwest. The angle relents and Beinn Bheag's summit is soon reached

(**10km; 420m; 3h**). There is more than one possible summit knoll (OS 1:25k and 1:50k maps show different points 200m apart), although on the ground the western one seems the highest and certainly makes the finer viewpoint. Particularly special are the views north to the turrets of An Teallach, ▶

South-west down Loch a' Bhraoin to Groban, left, and Beinn Bheag (Jim Teesdale)

Groban, left, and Beinn Bheag from the north (Rab Anderson)

the nearer slabby quartzite flanks of Sgùrr Bàn and Mullach Coire Mhic Fhearchair, and the glimpse to Lochan Fada with the pointed craggy peak of Slioch beyond.

Head east down steep grassy slopes to the Bealach Gorm (c470m), then ascend the north-west shoulder of Groban to its summit (**12km; 700m; 4h**). Being a little further removed from the most spectacular hills, Groban's view is not as good as Beinn Bheag's despite its extra height.

The best descent line will be between north and north-east depending on the level of the Abhainn Loch a' Bhraoin which must be forded to regain the approach path. Potentially high, it is best to make the crossing about 1.5km west of Lochivraon, upstream of some meandering loops. Return along the loch (**21.5km; 730m; 6h**).

Those for whom the two Grahams have made a good *hors d'oeuvre*, can make a great return over the western Fannaichs. From the summit of Groban, drop south-east to the Bealach na h-Imrich and either include the interesting Meallan Chuaich (690m) by its sinuous north ridge, or skirt it and head directly towards A' Chailleach. The ascent begins easily but the upper slopes rear up steeply to Ceann Garbh a' Chaillich (908m) where the ridge then leads to A' Chailleach (997m).

Continue to Sgùrr Breac (999m) then descend to the east end of Loch a' Bhraoin, either by backtracking to Toman Coinnich and down the Druim Reidh, or by continuing east to the col with Sgùrr nan Clach Geala and down the stalkers' path.

Another useful extension links Creag Rainich, a Corbett, into a round of the two Grahams, starting with Groban. On the descent from Beinn Bheag aim for the ruin of Feinasheen (NH092730) then climb to the summit of Creag Rainich (807m). Head south-east to Meall Dubh and either drop to the bothy, or descend diagonally to Loch a' Bhraoin, or continue along the ridge before descending.

A longer but perhaps even better day can be enjoyed from Kinlochewe to the south, on a route where a mountain bike is recommended. Start from the Incheril car park at NH037624 and head east up the pretty glen by the Abhainn Bruachaig track. At the Heights of Kinlochewe, fork left up the Gleann na Muice track to its end at NH070667; bikes are left here (**7km; 1h**).

Rather than approach the hills directly by the Meallan Odhar stalkers' path, it is better to continue up the Gleann na Muice path which has been upgraded for its initial 1.5km to a gate at NH063681. Continue on the path towards Lochan

Fada and 1km beyond the gate, strike north over the rough heathery ground of Sìthean Bìorach. There is a sense here of being amongst great and wild mountains; Slioch and A' Mhaighdean across Lochan Fada, the south-west corries of Beinn Tarsuinn and Mullach Coire Mhic Fhearchair ahead.

A line of small cairns marks a sketchy stalkers' path which continues below and east of Loch Meallan an Fhùdair. Drop diagonally to the burn leading to the Bealach na Croise and another vague path is picked up on its east side. Gain the bealach (c420m), or strike uphill earlier, and climb steeply to Beinn Bheag's west top (615m). There is then an easy stroll along the ridge by an old fenceline to the main summit (**14km; 720m; 4h 20min** on foot).

Continue to Groban as already described (**16km; 1000m; 5h 20min**). The descent is via the long south-west slope, following the side of a prominent washed-out gully lower down, to gain the upper flats of Gleann Tanagaidh. Cross the river and locate the end of the stalkers' path at NH081683. If the river is high, use the unmarked bridge at NH082679. This upgraded path climbs over Meallan Odhar then drops to rejoin the track end in Gleann na Muice (**28km; 1140m; 8h 30min** of which 14km can be done by bike).

Beinn a' Mhùinidh; 692m; (G114); L19; NH032660; mountain of pissing. (The huge waterfall dropping to Loch Maree is Allt na Still, burn of spouting)

Sitting at the south-east end of Loch Maree, Beinn a' Mhùinidh has been subjected to massive geological forces. It leans to the east displaying steep crags north-west towards Slioch (the Bonaid Dhonn) and south-west over Loch Maree, the latter containing the impressive Allt na Still waterfall. By contrast, the eastern aspects slope away into rolling moorland and small lochans.

Start from the Incheril car park at NH037624, 1km north-east of Kinlochewe. The best route follows the Loch Maree (and Slioch) footpath north-west for 3km to the burn which descends from the waterfall. Climb by a faint path up through steep heather and bracken on the south side of the burn. Bypass the crags by a heathery gully just south of the waterfall, up which gain a further 100m of height. The angle suddenly eases above the waterfall, on a shelf known as Coire Each.

A fine way to the top is to make a rising traverse of the shelf, trending north for 1km, then scramble through the upper quartzite tier at NH024658. A gentle ridge then leads north-east to the summit in a further 1km (**5.5km; 680m; 2h 20min**). Throughout the ascent there are great views of Slioch and Beinn Eighe, as well as down the length of Loch Maree. The summit adds the Fisherfield and the Fannaichs to the panorama, and all four Grahams covered earlier in this section.

Descend south for just over 2km, passing Meallan Ghobhar on its east – as the name suggests, feral goats may well be seen hereabouts. The direct return crosses the Allt Chnaimhean at around NH038638, where a rough trod traverses above the south side of the burn until clear of the gorge below. Finally, drop steeply down to the Loch Maree path and follow this back to Incheril (10km; 690m; 3h 30min).

An easier descent, and a possibly

tedious route of ascent, can be made to or from the Heights of Kinlochewe track about 1.5km east of the Incheril car park (**6km; 650m; 2h 25min**); (**12km; 650m; 3h 45min**).

The summit of Beinn a' Mhùinidh, centre, and the Allt na Still waterfall (Tom Prentice)

Meall Mhèinnidh, right, and Beinn Làir from the approach (Jim Teesdale)

> **Meall Mhèinnidh; 722m; (G61); L19; NG954748; hill of mining (bog iron was smelted beside Loch Maree)**

To the north of Loch Maree lies a wild and empty area which stretches for more than 20km and flanks the loch with steep slopes rising to a line of stunning mountains, of which Meall Mhèinnidh is the lowest. From the south side of Loch Maree, the hill appears as a gentle cone, sandwiched between its better-known Corbett neighbours Beinn Làir and Beinn Àirigh Charr and its ascent is often combined with one or other of these two hills.

A one-day ascent begins from the car park north of the River Ewe bridge in Poolewe at NG858808 and a bike is recommended. A tarmac road follows the north-east bank of the river for 2km, then a track continues to the keeper's cottage at Kernsary. After a further 500m, take a right fork to enter the forest, where the track deteriorates.

An excellent new footpath (not shown on the OS 1:50k map) exits the forest at NG909789 and regains the line of the original path. Follow this past Loch an Doire Crionaich. The scenery is fabulous, particularly the craggy north face of Beinn Àirigh

Charr above. Continue to Srathan Buidhe and cross the burn by the direct line of the new path; there is a bridge a little further upstream if the water level is high.

Immediately after the crossing, leave the path and gain Meall Mhèinnidh's prominent north-west ridge. Climb this to the top over rough ground, which gives some scrambling on its occasional outcrops (**13.5km; 740m; 4h 15min** on foot). The summit provides a superb view across the Fionn Loch to Ruadh Stac Mòr and A' Mhaighdean, and south across Loch Maree to Torridon. The obvious return is to retrace the outward route (**27km;**

760m; **7h 30min** on foot).

However, an excellent alternative is to drop roughly and directly into Srathan Buidhe and climb Beinn Àirigh Charr (791m) by its easy south-east corrie (**16.5km; 1280m; 6h** on foot).

Descend west, bypassing Spidean nan Clach on its south side, to pick up the stalkers' path at NG923761 which extends further uphill than the map shows. Join a traversing path at NG910771 which can either be followed east to the path junction at NG927773, or west to the Ardlair track at NG893768. Return to Kernsary and Poolewe (**29km; 1300m; 9h** on foot).

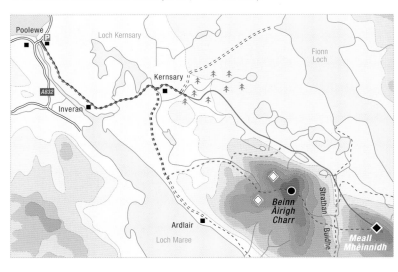

Beinn a' Chàisgein Beag; *682m; (G126); L19; NG965821; possibly big mountain of the tufts from Gaelic 'ceasg', plural 'ceasgan'*

A satellite cone of remote Beinn a' Chàisgein Mòr, any ascent of Beinn a' Chàisgein Beag will be earned the hard way. All one day approaches are long and combinations with its neighbours longer still.

Start from the A832 at NG961912 where a track runs alongside the west bank of the Gruinard River; verge parking. A mountain bike is recommended. The track is rough but there is time to enjoy the beautiful glen and the fine views to Beinn Dearg Bheag. Leave the track after 7km at NG994855, at a bridge over the Allt Loch Ghiubhsachain.

Follow the east bank of the burn and cross it after 1.5km at NG998840. Make a rising traverse southwards across the rough hillside to gain the end of a stalkers' path at the foot of an outcrop at NG994833. Follow this path round to where Beinn a' Chàisgen Beag at last comes into view, and drop down to cross the Uisge Toll a' Mhadaidh. Continue uphill for 1km, passing an unlikely chalet off to the side at NG980821, to a col below the final slope.

Leave the path and climb north-west over heather then mossy

boulders to Beinn a' Chàisgein Beag's trig point; the high point is a few metres south (**13.5km; 720m; 4h 15min** on foot). An isolated summit, the viewpoint is superb, particularly out to sea and across the Fionn Loch to Beinn Àirigh Charr and Beinn Làir with the Graham Meall Mèinn-didh in between.

Return the same way (27km; 790m; 7h 30min on foot, of which 14km can be biked). However, it is worth continuing south from the col over easy slopes to Beinn a' Chàisgein Mòr (856m) then returning by Creag-mheall Mòr (628m) and the rough ridge enclosing Loch Toll a' Mhadaidh. The descent off the north end of this ridge is slow, but leads to the eastern end of the stalkers' path used on the ascent (an added 10km; 520m; 3h 10min).

Another approach starts from the Gruinard beach car park at NG952899. Take the path on the east side of the Inverianvie River to Loch a' Mhadaidh Mòr then cross the Uisge Toll a' Mhadaidh to gain Ceann Caol Beinn a' Chàisgein and climb south up the final slopes (**9.5km; 700m; 3h 20min**); (19km; 720m; 5h 30min).

Beinn a' Chàisgein Beag across Fionn Loch (Jim Teesdale)

Beinn Ghobhlach from Loch Kanaird (Rab Anderson)

Beinn Ghobhlach; *635m; (G192); L19; NH055943; forked mountain*

Beinn Ghobhlach is a distinctive twin-topped hill which sits across the water from Ullapool on a peninsula sandwiched between Loch Broom and Little Loch Broom. Its ascent gives a rewarding and scenic outing. Take the unclassified single track road which branches off to the north of the Corrie Hallie car park before Dundonnell. This crosses the river and leads past Dundonnell House through Strath Beag, climbing to 240m before dropping back down again, to end on the north side of Little Loch Broom at Badrallach. There is parking at the road end about 1km beyond the camp site and bothy; keep the turning circle free. A track continues from here to the remote community of Scoraig.

Follow the Scoraig Path for about 1km, to the end of the fence on the left, then leave it and climb directly up the steep south-facing hillside without any real feature to aim for; stiff but mercifully short, although height and views are gained quickly. Emerge onto a ridge just east of point 338m with the fine sight of Beinn Ghobhlach ahead, rising above two lovely lochans. Drop down and cross the isthmus between Loch na Coireag and Loch na h-Uidhe then climb the increasingly rocky sandstone slope beyond onto the summit shoulder where a final steep section gains the top (**3.5km; 660m; 2h**). There are fine panoramic views, especially to Ben More Coigach to the north, Ben Dearg and the Inverlael Hills to the southeast, then Sàil Mhòr and An Teallach to the south.

Rather than return the same way (**7km; 730m; 3h 10min**), swing around the head of the west facing Coire Dearg and walk out to the north-west top above an impressive drop north down Coire nan Cnaimhean to Annat Bay. There is a distinct island feel out here and the view now extends over the end of the peninsula to a sea studded with islands. These are the lovely Summer Isles, through which the Ullapool to Stornoway ferry can often be seen threading a route on its way to the Isle of Lewis, visible to the west together with the hills of Harris.

Continue west a short way to the end of the ridge. The initial descent from here must be made in a slight south-easterly direction, heading towards the inner coire of Coire Dearg and the summit of Beinn Ghobhlach. Attempting to head west, or north-west, or north will end up in dangerous ground. Drop steeply down for about 100m or so then swing round and descend south-west, with the angle gradually easing, to pick up the burn draining from the corrie. This is the Allt an Uisge Mhaith and is descended all the way to the Scoraig Path 30m above the sea. Follow this fine path which rises above

Creag a' Chahda and leads around the point back to the start (9.5km; 730m; 3h 40min).

Another alternative is to take in Cnoc a' Bhaid-rallaich, the sub-2000 foot Marilyn to the south-east.

Loch na Coireag and Loch na h-Uidhe below the summit of Beinn Ghobhlach (Jim Teesdale)

SECTION 15
Loch Broom to the Cromarty Firth

Beinn Bhreac; 667m; (G149); L20; NH225886; speckled mountain

Beinn Bhreac is not named on any maps. In the past this hill has been known as Meall Dubh, the name applied by OS maps to the north-west top, some 2km away. Beinn Bhreac, along with Meall Dubh and Càrn Mòr the southern top, occupies a tract of high ground above Inverlael, between the Beinn Dearg hills and Ullapool. It is a retiring and difficult to discern summit; a great rounded featureless lump.

However, it provides a quite magnificent panorama of some of the finest hills in Scotland. From Ben More Assynt to the north, this includes, Ben Loyal, Ben Hope, Seana Bhraigh, the Beinn Dearg group, The Fannaichs, the Fisherfield mountains, An Teallach, Beinn Ghoblach, Ben More Coigach, Stac Pollaidh, Cùl Beag, Cùl Mòr, Suilven, and Canisp. So, it is worth saving for a good day.

There are two approaches, both from the shores of Loch Broom. The principal route starts from the walkers' car park at Inverlael (NH182854) and follows the track east into Inverlael Forest. Shortly after going through a gate into the forest, break off left and take a track over a bridge, crossing the twin ravines of the River Lael, then go

right on the main track running up the glen beside the river. After about 1km pass a path off right to a bridge over the river and a track off left, staying with the main track as it swings round uphill above the ruins of Glensquaib.

Just above a cleared area, go left onto an overgrown track where a hidden track is revealed ahead. This hidden track zigzags steeply up through younger trees to emerge on the upper forest track (a point that can be reached by a longer zigzag route by going left from the bridge over the river at the start). Climb the steep track opposite and leave the forest by a walkers' gate to the side of the vehicle gate.

Follow the track up and right across the hillside to where it eases above a steep drop into the Allt Badan Seasgach and the rounded summit of Beinn Bhreac comes into view. Where the track ends in boggy flat ground, cross a burn then continue on an atv track for 200m or so and break off left on an indistinct path, which soon fades. Climb the hillside onto the flat summit area, occupied by a small lochan. The top is on a small rise just to the north-east (**7km; 660m; 2h 40min**).

Return the same way (**14km; 660m; 4h 20min**). Alternatively, drop off south-east to cross the Allt na Lairige, following an atv track across grassier ground, and climb onto Càrn Mòr (649m). Descend south-west from here to join the Seana Bhraigh path which is followed pleasantly back with the fine sight of An Teallach ahead (**18km; 830m; 5h 30min**).

Another route starts from Leckmelm at NH171901, gained by turning north off the A835 at the sign for Leckmelm and parking just beyond some cottages. Climb a track (shown as a path on some maps) steeply uphill through the forest above the Allt Raon a' Chroisy, swinging up left to emerge from the forest through a gate. Continue past a shed then through some forestry into Strath Nimhe. At NH193903 break off right across the burn and follow a track up the other side to a bend in front of a small gully come waterslide. Ascend the slope up the left side of this and continue up the hillside to go through a decrepit deer fence. Meall Dubh, the north-west top, is gained via an obvious weakness on its north side; the 646m high point is 500m away at NH214900.

Beinn Bhreac itself lies some 2km to the south-east and is gained by initially heading south between two small lochans. The intervening ground is perhaps easier crossed slightly to the left, away from some fence posts, where traces of an atv track lead towards the summit (**7km; 670m; 2h 40min**). Return almost the same way (**13.5km; 670m; 4h 20min**).

Beinn Bhreac, with the snowy Beinn Dearg hills behind (Rab Anderson)

Meall Doire Faid and An Teallach (Meryl Marshall)

Meall Doire Faid; *729m; (G52); L20; NH220792; hill of the prophet's grove*

Lying above Braemore Junction at the head of Loch Broom, Meall Doire Faid is a satellite of the Corbett Beinn Enaiglair which can easily be included by extending either of the two suggested routes.

Both hills offer fine views to the south and to the west, where An Teallach looks magnificent and on a good day the Outer Hebrides can be seen.

The circuit of Coire Leacachain, to the east of the hill, offers a good high-level walk, maintaining a height of 600m for at least 7km and utilising stalkers' paths for half of that. Park in a layby 2km east of Braemore Junction, at NH229765. Cross the road and ascend the broad south-east ridge ahead, passing over Meall nan Doireachan (713m) to reach Meall Doire Faid (**3.5km; 620m; 1h 50min**). The north side drops steeply from the summit cairn and care is needed, particularly in poor visibility, when the onward descent is made to the Bealach nam Bùthan. To do this, go east for 200m and find easier ground, then turn west and bypass the steep craggy terrain immediately above the bealach on its west side. From the bealach a good stalkers' path is followed eastward for 1.5km to a junction of paths at NH238796 and then south-east for a further 2km along a broad ridge to

Meallan Mhurchaidh (625m).

Beinn Enaiglair's summit lies directly above the Bealach nam Bùthan and can be quickly climbed from there (**1km; 340m; 45min**), descending the south-east ridge to the junction of paths (adding **2.5km; 340m; 1h 10min**) then continuing along the ridge to Meallan Mhurchaidh.

From Meallan Mhurchaidh, the most direct route to the starting point heads south-west down the Allt

Leacachain, although the circuit continues onto Meall Leacachain (621m) then descends to the road at the start (11km; 820m; 4h 10min). A longer and more pleasant route descends the stalkers' path south-east to Loch Droma, after which the line of the old road which runs parallel and to the north of the A835 can be followed back to the starting point (13.5km; 710m; 4h 20min).

Meall Doire Faid can also be climbed from Braemore Junction where a path, marked by posts, climbs the hillside to the east of the forest plantation. The path passes to the east of Home Loch before joining a stalkers' path up the Allt a' Chumhainn. Leave this path at the 500m contour and go south-east to ascend the broad gully below the craggy north face of Meall Doire Faid. This face does not ease off until east of the summit, from where it is an easy climb westwards (**4.5km; 540m; 1h 55min**). Returning by the same route is perhaps preferable to the direct thrash down the south-west slopes (9km; 540m; 3h).

Again, Beinn Enaiglair can be included (**1km; 340m; 45min**) although it is better to descend the north-west ridge onto a stalkers' path then traverse round the hill to join the upward route at NH208798 (4.5km; 340m; 1h 35min). There are some newer tracks on this side of the hill.

Meall a' Chaorainn from the track to Loch Vaich (Rab Anderson)

Meall a' Chaorainn; 632m; (G195); L20; NH360827; hill of the rowan tree
Beinn Tharsuinn; 710m; (G81); L20; NH412829; transverse hill

Meall a' Chaorainn is a small hill, the northernmost summit of the crescent-shaped range of great rounded hills curving around Loch Vaich, with the Munro, Am Faochagach forming the highest peak. Beinn Tharsuinn sits tucked away on the opposite side of Strath Vaich, some 5km to the east of Meall a' Chaorainn and is the higher of the pair.

These are remote hills. Fortunately a private road then track cross 28km through the wilds from Black Bridge on the A835 Garve to Ullapool road, to the public road in Strathcarron, inland from Ardgay. This gives access to the hills from west or east and since it passes between them, it means they can conveniently be climbed as a pair, especially with the help of a mountain bike. Both ways in are almost equidistant, although it is the Black Bridge approach that is favoured. Any approach on foot is likely to entail an overnight stay.

There is ample parking at Black Bridge at the start of the road up Strath Vaich. After 3.5km, take the rougher track up the glen where the tarred road crosses the river towards Strathvaich Lodge and the hydro-dam. After a short steep climb this track drops gently down again, following the western shore of Loch Vaich, with fine views of the surrounding hills. A long gradual climb then leads to the south-east shoulder of Meall a' Chaorainn. The high point of the track is at the watershed at 369m, where a track branches off right to the burn draining from Cròm Loch beneath Beinn Tharsuinn. Bikes are left here (**13.5km; 210m; 1h 40min** by bike, **3h 20min** on foot). Times given from here are on foot, although after descending Meall a' Chaorainn it is possible to bike another 1km towards Beinn Tharsuinn.

▶

Beinn Tharsuinn above the Cròm Loch (Rab Anderson)

A short and ferociously steep climb north-west through heather gains the summit of Meall a' Chaorainn (**500m; 260m; 35min**). Due to the hill's size and its location the views are somewhat truncated; Beinn Tharsuinn is a superior viewpoint. Return to the foot of the slope then climb Beinn Tharsuinn by following the track which goes east then north, traversing the hillside to a small hydro installation at NH373832; the end of the road for wheels. Follow the north side of the burn, upstream to Cròm Loch, skirting the loch to the north (rough going) to gain the easy summit slopes that lead to the top (**6.5km; 610m; 2h 35min**). The return to the track can be varied and with a bike nearby the Corbett Beinn a' Chaisteal (1h 40min)

might tempt some. Otherwise descend the same way (11.5km; 620m; 4h). Return down Strath Vaich (27km; 280m; 3h by bike, 6h 30min on foot).

The same point between these hills can be gained from Ardgay on the east, by following the road signposted to Croick, then turning left to pass Amat Lodge to reach the road end at Glencalvie Lodge; there is parking at the junction. Follow the estate track west along the river towards Alladale Lodge. After 2.5km, just before the lodge, take the track on the left across the bridge over the river and continue up Gleann Mòr to join the Strath Vaich track just beyond Deanich Lodge, at the junction with Gleann Beag. The same approach and ascent times apply.

Càrn Loch nan Amhaichean; 697m; (G110); L20; NH411757; hill of the loch of the necks (isthmuses)

Beinn nan Eun; 743m; (G25); L20; NH448759; mountain of the birds

These hills share a remote location with fine views and can be climbed together, especially with the help of a bike. The best approach is from the A835 Garve to Ullapool road where a track leaves the road about 100m to the west of the Inchbae Lodge Hotel. There is parking 100m further west, just over the bridge, and it appears acceptable to drive up the track for 200m and park by a log stack.

Follow the river north up Strath Rannoch through forestry plantations then open moorland. Just beyond Strathrannoch Farm leave the track at a sharp bend (NH388747) in the corner of a small plantation (**6km; 130m; 40min** by bike, **1h 35min** on foot). Walk times are given from here.

A short section of track then a faint path lead up the north-west side of the Allt a' Choire-rainich, through an attractive rocky defile. Upstream of this, cross the burn by boulder

Beinn nan Eun across Loch nan Amhaichean (Rab Anderson)

south-west shore of Loch Glass to Wyvis Lodge where a rougher track continues 4km up the glen to an attractive waterfall (**12.5km, 150m; 1h 20min** by bike, **3h** on foot). Walk times are given from here.

Depending on the state of the Abhainn Beinn nan Eun either cross early and climb the south-east slopes to the summit of Beinn na Eun (**2km; 420m; 1h 10min**), or follow the stalkers' path upstream to join the route already described up the western spur. From the summit, head west round the north side of the loch to climb Càrn Loch nan Amhaichean by its north ridge (**6.5km; 650m; 2h 40min**).

Either return past the loch to gain the upper Abhainn Beinn nan Eun and then the path, or descend the south ridge then cut across east and descend a burn to the path leading back to the waterfall (**11.5km; 650m; 3h 50min**). Return along Loch Glass (**25km; 170m; 2h 40min** by bike, **6h** on foot).

hopping then climb the heathery hillside in a north-easterly direction, heading for a distinctive huge boulder on the skyline. The summit of Càrn Loch nan Amhaichean lies just beyond, with fine views of the neighbouring Easter Ross summits (**3km; 410m; 1h 20min**).

To continue to Beinn nan Eun, descend the north ridge, almost to a tiny lochan, then drop to the north shore of Loch nan Amhaichean and follow its eastern outflow for 1km until it joins the Abhainn Beinn nan Eun. On the other side, the easy western spur leads to the summit (**7.5km; 680m; 3h**). Less shapely than its near neighbour, Beinn nan Eun has a more extensive view, from Morven and the Caithness hills some 76km to the north-east, around to Strath Spey's Ben Rinnes 90km to the south-east.

Return west to the tiny lochan at the foot of the north ridge of Càrn Loch nan Amhaichean then drop to the path down the Allt a' Choirerainich and descend to Strathrannoch (**14.5km; 750m; 4h 45min**). Return along Strath Rannoch (**12km; 130m; 1h 20min** by bike, **3h 10min** on foot).

These hills can also be approached from the east by bike. The public road

from Evanton climbs up Glen Glass as far as the bridge at Eileanach Lodge where there is parking. A private track continues upstream, following the

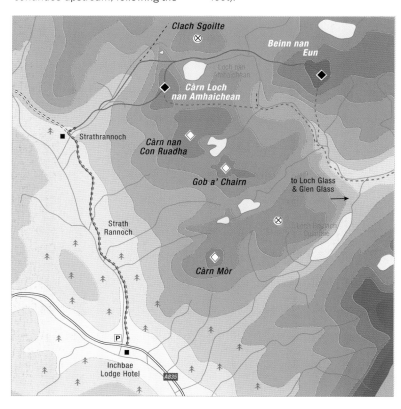

Meall Mòr; 738m; (G35); L20; NH515745; big hill

Meall Mòr's steep southern flanks present an impressive profile above the northern shore of Loch Glass. By way of contrast its summit ridge is open, grassy and rounded, making it prime wind turbine country. Not surprisingly perhaps, the lower top of Meall an Tuirc is populated by an extensive turbine development; the Novar Wind Farm.

Leave the B817 just north of Evanton and follow the minor road up Glen Glass to park short of the white iron gates and bridge over the River Glass, leading to Eileanach. Go over the bridge, past Eileanach Lodge and turn right onto a track leading north-west through forestry alongside the River Glass. At NH536701 turn right onto a short section of track leading to a deer fence and rickety stile and a concrete bridge over the River Glass. Meall Mòr is now clearly visible to the north-west. Cross the bridge and continue past a white building to a track junction. Turn left here and carry on to another track junction, where a grassy track on the right is ascended through conifers.

Keep left at the next junction, then right at the next, beyond which the upper level of the forestry has been felled, revealing the wind turbines on the flanks of Meall an Tuirc above. Exit the forest and descend slightly to join another track coming up from Loch Glass and follow that up right to a four-way junction on the western side of Meall an Tuirc, above the col with Meall Mòr. Turn right and ascend the turbine access track then a short section of hillside to the rounded top of Meall an Tuirc (**6km; 420m; 2h**). Return to the four-way junction and continue down past the turbines to the col. Pick your way through the peat hags to gain the broad south-east ridge of Meall Mòr and go over rounded Pt.717m to meet a ramshackle fence which is followed north-west then south-south west to the trig point on the summit (**9.5km; 600m; 3h 5min**). Return by the same route (**18km; 650m; 5h 15min**).

The whale-backed mass of the Graham Beinn Tharsuinn can be seen across Loch Morie to the north-east and the rocky top of Càrn Salachaidh

due north, beyond and right of the distinctive twin tops of the Corbett Càrn Chuinneag. However, all rather pale beside the massive presence of Ben Wyvis's Glas Leathad Beag, Tom a' Choinnich and Glas Leathad Mòr to the south across Loch Glass.

The track on the west side of the loch provides an alternate route to Beinn nan Eun (see previous page) which lies north of the Ben Wyvis massif.

Meall Mòr from the southern end of Loch Glass (Tom Prentice)

Tòrr Leathann, left, and Beinn Tharsuinn from the approach up Strath Rory (Rab Anderson)

Beinn Tharsuinn; 692m; (G113); L21; NH606792; transverse hill; **Sìdhean a' Choin Bhàin** (twin); 692m; L21; NH600803

Beinn Tharsuinn is the culmination of a mass of rounded, largely grassy hills lying between the Dornoch and Cromarty Firths. It affords a fine bird's-eye view of the two firths and their associated features. The top is a broad plateau of undulating terrain where OS maps show two points of the same height, 1.3km apart. It is easy enough to climb both, although an unratified survey has found the northerly Sìdhean a' Choin Bhàin to be the lower of the two at 688.9m. The only other break in this otherwise feature-less countryside is a high wind farm, 2km to the north-east of the summit.

The most pleasant ascent starts at a bridge (NH660777) over the Strathrory River on the B9176, the old A9 Struie Hill road, where there is a large car park. Head north-west on a good track which ends at a quarry after 4km. Climb the broad north-east ridge leading to the summit of Tòrr Leathann (637m); initially following a line of old turf shooting butts. It is reasonably easy going but marshy and tussocky in places.

Beinn Tharsuinn lies 1km to the north-west and is gained after a short descent to a col then a re-ascent over peat hags to reach the trig point (**7km; 570m; 2h 30min**). Four of the

other Grahams in this section are identifiable, from Càrn Salachaidh to the north-west, with the distinctive double breasted Corbett Càrn Chuin-neag between it and the other Beinn Tharsuinn, then Beinn nan Eun and closer to the south-east Meall Mòr with Ben Wyvis behind it.

A 20min walk gains the north-west top, Sìdhean a' Choin Bhàin. Either descend east, then south-east to follow the burn down, or return to the trig point and descend the east flank

to reach the burn then the Strathrory River and the approach track (16km; 630m; 4h 40min).

An alternative starting point is Baldoon on the south-east side of the hill where a peat road can be followed for 2.5km to the foot of the hill. The slopes on this side are heavy going with tussocky grass and heather and it is probably better to follow the old stalkers' path, which contours the base, to the quarry where the previous route is joined.

The rocky summit of Càrn Salachaidh, centre, viewed from Croick (Rab Anderson)

Càrn Salachaidh; *647m; (G178); L20; NH518874; filth mountain*

Viewed from Ardgay and Lower Gledfield on the northern approach up Strathcarron, Càrn Salachaidh's pointed double summit presents a distinctive profile. A similar profile can be seen from Croick to the north-west, but from most easily accessed locations, Càrn Salachaidh is obscured by the extensive high moorland which surrounds it.

The hill can be approached on foot from Strathcarron in the north via 6.5km of track and moorland, or from the south up Strath Rusdale to Lochan a' Chairn with the aid of a mountain bike, via 13.5km of track and open moorland. The latter saves about 12 miles (20km) of driving when approaching from the south and allows the Corbett of Càrn Chuinneag to the south-west, to also be climbed.

Approaching from the north, park at NH524921 about 100m west of the entrance to Gruinards Estate in a passing place on the south side of the road, opposite a post box and metal pedestrian gate leading to Gruinards Lodge. There is room for passing and about two parked cars. Do not restrict access to the track. Passing places offer the only viable parking for some distance along this road in both directions.

From the passing place follow the track south through woodland to a deer gate giving access to the open hillside. Càrn Salachaidh is now obvious straight ahead. Follow the track round Càrn Mòr to gain the deeply-cut river bed of the Allt a' Ghlinne. Cross over and follow assorted animal paths up the hillside, initially to the right of the Allt Coire Sheilich draining from Càrn a'

Bhealaich, then to its left.

Gain the top of Càrn a' Bhealaich (508m) and follow the high ground to reach the broad north ridge of Càrn Salachaidh. Ascend this over granite slabs and boulders aiming south for Pt.633m, the rocky west peak, topped with an impressively perched granite slab and a small cairn.

From here follow the summit ridge east to the trig point (646m) on Càrn Salachaidh. The OS 1:25k map indicates the 647m summit lies about 45m to the north-east (**6.5km; 620m; 2h 30min**). Descend south-east between small granite outcrops to a col and ascend to the east top of Càrn Bhrain (635m). Rather than returning over Càrn Salachaidh to the track, it is easy to descend west into the shallow corrie and traverse below the main peak at about the 580m contour to gain the north ridge from where Càrn a' Bhealaich and the outward route lead back to the start (**14km; 680m; 4h 30min**).

Càrn Salachaidh can also be approached up Glen Calvie from Glencalvie Lodge at the very west end of Strathcarron, again using a mountain bike. This also allows Càrn Chuinneag to be climbed, but involves even more driving.

Càrn a' Choin Deirg; 701m; (G103); L20; NH397923; hill of the red dogs

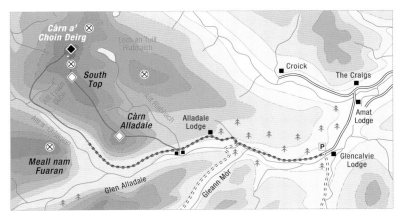

Càrn a' Choin Deirg is the most easterly summit of the range of hills known as the Freevater Forest and is situated inland to the west of Ardgay at the head of the Dornoch Firth. The summit sits at the north end of a curving undulating ridge some 3km in length and gives good views of the Sutherland hills to the north and Seana Bhraigh to the west.

The best approach is past Alladale Lodge to the south-east. This route affords some dramatic scenery with fine stands of Scots pine trees and good examples of U-shaped valleys. The Alladale Estate is creating a wilderness reserve with plans to introduce European elk, wolves, lynx and bears, initially in a 500 acre enclosure situated on the spur of wooded hillside south of the described route.

From Ardgay, take the turn signed to Croick, along the north side of the River Carron. Turn left at the telephone box before Croick and pass Amat Lodge to reach the road end at the Glencalvie Lodge junction (NH464892) where there is parking. Glen Calvie was subjected to an infamous clearance of its people in 1844 and an account in *The Times* brought this to the nation's attention and caused a considerable stir.

From the junction go west on the estate road into Glen Alladale for 4km, passing the track off left to Gleann Mòr then on the right Alladale Lodge. Cross the Allt Riabhach (NH426895) at the holiday lodges, a bike can be useful for this section, then strike up the hill over easy grass and heather to gain the summit of Càrn Alladale (635m). Descend north-west and traverse the broad ridge of Càrn a' Choin Deirg for 3km over several intervening tops. In the dip before the final rise to the trig point there is a small lochan (**9km; 720m; 3h 10min**).

The return to Glen Alladale can be made by the Allt a' Chlaiginn to the south-west. Descend to the small lochan then contour onto the spur of Leathad nan Con Dearga and drop down easy slopes on the west side of the Allt Easan Dubh with its waterfall. Pick up a stalkers' path which becomes an estate track after 2km and return beneath Càrn Alladale (**20km; 720m; 5h 50min**).

Càrn a' Choin Deirg from the long south-east ridge (Meryl Marshall)

SECTION 16
Loch Broom to the Pentland Firth

Ben More Coigach and Sgùrr an Fhidhleir, far left, from Speicein nan Garbh-choireachan (Noel Williams)

Ben More Coigach; *743m; (G23); L15; NC093042; big mountain of the Coigach district*
Sgùrr an Fhidhleir; *705m; (G94); L15; NC094054; peak of the fiddler*

Ben More Coigach's unmistakable profile dominates the landscape on the road north from Ullapool. Looking like the vast hull of an upturned boat, it presents a long, forbidding buttressed wall beneath a high-level ridge. However, this conceals the fact that there are two Grahams here which are part of a complex massif of seven separate summits, all over 500m in height. The views to mountain and sea, and the terrain, at times like a lunar landscape, are quite magnificent.

There are two principal approaches for climbing both Grahams, each with its own merits. A series of wild north-east facing corries containing the impressive rock prow of Sgùrr an Fhidhleir makes an approach from that direction an attractive option.

However, it is perhaps better to drive the extra distance around the massif to the road end near Culnacraig where the full length of Ben More Coigach's ridge can be combined into a fabulous round of all

seven summits. There is a parking area at NC062041, at the highpoint of the road before it turns the corner to run downhill to the road end; there is verge parking here also.

Walk towards the road end and on the other side of the bridge follow a path straight up the steep hillside. Where the angle eases at NC071042 break off the main path, which continues up the centre of the spur towards Sgùrr an Fhidhleir, and traverse rightwards on a vague path above the steeper slopes, heading towards the end of the ridge ahead. Drop down and cross the upper part of the Allt nan Coisiche ravine then continue to the foot of Garbh Choireachan. Although somewhat intimidating, with care, the ridge provides a relatively straightforward route. Once up, the path leads along a superb knife-edged ridge over Speicein nan Garbh-choireachan (738m) to reach the summit of Ben More Coigach, which is set back from the edge of the steep southern slopes on

a promontory (**4.5km; 690m, 2h 10min**).

Regain the edge to complete the traverse, then detour south-east and drop down to ascend the fine conical peak of Speicein Còinnich (717m), which marks the end of the ridge. Return north-west and descend to the foot of Sgùrr an Fhidhleir. Climb the slope and walk out to the summit of the Fhidhleir, which is in an exposed position, perched on the point with dizzy drops on two sides (**8.5km; 930m; 3h 15min**).

Descend to the col to the north-west by heading south-west for 500m or so before swinging round north. The flat top of Pt.648m is easily gained and offers more fine views. Now head south-west to take in Beinn nan Caorach (649m) before descending west-north-west to climb Cairn Conmheall (541m), the final summit (**12.5km; 1170m; 4h 40min**). There is steep rock at the western termination, so return towards the col then descend steeply to the side of

▶

Ben More Coigach, left, and Speicein nan Garbh-choireachan (Rab Anderson)

the Allt Tarsuinn to reach the road (**14.5km; 1170m; 5h 20min**).

The easiest and quickest way of climbing both Grahams is to start as for the above route but stay on the initial path which climbs to Sgùrr an Fhidleir. Drop off this and climb Ben More Coigach then return to the approach path to descend. This is quick and easy, but an inferior route.

The other favoured route starts as for Beinn an Eoin, (see p266, for details of parking and the initial approach). The path up the left side of the Allt Claonaidh leads through a gate in a deer fence to reach lovely Lochan Tuath where the mighty prow

of Sgùrr an Fhidhleir rears up ahead. Go round the south side of the lochan and continue up into the corrie to climb up the side of the burn beneath the peak. Towards the top, pass a stone gateway to emerge onto the shoulder and climb to the top of the Fhidleir (**5.5km; 650m; 2h 20min**).

It is possible to take in some of the peaks to the north and west but this involves some back tracking. Otherwise, return to the head of the corrie then continue over onto Ben More Coigach (**8.5km; 840m; 3h 20min**). The ridge is easily traversed but again involves back tracking.

On the return, the fine conical peak of Speicein Còinnich is worth climbing with a descent made back to the col at its base. From here, rather than return via the approach route down the corrie by the Fhidleir, descend a steep grassy slope north-east to go through a deer fence and climb onto Beinn Tarsuinn. Drop off this avoiding any craggy sections to rejoin the path alongside the Allt Claonaidh (**14.5km; 970m, 5h**). The eastern termination of Beinn Tarsuinn is rockier than the map suggests.

Although Beinn an Eoin gives a nice round on its own (see p266), it can be included with this round from Loch Lurgainn. If climbed on the way in, then it is best to return south-east from the summit for some way before descending to regain the path at the eastern end of Lochan Tuath. The steep ground directly above the loch is awkward to descend. If it is climbed on the way back then a number of ascent lines are possible but will always be easier further east.

From the south, Ben More Coigach can be climbed from the parking area at Blughasary just off the A835, by following the track up the River Runie then round to Loch Eadar dha Bheinn. From the east end of the loch climb onto the shoulder of Speicein Còinnich then over its summit to reach Ben More Coigach. Return the same way.

Ben More Coigach across Loch Kanaird from Ardmair (Rab Anderson)

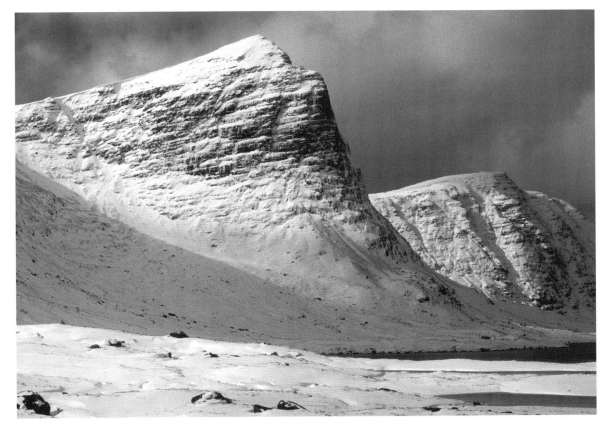

The impressive rock prow of Sgùrr an Fhidhleir above Lochan Tuath (Jim Teesdale)

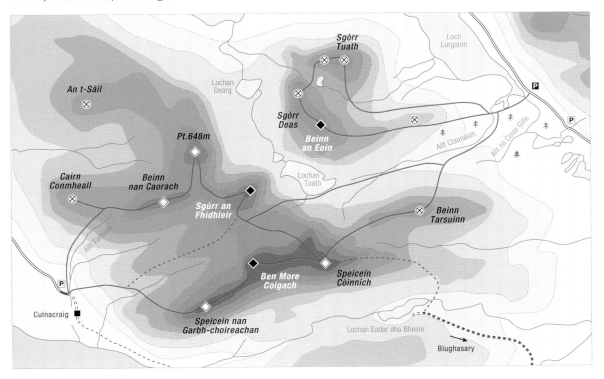

> **Beinn an Eoin**; *619m; (G208); L15; NC104064; mountain of the bird*

Beinn an Eoin is a small but distinctive twin-peaked hill overlooking Loch Lurgainn, opposite Cùl Beag and Stac Pollaidh. It is cradled by bigger Ben More Coigach and Sgùrr an Fhidhleir behind and a link with these is possible for a three Graham tick (see p263). However, this would miss out on what is a great little horseshoe walk taking in the northern top of Sgòr Tuath and also miss out on the best round of Coigach and the Fhidhleir.

Start from a passing place at the head of Loch Lurgainn (NC139067); it is possible to squeeze a car in off the road here and in nearby passing places. Otherwise, the nearest suitable parking is 1km back up the road, either side of the burn at NC145062. A path leads to a gate in a deer fence, then stepping stones across the Allt na Croise Gille flowing into Loch Lurgainn. If the river is high there is a bridge on the other side of the deer fence for access to a boat house but this means that the deer fence then has to be climbed. The path leads to the Allt Claonaidh and an atv track which fords the burn at this point (NC133064). If a crossing is not made here (take footwear and a towel) and the path is followed up into the corrie, then the next easy crossing may not be until further upstream where the burn forks. It is also possible to get over the burn to the north, where the deer fence crosses.

Cross over on the atv track and head uphill to the left of the steep nose of Cioch Beinn an Eoin to gain the ridge. Due to forestry planting somewhat tedious ground has to be crossed to reach the steeper slopes. The view is dominated by the immense rock prow of Sgùrr an Fhidhleir. Follow the rounded ridge to the top (**4km; 560m; 1h 50min**).

Drop down northwards between bluffs of eroded sandstone and head out onto a little top. Descend off the southern peak, Sgòrr Deas, towards a lovely lochan nestling in the col, taking care not to stray too far north since there are cliffs at the end of the ridge. Cross over to the west of the lochan then climb steeply onto the northern peak, Sgòrr Tuath, dodging in and around little rock steps and boulders. A lower top is crossed which has a curious deep fissure splitting it; take care under cover of snow! The slope to the north falls steeply to Loch Lurgainn and the view to Stac Pollaidh, Suilven, Cùl Mor and Cùl Beag is magnificent. Traverse east past the head of an open gully with some fine pinnacles and climb to the summit (**6km; 720m; 2h 35min**).

The best descent is to head straight down south, towards the lip of the corrie. Stay fairly high to cross the burn then follow its right side aiming for some obvious boulders beneath Cioch Beinn an Eoin where a shelf traverses around the hillside. Again, planting has made the terrain awkward here. Re-cross the Allt Claonaidh and return to the road (**10km; 730m; 3h 45min**).

Map on previous page

The summit of Beinn an Eoin, right, and pointed Sgùrr Tuath from Sgùrr an Fhidhleir (Iain Thow)

Stac Pollaidh from the south (Rab Anderson)

Stac Pollaidh; *612m; (G219); L15; NC107106; steep mountain at the pool*

Stac Pollaidh stands proud, a mountain in miniature, thrusting its weathered and battered Torridonian sandstone rock ramparts skywards, in defiance to the elements that have worn it down over the millennia. There is a lot of rock on the summit ridge, much of which can be bypassed. However, attaining the summit itself involves some unavoidable exposed scrambling, probably making it the most technically difficult summit on the mainland. Many don't quite make the top, although getting close is good enough and certainly not without its excitement.

Start part way down Loch Lurgainn, from a sizeable car park at the foot of the hill. Cross the road and go through a gate in the deer fence and follow a well-engineered footpath up through the trees. When the path splits, take the right branch and go through a gate onto the open hillside to continue up and across the southeastern shoulder to the back of the hill. The views on this section are dominated by Cùl Beag and beyond this over the head of the loch to Seana Braigh and Beinn Dearg. Around the shoulder, Cùl Mòr appears, followed by Canisp and Suilven.

Take the left fork of the path which slants steeply up towards a fenced enclosure with the odd zigzag to reach the narrow crest of the ridge at the central saddle (**1.5km; 460m; 1h**

10min). The Grahams on the opposite side, Beinn nan Eun, Sgùrr an Fhidleir and Ben More Coigach loom into view across the loch.

The East Top is only a short distance away and gives a fine perspective of the tower and pinnacle bristling ridge in front. There is a Far East Top but from here the scramble descent into the notch is quite difficult, especially if wet. A narrow traverse path on the north side leads to this top from the central saddle, avoiding all difficulty and the need for any scrambling. It is much the safer way if one wishes to include the Far East Top. However, for the scrambler there are two options for the down climb (Grade 3), neither recommended for the inexperienced. From a boulder on the north-east corner go right and down fairly smooth slabs. Better is to go left behind the boulder and using holds climb down, then step left across to the bottom of the other route to reach the base of the notch. The scramble up the other side and back down is easy.

▶

Stac Pollaidh from the flanks of Cul Mòr to the north-east (Tom Prentice)

To continue from the central saddle, walk across to a flat area in front of the first tower which bars progress along the ridge. The easiest scrambling options on the south side are described, although much can be by-passed on the north side by various traverse lines. Pass the tower on the left side (south) and continue past the first steep gully, then two more open ones.

At the third open gully, which is at the far side of a major gully coming up from below, there are two options. One is to traverse a path left around the edge past some boulders into a wide, loose gully and climb this easily to the crest. The other is to go up the gully to just beneath a steepening with a small jammed boulder and traverse out left on a path, then around the edge past some boulders into the wide loose gully and climb its right side over an easy step to gain the crest.

Either way, the right side of the ridge leads easily upwards past a cairned top to a tower. Here an awkward sidle has to be made across a short rounded slab above a gully – there is a good handhold for this short move. This allows a second cairned top to be reached. This short bit can be avoided by dropping down a gully on the left (south) and then ascending the gully on the other side until a traverse path leads up left onto the crest in front of the second cairned top. Ahead is a large and fine rock wall, above which is the high point.

To reach the summit, drop to an airy col in front of a tower barring further access. Many get no further than this point; the knowledgeable use of a short rope here could be beneficial. This is perhaps the Grahams' version of the Inaccessible Pinnacle!

The tower can be climbed directly by a few moves graded Difficult. An easier option is to go down left (south) a short way to gain slabby rock and the base of a slanting, flared chimney-groove. An awkward move (squirm) gains a good hold, which enables one to pull up and pass through an easier narrowing to gain the crest behind the tower; take care on the final move back down this way. Remember the moves well for they have to be reversed!

To return, retrace ones steps to the central saddle (**2.5km; 560m; 2h 10min**), avoiding the temptation to descend north earlier since this will add to the hills erosion problem. From the saddle, descend north and follow the left-hand path which slants down beneath the ridge around the north-west shoulder, then back to the start (**4.5km; 560m; 3h 20min**).

Stac Pollaidh from Badnagyle to the west (Tom Prentice)

SUILVEN; *pillar mountain, from Old Norse 'sulr', pillar and Gaelic 'beinn', lenited as 'bheinn'*
Caisteal Liath; *731m; (G49); L15; NC153183; grey castle*

Not only is Suilven one of the finest Grahams but it ranks as one of the best of all Scottish mountains. It is a mountain of superlatives and a much prized ascent. There are two principal approaches, both from the west near Lochinver. These are long but they allow time to enjoy the hill and the passage through a wonderful landscape.

The Inverkirkaig approach starts from a good car park (NC085194) beside the River Kirkaig to the southeast of Inverkirkaig. There is a café and bookshop up the hill above the car park. Cross the road and follow a signposted path to the Falls of Kirkaig, through lovely wooded terrain to reach the point where a path descends to the falls at NC111180 (55min). It is worth visiting the fall but the hill is a long way off and it's better to save this for the return. Continue for a further 800m, keeping an eye out for a cairn and a path up the banking on the left at NC118177, opposite a rapid on the river. Take this path which cuts over the peninsula to cross the head of Fionn Loch. On the other side it loops round and after 1km crosses a flat area.

At the back of a knoll, Creag a' Choire Mhòir, at NC132179, take a cairned rough path which breaks off left and climb steeply through a craggy area. A vague path leads gradually up and across the slope with the majestic sight of sphinx-like Suilven ahead. This joins a path coming up from further along the lochside path (longer and perhaps less scenic) at a ▶

The impressive cliffs of Caisteal Liath, Suilven, from the Inverkirkaig approach (Noel Williams)

Meall Meadonach (Rab Anderson)

burn beneath the Bealach Mòr; the saddle in the middle of Suilven and the only chink in the hills defences.

A steep and eroded path leads to the saddle, which sits on a knife edge where the route from Lochinver comes up. Head north-west through a wall that has been built here and climb to the fabulous summit of Caisteal Liath (**10.5km; 800m; 3h 45min**). There are a few rock steps to be negotiated and some exposed sections which require care, especially in winter. There is a definite sense of achievement in attaining this spot. Return the same way (21km; 860m; 6h 15min).

The other approach starts from the end of the road which leaves Lochinver on the north side of the Culag River where there is parking for perhaps five cars (NC108220). Take the road, not the track, and walk past Glencanisp Lodge, ignoring a path off left (the River Inver Loop), to head south-east on a good stalkers' path

with the prow-like bastion of Caisteal Liath looking some way off. Pass a path off left to Suileag Bothy (1h) and continue for 2km to reach a

substantial bridge over the river. Carry on for another 500m, uphill around the corner then down to a burn. Break off right here (NC168197) on a path that climbs towards the Bealach Mòr and passes between two lochans, Loch na Barrack and Loch a' Choire Dhuibh, to reach the foot of the slope. The path climbs steeply up a shallow gully to join the Inverkirkaig route at the saddle and continues to the top (**9.5km; 700m; 3h 20min**); (19km; 760m; 5h 45min).

Some may wish to prolong the experience and take in the two central Graham Tops, however the second of these involves some scrambling. A path leads easily up onto and along the splendid crest of Meall Meadonach West then down to a col. A steeper section follows with scrambling, where care should be taken in finding the easiest route and remembering the way back. The flat summit table is one of Suilven's most prominent features when viewed from the surrounding hills.

Anyone wishing to take in Meall Beag, the final Graham Top, might balk at the exposed descent down a noticeably less travelled route to the next col and at the equally exposed tricky scramble to gain the sanctuary of the top of Suilven's tail fin. The descent off the back is easy but a gully cleft that cuts into the top has to be watched out for.

Caisteal Liath, with its transverse wall (Rab Anderson)

Ben Stack from the A894 near Laxford Bridge (Rab Anderson)

Ben Stack; 720m; (G66); L9; NC269422; steep mountain

Rising from the rugged Sutherland landscape, this majestic little mountain presents a distinctive conical profile, particularly when seen from the north-west. From this direction Ben Stack bears an uncanny resemblance to the mountain in the Paramount Pictures logo. There are two principal ascent routes, taking either the north-west or the south-east ridges. However, these are just up and down the same way routes, which do little justice to such a fine mountain. A better circuit which combines these ridges starts from Achfary to the south-east where there is parking in front of the estate office. The approach is made through Strath Stack.

Walk south past the school and turn right up a gravel track beside the public telephone box. Pass between the houses and the garages then go through a gate into the forest. The Allt Achadh Fairidh tumbles through the floor of the glen below and soon the track emerges into the open and continues alongside the top edge of the forestry plantation. About 500m past the last of the trees, opposite a cascade on the other side of the glen,

break off right (NC263412) and follow the right bank of a burn up onto flatter ground.

Continue north out in front of the steeper slopes and ascend beside another burn, passing a distinctive large boulder with a small boulder perched on its top, to reach the north-west shoulder of the hill. The rough ascent path which comes up from Loch na Seilge is joined here and leads steeply up the splendid rocky ridge. At first sight this can look intimidating but it's straightforward with fine situations and superb views

across to Foinaven and Arkle. Traverse the airy but easy knife-edged crest past the summit cairn then an incongruous solar powered police aerial to reach the slightly lower trig point 100m or so to the south-east (**6km; 680m; 2h 30min**). The crest is split by a curious landslip fissure.

Descend the south-east ridge steeply to a small knoll, beneath which the slope fans out. Continue in the same line, down the prominent rock dyke of the Leathad na Stioma, to reach boggy ground, then a short section of track and the road leading back to the start (**10km; 690m; 3h 30min**). The above descent can be used to climb the hill since it provides the least intimidating route, although boggy ground is crossed at the start (**4km; 680m; 2h**); (**8km; 690m; 3h**).

The northern route starts at a small building beside the road where there is space for a few cars (NC266437). Ascend the track up the hillside to the west and leave this at NC258432 after crossing the burn that runs into Loch na Seilge. Follow the path and ascend the north-west ridge as for the previous route (**3km; 680m; 1h 50min**); (**6km; 680m 2h 45min**).

Sàbhal Beag; *732m; (G48); L9; NC373429; little barn*

Sàbhal Beag is the northernmost Graham, a lonely lump of a hill to the south-east of its much finer neighbours, Foinaven and Arkle. In itself it does not have much to offer apart from good views of the neighbouring hills. However, when combined with Sàbhal Mòr, which in spite of its name is lower than Sàbhal Beag, and the Corbett, Meall Horn, it provides a very satisfying day.

Begin at the south end of Loch Stack, 1km north of Achfary, where there is parking at the start of an estate road which crosses the river. A bike is useful for the first part of the route. Go along the estate road for 3km to Lone and thereafter on a good track that heads east up Srath Luib na Seilich. After an initial steep section the glen flattens out and the track can be followed for 6km to the Bealach na Fèithe. A mountain bike can be used on much of this track but it is rutted and steep in places. Timings given are on foot.

From the bealach, climb north up steep grassy slopes which ease higher up; a small cairn tops the broad flat summit (**11km; 710m; 3h 40min**). The views of Ben Hope and

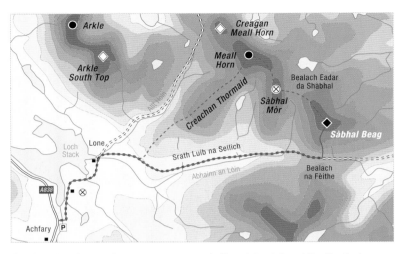

Ben Loyal to the north-east are outstanding and almost the whole of the north-west corner of Scotland is spread out before you. The neighbouring Grahams of Ben Stack and Càrn an Tionail can be identified to the west and south-east. Descend the same way (**22km, 730m; 6h 20min**).

A more complete circuit takes in Sàbhal Mòr (703m) and the Corbett, Meall Horn (777m). From the summit of Sàbhal Beag go northwards over stony ground and descend to the boiler plate slabs of the Bealach Eadar da Shàbhal. Easily climb Sàbhal Mòr and follow the broad south-east ridge onto Meall Horn (**14km; 950m; 4h 50min**). Descend the south-west slopes and the ridge of Creachan Thormaid back to Lone then the starting point (**23.5km; 1010m; 7h 15min**).

A return can also be made over Creagan Meall Horn to the track at the Bealach Horn which offers the option of including Arkle in the round.

Sàbhal Mòr and Sàbhal Beag, right, from Strath Luib na Seilich (Meryl Marshall)

Beinn Direach, left, and Meall a' Chlèirich from the track above West Merkland (Rab Anderson)

Càrn an Tionail; *759m; (G6); L16; NC392390; hill of the gathering (of deer, etc)*
Beinn Direach; *688m; (G120); L16; NC406380; steep or perpendicular mountain*

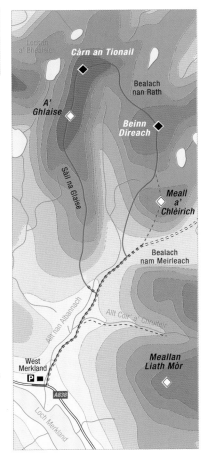

These two hills lie north of Loch Merkland on the A838 between Lairg and Laxford Bridge, at the southern end of the range of hills that include Foinaven, Arkle and several other Corbetts, as well as the Graham Sàbhal Beag. Càrn an Tionail is the higher of the pair with a fine and airy south ridge some 3km in length, whilst Beinn Direach is smaller and more rounded. Both hills give relatively easy going with grassy slopes and stony upper reaches. A circuit combining the two provides a very pleasant horseshoe with good panoramic views of the surrounding hills.

Approach from West Merkland, towards the northern end of Loch Merkland, starting from the west side of the bridge over the Allt nan Albannach. Just past the entrance to the cottage there is limited parking around the edges of a track with a gate.

Walk back over the bridge and follow a good track up the Allt nan

Albannach for 2km. This track continues over the Beallach nam Meirleach, the Robbers Pass, to the road which runs beneath Ben Hope in Strath More and was originally an old droving route.

A few hundred metres after crossing the Allt Coir' a' Chruiteir, which is the route of the path to the summit of the Corbett Ben Hee, break off left on a track which descends to a metal bridge over the Allt nan Albannach. Cross over, then head north up the grassy slopes of Sàil na Glaise, the long ridge which leads to A' Ghlaise, the southern top of Càrn an Tionail. It is quite a steep initial ascent, although an atv track may be picked up from time to time, which helps the climb.

Once on the ridge the going is easier and a splendid walk along the edge of a steep drop-off into the corrie to the east leads to the top of A' Ghlaise (750m). Càrn an Tionail lies just over 1km away to the north and is easily ▶

Looking west to Meallan Liath Coire Mhic Dhughaill (Rab Anderson)

reached after a short descent and re-ascent (**7km; 700m; 2h 45min**).

Large numbers of deer gather to graze on the steep slopes beneath the ridge and in the corrie, hence the name of the hill. The stony ground on the upper slopes gives a good habitat to several flocks of ptarmigan; also of note are a couple of small stone shelters just under the summit.

The view is grand, particularly north to Ben Hope and Ben Loyal, then west to the complex system of tops, ridges and corries that make up the Corbett Meallan Liath Coire Mhic Dhughaill. It is worth walking downhill a little to the west for the fine view over Lochan a' Bhealaich into the lovely corrie containing Coire Loch. To the north-west over the rounded and less defined neighbouring Graham of Sàbhal Beag lies the Corbett Meall Horn with Arkle and Fionaven beyond.

Descend the broad north-east ridge for 400m and then curve round to the south making for the slabby rocks at the remarkably rugged and scoured Bealach nan Rath, avoiding a line of crags on its north side. Beinn Direach rises ahead and the angle of the slope, together with the minimum re-ascent, means it is a quick and easy climb to the broad and flat summit (**9km; 850m; 3h 40min**).

The descent is made by going south down the short spur of Ceann Garbh na Beinne Dìrich towards the massive bulk of Ben Hee to reach a broad bealach. From here the Graham Top Meall a' Chlèirich (631m) can be climbed although the descent south to the track below is quite steep. A descending traverse around the west side of Meall a' Chlèirich enables an atv track to be joined which leads to the Allt na Glaise draining the corrie, then to the main track just west of the Bealach nam Meirleach.

The fact that it is a 600m ascent from here to the summit of Ben Hee is likely to put most off any thought of attempting to include this in the round. A pleasant 3km walk leads back down the track to West Merkland (**15km; 850m; 5h 15min**).

Càrn an Tionail from A' Ghlaise (Rab Anderson)

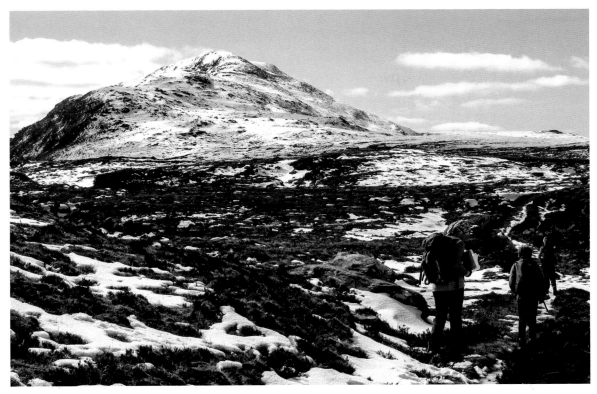

Meallan a' Chuail from the stalkers' path to the north (Grahame Nicoll)

Meall an Fheur Loch; 613m; (G216); L16; NC361310; *hill of the grassy (reedy) loch*
Meallan a' Chuail; 750m; (G11); L15; NC344292; *little hill of coal (peat supplies?)*

The ascent of this pair of Grahams gives a very good and scenic outing with the possibility of including the Corbett, Beinn Leòid. Start from the single track A838 between Loch Merkland and Loch More, just west of the high point where there is a small parking area at a passing place (NC358333).

Walk west along the road for 100m to where a wooden bridge gives access to a stalkers' path which zigzags uphill between a break in the forestry. Height is gained quickly and the angle eases right off. At a flattish section, where there is a small, normally dried-up lochan, head up the slope on the left. At this point there is a boulder on the left and the stalkers' path veers away from the hillside crossing some stepping stones.

Ascend the slope past two tiny lochans to climb easily up the rounded ridge with views across to the two neighbouring Grahams, Càrn an Tionail and Beinn Direach, as well as back to Ben Stack and Arkle. The

summit of Meall an Fheur Loch is flat and the cairn, which lies over to the

▶

Meall an Fheur Loch above Loch a' Ghriama from the A838 (Jim Teesdale)

Meall an Fheur Loch from the north ridge of Meallan a' Chuail (Rab Anderson)

left, could be difficult to find in mist (**3km; 490m; 1h 30min**). Ahead, Meallan a' Chuail's fine east face rises above the two lochans in its corrie; Ben More Assynt lies beyond.

Head south-west off the top, down the curving ridge to a flatter section and a point where there is a view out over steeper slopes dropping to Loch Iol-ghaoith below. On the other side, a waterfall tumbles down the hillside from the lochan nestling in the corrie beneath the summit of Meallan a' Chuail. Swing round and descend westwards to the southern tip of Loch Cùl a' Mhill. Take care not to stray south here in poor visibility.

Cross the outflow at the end of the lochan and climb steeply to gain the narrow northern ridge of Meallan a' Chuail which then leads to the summit, perched on the edge over-looking the lochans below (**6km; 790m; 2h 40min**).

A better alternative is to ascend the slope a short way from Loch Cùl a'

Mhill, then cut south across the steep slope via a deer track to ascend past some boulders to reach idyllic Lochan Meallan a' Chuail. Go around the east side of this lochan and the unnamed lochan to its south then ascend the steep south-east ridge to the summit (about 1km and 15min longer). This is also better if taking in Beinn Leòid.

Descend the long north ridge and continue north off the end above Loch Cùl a' Mhill on the higher ground, thereby avoiding most of the boggy terrain. The stalkers' path is reached a few hundred metres before a small lochan. Follow the path to the dried-up lochan then downhill to the start (**11km; 800m; 4h**).

Beinn Leòid can be included (**2.5km; 250m 1h 5min** from Meallan a' Chuail). It is perhaps better to return over Meallan a' Chuail, rather than descend the path north from the col which then has to be left to climb featureless rough ground to get back to the approach route.

Beinn Dhorain; 628m; (G197); L17, NC925156; mountain of the wet place

This summit forms the highest point of a large tract of hill country south of the Strath of Kildonan. It gives distant views of the Moray coast and most of the hills in the north-east part of Scotland, including the Cairngorms. The hills in this area are generally rounded and heathery but an exception to this is the steep east face of Beinn Dhorain.

The ascent is best made from Glen Loth where a small surfaced road climbs to a height of 340m, cutting off the corner between the A9 and the Strath of Kildonan. Glen Loth is uninhabited but at one time it held a considerable population. They were cleared to make way for sheep by the notorious Patrick Sellar, factor of the Duke of Sutherland and the remains of their settlements, as well as other archaeological features which indicate that the glen was settled in prehistoric times, can be seen. A visit to puzzle over the impressive Clach Mhic Mhios standing stone at NC941151 is worthwhile; park as for the short route to the top.

A pleasant route starts further down Glen Loth, some 200m north of a bridge over the Sletdale Burn, where a grassy track climbs the southern slopes of Druim Dearg. There is parking on the grass opposite the gate at the start of the track (NC936129). Follow the right fork of the track and go over Druim Dearg to gain the saddle to the south of Beinn Dhorain then climb to the top. Veer right to the east top for the view down into Glen Loth then gain the summit to the north-west (**4km; 530m; 1h 45min**).

Continue across to Ben Uarie (623m) with its trig point, less than 1km to the north, where there are rewarding views into the Strath of Kildonan and to the splendid conical peak of Morven. The descent can be made from the col between the hills via the steep east facing corrie and although this involves a 3km walk back down the road it can be combined with a visit to the Clach Mhic Mhios standing stone (**10km; 530m; 3h 15min**). An alternative is to head south-west across easy featureless ground into Glen Sletdale and follow the burn, picking up a well-made track for the last 2km, to regain the starting point (**12km; 530m; 3h 45min**).

For those intent on bagging the summit quickly, the left side of the northernmost of the shallow corries on the east side of Beinn Dhorain

provides a steep, heathery ascent. Opposite a small parking area at NC937155 there is a stile over the fence. Cross this and ascend the slope to reach the east top then the summit (**1.5km; 360m; 1h**). Continue to Ben Uarie then, either descend steeply east to the side of a rocky band, or from the col between the hills (**4km; 360m; 1h 40min**).

Beinn Dhorain from Glen Loth (Rab Anderson)

Creag Mhòr, left and Creag a' Choire Ghlais – Ben Armine, from the south-east (Rab Anderson)

BEN ARMINE; *mountain of the hero, chieftain, steward*
Creag a' Choire Ghlais; *705m; (G91); L16; NC694273; cliff of the grey-green corrie*
Creag Mhòr; *713m; (G75); L16; NC698240; big cliff*

These retiring and somewhat dull looking hills are amongst the most remote Grahams. However, they are easily approached by mountain bike and the resultant walk over their summits ends up providing an excellent day out in the rugged far north. The start point for the hills is normally reached by a lovely drive up the A897 beside the River Helmsdale through the Strath of Kildonan, then via the B871 up Strath Beg. To the south of Badanloch Lodge an estate track begins at NC801330, at the entrance to which there is good parking. The track runs west past Loch Badanloch, Loch an Alltan Fheàrna then on to Loch Choire Lodge at the head of Loch Choire beneath Ben Klibreck.

Bike along this track to NC687310 where a good stalkers' path heads south-south-east to run beneath the steep east-facing slopes of both hills (**13.5km; 70m; 1h 30min** by bike, **3h** on foot). The best route is probably to

climb across the hills and to return by this path. Times given are now on foot, from and back to here.

Strike off up the hillside to gain a slight spur descending from Meall nan Aegean. Swing right before the summit of this to reach a col then make the short ascent west onto Creag na h-Iolaire (**3km; 500m; 1h 30min**). A lovely cover of moss carpets

The summit of Creag Mhòr, Morven in the distance (Rab Anderson)

the ground, a feature of the hilltops on this round. The view across the top of Scotland is expansive; Ben Klibreck is close and large, Ben Hope, Ben Loyal, the island of Hoy, Ben Griam Mòr and Ben Griam Beag rising out of the flatland. Creag Mhòr looks a long way from here but the intervening terrain is generally good for walking and can be crossed with and make a long but steady climb to the trig point on the summit of Creag Mhòr (**9km; 800m; 3h 40min**). Over to the east is the final pocket of mainland Grahams, Beinn Dhorain, Scarben and majestic Morven.

On the descent the natural drift is to initially head down the north-east shoulder past a large cairn to a point where the map suggests a steep drop north-east to the stalkers path below. However, it is perhaps better to avoid the re-ascent that this entails and to continue north-north-west down the slight spur, not far from the line of ascent. Swing round across Coir' an Eas and make a descending traverse to join the stalkers' path that crosses between the hills, then descend a short way to the junction with the northbound stalkers' path at NC703261.

This excellent path leads above Gorm-loch Beag, through a dip in front of Coire na Saidhe Duibhe, back to the track. It is a long but pleasant walk of 5.5km (**17.5km; 850m; 5h 50min**), aided by the knowledge of what turns out to be swift and enjoyable bike ride back (**27km; 90m; 3h by bike, 6h on foot**).

ease. There are some peat hags but these are easily crossed, or avoided.

Return to the col and climb east onto Meall nan Aegean (695m), then drop south-east to a col where hag riven ground looks like it will be a problem. However, the hags are small and a line through them easily found to gain the mossy dome of Ben Armine and the summit, named Creag a' Choire Ghlais on OS maps (**5.5km; 650m; 2h 30min**).

Descend south-south-west across a stalkers' path passing between the hills, then head south across the col. Avoid the hags on the right, or left,

Looking towards Creag a' Choire Ghlais, Ben Armine from Creag Mhòr (Rab Anderson)

Scaraben, centre, from Smean to the north-west (Jim Teesdale)

Scaraben; *626m; (G200); L17; ND066268; incised mountain, from old Norse 'skora' and Gaelic 'bheinn'*

In complete contrast to the neighbouring peak of Morven, Scaraben is a linear quartzite ridge with three distinct rounded tops. The summit is in the middle and the traverse of all three tops gives a pleasant walk. Start from Braemore where there is a small parking area at the end of the minor road which leaves the A9 on the edge of Dunbeath. The Morven approach starts here too.

Cross the bridge then turn off left along another track and head for the second farm before climbing south on a gradually steepening slope, crossing quartz scree to gain the top of East Scaraben (590m). Head westwards to the main central summit and trig point (**5km; 560m; 2h**) then drop down and climb onto West Scaraben (609m).

Descend by the north spur, avoiding a steeper section lower down on the east, and head for the Morven track, avoiding the fields at Braeval to the west (**11.5km; 650m; 3h 50min**). It is possible to carry on via Smean to Morven but this makes for quite a big day. However, Smean and, or, Maiden Pap are more easily included in a return route.

Morven; *706m; (G89); L17; ND004285; big mountain*

Morven is the highest point of Caithness and one of Scotland's most prominent mountains; a great conical mass rising out of the water-logged flatness of the Caithness Flow Country, the largest expanse of blanket bog in Europe. Its distinctive shape can be seen from as far away as the Moray coast and the Cairngorms beyond. There is a sense of space here and the expansive view extends from the Sutherland hills in the west, along the Caithness coast in the north to the islands of Orkney and Hoy, with its sea-stack the Old Man of Hoy, then east to the rigs of the Beatrice oilfield with its experimental deep water wind turbines.

Start from the road end at Braemore, as for Scaraben. Follow the track over the bridge then west through Braeval to pass beneath the impressive mini-peak of Maiden Pap to reach the end of the track at Corrichoich. Head south-west over moorland following a rough atv track, then a vague path to gain the saddle east of Morven. A steep 350m ascent over heather and scree, where a rough path might be found to ease some of the way, gains the shoulder. Pass south of a rock tor then climb easy slopes to the final rise and a fabulous summit (**8km; 590m; 2h 45min**). Return the same way (**16km; 620m; 4h 50min**).

Alternatively, for a three Marilyn day, climb east onto the rocky top of Càrn Mòr then traverse across onto the fine tor-topped summit of Smean (509m); (**11.5km; 850m; 4h**). Descend steeply to the north-east then cross the intervening flat ground to reach the Maiden Pap which is climbed via the obvious line of weakness on its south side. This leads to a narrow col from where a final short climb gains an impressive little summit (484m); (**14.5km; 1020m; 5h 15min**). Return to the col then descend steeply to the north on a path to regain the track of the outward route beside a forestry plantation and return to Braemore (**18km; 1020m; 6h 15min**). From Smean it is possible to ascend Scaraben but this makes for quite a long day and Maiden Pap is awkward to include, being a detour off the natural round.

An interesting and unusual route to Morven is from the south via the track along the Langwell Water; a bike is useful. Park at the Berriedale bridge and take the estate road (ND118226) for Langwell House. A locked gate at the edge of the wood necessitates a high lift of the bikes, thereafter take the middle of three tracks.

Leave the bikes at Wag (**13km; 180m; 1h 30min by bike, 3h 10min on foot**). Head north over rough moorland making for homesteads marked on the map then go north-west up an obvious shallow gully, a steep and sustained climb of 450m, to the summit (**3km; 520m; 1h 30min**). Return the same way (**6km; 520m; 2h 30min**); (**26km; 180m, 2h 45min by bike, 6h 20min on foot**). This can be extended east to take in Smean, or west then south to include Creag Scalabsdale.

Morven from the approach track to Corrichoich (Jim Teesdale)

SECTION 17
The Islands: Arran, Jura, Mull, Rum, Skye, South Uist & Harris

Mullach Buidhe, centre, from Casteal na h-Iolaire (Tom Prentice)

ARRAN

Mullach Buidhe; *721m; (G65); L62, 69; NR901427; yellow mountain*

Arran's western hills lack the jagged peaks and alpine ambiance of the main range, being rather more rounded in appearance. Nevertheless, they harbour some rocky ridges and corries which would not be out of place in the Cairngorms.

The village of Pirnmill on the west coast offers the most direct access to Mullach Buidhe. Park at the southern end of the village in a roadside layby just north of Pirnmill Village Store and Post Office and the bridge over the Allt Gobhlach. The footpath is sign-posted from here.

Ascend the access road directly opposite the parking area, first diagonally left then more directly. Where it starts to curve left, look out for a foot-path sign on the right on the edge of woodland. The path leads through scrubby birch, muddy in places, to gain the Allt Gobhlach. Ascend over various stiles and alongside a deer fence to leave the trees and get the first view of the hills. Continue past a waterfall on the right then alongside the burn, now flowing through a narrow wooded gorge, to a point directly below the nose of Coire Roinn's right-hand ridge, which descends from the Graham Top of

Beinn Bharrain (717m). The left-hand ridge offers an alternative scrambling ascent (see next page).

At the head of a track by a small dam, cross the burn and the moor-land to gain the ridge. A path appears

as the ridge becomes better defined and leads round the top of Coire Roinn to the cairn on the summit of Beinn Bharrain. Continue east then north-east over the prominent granite tor of Casteal na h-Iolaire, then

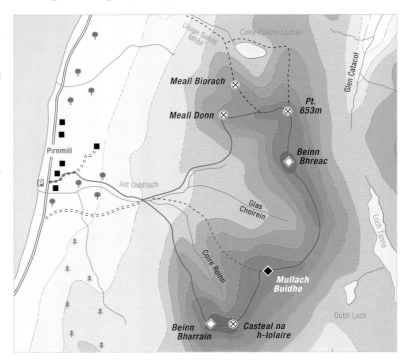

The Islands
Caledonian MacBrayne is the major operator of ferries to the islands <www.calmac.co.uk>. Highland Council operates a few small crossings and there are some private companies operating crossings. Online searches for ferry crossings to the island name should reveal the relevant information. The Caledonian MacBrayne website timetable contains a section 'Useful Ferry Timetables (Non Calmac)' which is certainly useful. In addition to the standard crossings, Caledonian MacBrayne offer a Hopscotch Ticket which covers various ferry crossings to from and between the islands, valid for a limited period.

Arran & The Inner Hebrides
The Isle of Arran, and the group of islands known as the Inner Hebrides contain a total of 11 Grahams on four islands. Arran has one Graham whilst Jura has two, Mull has seven and Rum has one.
***Arran** is reached by Caledonian MacBrayne ferry from Ardrossan to Brodick. Another ferry crosses from Claonaig on the Kintyre Peninsula to Lochranza <www.calmac.co.uk>.*
***Jura** is reached by Caledonian MacBrayne ferry from Kennacraig at the northern end of the Kintyre Peninsula, either to Port Ellen or Port Askaig on Islay <www.calmac.co.uk>. Another ferry crossing is required from Port Askaig to Feolin on Jura; (ASP Ship Management Ltd) details on <www.jurainfo.com> and in the Caledonian MacBrayne timetable. A passenger only ferry crosses directly to Craighouse on **Jura** from Tayvallich (NR742782) on Knapdale, details on <www.jurapassengerferry.com> and on <www.calmac.co.uk>.*
***Mull** can be reached by ferry from Oban to Craignure, although the more convenient and less expensive crossing from Lochaline on Morvern (probably gained via the Corran ferry crossing operated by Highland Council) to Fishnish makes day trips possible. There is a spring, summer and autumn only crossing to Tobermory from Kilchoan on Ardnamurchan. The Mull crossings are operated by Caledonian MacBrayne <www.calmac.co.uk> where details of the Corran ferry can also be found.*
***Rum** contains one solitary Graham and the island can be reached by ferry crossing from Mallaig via the Caledonian MacBrayne Small Isles service <www.calmac.co.uk>.*

Isle of Skye
The Isle of Skye contains 10 Grahams and most walkers will choose arrive on the island via the Skye Bridge from Kyle of Lochalsh. However, the Kylerhea ferry crossing from near Glenelg is an alternative. This ferry takes vehicles but it is also possible to cross as a foot passenger and climb the three easternmost Grahams on Skye; Beinn na Caillich, Sgùrr na Coinnich and Ben Aslak. The ferry is operated by the Isle of Skye Ferry Community Interest Company <www.skyeferry.com>. Details are on the Caledonian MacBrayne website <www.calmac.co.uk> who also operate a ferry crossing from Mallaig to Armadale.

The Outer Hebrides
Despite their size and their hilly nature, in contrast to the islands of the Inner Hebrides, the islands of the Outer Hebrides only contain four Grahams ; Beinn Mhòr on South Uist then Uisgneabhal Mòr, Òireabhal and Tiorga Mòr on Harris. Caledonian MacBrayne <www.calmac.co.uk> is the sole ferry operator.
***South Uist** can be reached from Oban on the mainland by ferry to Lochboisdale on South Uist, a service which alternates with Castlebay on Barra. A ferry also crosses between Barra and Eriskay, connected by causeway to South Uist. Another ferry crosses from Uig on Skye to Lochmaddy on North Uist, connected by road with South Uist. A ferry also provides a link between The Uists and Harris, see below.*
***Isle of Harris** can be reached from Uig on Skye by ferry to Tarbert. A ferry crosses from Ullapool on the mainland to Stornoway on the Isle of Lewis, which is joined to the Isle of Harris. The final link is a ferry between Leverburgh on Harris and the island of Berneray, connected to The Uists by causeway.*

descend slabby ground to the corrie edge and follow it to the cairn and trig point on Mullach Buidhe, overlooking Glas Choirein (5km; 780m; 2h 25min).

An alternative approach can be made up the north ridge (the left-hand of the two ridges enclosing Coire Roinn), which is easily gained from the Allt Gobhlach and offers an excellent Grade I/II scramble on rough granite. The main difficulties are near the top and would be awkward to avoid, however the exposure is moderate and the scrambling is not sustained. Descending by this route is not recommended.

A return can be made back over Beinn Bharrain, but it is more enjoyable to continue north round Glas Choirein to Beinn Bhreac, at 711m a Graham Top, then on to the smaller summit of Pt.653m. From here traverse west round the corrie overlooking picturesque Coire-Fhionn Lochan to spot height 586m, where the path makes a distinct turn to the north-west and contours round the corrie towards Meall Biorach. Do not follow this route, but leave the path at NR901542 and descend in a south-westerly direction towards Meall Donn, from where heather and grass lead down to a path on the north bank of the Allt Gobhlach, which leads back to the main path to Pirnmill (13km; 960m; 4h 45min).

It is also possible to descend north to Coire-Fhionn Lochan from Pt.653m and Meall Biorach and follow a well-travelled path beside the Uisige Soluis Mhòir to Mid Thundergay on the coast road, 2.5km north of Pirnmill. This traverse is popular with walkers using the coastal bus service for transport, rather than private car.

> **JURA**
> **Beinn Shiantaidh**; *757m; (G7); L61; NR513747; Probably holy mountain; locally 'a' bheinn sheunta'*
> **Beinn a' Chaolais**; *733m; (G41); L60, 61; NR488734; mountain above the narrows*

Jura's mountains have a reputation for uncompromising toughness requiring similar stamina and mountain skills to another great island round in this guide; the Cuillin of Rum. Known by all as the Paps of Jura, there are actually three main mountains and a lesser outlier, rather than the two that might be expected from the 'breasts' of the Gaelic title.

The two Grahams and Beinn an Oir, the Corbett in between, form the north and west sides of Gleann an t-Sìob, making a round of all three the logical expedition for most hillwalkers. Just 52m separates the highest and lowest of the three and the amount of ascent from the cols in between ranges from 330m –350m. Effort is fairly evenly distributed through the day, but when combined with 10km of approach and descent, ankle-twisting scree, some ill-defined paths and mountain route finding, it is easy to see where Jura's reputation comes from.

The most popular ascent begins from the car park on the north side of the Corran River (NR545721) at the start of the minor road to Knockrome. From here there are two options.

The main route crosses back over

Beinn Shiantaidh from the head of Gleann an t-Sìob (Tom Prentice)

the bridge and follows the signposted path and subsequent atv track on the west side of the Corran River, first north then west towards Loch an t-Sìob. The route is extremely marshy in places, but leads directly to obvious stepping stones at the eastern end of Loch an t-Sìob. Ascend Beinn Shiantaidh from here, directly north-west on ill-defined paths through heather and scree tongues to gain the west side of south-east ridge where the scree starts in earnest and the path becomes more obvious.

Gain the south-east ridge and follow it to a levelling out which leads south-west over grass and scree mounds to the cairn (**4.5km; 740m; 2h 15min**).

The alternative is via the signposted 'Evans's Walk' which starts opposite the car park at NR550731 and is reached by walking north up the road. This route is less marshy, the best approach if including Corra Bheinn in the round and also misses out the lower flanks of Beinn Shiantaidh. However, it is slightly longer and requires a little more route

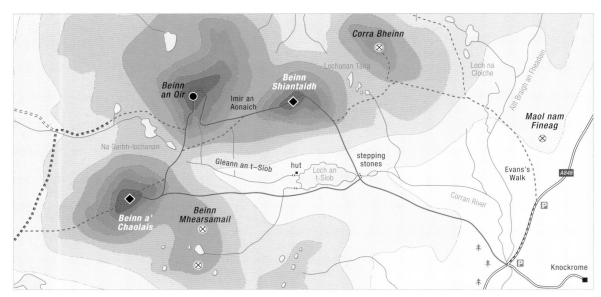

finding. Follow the left-hand path when the route divides near the start and leave it at a small cairn (NR539747), just before it bends sharp right and ascends north towards Loch na Cloiche. Traverse north-west on animal tracks to the base of Corra Bheinn, which can be climbed up and down via the same route in 50min from here; 1.5km. From the Lochanan Tanna lochans a distinct path follows the screeline south-west below Beinn Shiantaidh's south-east ridge to the join the previously described ascent route. Excluding Corra Bheinn, this route is 1.5km longer than via the River Corran but with the same height gain and takes an extra 20min.

From the summit of Beinn Shiantaidh descend west on an initially well-defined ridge which broadens into a mixture of grass and scree to gain and follow a shallow gullyline to the Imir an Aonaich col. Beyond the col a clear path traverses the southern flanks of Beinn an Oir to a burn draining the shallow corrie between the peak's twin south ridges.

Follow the path up the right bank of the burn into the upper corrie to a

stone shelter where the scree starts. From there ascend grass directly below an obvious tor formed by an igneous sill, to reach a further two stone shelters, believed to be the remains of a 'Colby Camp' occupied by the Ordnance Survey during the first Triangulation of Great Britain in the first half of the 19th century. A well-defined path leads south-west to the trig point (**7km; 1070m; 3h 30min**).

Descend south on a superb ridge of blocky quartzite with fine views west to the Sound of Islay and south-west to Beinn a' Chaolais, then veer south-west onto a subsidiary ridge and weave down through scree and crags to skirt the lochans of Na Garbh-lochanan to the south.

A direct ascent can be made of the east face of Beinn a' Chaolais from here following a line left of the scree, but it is easier perhaps to traverse round the base of the east ridge, then ascend gentler-angled scree, heather and rock to its crest and follow that to the summit (**9km; 1430m; 4h 45min**). Go back down the east ridge or down the scree of the east face to the head of Gleann an t-Siob and pick up a wet, muddy path along southern edge

of Loch an t-Siob to reach the stepping stones at its east end and the main path back to the start (**15.5km; 1430m; 6h 30min**).

It is also possible to approach the mountains directly from the Feolin Ferry. Follow the bikeable track north above the shore through woodland to a track crossroads. Take the track that leads east, uphill to the Lochan Gleann Astaile dam then follow the track on the other side a short way before climbing to the summit of Beinn a' Chaolais via its south-west ridge (**8km; 730m; 3h**).

Descend the scree of the north-east face to the col then drop down a bit and cut across the front of Beinn an Oir to climb Beinn Shiantaidh (**11km; 1140m; 4h 30min**). Return to below Beinn an Oir and ascend it as previously described (**13.5km; 1470m; 5h 45min**), then descend the south ridge to regain the Beinn a' Chaolais col. Skirt the lochans of Na Garbh-lochanan to the north and descend by the burn to gain a track. Continue to NR499744 then cross the burn and take the track south to rejoin the approach route at the dam (**24.5km; 1500m; 8h 30min**).

Beinn a' Chaolais and Islay from the south ridge of Beinn an Oir (Tom Prentice)

Creach Beinn from Loch Buie (Tom Prentice)

MULL
Creach Beinn; *698m; (G108); L49; NM642276; craggy mountain*
Ben Buie; *717m; (G70); L49; NM604270; yellow mountain*

Creach Beinn and Ben Buie are the biggest hills in the south of Mull. They have a lot of steep, exposed gabbro giving them the appearance of rugged little mountains, in contrast to the rounded, grassy hills just to the north. Creach Beinn lies above the sheltered, wooded fresh water loch, Loch Uisg whilst Ben Buie overlooks the marine loch, Loch Buie, which is surrounded by yellow gorse blooms. Loch Spelve, Loch Uisg and Loch Buie are part of the Great Glen Fault which runs from Inverness.

Start on the east side of a small bridge in Gleann a' Chaiginn Mhòir, about 1km from the road end at Loch Buie; there is a small parking area at NM615256, used by people visiting the Lochbuie Stone Circle. This glen runs between the two hills and is more interesting than many on Mull, containing several small crags of glacier smoothed gabbro with a few hardy holly trees clinging to them. Fallow deer have been introduced here whilst those at Gruline near Salen have been established for longer. Mull is well known nowadays for white tailed eagles but these hills are the territory of golden eagles, with both hills having high points named Creag na h-Iolaire (Eagle's Cliff) on their northern flanks.

Climbing Creach Beinn first, go through a gate on the opposite side of the road and follow a stalkers' path that runs gently up to the east of the burn leading through the glen towards Loch Airde Glais, the first of

The Loch Uisg flanks of Creach Beinn (Tom Prentice)

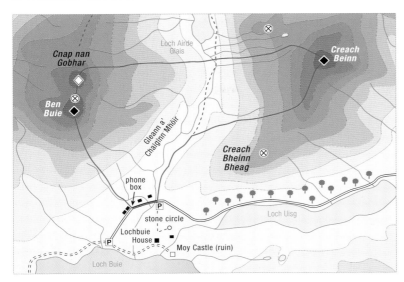

of similar height. Continue south for 500m over the central top (700m) to reach the large cairn on the main summit overlooking Loch Buie (**8.5km; 1310m; 4h 20min**).

There are cliffs below the summit, to the south and east, so care is needed to descend. A path just south of the summit runs down to the right (west) under the cliffs. Alternatively, walk down to the west to avoid the cliffs then walk back east. Descend the rounded ridge with scree soon giving way to vegetation. Continue down overlooking the burn of the Allt a' Ghoirtein Aird then avoid the houses just before reaching the road on the bend by the telephone box. A short walk along the road leads back to the car park (**11.5km; 1310m; 5h 20min**).

These hills can also be ascended from the top of Glen More on the A849 to the north using public transport. Start from the high point at NM617303; there is also a layby for parking at NM622394. The top of Ben Buie is easily reached via Creag na h-Iolaire. Return over Cnap nan Gobhar before dropping east to reverse the previously described ascent route to climb Creach Beinn. It is perhaps best to descend this via the line of ascent then traverse along either side of Loch Airde Glais.

'the three lochs'. After less than 2km of gentle walking, above a step in the floor of the glen, break off right and climb steeply to reach the easy broad ridge which is followed north-east to the summit of Creach Beinn (**4km; 690m; 2h**). There is a cylindrical trig pillar then a small ring cairn just to the east which offers a little shelter. This is a good viewpoint for the mainland hills such as Ben Nevis, Beinn Sgulaird, Ben Cruachan and also Rum to the north and Jura to the south.

To descend it is best to first walk north-west from the summit then drop west back down to the glen. Descending to the west from the summit leads to scree covered slab and whilst this can be descended with care, it is unpleasant. Continue down to the glen past various crags to join the vague path just south of Loch Airde Glais.

Climb the broad ridge ahead which leads up to the north of Ben Buie; some of the ridge is on perfect gabbro slabs. From the top of the ridge a short walk leads south to Cnap nan Gobhar (714m), the north top of Ben Buie. There are three tops

Ben Buie from the Loch Buie seashore (Tom Prentice)

Beinn Talaidh from Glen More (Colin Moody)

MULL
Beinn Talaidh; 761m; (G1); L49; NM625347; possibly mountain of the view, from Gaelic 'beinn an t-seallaidh'
Sgùrr Dearg; 741m; (G30); L49; NM665339; red mountain

Beinn Talaidh is a somewhat enigmatic hill, laying claim to being a Graham (the highest) and perhaps a Corbett (the lowest). Much internet space has been devoted on the subject, however its most recent measurement gives it a height of 761.70m which makes it 299mm below Corbett height!

Together with its neighbour Sgùrr Dearg, these two hills dominate the head of Glen Forsa and provide a short but very energetic outing from Glen More. The lowest point for the crossing between the two hills is only 80m above sea level which is lower than the starting point of the walk!

Start in Glen More, at the junction of a forestry track and the A849 at NM642328 where there is space for several cars. Less than 100m up the forestry track at a slight bend, a vague atv track/path runs off to the left. Follow this to quit the forestry at a stile where a steep, grassy hillside leads to the shoulder of Maol nam Fiadh and the start of the curving south ridge of Beinn Talaidh. This gives a gradual ascent to the broad summit dome (**3km; 650m; 1h 45m**). A cylindrical trig pillar sits on the top, from where there are stunning views.

For those wishing to ascend the outlier Beinn Bheag (537m) a steep, straight descent over scree gives access to the linking col, from where Beinn Bheag is a short ascent. Immediately north of the col, at the very head of Gleann Lèan, lie the remains

Beinn Talaidh from Cruach Choireadail (Graham Little)

of a Dakota aircraft which crashed at the col in 1945, en route from Iceland to Prestwick. From the summit descend the steep south ridge, then skirt the foot of Beinn Bheag northwards to a wide break in the forestry in the glen.

The same point can be reached with more ease from the trig pillar on Beinn Talaidh, by initially heading south-east then swinging east to descend grassy terrain between the two main burns in Coire Ghaibhre.

The right side of the forest break is less boggy, but crossing the burn here after heavy rain would be problematic since there is no footbridge. In these circumstances it might be better to head back to the car then climb Sgùrr Dearg from the road. Continuing though, head up the hillside to follow a slight burn (not shown on OS maps) and thence onto the craggy nose of Beinn Bhearnach. A wide, gently rising ridge of about 1km, leads to the summit cairn of Sgùrr Dearg which lies close to the edge of its precipitous north face (**8km; 1310m; 4h 20min**).

Descend the south ridge towards the other Beinn Bhearnach until a strange tumbled down wall is encoun-

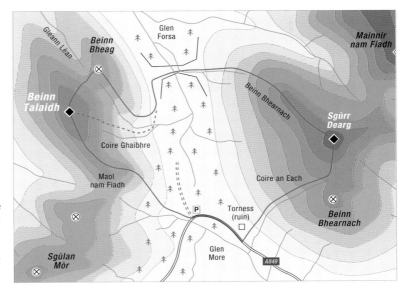

tered. Follow the wall into Coire nan Each and then descend the north bank of the Allt Caisreagach passing some attractive cascades, to reach the A849 at the roadside ruins of Torness. A short walk along the road leads back to the starting point (11km; 1310m; 5h 20m).

A significantly longer, but in some ways more satisfying ascent of these hills can be effected from the north

starting at the bothy of Tomsleibhe, accessed by mountain bike type track from the main road near the Glen Forsa Hotel. The classic north ridge of Beinn Talaidh is climbed and Glen Forsa crossed via the aforementioned forestry break. A return from Sgùrr Dearg gives rough walking above the forestry along the east side of Glen Forsa via the ancient settlement of Rhoail.

Sgùrr Dearg, right, and the firebreak below the craggy north-west shoulder of Beinn Bhearnach (Graham Little)

Cruachan Dearg, Corra-bheinn, Beinn a' Mheadhain and Cruach Choireadail from Glen More (Colin Moody)

MULL

Corra-bheinn; *704m; (G95); L48; NM573321; steep mountain;* **Cruachan Dearg** *(twin); 704m; L48; NM568332*

Cruach Choireadail; *618m; (G212); L48; NM594304; heap above An Coireadail (perhaps 'coire na dail', corrie of the meadow)*

These fine hills, whose rocky southern flanks give depth and atmosphere to the northern side of Glen More, are infrequently ascended and consequently have no established ridge paths. Although somewhat dominated by Ben More to the west, they give splendid walking with ever changing views. The so-called twin peaks of Corra-bheinn and Cruachan Dearg, with summits over 1km apart, do have similarities of form although the former is undoubtedly the most striking and elegant.

Start at the western end of Glen More, at a prominent holly tree and stone bridge carrying the old road over the Allt Teanga Brideig burn, at the ruins of Teanga Brideig (NM563306). There are several parking spaces on the old road, just west of the stone bridge. Take the track over the bridge to the ruins and follow a wet path leading up the

east side of the glen to the col of Càrn Cul Righ Albainn (330m). Head eastwards, contouring around rocky knolls, then climb the steep west

flank to the summit of Cruachan Dearg (**4.5km; 670m; 2h 5min**). An unratified survey measures Cruachan Dearg at 704.1m and

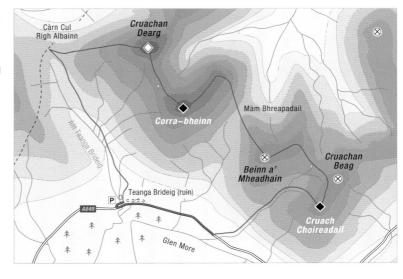

confirms Corra-bheinn as the higher of these twins at 704.9m.

Descend south and cross the Màm a' Choir' Idhir col (570m) to climb past a tiny lochan onto the dark twin summit of Corra-bheinn. Traverse along the wide north-east ridge for about 500m to just before it is truncated by the rugged little Coire na Lice Duibhe. Descend south over scree, linking grass patches, to the pass of Màm Bhreapadail (390m), where an ancient path links Glen More and Glen Cannel.

The bonus hill of Beinn a' Mheadhain (602m) lies straight ahead, with its distinctive north-west spur giving a 210m ascent directly to the top. The straightforward descent east then south-east to the col of Màm Choireadail (464m) is followed by a southward ascent, largely over grass, to the summit of Cruach Choireadail (**9.5km; 1170m; 4h 15min**). Cruachan Beag (596m) can be taken in if desired.

Descend north-west to the near level floor of An Coireadail (a hanging valley) and then head down the glen. Just beyond the lip of the hanging valley a fine little waterfall drops over an overhanging barrier into a deep

Cruachan Dearg, right, and Beinn Fhada (Graham Little)

pool – the perfect place to cool off on a hot summer's day!

A short distance below, the Uisgeacha Geala cascades over gabbro walls and slabs. These can be avoided by descending on the north side of the burn, passing a prominent perched block lower down and thence to the road. Teanga Brideig is a 20min walk along the road (**13.5km; 1170m; 5h 25min**).

An even more challenging circuit of these hills can be made from the north by starting at the ruin of Gortenbuie at the head of Glen Cannel; a 7.5km mountain bike ride from Knock along the south side of Loch Bà. The circuit, probably best done by starting with Cruach Choireadail, gives a splendid wilderness experience (**12km; 1230m; 5h 20min from Gortenbuie**).

Cruach Choireadail from the south-east (Grahame Nicoll)

Approaching the stepped nose, with the summit tower of Beinn Fhada beyond (Andrew Fraser)

MULL
Beinn Fhada; *702m; (G98); L47, 48; NM540349; long mountain*

While many hillwalkers will link Beinn Fhada with the nearby Munro of Ben More, it is also easily combined with its two northerly lower neighbours to make an excellent round in its own right.

It is an impressive and surprisingly rocky peak, every bit as good as its more illustrious neighbour and, as with all Grahams, the lower altitude means it is often clear when Ben More is cloud bound.

Park at NM516374 on the north side of the B8035 in the vicinity of a Mile Post, some 200m south of the bridge over the Scarisdale River. There is ample parking on the grassy coastal pasture. Cross the heather moorland, wet initially, in a south-easterly direction to gain Beinn Fhada's prominent north ridge and make the steep ascent to the summit of Pt.563m, admiring the fine sea views north-west across Loch na Keal to the islands of Eorsa and Ulva.

Climb the ridge left of a lochan to a stepped nose leading to a broader ridge and follow that over grass and rock towards the summit cone. After

the larger of two lochans, a short section of scrambling gains the final ridge leading to the summit cairn (**4km; 740m; 2h 5min**).

Continue eastwards from the summit, then north-east past the col below An Cruachan, to grassy slopes leading north to the col below Beinn nan Gabhar. From here ascend north then north-west to the cairn marking the highest point on the broad, rocky ridge of Beinn nan Gabhar (572m). Return south-east for about 250m, then east down scree and cross the infant Scarisdale River at the head of the corrie.

A line of small cliffs form a distinctive feature slicing straight up the southern side of Beinn a' Ghraig. Ascend left of these to quickly gain the long ridge and follow it over rocky tops and the 591m summit (a Sub 2000ft Marilyn) to the final lower cairned top, which is separated from the main ridge by a col. Descend west from the cairn, weaving through areas of steep ground divided by slabby rock steps. In poor visibility or wet weather, care is needed here in order to find the easiest route to the grassy runnels and scree at their base.

Continue descending west towards the coast to pass through a boundary wall, beyond which the driest line is

The distinctive summit tower of Beinn Fhada from the west (Colin Moody)

taken across rough sheep pasture to the road and back to the start (11km; 950m; 4h 15min).

Ben More can be included by descending south-west from the summit of Beinn Fhada to a col reached by walkers making a circuit of Ben More from the road. Climb the north ridge of A' Chioch (867m) to its top, then descend west to the base of

Ben More's steep east ridge and climb it to the summit (**7km; 1280m; 3h 45min**).

The standard route up Ben More is now followed north-west then west down to the Abhainn Dhiseig. Cross over and continue to reach the track to Dhiseig and the road, which is followed back to the start (14.5km; 1280m; 5h 45min).

The far west top of Beinn a' Ghraig and Loch na Keal from the flanks of Beinn Fhada (Tom Prentice)

RUM
Trollabhal; 702m; (G101); L39; NM377952; troll fell

Trollabhal is the only Graham on the island and one of the six principal hills forming the Rum Cuillin ridge. Two of these hills, Askival and Ainshval are Corbetts, while Hallival and Sgùrr nan Gillean, the first and last of the round of six when starting from Kinloch, are fine summits in their own right. The latter is a Corbett Top whilst Hallival and Pt.759m between Ainshval and Sgùrr nan Gillean are Graham Tops.

Getting to Rum requires effort and planning and most hillwalkers will want to make the most of their visit,

especially if it coincides with good weather. A full round of the Rum Cuillin ridge is usually the objective, or at the very least, an ascent of Trollabhal and the two Corbetts. Accordingly, a full round is described here, along with a variety of alternative return routes and descents which can be utilised to climb Trollabhal, with or without Askival and Ainshval, should time and weather be against you.

The route starts just south of Kinloch Castle on the main vehicle track, just north of the bridge over the Allt Slugan a' Choilich. Turn left

onto a path signposted Rum Cuillin and follow it beside the river and past the castle to a gate, then through woodland passing to the left of the powerhouse building. Exit the woodland and ascend the track and the path beyond to reach a hydro dam which provides Kinloch with some of its electricity.

Above this, pass through a deer fence and continue up into Coire Dubh to a causeway breached by the burn. This is the old dam which once supplied Kinloch Castle with water for electricity, the first Scottish castle to be lit this way. The paths now become less distinct, one branch continuing up the corrie to Bealach Bairc-mheall, the other veering to the south-east (left). Follow the left-hand path up beside a small burn to the col named Cnapan Breaca, then ascend the rocky hillside to the south passing over Pt.518m to gain the lower north-west ridge of Hallival, a short way above the Bealach Bairc-mheall.

Ascend the ridge, at first grassy then steeper and rocky, to reach Hallival's summit (**4.5km; 720m; 2h 10min**), from where there are fine views south to Askival and the hills of Mull beyond, plus the mainland hills to the east, with the island of Eigg 'afloat' in the sea below.

Descend south from Hallival, steeply at first down rocky steps, then a narrow grassy ridge to the col. From here the north ridge of Askival is narrow and rocky but relatively easy and leads up past the Askival Pinnacle (more of a slab than a pinnacle) via a cairned zigzag path, followed by steep but easy scrambling to the summit (**5.5km; 933m; 2h 50min**).

From Askival, a steep though straightforward descent of the mostly gravelly west ridge leads to the Bealach an Oir. The broad east ridge of Trollabhal lies ahead and is easily ascended despite its rocky profile, to gain the south-eastern and slightly lower summit. The main summit lies some 50m further on to the north-west and is climbed by a short but exposed scramble up rock and grass to reach the top of one of the most impressive summits among the Grahams (**7.5km; 1180m; 3h 50min**).

The views on a clear day are truly

Approaching the summit of Trollabhal (Noel Williams)

superb. The lower south-eastern summit is in the foreground with Askival beyond to the east and Ainshval to the south, these two hills enclosing Rum's remote and dramatic Glen Dibidil with, again, the island of Eigg framed in blue sea below.

Return to the lower summit and descend the south ridge first south-east then weaving south-west and south between small rock steps to the Bealach an Fhuarain. From the bealach, avoid the steep lower buttress of Ainshval's north ridge by traversing westwards (right) for a short way then zigzagging up the left side of the screes via a well-worn line to gain a grassy col higher up on the ridge.

From here, follow the ridge taking care in the upper half which is narrow and while only of moderate scrambling difficulty, can be tricky and awkward when wet. However, this section of the ridge is easily bypassed to the east (left) via a small path up the corrie to the grassy summit close to the Ainshval cairn (**8.5km**; **1445m**; **4h 35min**).

A return can be made to the Bealach an Fhuarain from here, but if continuing to Sgùrr nan Gillean,

descend the grassy ridge south to a col from where a pleasantly airy ridge leads to the broad summit of Pt.759 and Sgùrr nan Gillean beyond (**10km**; **1524m**; **5h 5min**).

From Sgùrr nan Gillean, there are three principal routes back to Kinloch. The first and probably the most popular is to descend the south ridge for about 600m to where the ground flattens at a tiny lochan at NM381925. The last 100m can involve scrambling down short rocky gullies and requires care. From the flatter ground, head east to pick-up the burn draining the east face and follow it south-east to Dibidil bothy from where a path, rough and boggy in places, leads round the coast to Kinloch (**20km**; **1524m**; **7h 40min**). It should be noted that Gillean's east ridge looks tempting as a direct descent, but leads to very steep and rocky ground and is not recommended.

The second is easier but longer. Return north to the col between Sgùrr nan Gillean and Pt.759m, then descend south-west and south to cross the Papadil burn and gain the coastal path to Dibidil bothy and

Kinloch (**23.5km**; **1524m, 8h 30min**).

The third is to return over Ainshval to Bealach an Fhuarain, from where there are two options. The first is to, traverse north-east round the base of Trollabhal to Bealach an Oir, followed by a long pathless traverse north round Atlantic Corrie, below the steep rock gullies and deceptively large boulder slopes of the western flanks of Askival and Hallival, to the Bealach Bairc-mheall. From there, descend into Coire Dubh to the path back to Kinloch (**18.5km**; **1650m**; **7h 10min**). This route is only recommended in good visibility. The second, and probably the best option if conditions are poor or darkness is approaching, is to descend east into pathless Glen Dibidil and follow that to Dibidil bothy and Kinloch (**23km**; **1650m**; **8h 20min**).

Anyone wishing to climb Trollabhal in isolation from the rest of the Rum ridge should ascend to the Bealach Bairc-mheall between Barkeval and Hallival and then traverse round Atlantic Corrie for the approach and return route (**6km**; **800m**; **2h 50min**); (**12km**; **850m**; **6h 5min**). However, this is only recommended in good visibility.

Beinn na Caillich from Sgùrr na Còinnich (Noel Williams)

SKYE

Beinn na Caillich; *732m; (G43); L33; NG770229; peak of the old woman; said to be named after the Norse princess who barred the Kyleakin narrows with a chain, to collect taxes*

Sgùrr na Còinnich; *739m; (G32); L33; NG762222; peak of the moss*

Ben Aslak; *610m; (G223); L33; NG750191; breast mountain, from Gaelic 'aslaich'. Mapped Ben Aslaig (1820)*

Situated in a fairly quiet and less frequented part of the Isle of Skye this cluster of hills is prominent in the view west from Glenelg on the mainland side of Kyle Rhea. The hills also feature in the view across Loch Alsh on the road to Kyle of Lochalsh and the most popular route onto the island via the Skye Bridge, which bypasses the hills to the north.

While Ben Aslak is included in this guidebook, an unratified survey has measured it at 609m, which would mean it is not high enough to be a Graham. Anyone wishing to miss it out would be best returning from Sgùrr na Còinnich by the ascent route.

A turntable vehicle ferry crossing to Skye still operates from April to October at the ancient Glenelg to Kylerhea crossing point. It is also possible to cross from the mainland as a foot passenger to climb all three hills. The road from Kylerhea climbs to a high point at Bealach Udal before

dropping through Glen Arroch to join the A87 north coast road between the Skye Bridge and Broadford.

The three hills can be approached most conveniently from Bealach Udal and this saves a considerable

amount of ascent. Indeed a popular option is to climb these hills in two separate outings, one either side of Bealach Udal. However, a better and rather more ambitious option is described here which starts from

Sgùrr na Còinnich from Beinn na Caillich (Jim Teesdale)

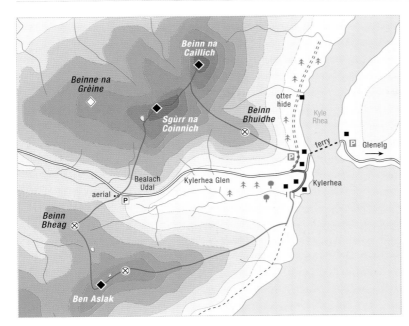

to the left here and after 100m descend more steeply to a dip. Continue heading in a south-easterly direction and go past a sizeable hidden lochan. On the final section, either make for a prominent grassy runnel and at the top turn right to reach the summit, or slant rightwards towards more rocky ground and find some pleasant scrambling which leads back left to the summit (**8.5km; 1230m; 4h 15min**).

Descend north-east to a dip and go past the right-hand edge of a lochan then continue easily onto the eastern top of the hill. The view to Sgùrr na Còinnich on the other side of the glen is good and on the mainland the Graham Beinn a' Chapuill can be seen with Beinn Sgritheall to its side. Now make a long descent of the east ridge, which is at a pleasant angle for most of the way. On the lower section go past a minor top on its northern flank and continue for another 500m. The bottom part of the ridge is rather steeper and the vegetated slope is hard going. Fight across the lower ground and head in the direction of a rusty metal shed. Pick up a faint path along the coast and follow this inland to a hidden bridge across the Kylerhea River at NG785284. Emerge between houses and turn right along a track which leads back to the road from the ferry then the start (**14km; 1300m; 6h**).

Kylerhea and visits all three summits in a single outing.

Start from a car park 300m up a side road, directly above the ferry slipway. The road is signposted 'Kylerhea Otter Haven'. Head directly up the heathery hillside on a slope with occasional rock outcrops. Some may be surprised to learn that these hills are built of Torridonian Sandstone, a rock more usually associated with the hills on the mainland further north.

Eventually the slope eases off at a broad stony flattening called Beinn Bhuidhe (488m). The twin peaks of Sgùrr na Còinnich and Beinn na Caillich lie straight ahead. Cross a shallow neck then head slightly rightwards towards the dip between the peaks called Bealach nam Mulachag. Once on this broad col turn right to ascend Beinn na Caillich. Climb a short section of scree at first then weave a way through the dipping rock strata. Continue more easily on the grassier ground above to the cairn on the summit (**3km; 690m; 1h 50min**). There are superb views north over Kyle Akin and the Skye Bridge.

Return to Bealach nam Mulachag and climb a grassy slope trending slightly rightwards at first to reach the cylindrical trig pillar on the summit of Sgùrr na Còinnich (**4.5km; 850m; 2h 30min**). Ben Aslak, the next objective,

is now conspicuous to the south on the other side of Bealach Udal.

Head south-west from the summit towards a small lochan, then descend southwards, as directly as possible to Bealach Udal and the high point on the road up the Kylerhea Glen. On the opposite side of the road there is a short section of rough track which leads to a mast. Follow this at first then continue up a broad slope in a south-westerly direction to a minor top called Beinn Bheag (468m). Turn

Ben Aslak from Sgùrr na Còinnich (Noel Williams)

SKYE

Beinn na Caillich; 732m; (G42); L32; NG601233; *peak of the old woman: a gigantic Fingalian woman (and a pot of gold) is said to be buried under the huge summit cairn*

Beinn Dearg Mhòr; 709m; (G84); L32; NG587228; *big red mountain*

These hills of the Red Cuillin form a distinctive backdrop to the west of Broadford, especially the conical Beinn na Caillich which is prominent when seen from the Skye Bridge crossing. The circuit of the two Grahams, together with the lesser Beinn Dearg Bheag, provides a splendid and scenic outing. It is a popular walk and there is a rough path in places, though not for all of the circuit.

It is possible to start the circuit by parking at NG620230, close to the end of cul-de-sac road to Old Corry, gained off the A87 to the west of Broadford. The parking is to the side of the bridge over the Allt a' Choire, however, space can be difficult to find at times and the end of the road is a turning circle. Another option starts from the B8083 to Torrin at NG627220 where there is good parking on the grass opposite a chambered cairn. A prepared path joins a track which leads to a footbridge over the Broadford River and the road end at Old Corry (about 15min). There is a good view of all three hills in the circuit from this approach.

From the road end at Old Corry, where the distance and times are given from, head north-west directly towards the summit of Beinn na Caillich, following a faint path then crossing a burn to continue up its south side. The going steepens and the path disappears as the upper cone-shaped slope of scree and boulders is gained. Height is attained quickly to reach the trig point and large cairn which sit on the summit (**2km; 710m; 1h 45min**).

Descend westwards out along the broad ridge to gain the low point between the hills then continue up the elegant ridge which curves round to the top of Beinn Dearg Mhòr (**3.5km; 860m; 2h 25min**). This sits at the head of the corrie and as well as offering fine views down this to the east, there is a tremendous view to the west over the head of Loch Slapin to Blàbheinn, Sgùrr nan Each, Garbh-bheinn then the Graham Belig which sits at the end of the ridge connecting this group. Poking up behind these peaks is the Cuillin.

Descend steeply down scree to the south-east to gain the Bealach Sgreamhach then climb the ridge onto 582m high Beinn Dearg (**4.5km; 970m; 3h**). Descend the long north-east ridge, cross the burn that issues from the corrie, the Allt Beinn Deirge, then continue across the slope to the road end at Old Corry (**8km; 970m; 3h 50min**).

A pleasant circuit of Beinn Dearg

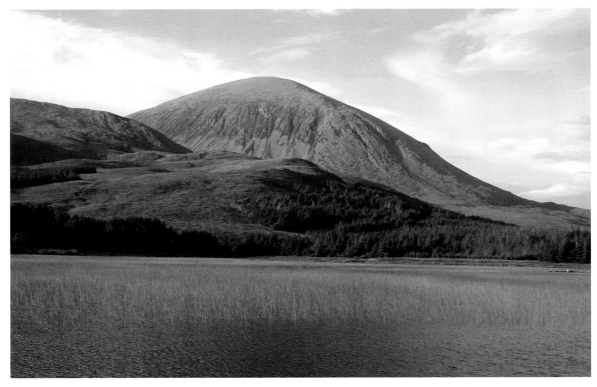

Beinn na Caillich above Loch Cill Chriosd (Rab Anderson)

Beinn Dearg Mhòr from Beinn na Caillich with the Cullin beyond (Rab Anderson)

Mhòr and Beinn na Caillich can also be made from north, around Coire Rèidh. The ascent begins from a section of the old road at Strollamus where there is parking at NG603267, just after a left-hand bend on the main road between Broadford and Portree. Walk west along a track for almost 1km to cross the Allt Strollamus then take to a path which runs up the side of the burn. Follow this for 800m or so, to where it forks, then go up beside the left fork, the Allt na Teangaidh. Gain Pt.535m above the prominent dark crag ahead, Creagan Dubh, by a grassy runnel on the left of the north-east ridge; there are some alternative scrambling options. Continue across a change in rock type and climb to the top of Beinn Dearg Mhòr (**5km; 720m; 2h 20min**).

Descend north-east, then east to cross the head of Coire Rèidh then climb to the top of Beinn na Caillich (**6.5km; 900m; 3h**). The descent is via the north-west ridge between Coire Rèidh and Coire Seamraig; the going is a little easier closer to the right-

hand edge. A descent down slabby rocks regains the Allt na Teangaidh

which is followed back as for the approach (**11.5km; 900m; 4h 40min**).

Belig, left, and Garbh-bheinn from the north (Rab Anderson)

SKYE

Belig; 702m; (G99); L32; NG544240; *fore tooth, perhaps, from Gaelic 'beulag'; or a corruption of Gaelic 'bealach', pass, from Bealach na Beiste high on its west flank*

Belig and its bigger neighbour, the Corbett Garbh-bheinn, occupy a prominent position overlooking the A87 where it loops around the head of Loch Ainort. The hills are joined by a fine ridge and although Belig gives a pleasant short outing on its own, it is normal to climb both hills together. The best starting point for this traverse is the long layby (NG534267) in front of the Eas a' Bhradain waterfall, just around the bend where the A87 straightens for the uphill climb. Starting here also enables Marsco to be included if desired.

Walk down the road and cross the bridge over the Abhainn Ceann Loch Ainort then leave the road and follow the left bank until a suitable place to cross the tributary which joins it can be found. This gains the slope at the foot of Belig's north ridge. It is possible to cut across to the ridge directly but the main burn, though not deep, might have to be waded. Climb the slope which gradually steepens and narrows to a rocky section. This is easiest bypassed via the scree slope to its right although if taken

more directly it gives a Grade 2 scramble; see the SMC guidebook *Skye Scrambles*.

Above this, the narrow, grassier crest is gained and leads to a fine summit (**3.5km; 690m; 1h 55min**). This point can also be reached by following the left-hand burn towards the col between Belig and Glas Bheinn Mhòr before climbing onto the shoulder at the top of the south-east ridge; also a possible descent should one wish.

Continuing with the round, descend towards Garbh-bheinn beside an old wall that runs down the rocky south-west ridge to gain the Bealach na Beiste. Any steeper ground is easily bypassed. It is possible to drop north into the corrie to return from here but this misses out on the splendid north-east ridge of Garbh-bheinn. It is a stiff but interesting 350m climb that passes remarkably quickly. The broad ridge starts easily, steepening to scree then narrowing to rockier ground with an easy but airy ridge to finish (**5km; 1040m; 3h**). Any difficulties are avoidable but if taken directly

they give a Grade 1 to 2 scramble. The views are stunning, especially south to the rocky Sgùrr nan Each, Clach Glas, Blàbheinn traverse and west to the main Cuillin ridge.

The descent curves around the corrie then drops down the long north ridge. Again, any difficulties can be avoided but if taken directly they give Grade 1 to 2 scrambling. The ridge kinks to the north-west for a 60m climb over Pt.489m then continues as the Druim Eadar Dà Choire which leads to the waterfall above the road at the start (**9km; 1100m; 4h 20min**). Cutting across west from Pt.489m gains the south-east ridge of Marsco

A circuit of Belig and Garbh-bheinn can also be made from the south-east, from the B8083 where it loops around the head of Loch Slapin just beyond Torrin. This is perhaps best done in an anti-clockwise direction starting with Belig, which also allows for variations or extensions at the end of the day. Either park at NG561224 on a loop of old road where a rough path heads across to the south-east ridge of Belig, or

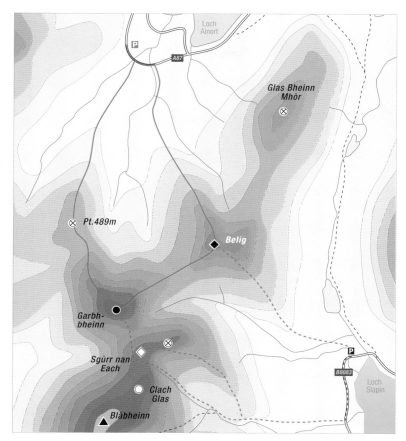

summit (**2.5km; 700m; 1h 45min**).

Descend the south-west ridge to the Bealach na Beiste then ascend the north-east ridge of Garbh-bheinn to reach that summit, as for the previous route (**4km; 1050m; 2h 50min**). From here, descend the rocky south-east ridge which has some Grade 1 scrambling to reach the col with Sgùrr nan Each. This peak can be skirted by a traverse south to reach the col with Clach Glas where a descent east down steep scree leads into Choire a' Càise to gain the Blàbheinn path where it runs down the burn back to the road (**8.5km; 1060m; 4h 10min**). If Sgùrr nan Each is to be included, the ridge leading to the summit beyond its small western top provides some Grade 1 to 2 scrambling. From a dip in front of the eastern top, descend the south-east ridge to join the Blàbheinn path (**9km; 1160m; 4h 30min**).

Although the traverse of Clach Glas is normally done in a north to south direction, climbing the north ridge with an onward continuation to Blàbheinn, this involves some tricky scrambling graded Moderate and Difficult on which a rope would prove useful, as well as p138 & p139 of *Skye Scrambles*). To finish this extension, Blàbheinn is descended by the standard east flank route.

in the main car park for Blàbheinn then walk north along the road to this point. Once across the Allt

Aigeinn the ridge quickly steepens and provides a stiff but fine route to first the east shoulder, then the

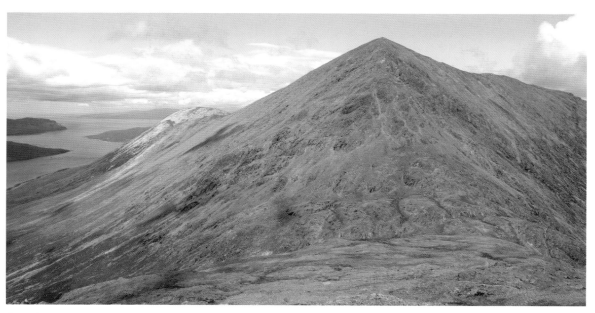

Belig from the flanks of Garbh-bheinn (Noel Williams)

The prominent profile of Beinn Dearg Mhòr viewed from Marsco, with Glamaig beyond (Noel Williams)

SKYE

Beinn Dearg Mhòr; *731m; (G50); L32; NG520285; big red mountain*

The hills of the Red Cuillin prominently form the east side of Glen Sligachan opposite the northern termination of the Cuillin Ridge. At the entrance to the glen is the great pyramidal cone of the Corbett Glamaig, then the two Grahams Beinn Dearg Mhòr, which has a subsidiary top in Beinn Dearg Mheadhonach, and Marsco. This whole group can be climbed in one fine outing but Marsco and Beinn Dearg Mhòr are described here as separate, more manageable walks.

Start the approach to Beinn Dearg Mhòr from the car park on the east side of the bridge in front of the Sligachan Hotel, beside the entrance of the road to Sligachan self catering bunkhouse and cottages. Walk along the old road towards the picturesque old bridge and take the Loch Coruisk footpath. Go through a gate and some 200m from the start, break off left to follow a smaller path up the side of the Allt Daraich gorge.

Further up, cross a fence, either by the gate, or a stile 100m to its right, whichever is the drier. Until the base of the ridge is reached the ground

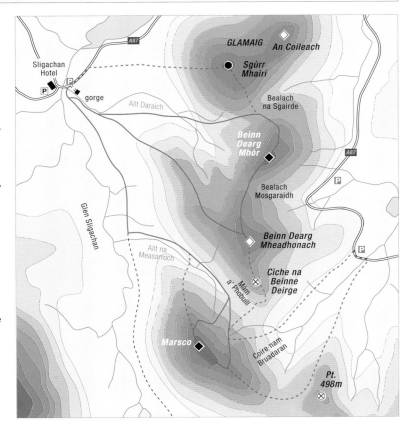

underfoot on this section can be fairly boggy. After the initial steepening, the ridge provides a fine highway leading to the final slopes of red coloured scree, up which the path zigzags onto Beinn Dearg Mheadhonach (651m), (**4.5km; 650m; 2h**). The actual top lies a short distance to the south-east and is worth walking out to for the view. Now head northwards around the edge of the eastern corrie, whose slopes plummet steeply to the road below, then descend to the Bealach Mosgaraidh.

The steep pyramidal cone above is climbed surprisingly quickly by a path which zigzags its way upwards through scree and juniper to reach the top of Beinn Dearg Mhòr (**6km; 870; 2h 45min**). Descend north and continue easily along the shoulder overlooking Coire nan Laogh, towards a small cairn at the end. Turn left towards Sligachan and drop down to pick up paths which descend steeply through scree to the Bealach na Sgairde.

Glamaig's long and very steep southern shoulder rises dauntingly upwards from here and for the fit this gives a steep, stony ascent to the western summit of Sgùrr Mhairi (1km; 360m; 50min). The east top of An Coileach can be taken in if desired. A

Steep scree runnels on the west face of Beinn Dearg Mhòr (Jim Teesdale)

punishing descent can be made directly towards Sligachan although it is perhaps easier to return to the bealach.

However, most will be content not to climb Glamaig but drop west off the Bealach na Sgairde to Sligachan. A path leads across to the spur between the burns and is descended to their junction at NG505292. Either cross over to the left bank to regain the upward route, or cross over the right-hand burn and follow the right bank then cut the corner to regain the car park (**11km; 870m; 4h 10min**).

Glamaig, left, Beinn Dearg Mhòr and Beinn Dearg Mheadhonach from Sgùrr nan Gillean (Rab Anderson)

Marsco from Glen Sligachan, flanked by Garbh-bheinn and Blàbheinn (Rab Anderson)

SKYE
Marsco; *736m; (G36); L32; NG507251; meaning obscure*

One of the finest Grahams, this shapely hill is a distinctive member of the Western Red Hills group. Its eastern flank is seen clearly from the A87 coast road where it runs alongside Loch Ainort. A more familiar view is the impressive profile seen from the Sligachan Hotel when looking south along Glen Sligachan.

An obvious crag stands out on its western flank, the Fiachlan Dearg.

The shortest approach is from the north-east but the route in Coire nam Bruardaran is rather boggy. A much better path runs along Glen Sligachan and this approach is preferred. Start from the same car park as for Beinn Dearg Mhòr (see p306), on the south

side of the road a short distance to the east of the bridge over the River Sligachan. There is a well-worn path up Glen Sligachan, which the Beinn Dearg Mhòr path breaks off from after 200m, but it is further than it looks and it takes an hour to reach the foot of the mountain. After 3km it is important to take the left fork in the path and stay on the north bank of the Allt na Measarroch, climbing steadily in a south-easterly direction to a broad bealach called Màm a' Phobuill.

Before the bealach is reached, a route can be taken up the steep northern end of the mountain, but it is slightly more interesting to continue to the bealach and ascend the faint north-eastern spur instead. To do so, slant off to the right just before the high point of the bealach and head towards a rather indistinct, broad, rocky spur which separates two shallow corries on the eastern flank of the mountain. The best way to tackle this spur is by a faint grassy ramp which slants gently upwards

The summit ridge, Sgùrr nan Gillean in the distance (Noel Williams)

from left to right.

When the slope steepens, ascend a grassy patch to the left of a train of boulders then clamber over boulders to reach the start of the ramp and follow this rightwards without undue difficulty. Eventually emerge in the upper part of the corrie where a distinctive reptilian-like rock can be seen in profile on the skyline. Continue up the slope above to gain the crest of the north ridge at the southern end of a horizontal section.

Turn left and ascend a pleasant stretch of ridge directly to the narrow summit marked by a small and precariously perched cairn (**6.5km; 730m; 2h 40min**). The views are breathtaking. The whole Cuillin range lies across Glen Sligachan to the west, Blàbheinn, Garbh-bheinn and Belig are close by to the south and the rest of the Western Red Hills lie to the north.

Descend the delightful south ridge with superb views straight ahead of Blàbheinn and its neighbours. At a dip (NG512249) before the small south-east top, turn left and descend northwards by a line of old fence posts back to Màm a' Phobuill. Partway down cross a burn before rejoining the path used in ascent (**13.5km; 730m; 4h 30min**).

From the bealach Màm a' Phobuill it is possible to link Marsco with Beinn Dearg Mhòr, via the small but

Marsco from the south-west (Noel Williams)

finely proportioned summit of Cìche na Beinn Deirge (509m) to the south-east of Beinn Dearg Mheadhonach. From the bealach ascend north-east to a path running east below the extensive screes on the south side of Cìche na Beinn Deirge. Follow this path, a little faint in places, round to the south-east face with views north-east to Loch Ainort, to gain heathery and rocky sections in the scree which can be ascended north with more ease to gain the cairned summit.

From here follow the broad ridge to a col, then ascend straight up Beinn Dearg Mheadhonach's south ridge to the summit (3km; 380m; 1h 35min

from Marsco). Continue to Beinn Dearg Mhòr and Glamaig if desired, as described for that route on p306.

The ascent of Marsco from the north-east starts from the car park at the bend in the road by the Eas a' Bhradain waterfall. Ascend the Druim Eadar Dà Choire ridge which extends from Garbh-bheinn, cutting off right before Pt.489m to gain the bealach, then climb the south-east ridge. Descend as for the main route then return alongside the boggy Allt Coire nam Bruadaran. Marsco can also be included in an extended round with Belig and Garbh-bheinn from this starting point.

See previous pages for map

Marsco, left, Beinn Dearg Mheadhonach in shade, Beinn Dearg Mhòr and Glamaig from Garbh-bheinn (Tom Prentice)

The Storr and the Old Man of Storr from across Loch Leathan (Rab Anderson)

> **SKYE**
>
> **The Storr**; 719m; (G68); L23; NG495540; *the steep high cliff, from Gaelic 'stòr'. Possibly a Gaelicisation of original old Norse 'stor', large*
>
> **Hartaval**; 669m; (G146); L23; NG480551; *hill of the stag. Old Norse 'fjall', mountain, has been Gaelicised to '-bhal', and Anglicised to '-val'*

The two Grahams of The Storr and its more retiring partner, Hartaval, form the highest points on the fabulous Trotternish Ridge which snakes its way up the length of the Trotternish Peninsula in northern Skye. The ascent to the summit of The Storr passes one of the island's most iconic landmarks, the leaning rock pinnacle of the Old Man of Storr. The scenery and the rock architecture of the landslip area around the Old Man is spectacular and one of the 'must see' places in Scotland. As a result the main car park is often busy. However there is a choice of parking depending on the route chosen.

There are two car parks, about 900m apart, a short distance to the north of Portree at the end of the Storr lochs, Loch Fada and Loch Leathan. There is an area of felled forest here which has somewhat affected the aesthetics of the surroundings, at least until new growth occurs.

The first car park at (NG502524)

which is gated and is the least used by tourists, is also perhaps the better if the circuit with a return via the Bealach Beag is intended. The route from here climbs northwards up the side of the felled area. Above this, a path can be picked up which leads

through the area known as The Sanctuary, heading for the Old Man of Storr who leans skywards from his somewhat precarious perch on a mound, amidst a mass of attendant pinnacles and twisted rock formations. Huge impregnable cliffs, riven

The Old Man of Storr (Iain Thow)

with dark gullies tower above and form an impressive backdrop to the chaotic landscape. Various paths allow the many nooks and crannies to be investigated.

The second car park is the busiest one and is located at NG509529, directly below the Old Man and the felled forestry plantation. From here a good path leads steeply through the felled area, then on up boulder-strewn slopes to The Sanctuary and the Old Man. Both routes join beyond the Old Man where the path to the summit of The Storr runs north between Needle Rock and the cliffs to make a rising traverse below the cliffs, which gradually diminish in height. Cross a fence, then the small rock band marking the end of the cliffs and emerge on the east shoulder of the hill.

There are two options from here. The easiest route, suited to those of a more nervous disposition, follows a fairly level path that makes a wide arc across Coire Scamadal to reach the north ridge on the corrie's far side. This ridge then leads pleasantly south up to the trig point on the amazingly flat grassy summit of The Storr, which sits on the very edge of the precipice high above The Sanctuary (**4km; 580m; 2h**).

A steeper and more direct line from the east shoulder follows the left-

Hartaval, centre, and The Storr, left, from the north (Tom Prentice)

hand edge above the cliffs. Traces of path lead up a barren slope of scree and through small rock bands where there is much overall looseness. It is a spectacular way to the top and passes the head of a number of impressive gullies that spilt the massive cliffs and offer glimpses of the Old Man far below. Towards the top it is possible to climb onto the pinnacle which is The Storr East Top (c710m), however this sits above big drops and although relatively easy, great care should be taken.

Beneath the top, traverse right and either go up a small rock bluff, or traverse beneath it then ascend to regain the path and a ladder of steps up the steep grassy slope in the shallow gully which forms an obvious break in the upper rocks. Emerge onto the flat grassy slopes leading to the summit. A slightly shorter but perhaps more time consuming route.

Descend north a short way along the rim of the corrie then drop more steeply west off the back to reach the Bealach a' Chuirn at the foot of Hartaval. Continue up the shoulder and follow a line of old fence posts up the hillside, crossing the head of a fine corrie to gain the summit of Hartaval (**6km; 760m; 2h 50min**).

Return to the bealach. Two options now exist. The first gains the northern shoulder of The Storr by climbing diagonally left up the slope above a rock outcrop, aiming for a small rock bluff, then traverse across Coire Scamadal back to the route of ascent and the Old Man of Storr (**11km; 860m; 4h 20min**).

The alternative is to contour south around the west flank of The Storr, initially following the fence posts, then a line below them to reach the Bealach Beag. Aim for the low point then pick up the burn and follow this steeply down a break in the cliffs with little rock steps. Care is required here although there is nothing of any diffi-culty. Beneath this, grassy slopes lead to the first car park (**10km; 760m; 4h**).

SOUTH UIST
Beinn Mhòr; *620m; (G205); L22; NF808310; big mountain*

A rugged chain of hills runs down the eastern side of The Uists and their highpoint on South Uist, Beinn Mhòr, is a fine hill with a splendid lofty ridge. On one side this looks out over a sprinkling of lochans and long sandy beaches into the Atlantic Ocean, whilst on the other it gives views over The Minch to Skye with the mainland beyond. The ascent of Beinn Mhòr provides a memorable day out and is best saved for good weather.

Start at the road end along the north side of Loch Aineort, taking care not to block the turning circle (NF788283). Walk east through the trees and fuchsias on a well-constructed footpath just above the sea, passing a ruin and crossing a bridge over the head of a small inlet. A little further on, at another ruined building there is a deeper inlet and the path, now less distinct, runs up the west side of this. Pass around the head of the inlet and cross the two burns that drain into it, then climb a stile over a low fence and continue up

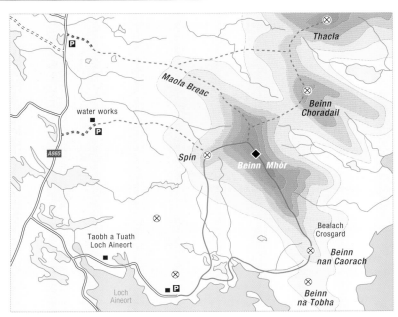

and around the other side to pick up a path. This traverses the slope away from the obvious notch of the Bealach Crosgard, which is the direction you feel you should be going in.

However, the direct approach to the bealach gives steeper and tougher going.

Cross a small bridge over the burn draining from Beinn nan Caorach and

The south ridge of Beinn Mhòr above Bealach Crosgard (Rab Anderson)

Looking south to Beinn Mhòr's summit and the Heileasdale Buttresses (Noel Williams)

Beinn na Tobha, then start to climb upwards beside the right-hand burn and curve up onto Beinn nan Caorach (347m) which is crossed to gain the Bealach Crosgard. Now with fine views opening up all around, climb grassy slopes onto the whaleback ridge which provides a pleasant climb past a false top to the trig point perched on the edge of some cliffs (**6km; 700m; 2h 40min**).

After a short descent, continue to the slight rise which is the northern top, along a splendid narrow ridge with steep slopes plummeting dramatically into Gleann Heileasdail to the east. Drop down steeply due west using the grassy slopes between the boulders to reach a small lochan then the top of the spur of Spin (356m). Descend, the broad rocky ridge south towards Loch Aineort. Cross the flats below and head between two small lochans to pass the western end of Loch nam Faoileann to reach the path at the first small inlet, which leads back to the start (**11.5km; 710m; 4h 15min**).

A quicker route, though not as good, starts from the road to the water works that goes through an unlocked gate to the side of the A865

past the standing stone at NF770322. This gains a helpful 50m of height. Go round the north side of the knoll of Beinn a' Charra then cross the burn and climb Spin via its north-west shoulder. Thereafter climb steeply to the north top of Beinn Mhòr and traverse the ridge to gain the summit (**4.5km; 590m; 2h**). Return the same way (**9km; 610m; 3h 20min**).

Another route uses the peat track which starts at NF768346 on the A865 at the north end of Loch Dòbhrain. This is the better start point for the fine round which takes in Beinn Corradail and Thacla. Follow the peat track to its end then pass a group of three small lochans to climb onto Maola Breac, the north-west ridge of Beinn Mhòr, and continue up the fine narrow upper section to gain the north top. Thereafter the splendid level crest leads to the summit (6km; 620m; 2h 25min).

Return to the north top then descend the north-east ridge to the Bealach Heileasdail. From there, gain the south-east ridge of Beinn Choradail by a slanting climb due east up its steep but easy south-west flank, crossing the small subsidiary grassy top Feith-bhealach, to reach

the 527m summit of Beinn Choradail (**9km; 870m; 3h 45min**).

To reach Thacla from here, it is important to avoid the steep buttresses that flank the north side of Beinn Choradail. Do this by first heading north-north-east for 50m or so along the short summit ridge from the summit cairn to find a small scree gully. Descend this to a sloping grassy traverse which leads down north-west to the broad bealach between the hills, at the head of Gleanns Usinis and Dorchaidh. The summit of Thacla (606m) is then easily reached by a steep, grassy and stony ascent of its south-west flank (**11.5km; 1170m; 5h**). The best descent is to return to the bealach then descend the north-west spur of Beinn Choradail, Maoladh Creag nam Fitheach and traverse west across the foot of the north-west ridge of Beinn Mhòr to the head of the peat track and follow this back to the road (**18km; 1170m; 6h 50min**).

The linear traverse of Beinn Mhòr, Beinn Choradail and Thacla, starting from Aridh nam Bàn and finishing at Loch Sgioport, is a splendid outing but with the obvious problem that the finish is some way from the start.

Uisgneabhal Mòr and Tèileasbhal from Aird Asaig to the south (Rab Anderson)

HARRIS

Uisgneabhal Mòr; *729m; (G55); L13, 14; NB120085; Old Norse 'fjall', mountain, has been Gaelicised to '-bhal'. The first element is probably old Norse but Gaelicised to 'uisge' water*

Uisgneabhal Mòr and its smaller neighbour Tèileasbhal form the central part of the beautiful and rugged North Harris Hills. They are a shapely pair of peaks that catch the eye when travelling north on the road from Tarbert, lying to the west of the higher An Cliseam group of hills and to the east of the other two Harris Grahams, Oireabhal and Tiorga Mòr.

Park either side of the bridge over the river at the sea inlet of Loch Mhiabhaig, at the start of the track up Gleann Mhiabhaig. This track is the return route past the mighty rock prow of Sròn Scourst, seen in profile ahead. Walk beside a fence on the east side of the river for 300m and where this veers off right, strike up the hillside. There is no path and initially the going is quite tough but once the knoll of Creag na Speireig is reached it becomes easier and the elegant south ridge of Uisgneabhal Mòr leads upwards with ever expanding views. Broad at first, the ridge gradually narrows down and here traces of a path are picked up and lead along the top of some cliffs to a large cairn

perched right on the edge (**4km; 730m; 2h 10min**). There are splendid views east across the narrow rift to Mulla bho Tuath and Mulla bho Deas in the An Cliseam group, as well as west to Oireabhal.

Descend north through a boulder-field, then down steep grassy slopes

around the edge of the corrie and down through another boulder-field to reach the col between the two peaks. The ascent to Tèileasbhal (697m) is steep but short-lived and a small crag which bars the way up the crest is easily bypassed (**5km; 870m; 2h 45min**).

A shorter return is possible but it is better to drop down and follow the summit spur north to its end before heading down the long north-west shoulder through boulders, aiming for two lochans that can be seen ahead at the end of track in the main glen. The line of descent runs along the head of the hanging-valley of Gleann Uisleitir, on the other side of which, the rocky profile of Sròn Scourst holds the view.

Eventually drop off this shoulder, just after a steepening, and descend to the burn which leads to the track in Gleann Mhiabhaig. A fairly level 4.5km walk along this track leads back to the start, passing beneath Sròn Scourst, whose rocky slopes tower above the track and the lochan at its foot (**12.5km; 870m; 4h 45min**).

HARRIS

Oireabhal; *662m; (G160); L13, 14; NB083099; Old Norse 'fjall', mountain, has been Gaelicised to '-bhal'. The first element is possibly Old Norse 'orri', moorfowl, i.e. red grouse. There are also two peaks of this name on Harris and one on Rum*

Tiorga Mòr; *679m; (G131); L13, 14; NB055115; Tiorga is obscure, 'mòr' is Gaelic for big*

Together with their satellite tops, these two Grahams lie either side of Gleann Chliostair and are the highest points of the westernmost hills of North Harris. Oireabhal forms part of a 7km ridge running along the east side of the glen which terminates with the great rock promontory of Sròn Uladal. Tiorga Mòr lies on the other side of the glen and is the higher and more rugged of the pair. The traverse of the hills on the east side of the glen, followed by a visit to view the dramatic cliffs of Sròn Uladal then the ascent of Tiorga Mòr gives a superb outing.

The views from these hills are stunning and extend north beyond the Harris Hills to the Uig Hills on Lewis then north-west to the sand-fringed island of Scarp. To the south is the island of Taransay, the sands of Luskentyre and hills of South Harris. If you are lucky, out west will be the islands of St Kilda, sitting on the edge of the Continental Shelf.

The best starting point for the full circuit is at the northern end of Loch nan Caor where there is off-road parking at a bend in the B887 (NB066073), about 1km to the west of the high point of the road at Cliasmol. Alternatively, park further west, at the start of the access road to Loch Chliostair (see below) and walk the 1.5km along the road at the start, rather than the end.

Climb east onto the south-west shoulder of Cleiseabhal (511m) and follow this to the trig point on the stony top (**2km; 460m; 1h 15min**). Crags fall steeply to the north of the summit and the route descends north-east onto the connecting ridge which runs north above crags on the east side to reach a well-defined bouldery bealach. From here, the ridge, continues north over the small intermediate summit of Bìdigidh (500m) then on to the summit of Oireabhal (**4km; 740m; 2h 15min**).

Drop down the slope to the north-north-east to gain the bealach then climb the ridge onto the fine Ulabhal (659m). Descend northwards towards the lesser top of Muladal then swing westwards and descend close to the burn to reach the path running along the floor of the glen at the north end of Loch Aiseabhat. The simple option from here is to make the 340m climb straight up the other side onto the ▶

Tiorga Mòr from Oireabhal across Gleann Chliostair (Grahame Nicoll)

Oireabhal and Bidigidh from near Amhuinnsuidhe (Rab Anderson)

unnamed rounded grassy top at NB061121, which is probably Tiorga Beag; the OS place this name further north where there is no summit. From here, a short drop south-west and a final 130m climb gain the trig point and cairn on Tiorga Mòr (**9.5km; 1210m; 4h 30min**).

However, a longer and better route descends the path north, out in front of the remarkable overhanging cliffs of Sròn Uladal which sits sphinx-like at the head of the glen. Regarded as the most impressive crag in the British Isles the Sròn is home to some of the hardest rock climbs in the country. Continue to Loch Uladal out in front of the nose itself, on the left of which is where pioneers in the late 1930s recorded the area's first climbs. Now, either retrace your steps to Loch Aiseabhat, or climb west up the steep hillside to gain a shallow col south of Màs a' Chnoic Chuairtich then traverse south along the rocky ridge above the crags of Creagan Leathan. Ascend Tiorga Beag and continue to Tiorga Mòr. This detour adds another (**4km; 180m; 1h 15min**) onto the round.

Two options exist for the descent off Tiorga Mòr. The most obvious is down the prominent south-east ridge to cross the dam at the south end of Loch Chliostair then follow the track back. However, although there are no real difficulties there is a lot of rough, rocky terrain which although of interest does require more concentration. Another option heads south down less complicated slopes, either directly to the track, or perhaps easier to the path through Gleann Leòsaid then the track. Follow the track to the road just to the east of the gates to Amhuinnsuidhe where a 1.5km walk along the road leads back to the start (**16.5km; 1250m; 6h 40min**). If the detour to view Sròn Uladal is made then the additional time for this needs added.

Oireabhal can be climbed on its own starting at (NB066073), as for the main traverse described above (**4km; 740m; 2h 15min**), then returning over Bìdigidh and descending south-west

Sròn Uladal with the summits of Ulabhal and Oireabhal beyond (Noel Williams)

from the bealach south of this, first steeply, then west more gently to the small Loch Collas Sgairbhe. From here, a descending traverse of the west flank of Cleiseabhal leads easily back to the start (8km; 780m; 3h 30min).

Another option is to park along the road signposted to Chliostair Power Station and Marine Harvest's Amhuinnsuidhe Hatchery. Do not park in the entrance since large vehicles require this for turning. There is limited space beside the gates to Amhuinnsuidhe and a short way up the track where the riverside verge is wide enough to accommodate a number of vehicles opposite a passing place. There is also limited parking at the locked gate 400m further on where the road forks right to the fish farm. Follow the track past Loch Leòsaid and the power station

Tiorga Mòr from the south (Rab Anderson)

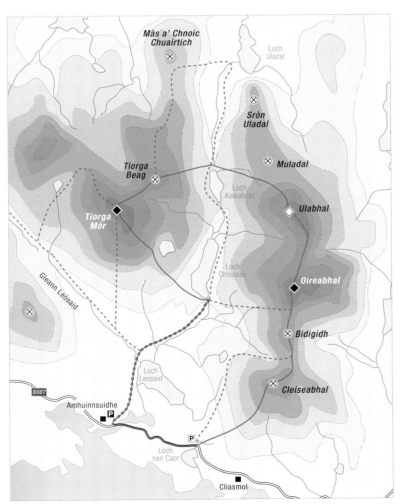

towards the dam, then head east to gain the south ridge of Oireabhal (**5km; 650m; 2h 10min**). Either of these options can be extended north over Ulabhal, with a possible visit to view Sròn Uladal, then a return past Loch Aiseabhat and Loch Chliostair.

To climb Tiorga Mòr on its own, park along the start of the track to Loch Chliostair and follow it to the bridge across the burn flowing into Loch Leòsaid. Head north-west up Gleann Leòsaid, picking up a path after 500m or so and following it for another 500m before striking north up the steep but easy south flank of Tiorga Mòr to reach the summit (**4km; 670m; 2h**). Alternatively, carry on up Gleann Leòsaid to the bealach at NB040111 then head north, first to the attractive small Loch Bràigh Bheagarais, then to the bealach with Ceartabhal. Now head south to climb the north-east ridge to the top of Tiorga Mòr (**7km; 670m; 2h 40min**).

Another option is to continue past the power station, cross the dam and climb the fine and prominent south-east ridge which gives some easy, though avoidable, scrambling (**5.5km; 670m; 2h 20min**). A return can be made by one of the other ascent options, or the outing can be extended down the north-east ridge to return past Loch Aiseabhat and Loch Chliostair.

Scottish Hills over 2000ft (609.60m) and less than 2500ft (762m) in Height

The Table that follows lists 224 Scottish hills which are over 2000ft (609.60m) and less than 2500ft (762m) in height, which have an all round drop, or prominence, of 150m. Despite the metrication of UK mapping, the traditional method of grouping hills into their original imperial measurement height bands in feet has prevailed, in accordance with the height Tables for The Munros and The Corbetts, albeit that this creates odd metric equivalents for use with contemporary maps.

Hugh Munro's *Tables Giving All the Scottish Mountains Exceeding 3000ft in Height* was published in 1891 and John Rooke Corbett's *List of Scottish Mountains 2500ft and Under 3000ft in Height* was published in 1952. However, unlike Munro before him, Corbett set a separation criterion to illustrate how distinct each hill on his list was from those around it. This was based on a set number of map contour rings, subsequently interpreted to mean that hills on his list had to involve a re-ascent of 500ft (152.4m) on all sides, thereby illustrating their prominence, or what has become known as their drop.

A definitive list of the hills between 2000ft and 2500ft was finally agreed in 1992 between Alan Dawson and Fiona Torbet (neè Graham). They too continued the practice of grouping hills within a height band measured in feet but a metric height separation criterion of 150m was applied, this being the closest round metric equivalent to 500ft. The hills were named The Grahams and this list is the one used for this book. Alan Dawson continues to maintain the official hill listing for The Grahams and that differs from the one here, principally because Dawson is actively resurveying hill heights and summit locations. However, at the time of writing, these surveys are not being carried out to Ordnance Survey standards and the results are not being sent to them for ratification and inclusion on their mapping.

The Ordnance Survey is the national mapping authority responsible for the maintenance of the definitive record of Britain's geographic features. Where the results of surveys have been carried out to OS standards and accepted by the OS for inclusion on its mapping, they are viewed as official and the SMC has used them as the basis for the information in this book. Where these surveys have not been carried out to OS standards and have not been sent to the OS for ratification, it is the SMC's view that they cannot be deemed to be official.

However, the SMC recognises that this unratified survey data might well be accurate and is therefore of relevance to hill-walkers. Where applicable, a note of such information is made in the walk description and in the Tables of Grahams and Donalds that follow. The SMC would like to thank Alan Dawson for providing his survey data. The SMC hopes that in the future this survey data, if validated, can be incorporated onto OS mapping for the benefit of all.

Table/Column Explanations

Section Number & Name: For the purpose of this guidebook, the layout of this Table of Grahams differs from that maintained by Alan Dawson, and that previously published by the SMC. The Grahams have been grouped into geographical Sections which correspond to the established 1-17 Sections used by the SMC for The Munros, with the addition of a Section 0 for the Lowland Hills, as in The Corbetts.

Where necessary, due to the size of a particular geographical Section and the resultant number of hills it contains, that Section has been subdivided by the use of an alphabetic letter. Section 0 has been divided into 0a, 0b and 0c, Section 1 into 1a and 1b and Section 10 into 10a and 10b. Due to the lack of Grahams, some Sections have been combined for this book, namely 2 & 3, and 5, 6 & 7.

As with previous SMC Tables, these Sections are generally ordered in a logical snake-like progression through Scotland from the south-west to the north-east, finishing with The Islands. The official Table of Grahams lists hills in each Section in descending order of height, however for ease of use in connection with this book the Table here lists hills in a geographic order. This has the advantage that hills which are generally linked and climbed together should appear together in the Tables.

Name: The name is generally that according to the OS. When there are two hills with the same name, standard brackets give a relevant location. When there is an overall name for a hill massif, or a second, or an alternative name for a hill, this is shown in square brackets.

Height: This is in metres and taken from OS maps. A letter in brackets refers to additional height information given in the notes at the end.

G No: Grahams in order of height, (G1) being the highest. The letter 'T' denotes a 'Twin' where current OS maps do not indicate which of two adjacent hills is the highest; unratified surveys have separated the four pairs of twins, see notes.

OS Map & Grid Ref: The first two digits refer to the relevant OS 1:50k Landranger series map which covers the hill. An eight figure OS grid reference, prefixed by two grid letters, is given in the following Table, which provides the location of a summit to within 10m, and a six figure grid reference has been given in the text, which provides the location of a summit to within 100m.

Munros Tables and Donalds Tables both included Tops. As a result Munro's Tables lists 508 summits, of which 282 are classed as separate mountains, or Munros, and 226 are subsidiary Munro Tops. Donald did the same but fortunately, Corbett did not do this and neither did Torbet and Dawson at the time, so Graham Tops are not listed here. For the uninitiated, Graham Tops do not just occur on Grahams, as indeed Munro Tops only occur on Munros, they occur on Grahams, Corbetts and Munros and they number around 1000. Being higher, Corbett Tops occur on Corbetts and Munros and number around 700. Complete lists of Grahams, Graham Tops and Corbett Tops are published by TACit Press.

Name	Height	G No	OS Map	Grid Ref	Page	Date climbed
SECTION 0a – Galloway & The Lowthers						
Cairnsmore of Fleet	711	(G79)	83	NX 5016 6707	14	
Lamachan Hill	717	(G71)	77	NX 4352 7690	16	
Millfore	657	(G169)	77	NX 4779 7545	16	
Mullwharchar	692	(G116)	77	NX 4542 8664	19	
Craignaw	645	(G180)	77	NX 4592 8333	19	
Windy Standard	698	(G109)	77	NS 6201 0146	30	
Blackcraig Hill	700 (a)	(G105)	71,77	NS 6476 0640	30	
Green Lowther	732	(G44)	71,78	NS 9003 1203	36	
Ballencleuch Law	689	(G119)	78	NS 9356 0497	34	
Queensberry	697	(G111)	78	NX 9890 9975	32	
SECTION 0b – The Borders						
Tinto	711	(G80)	72	NS 9532 3437	40	
Culter Fell	748	(G15)	72	NT 0528 2908	42	
Gathersnow Hill	688	(G121)	72	NT 0587 2570	44	
Andrewhinney Hill	677	(G137)	79	NT 1975 1387	46	
Croft Head	637	(G188)	79	NT 1530 0565	48	
Capel Fell	678	(G133)	79	NT 1639 0690	48	
Ettrick Pen	692	(G115)	79	NT 1999 0765	48	
Dun Rig	744	(G22)	73	NT 2534 3155	64	
Blackhope Scar	651	(G174)	73	NT 3152 4833	66	
Windlestraw Law	659	(G162)	73	NT 3712 4309	68	
Cauldcleuch Head	619	(G209)	79	NT 4565 0068	70	
SECTION 0c – The Midland Valley						
Ben Cleuch	721	(G62)	58	NN 9027 0063	73	
Uamh Bheag	664 (b)	(G156) T	57	NN 6911 1185	77	
Uamh Bheag East Top	664 (b)	(G156) T	57	NN 6961 1193	77	
SECTION 1a – Loch Fyne to Loch Lomond						
Cruach nan Capull	611	(G220)	63	NS 0957 7954	79	
Creag Tharsuinn	643	(G184)	56	NS 0882 9136	83	
Beinn Mhòr	741	(G29)	56	NS 1078 9081	81	
Beinn Bheag	618	(G210)	56	NS 1259 9320	81	
Beinn Ruadh	664	(G155)	56	NS 1557 8837	80	
Beinn Lochain	703	(G97)	56	NN 1602 0062	84	
Stob na Boine Druim-fhinn	658	(G163)	56	NN 1688 0253	84	
Cruach nam Mult	611	(G221)	56	NN 1689 0559	86	
Stob an Eas	732	(G47)	56	NN 1853 0738	88	
Cnoc Còinnich	761	(G2)	56	NN 2335 0075	88	
Beinn Chaorach	713	(G74)	56	NS 2875 9236	90	
Beinn a' Mhanaich	709	(G86)	56	NS 2691 9460	90	
Beinn Eich	703	(G96)	56	NS 3021 9467	92	
Cruach an t-Sìdhein	684	(G123)	56	NS 2752 9651	92	
Doune Hill	734	(G39)	56	NS 2906 9713	92	
Mid Hill	657	(G168)	56	NS 3214 9626	92	
Tullich Hill	632	(G196)	56	NN 2935 0064	95	
Beinn Bhreac	681	(G127)	56	NN 3213 0005	95	
Beinn Damhain	684	(G124)	50,56	NN 2820 1730	97	
Beinn Bhalgairean	636 (c)	(G189)	50	NN 2026 2410	100	
Meall nan Gabhar	744 (d)	(G21)	50	NN 2357 2402	100	
Meall Odhar	656	(G171)	50	NN 2980 2984	99	
Fiarach	652	(G173)	50	NN 3448 2615	98	
SECTION 1b – Loch Lomond to Loch Tay						
Cruinn a' Bheinn	632	(G194)	56	NN 3654 0514	103	
Ben Venue	729	(G53)	57	NN 4746 0633	104	
Meall Mòr	747	(G17)	50,56	NN 3837 1515	106	

Name	Height	G No	OS Map	Grid Ref	Page	Date climbed
Stob Breac	688	(G122)	57	NN 4473 1661	*111*	
The Stob	753 (e)	(G10)	51	NN 4913 2318	*110*	
Creag Mhòr	658	(G164)	57	NN 5103 1851	*108*	
Sgiath a' Chaise	645 (f)	(G181)	57	NN 5836 1694	*107*	
Mòr Bheinn	640	(G186)	51,57	NN 7162 2117	*113*	
Beinn Dearg	706 (g)	(G87)	57	NN 6967 1975	*112*	
Meall Buidhe	719	(G67)	51	NN 5768 2757	*114*	
Creag Gharbh	637	(G187)	51	NN 6323 3273	*115*	
Creag Each	672 (h)	(G143)	51	NN 6525 2637	*116*	
Creag Ruadh	712	(G77)	51	NN 6742 2925	*116*	
Ciste Buide a' Claidheimh [Shee of Ardtalnaig]	759	(G5)	51,52	NN 7295 3515	*118*	
Beinn na Gainimh	730	(G51)	52	NN 8372 3446	*119*	
Meall nan Caorach	623 (i)	(G201)	52	NN 9286 3389	*120*	
Meall Reamhar	620 (j)	(G206)	52	NN 9220 3326	*120*	
Meall Dearg	690	(G117)	52	NN 8865 4149	*121*	

SECTION 2 & 3 – Loch Tay to Loch Linnhe

Name	Height	G No	OS Map	Grid Ref	Page	Date climbed
Meall a' Mhuic	745	(G18)	42,51	NN 5793 5080	*123*	
Beinn na Sroine	636	(G190)	50	NN 2339 2894	*126*	
Beinn Donachain	650	(G176)	50	NN 1988 3165	*127*	
Màm Hael	726	(G57)	50	NN 0085 4089	*132*	
Beinn Mòlurgainn	690	(G118)	50	NN 0195 4006	*132*	
Beinn Mheadhonach	715	(G73)	50	NN 0198 3689	*132*	
Beinn nan Lus	709	(G85)	50	NN 1307 3757	*131*	
Meall Garbh	701	(G102)	50	NN 1679 3672	*130*	
Beinn Suidhe	676	(G139)	50	NN 2117 4004	*129*	
Meall Tairbh	665	(G154)	50	NN 2509 3758	*128*	
Sgòrr a' Choise	663	(G159)	41	NN 0844 5515	*134*	
Meall Mòr	676	(G141)	41	NN 1061 5596	*134*	
Sgòrr na Cìche [Pap of Glencoe]	742	(G28)	41	NN 1252 5943	*136*	
Stob na Cruaiche [A' Chruach]	739	(G34)	41	NN 3636 5710	*124*	

SECTION 4 - Loch Linnhe to Loch Ericht

Name	Height	G No	OS Map	Grid Ref	Page	Date climbed
Beinn na Gucaig	616	(G213)	41	NN 0629 6533	*139*	
Tom Meadhoin	621	(G204)	41	NN 0873 6210	*139*	
Beinn na Cloiche	646	(G179)	41	NN 2847 6487	*140*	
Creag Ghuanach	621	(G203)	41	NN 2999 6900	*140*	
Cnap Cruinn	742	(G27)	41	NN 3028 7748	*142*	
Binnein Shuas	747	(G16)	34,42	NN 4630 8268	*143*	
Binnein Shios	667	(G150)	34,42	NN 4924 8571	*143*	
Meall nan Eagan	658	(G165)	42	NN 5967 8747	*145*	

SECTION 5, 6 & 7 – Loch Ericht to Glen Esk

Name	Height	G No	OS Map	Grid Ref	Page	Date climbed
Creag a' Mhadaidh	612	(G217)	42	NN 6346 6501	*147*	
Creag Ruadh	658	(G166)	42	NN 6852 8821	*148*	
Blath Bhalg	641	(G185)	43	NO 0194 6112	*149*	
Mount Blair	744	(G20)	43	NO 1674 6297	*150*	
Duchray Hill [Mealna Letter]	702	(G100)	43	NO 1615 6725	*150*	
Badandun Hill	740	(G31)	44	NO 2074 6788	*152*	
Cat Law	671	(G145)	44	NO 3188 6108	*153*	
Corwharn	611 (k)	(G222)	44	NO 2886 6511	*153*	
Hill of Wirren	678	(G134)	44	NO 5228 7393	*154*	
Hunt Hill	705	(G92)	44	NO 3800 8053	*156*	

SECTION 8 – Deeside to Speyside

Name	Height	G No	OS Map	Grid Ref	Page	Date climbed
Creag Bhalg	668	(G148)	43	NO 0917 9123	*159*	

Name	Height	G No	OS Map	Grid Ref	Page	Date climbed
Geallaig Hill	743	(G24)	37,44	NO 2979 9817	160	
Mona Gowan	749	(G14)	37	NJ 3359 0583	161	
Pressendye	619	(G207)	37	NJ 4903 0897	162	
Cnap Chaochan Aitinn	715	(G72)	36	NJ 1458 0996	165	
Ladylea Hill	610 (l)	(G224)	37	NJ 3431 1682	164	
The Buck	721	(G63)	37	NJ 4121 2339	163	
Creagan a' Chaise	722	(G60)	36	NJ 1042 2415	167	
Càrn a' Ghille Chearr	710	(G82)	36	NJ 1396 2985	167	
Cook's Cairn	755	(G9)	37	NJ 3022 2783	166	

SECTION 9 – Speyside to the Great Glen

Name	Height	G No	OS Map	Grid Ref	Page	Date climbed
Càrn Glas-choire	659	(G161)	35,36	NH 8915 2916	171	
Càrn nan Tri-tighearnan	615	(G214)	27	NH 8231 3903	172	
Càrn na h-Easgainn	618	(G211)	27	NH 7440 3207	173	
Creag Liath	743	(G26)	35	NH 6637 0077	174	
Creag Dubh (Newtonmore)	756	(G8)	35	NN 6780 9723	175	
Creag Ruadh	622	(G202)	35	NN 5580 9138	176	
Creag Dhubh (Glen Spean)	658	(G167)	34,41	NN 3226 8245	177	
Leana Mhòr (west)	684	(G125)	34,41	NN 2847 8787	178	
Leana Mhòr (east)	676	(G140)	34,41	NN 3171 8791	179	

SECTION 10a – Loch Linnhe to Glenfinnan

Name	Height	G No	OS Map	Grid Ref	Page	Date climbed
Beinn Mheadhoin	739	(G33)	49	NM 7991 5144	181	
Beinn na Cille	652	(G172)	49	NM 8543 5420	182	
Druim na Sgriodain	734	(G40)	40	NM 9784 6561	183	
Sgòrr Mhic Eacharna	650	(G177)	40	NM 9284 6304	184	
Beinn Bheag	736	(G38)	40	NM 9145 6353	184	
Sgùrr nan Cnamh	701	(G104)	40	NM 8866 6432	186	
Sgùrr a' Chaorainn	761	(G3)	40	NM 8950 6620	187	
Stob Mhic Bheathain	721	(G64)	40	NM 9140 7139	188	
Meall nan Damh	723	(G59)	40	NM 9194 7450	190	
Glas Bheinn	636	(G191)	40	NM 9388 7584	190	
Beinn Gàire	666	(G152)	40	NM 7811 7488	192	
Croit Bheinn	663	(G158)	40	NM 8108 7733	192	

SECTION 10b – Glenfinnan to Glen Shiel

Name	Height	G No	OS Map	Grid Ref	Page	Date climbed
Sgùrr na Maothaich [Meith Bheinn]	710	(G83)	40	NM 8215 8725	199	
An Stac	718	(G69)	40	NM 8667 8890	204	
Glas-charn	633	(G193)	40	NM 8464 8373	198	
Aodann Chlèireig	663	(G157)	40	NM 9946 8254	196	
Meall Onfhaidh	681	(G128)	41	NN 0104 8408	196	
Mullach Coire nan Geur-oirean	727	(G56)	41	NN 0490 8927	200	
Stob a' Ghrianain [Druim Fada]	744	(G19)	41	NN 0870 8240	195	
Meall Blàir	656	(G170)	33	NN 0774 9503	203	
Sgùrr Chòinnich	749	(G13)	34	NN 1277 9497	202	
Glas Bheinn	732	(G46)	34	NN 1715 9189	201	
Slat Bheinn	700	(G106)	33	NG 9100 0274	206	
Meall nan Eun	667	(G151)	33	NG 9035 0522	206	
Druim Fada	713	(G76)	33	NG 8946 0833	211	
Beinn Clachach	643	(G183)	33	NG 8859 1091	209	
Beinn a' Chapuill	759	(G4)	33	NG 8351 1485	208	
Biod an Fhithich	644 (m)	(G182)	33	NG 9508 1473	212	

SECTION 11 – Glen Shiel to Loch Mullardoch (or Glen Cannich)

Name	Height	G No	OS Map	Grid Ref	Page	Date climbed
Càrnan Cruithneachd	729 (n)	(G54)	25,33	NG 9944 2582	215	
Càrn a' Chaochain	706	(G88)	34	NH 2351 1778	221	
Càrn Mhic an Toisich	678	(G135)	34	NH 3105 1858	217	

Name	Height	G No	OS Map	Grid Ref	Page	Date climbed
Meall a' Chràthaich	679	(G130)	26	NH 3607 2209	*217*	
Meall Fuar-mhonaidh	699	(G107)	26	NH 4570 2221	*219*	
Glas-bheinn Mhòr	651	(G175)	26	NH 4368 2316	*219*	
Beinn a' Mheadhoin	613	(G215)	25	NH 2186 2555	*223*	

SECTION 12 – Loch Mullardoch (or Glen Cannich) to Glen Carron

Name	Height	G No	OS Map	Grid Ref	Page	Date climbed
Creag Dhubh Mhòr	612 (o)	(G218)	25	NG 9828 4047	*233*	
Càrn na Breabaig	679	(G132)	25	NH 0667 3015	*225*	
An Cruachan	705	(G90)	25	NH 0937 3587	*229*	
Beinn na Muice	695	(G112)	25	NH 2188 4023	*228*	
Càrn Gorm	677	(G138)	26	NH 3286 3551	*226*	
Beinn Mheadhoin	665	(G153)	25	NH 2588 4777	*232*	
Meall na Faochaig	681	(G129)	25	NH 2575 5251	*231*	
Càrn na Còinnich	673 (p)	(G142) T	26	NH 3245 5105	*230*	
Meall nan Damh	673 (p)	(G142) T	26	NH 3529 5222	*230*	

SECTION 13 – Glen Carron to Loch Maree

Name	Height	G No	OS Map	Grid Ref	Page	Date climbed
Beinn a' Chlachain	626	(G199)	24	NG 724 4905	*238*	
Sgùrr a' Gharaidh	732	(G45)	24	NG 8841 4436	*237*	
Beinn na h-Eaglaise	736	(G37)	25	NG 9088 5235	*239*	
Càrn Breac	678	(G136)	25	NH 0451 5300	*235*	
Beinn na Feusaige	627	(G198)	25	NH 0900 5423	*235*	
An Ruadh-mheallan	671	(G144)	19,24	NG 8361 6148	*240*	
Beinn a' Chearcaill	725	(G58)	19	NG 9306 6378	*241*	

SECTION 14 - Loch Maree to Loch Broom

Name	Height	G No	OS Map	Grid Ref	Page	Date climbed
Meall a' Chaorainn	705	(G93)	19	NH 1360 6041	*243*	
Beinn a' Mhuinidh	692	(G114)	19	NH 0321 6604	*247*	
Beinn nan Ramh	711	(G78)	19	NH 1396 6615	*244*	
Beinn Bheag	668	(G147)	19	NH 0859 7138	*245*	
Groban	749	(G12)	19	NH 0997 7089	*245*	
Meall Mhèinnidh	722	(G61)	19	NG 9549 7484	*248*	
Beinn a' Chàisgein Beag	682	(G126)	19	NG 9655 8214	*249*	
Beinn Ghobhlach	635	(G192)	19	NH 0557 9435	*250*	

SECTION 15 – Loch Broom to the Cromarty Firth

Name	Height	G No	OS Map	Grid Ref	Page	Date climbed
Beinn Bhreac	667	(G149)	20	NH 2257 8865	*253*	
Meall Doire Faid	729	(G52)	20	NH 2208 7920	*254*	
Meall a' Chaorainn	632	(G195)	20	NH 3600 8272	*255*	
Beinn Tharsuinn (Strath Vaich)	710	(G81)	20	NH 4125 8294	*255*	
Càrn Loch nan Amhaichean	697	(G110)	20	NH 4112 7576	*256*	
Beinn nan Eun	743	(G25)	20	NH 4482 7597	*256*	
Meall Mòr	738	(G35)	20	NH 5153 7455	*258*	
Beinn Tharsuinn (Strath Rory)	692 (q)	(G113) T	21	NH 6063 7928	*259*	
Sìdean a' Choin Bhàin	692 (q)	(G113) T	21	NH 6000 8031	*259*	
Càrn Salachaidh	647	(G178)	20	NH 5188 8744	*260*	
Càrn a' Choin Deirg	701	(G103)	20	NH 3975 9234	*261*	

SECTION 16 – Loch Broom to The Pentland Firth

Name	Height	G No	OS Map	Grid Ref	Page	Date climbed
Ben More Coigach	743	(G23)	15	NC 0939 0426	*263*	
Sgùrr an Fhidhleir	705	(G94)	15	NC 0944 0545	*263*	
Beinn an Eoin	619	(G208)	15	NC 1049 0643	*266*	
Stac Pollaidh	612	(G219)	15	NC 1071 1061	*267*	
Caisteal Liath [Suilven]	731	(G49)	15	NC 1532 1836	*269*	
Ben Stack	720	(G66)	9	NC 2693 4229	*271*	
Sabhal Beag	732	(G48)	9	NC 3732 4291	*272*	
Càrn an Tionail	759 (r)	(G6)	16	NC 3923 3903	*273*	
Beinn Direach	688 (s)	(G120)	16	NC 4061 3806	*273*	
Meallan a' Chuail	750	(G11)	15	NC 3446 2923	*275*	

Name	Height	G No	OS Map	Grid Ref	Page	Date climbed
Meall an Fheur Loch	613	(G216)	16	NC 3619 3107	275	
Beinn Dhorain	628	(G197)	17	NC 9253 1566	277	
Creag a' Choire Ghlais						
[Ben Armine]	705	(G91)	16	NC 6948 2732	278	
Creag Mhòr	713	(G75)	16	NC 6984 2401	278	
Morven	706	(G89)	17	ND 0047 2854	281	
Scaraben	626	(G200)	17	ND 0661 2684	280	

SECTION 17 – The Islands: Arran, Jura, Mull, Rum, Skye, Uist & Harris

Name	Height	G No	OS Map	Grid Ref	Page	Date climbed
Mullach Buidhe (Arran)	721	(G65)	62,69	NR 9018 4278	286	
Beinn a' Chaolais (Jura)	733	(G41)	60,61	NR 4888 7344	288	
Beinn Shiantaidh (Jura)	757	(G7)	61	NR 5134 7477	288	
Beinn Fhada (Mull)	702	(G98)	47,48	NM 5400 3490	296	
Corra-bheinn (Mull)	704 (t)	(G95) T	48	NM 5732 3218	294	
Cruachan Dearg (Mull)	704 (t)	(G95) T	48	NM 5684 3320	294	
Cruach Choireadail (Mull)	618	(G212)	48	NM 5947 3048	294	
Ben Buie (Mull)	717	(G70)	49	NM 6041 2701	290	
Creach Beinn (Mull)	698	(G108)	49	NM 6427 2762	290	
Beinn Talaidh (Mull)	761 (u)	(G1)	49	NM 6255 3470	292	
Sgùrr Dearg (Mull)	741	(G30)	49	NM 6654 3399	292	
Trollabhal (Rum)	702	(G101)	39	NM 3773 9520	298	
Marsco (Skye)	736	(G36)	32	NG 5075 2519	308	
Beinn Dearg Mhòr (Sligachan-Skye)	731	(G50)	32	NG 5203 2849	306	
Belig (Skye)	702	(G99)	32	NG 5440 2405	304	
Beinn Dearg Mhòr (Broadford-Skye)	709	(G84)	32	NG 5877 2285	302	
Beinn na Caillich (Broadford-Skye)	732	(G42)	32	NG 6014 2330	302	
Ben Aslak (Skye)	610 (v)	(G223)	33	NG 7507 1912	300	
Sgùrr na Coinnich (Skye)	739	(G32)	33	NG 7624 2225	300	
Beinn na Caillich (Kylerhea-Skye)	732	(G43)	33	NG 7704 2297	300	
Hartaval (Skye)	669	(G146)	23	NG 4800 5510	310	
The Storr (Skye)	719	(G68)	23	NG 4954 5404	310	
Beinn Mhòr (South Uist)	620	(G205)	22	NF 8085 3109	312	
Tiorga Mòr (Harris)	679	(G131)	13,14	NB 0555 1150	315	
Oireabhal (Harris)	662	(G160)	13,14	NB 0839 0997	315	
Uisgneabhal Mòr (Harris)	729	(G55)	13,14	NB 1209 0858	314	

(a) Unratified height of 700.9m; (b) Unratified survey confirms the west top as 665.6m and the summit. The east top as 663.4m and the trig point between the two as lower again; (c) Unratified height of 636.7m; (d) Height from OS 1:10k confirmed by unratified survey (1:25k & 1:50k give 743m at NN23452418); (e) Unratified height of 753.6m; (f) Unratified height of 644.1m; N. Top given 642.7m; (g) Unratified height of 708.3m at NN68511900 Stùc na Cabaig; (h) Unratified height of 673.7m; (i) Unratified height of 623.7m; (j) Unratified height of 617.8m; (k) Unratified height of 609m which is below Graham height; (l) Unratified height of 609.1m which is below Graham height; (m) Unratified summit height of 645.9m & col height of 491.8m, giving a 154.1m drop; (n) Unratified height of 727.8m; (o) Unratified height of 610.9; (p) Unratified height of 673.4m for Càrn na Coinnich and 670.1m for Meall nan Damh de-twins these, confirming Càrn na Coinnich as the summit; (q) Unratified height of 688.9m for Sìdean a' Choin Bhàin de-twins these; (r) Unratified height of 785.5m; s) Unratified height of 688.9m; (t) Unratified height of 704.9m for Corra-bheinn and 704.1m for Cruachan Dearg de-twins these, confirming Corra-bheinn as the summit; (u) Ratified height of 761.7m which is below 2500ft.; (v) Unratified height of 609.0m is lower than Graham height.

All Hills in the Scottish Lowlands, 2000ft (609.60m) in Height and Above

Percy Donald's *Tables Giving All Hills in the Scottish Lowlands 2000ft in Height and Above* was first published in the Scottish Mountaineering Club Journal in 1935. This list was subsequently published by the SMC in its book *Munro's Tables and Other Tables of Lower Hills* and has been maintained by them ever since.

Percy Donald visited every elevation over 2000ft in what he considered The Scottish Lowlands. He developed a complex formula to distinguish between those points which he classified as Hills and those which he considered to be Tops. The format of his list was similar to the earlier Munro's Tables where summits were classified as Hills and Tops, now simply known as Munros and Munro Tops. Likewise the summits on Donald's List once classified as Hills and Tops are now simply known as Donalds and Donald Tops.

It has been suggested that Donald's List should conform to a metric equivalent and that the definition should be more precise and relate to a specific measure of re-ascent from neighbouring summits. However, albeit antiquated, it is felt that Percy Donald left us a clear definition of his categorisation which has produced a list of historical interest that is still relevant to today's hillwalker. It would be an aberration for The Munros to be forced down this route in order to conform to a more precise definition. So, like The Munros, the table that follows adheres to the traditional definitions. This is Donald's List and these are The Donalds. Those who complete the list are known as Donaldists.

An interesting point about Donald's Tables is that they are seen as a complete entity. So, most of those collecting The Donalds elect to climb all 140 Hills and subsidiary Tops on Donalds list; the Donalds and Donald Tops. This is unlike the Munros where the majority complete only the 282 principal Hills, or the Munros as they are known, and a remarkably low percentage, perhaps less than 20%, complete the 226 subsidiary Munro Tops as well.

The exact geographic compass of Donald's Tables was never made clear but the inclusion of the Ochill Hills suggests that his definition of Lowland was a geological one; namely, all of the country south of the Highland Boundary Fault. If this definition is strictly applied, it is clear that Donald overlooked a small group of hills lying to the south of Glen Artney which rise above the 2000ft level. Although appearing to be part of the Highlands, this group of two Hills and two Tops lies south of the Highland Boundary fault and was subsequently added to the tables.

Hills and Tops were determined by Percy Donald in accordance with the following rules: *Tops are all elevations with a drop of 100ft (30.48m) on all sides and elevations of sufficient topographical merit with a drop of between 100ft and 50ft (15.24m) on all sides. Grouping of Tops into Hills, except where inapplicable on topographical grounds, is on the basis that Tops are no more than 17 units from the main top of the Hill to which they belong; where a unit is either one twelfth of a mile measured along the connecting ridge or one 50ft contour between the lower Top and its connecting col.*

While the rules as they stand lack mathematical precision, the actual result of their application is that, with but few exceptions, an 80ft (24.38m) drop determines a Top and the 17-unit rule a Hill.

Table/Column Explanations

Section Number & Name: Section 0 – The Lowlands has been split into three; 0a, 0b (effectively west and east of the M74 corridor) and 0c (north of the M8).

Name & Height: Ordnance Survey spellings and heights in metres have been used. Survey information that has not been ratified by the OS has been noted.

Hill No & Top No: Hill No refers to the actual Donalds (D1) to (D89) and Top No refers to a summit placing in the full list of Donalds and Donald Tops, 1 -140.

OS Map & Grid Ref: The first two digits refer to the relevant OS 1:50k Landranger series map which covers the hill. An eight figure OS grid reference, prefixed by two grid letters, is given in the Table below, which provides the location of a summit to within 10m, and a six figure grid reference has been given in the text, which provides the location of a summit to within 100m.

Name	Height	Hill No	Top No	OS Map	Grid Ref	Page	Date climbed
SECTION 0a – Galloway & The Lowthers							
Galloway Hills							
Cairnsmore of Fleet	711	(D28)	42	83	NX 5016 6707	14	
Knee of Cairnsmore	657		88	83	NX 5096 6563	14	
Meikle Mulltaggart	612		137	83	NX 5120 6781	14	
Larg Hill	676	(D49)	67	77	NX 4247 7574	16	
Lamachan Hill	717	(D26)	39	77	NX 4352 7690	16	
Curleywee	674	(D51)	71	77	NX 4546 7695	16	
Millfore	657	(D62)	86	77	NX 4779 7545	16	
The Merrick	843	(D1)	1	77	NX 4275 8554	19	

Name	Height	Hill No	Top No	OS Map	Grid Ref	Page	Date climbed
Benyellary	719		37	77	NX 4148 8390	19	
Kirriereoch Hill	786	(D11)	13	77	NX 4209 8700	22	
Tarfessock	697	(D35)	50	77	NX 4090 8919	22	
Tarfessock South Top	620		129	77	NX 4136 8862	22	
Shalloch on Minnoch	775	(D13)	15	77	NX 4075 9056	22	
Caerloch Dubh	659		84	77	NX 4001 9202	22	
Craignaw	645	(D68)	94	77	NX 4592 8333	19	
Dungeon Hill	620	(D83)	128	77	NX 4604 8507	19	
Mullwharchar	692	(D39)	54	77	NX 4542 8664	19	
Meikle Millyea	746 (a)	(D15)	20	77	NX 5183 8288	26	
Milldown	738	(D18)	24	77	NX 5112 8394	26	
Millfire	716		41	77	NX 5082 8479	26	
Corserine	814	(D6)	6	77	NX 4978 8706	26	
Carlin's Cairn	807	(D8)	9	77	NX 4969 8836	24	
Meaul	695	(D37)	52	77	NX 5005 9098	24	
Cairnsgarroch	659	(D60)	83	77	NX 5155 9135	24	
Corran of Portmark	623	(D80)	122	77	NX 5092 9367	24	
Bow	613		135	77	NX 5080 9282	24	

Carsphairn Hills

Name	Height	Hill No	Top No	OS Map	Grid Ref	Page	Date climbed
Cairnsmore of Carsphairn	797	(D10)	12	77	NX 5946 9799	28	
Beninner	710		44	77	NX 6057 9716	28	
Moorbrock Hill	650	(D65)	91	77	NX 6206 9838	28	
Windy Standard	698	(D33)	48	77	NS 6201 0146	30	
Keoch Rig	611		139	77	NX 6170 9998	28	
Alhang	642	(D71)	100	77	NS 6422 0102	30	
Alwhat	628		114	77	NS 6466 0203	30	
Meikledodd Hill	643		98	77	NS 6609 0276	30	
Blacklorg Hill	681	(D45)	62	77	NS 6538 0423	30	
Blackcraig Hill	700 (b)	(D30)	45	71,77	NS 6476 0640	30	

Lowther Hills

Name	Height	Hill No	Top No	OS Map	Grid Ref	Page	Date climbed
Queensberry	697	(D34)	49	78	NX 9890 9975	32	
Earncraig Hill	611	(D88)	138	78	NX 9732 0137	32	
Gana Hill	668	(D54)	76	78	NS 9543 0107	32	
Wedder Law	672	(D52)	72	78	NS 9387 0251	34	
Scaw'd Law	663	(D58)	81	78	NS9226 0350	34	
Glenleith Fell	612		136	78	NS 9223 0238	34	
Ballencleuch Law	689	(D42)	57	78	NS 9356 0497	34	
Rodger Law	688		60	71,78	NS 9453 0580	34	
Comb Law	645	(D67)	93	71,78	NS 9438 0738	34	
East Mount Lowther	631	(D76)	112	71,78	NS 8785 1000	36	
Lowther Hill	725	(D23)	32	71,78	NS 8900 1075	36	
Cold Moss	628		115	71,78	NS 8989 0947	36	
Green Lowther	732	(D21)	30	71,78	NS 9003 1203	36	
Dun Law	677	(D48)	66	71,78	NS 9166 1364	36	
Lousie Wood Law	618	(D86)	132	71,78	NS 9319 1527	36	

SECTION 0b – The Borders

Tinto & Culter Hills

Name	Height	Hill No	Top No	OS Map	Grid Ref	Page	Date climbed
Tinto	711	(D29)	43	58	NS 9532 3437	40	
Hudderstone	626	(D78)	119	72	NT 0221 2714	46	
Culter Fell	748	(D14)	19	72	NT 0528 2908	42	
Chapelgill Hill	696	(D36)	51	72	NT 0665 3037	42	
Cardon Hill	675		70	72	NT 0652 3148	42	
Hillshaw Head	652	(D63)	89	72	NT 0483 2460	44	

Name	Height	Hill No	Top No	OS Map	Grid Ref	Page	Date climbed
Coomb Dod	635		108	72	NT 0461 2383	44	
Gathersnow Hill	688	(D43)	58	72	NT 0587 2570	44	
Coomb Hill	640		102	72	NT 0695 2636	44	
Moffat Hills							
Swatte Fell	729 (c)	(D22)	31	78	NT 1203 1154	50	
Nether Coomb Craig	724		34	78	NT 1293 1097	50	
Falcon Craig	724		33	78	NT 1223 1272	50	
Hart Fell	808	(D7)	8	78	NT 1136 1357	50,52	
Whitehope Heights	637	(D73)	106	78	NT 0956 1389	52	
Under Saddle Yoke	745	(D16)	21	78	NT 1424 1262	50	
Saddle Yoke	735 (d)		27	78	NT 1440 1239	50	
Cape Law	722	(D24)	35	78	NT 1311 1508	56	
Din Law	667		77	78	NT 1242 1568	56	
Garelet Dod	698	(D32)	47	78	NT 1262 1726	56	
Erie Hill	690	(D41)	56	78	NT 1241 1873	56	
Laird's Cleuch Rig	684		61	78	NT 1250 1959	56	
Garelet Hill	680		63	72	NT 1240 2015	56	
White Coomb	821	(D4)	4	79	NT 1632 1509	54,56	
Carrifan Gans	757		18	79	NT 1593 1388	54,56	
Firthhope Rig	800		10	79	NT 1535 1539	54,56	
Great Hill	774 (e)		16	78	NT 1459 1639	56	
Molls Cleuch Dod	785	(D12)	14	79	NT 1511 1794	56	
Carlavin Hill	736		26	78	NT 1420 1887	56	
Lochcraig Head	801 (f)	(D9)	11	79	NT 1670 1761	54	
Nickies Knowe	761		17	79	NT 1639 1915	54	
Ettrick Hills							
Croft Head	637	(D72)	105	79	NT 1530 0565	48	
Loch Fell	688	(D44)	59	79	NT 1701 0472	48	
West Knowe	672		73	79	NT 1630 0524	48	
Capel Fell	678	(D46)	64	79	NT 1639 0690	48	
Smidhope Hill	644		96	79	NT 1681 0767	48	
White Shank	622		126	79	NT 1690 0830	48	
Wind Fell	665	(D56)	79	79	NT 1789 0613	48	
Hopetoun Craig	632		109	79	NT 1876 0679	48	
Ettrick Pen	692	(D38)	53	79	NT 1999 0765	48	
Bodesbeck Law	665 (g)	(D55)	78	79	NT 1699 1040	46	
Mid Rig	616		133	79	NT 1802 1227	46	
Bell Craig	623	(D79)	121	79	NT 1864 1286	46	
Andrewhinney Hill	677	(D47)	65	79	NT 1975 1387	46	
Trowgrain Middle	628 (h)		116	79	NT 2066 1503	46	
Herman Law	614	(D87)	134	79	NT 2135 1570	46	
Manor Hills							
Talla Cleuch Head	691	(D40)	55	72	NT 1334 2183	58	
Broad Law	840	(D2)	2	72	NT 1464 2353	58	
Cramalt Craig	831 (i)	(D3)	3	72	NT 1684 2473	58	
Hunt Law	639		103	72	NT 1500 2646	58	
Clockmore	641		101	72	NT 1831 2287	58	
Dollar Law	817	(D5)	5	72	NT 1780 2783	62	
Fifescar Knowe	811		7	72	NT 1751 2708	62	
Notman Law	734		28	72	NT 1850 2602	62	
Middle Hill	716 (j)	(D27)	40	72	NT 1594 2946	60	
Taberon Law	636 (k)		107	72	NT 1464 2888	60	
Drumelzier Law	668	(D53)	75	72	NT 1494 3121	60	
Pykestone Hill	737	(D19)	25	72	NT 1730 3125	60	

Name	Height	Hill No	Top No	OS Map	Grid Ref	Page	Date climbed
The Scrape	719		38	72	NT 1760 3241	60	
Greenside Law	643	(D70)	97	72	NT 1979 2562	62	
Black Law	698	(D31)	46	73	NT 2226 2793	62	
Conscleuch Head	624		120	73	NT 2203 2627	62	
Deer Law	629		113	73	NT 2229 2555	62	
Black Cleuch Hill	675		69	73	NT 2222 2900	62	
Dun Rig	744	(D17)	22	73	NT 2534 3155	64	
Glenrath Heights	732	(D20)	29	73	NT 2416 3226	64	
Stob Law	676	(D50)	68	73	NT 2301 3327	64	
Birkscairn Hill	661	(D59)	82	73	NT 2747 3317	64	
Moorfoot Hills							
Dundreich	623	(D81)	123	73	NT 2746 4908	66	
Bowbeat Hill	626	(D77)	118	73	NT 2920 4690	66	
Blackhope Scar	651	(D64)	90	73	NT 3152 4833	66	
Whitehope Law	623	(D82)	124	73	NT 3303 4456	68	
Windlestraw Law	659	(D61)	85	73	NT 3712 4309	68	
Bareback Knowe	657 (l)		87	73	NT 3622 4206	68	
Roxburgh & Cheviot Hills							
Cauldcleuch Head	619	(D84)	130	79	NT 4565 0068	70	
Windy Gyle	619	(D85)	131	80	NT 8553 1521	70	
Cairn Hill West Top	743 (m)		23	80	NT 8957 1930	70	
SECTION 0c – The Midland Valley							
Ochil Hills							
Blairdenon Hill	631	(D75)	111	58	NN 8657 0185	75	
Ben Ever	622		125	58	NN 8933 0010	73	
Ben Cleuch	721	(D25)	36	58	NN 9027 0063	73	
The Law	638		104	58	NS 9102 9965	73	
Andrew Gannel Hill	670		74	58	NN 9185 0060	73	
King's Seat Hill	648	(D66)	92	58	NN 9337 9998	73	
Tarmangie Hill	645	(D69)	95	58	NN 9421 0140	76	
Whitewisp Hill	643		99	58	NN 9551 0136	76	
Innerdownie	610	(D89)	140	58	NN 9666 0315	76	
Glen Artney Hills							
Meall Clachach	621 (n)		127	57	NN 6883 1258	77	
Uamh Bheag	664 (o)	(D57) T	80	57	NN 6911 1185	77	
Uamh Bheag East Top	664 (o)	(D57) T	80	57	NN 6961 1193	77	
Beinn Odhar	626		117	57	NN 7144 1277	77	
Beinn nan Eun	631	(D74)	110	57	NN 7236 1312	77	

(a) Harvey map gives 749m 400m south-west at NX516825; (b) Unratified height 700.9m; (c) Unratified height 729.9m 200m south-west at NT11841138 (OS 1:50k marks summit here); (d) Unratified height 735.5m; (e) Unratified height 774.7m at NT14591639; (f) High point apparently 100m further north at NT16661774; (g) Unratified height 664.2m; (h) Summit lies 150m north-west of cairn and fence; (i) Unratified height 830.2m; (j) Unratified height 717.1m; (k) Unratified height 636.7m; (l) Unratified height 656.0m; (m) The highest point on the border between Scotland and England. It is not an actual summit and cannot therefore be classified as a separate 'hill'; (n) Unratified height 618.9m; (o) Unratified survey confirms the west top as 665.6m and the summit. The east top as 663.4m and the trig point between the two as lower again

G No	Name	Height	Page	G No	Name	Height	Page
G1	Beinn Talaidh	761m (a)	292	G60	Creagan a' Chaise	722m	167
G2	Cnoc Còinnich	761m	88	G61	Meall Mhèinnidh	722m	248
G3	Sgùrr a' Chaorainn	761m	187	G62	Ben Cleuch	721m	73
G4	Beinn a' Chapuill	759m	208	G63	The Buck	721m	163
G5	Ciste Buide a' Claidheimh [Shee of Ardtalnaig]	759m	118	G64	Stob Mhic Bheathain	721m	188
				G65	Mullach Buidhe	721m	286
G6	Càrn an Tionail	759m (b)	273	G66	Ben Stack	720m	271
G7	Beinn Shiantaidh	757m	288	G67	Meall Buidhe	719m	114
G8	Creag Dubh (Newtonmore)	756m	175	G68	The Storr	719m	310
G9	Cook's Cairn	755m	166	G69	An Stac	718m	204
G10	The Stob	753m (c)	110	G70	Ben Buie	717m	290
G11	Meallan a' Chuail	750m	275	G71	Lamachan Hill	717m	16
G12	Groban	749m	245	G72	Cnap Chaochain Aitinn	715m	165
G13	Sgùrr Chòinnich	749m	202	G73	Beinn Mheadhonach	715m	132
G14	Mona Gowan	749m	161	G74	Beinn Chaorach	713m	90
G15	Culter Fell	748m	42	G75	Creag Mhòr (Sutherland)	713m	278
G16	Binnein Shuas	747m	143	G76	Druim Fada (Kinlochhourn)	713m	211
G17	Meall Mòr (Loch Katrine)	747m	106	G77	Creag Ruadh (Loch Earn)	712m	116
G18	Meall a' Mhuic	745m	123	G78	Beinn nan Ramh	711m	244
G19	Stob a' Ghrianain [Druim Fada]	744m	195	G79	Cairnsmore of Fleet	711m	14
G20	Mount Blair	744m	150	G80	Tinto	711m	40
G21	Meall nan Gabhar	744m	100	G81	Beinn Tharsuinn (Strath Vaich)	710m	255
G22	Dun Rig	744m	64	G82	Càrn a' Ghille Chearr	710m	167
G23	Ben More Coigach	743m	263	G83	Sgùrr na Maothaich [Meith Bheinn]	710m	199
G24	Geallaig Hill	743m	160	G84	Beinn Dhearg Mhòr (Broadford)	709m	302
G25	Beinn nan Eun	743m	256	G85	Beinn nan Lus	709m	131
G26	Creag Liath	743m	174	G86	Beinn a' Mhanaich	709m	90
G27	Cnap Cruinn	742m	142	G87	Beinn Dearg	706m (e)	112
G28	Sgòrr na Cìche [Pap of Glencoe]	742m	136	G88	Càrn a' Chaochain	706m	221
G29	Beinn Mhòr (Cowal)	741m	81	G89	Morven	706m	281
G30	Sgùrr Dearg	741m	292	G90	An Cruachan	705m	229
G31	Badandun Hill	740m	152	G91	Creag a' Choire Ghlais [Ben Armine]	705m	278
G32	Sgùrr na Còinnich	739m	300	G92	Hunt Hill	705m	156
G33	Beinn Mheadhoin (Kingairloch)	739m	181	G93	Meall a' Chaorainn (Achnasheen)	705m	243
G34	Stob na Cruaiche [A' Chruach]	739m	124	G94	Sgùrr an Fhidhleir	705m	263
G35	Meall Mòr (Loch Glass)	738m	258	G95	Corra-bheinn	704m (f)	294
G36	Marsco	736m	308	G96	Beinn Eich	703m	92
G37	Beinn na-h Eaglaise	736m	239	G97	Beinn Lochain	703m	84
G38	Beinn Bheag (Ardgour)	736m	184	G98	Beinn Fhada	702m	296
G39	Doune Hill	734m	92	G99	Belig	702m	304
G40	Druim na Sgriodain	734m	183	G100	Duchray Hill [Mealna Letter]	702m	150
G41	Beinn a' Chaolais	733m	288	G101	Trollabhal	702m	298
G42	Beinn na Caillich (Broadford)	732m	302	G102	Meall Garbh	701m	130
G43	Beinn na Caillich (Kylerhea)	732m	300	G103	Càrn a' Choin Deirg	701m	261
G44	Green Lowther	732m	36	G104	Sgùrr nan Cnamh	701m	186
G45	Sgùrr a' Gharaidh	732m	237	G105	Blackcraig Hill	700m (g)	30
G46	Glas Bheinn (Loch Arkaig)	732m	201	G106	Slat Bheinn	700m	206
G47	Stob an Eas	732m	88	G107	Meall Fuar-mhonaidh	699m	219
G48	Sàbhal Beag	732m	272	G108	Creach Beinn	698m	290
G49	Caisteal Liath [Suilven]	731m	269	G109	Windy Standard	698m	30
G50	Beinn Dhearg Mhòr (Sligachan)	731m	306	G110	Càrn Loch nan Amhaichean	697m	256
G51	Beinn na Gainimh	730m	119	G111	Queensberry	697m	32
G52	Meall Doire Faid	729m	254	G112	Beinn na Muice	695m	228
G53	Ben Venue	729m	104	G113	Beinn Tharsuinn (Strath Rory)	692m	259
G54	Càrnan Cruithneachd	729m (d)	215	G114	Beinn a' Mhùinidh	692m	247
G55	Uisgneabhal Mòr	729m	314	G115	Ettrick Pen	692m	48
G56	Mullach Coire nan Geur-oirean	727m	200	G116	Mullwharchar	692m	19
G57	Màm Hael	726m	132	G117	Meall Dearg	690m	121
G58	Beinn a' Chearcaill	725m	241	G118	Beinn Mòlurgainn	690m	132
G59	Meall nan Damh	723m	190	G119	Ballencleuch Law	689m	34

G No	Name	Height	Page
G120	Beinn Direach	688m (h)	273
G121	Gathersnow Hill	688m	44
G122	Stob Breac	688m	111
G123	Cruach an t-Sidhein	684m	92
G124	Beinn Damhain	684m	97
G125	Leana Mhòr (west)	684m	178
G126	Beinn a' Chaisgein Beag	682m	249
G127	Beinn Bhreac (Loch Lomond)	681m	95
G128	Meall Onfhaidh	681m	196
G129	Meall na Faochaig	681m	231
G130	Meall a' Chrathaich	679m	217
G131	Tiorga Mòr	679m	315
G132	Càrn na Breabaig	679m	225
G133	Capel Fell	678m	48
G134	Hill of Wirren	678m	154
G135	Càrn Mhic an Toisich	678m	217
G136	Càrn Breac	678m	235
G137	Andrewhinney Hill	677m	46
G138	Càrn Gorm	677m	226
G139	Beinn Suidhe	676m	129
G140	Leana Mhòr (east)	676m	178
G141	Meall Mòr (Glen Coe)	676m	134
G142	Càrn na Còinnich	673m	230
G143	Creag Each	672m (i)	116
G144	An Ruadh-mheallan	671m	240
G145	Cat Law	671m	153
G146	Hartaval	669m	310
G147	Beinn Bheag (Letterewe)	668m	245
G148	Creag Bhalg	668m	159
G149	Beinn Bhreac (Loch Broom)	667m	253
G150	Binnein Shios	667m	143
G151	Meall nan Eun	667m	206
G152	Beinn Gàire	666m	192
G153	Beinn Mheadhoin (Strathconon)	665m	232
G154	Meall Tairbh	665m	128
G155	Beinn Ruadh	664m	80
G156	Uamh Bheag	664m (j)	77
G157	Aodann Chleireig	663m	196
G158	Croit Bheinn	663m	192
G159	Sgòrr a' Choise	663m	134
G160	Oireabhal	662m	315
G161	Càrn Glas-choire	659m	171
G162	Windlestraw Law	659m	68
G163	Stob na Boine Druim-fhinn	658m	84
G164	Creag Mhòr (Balquhidder)	658m	108
G165	Meall nan Eagan	658m	145
G166	Creag Ruadh (Dalwhinnie)	658m	148
G167	Creag Dhubh (Glen Spean)	658m	177
G168	Mid Hill	657m	92
G169	Millfore	657m	16
G170	Meall Blàir	656m	203
G171	Meall Odhar	656m	99
G172	Beinn na Cille	652m	182
G173	Fiarach	652m	98
G174	Blackhope Scar	651m	66
G175	Glas-bheinn Mhòr	651m	219
G176	Beinn Donachain	650m	127
G177	Sgòrr Mhic Eacharna	650m	184
G178	Càrn Salachaidh	647m	260
G179	Beinn na Cloiche	646m	140

G No	Name	Height	Page
G180	Craignaw	645m	19
G181	Sgiath a' Chaise	645m (k)	107
G182	Biod an Fhithich	644m (l)	212
G183	Beinn Clachach	643m	209
G184	Creag Tharsuinn	643m	83
G185	Blath Bhalg	641m	149
G186	Mòr Bheinn	640m	113
G187	Creag Gharbh	637m	115
G188	Croft Head	637m	48
G189	Beinn Bhalgairean	636m (m)	100
G190	Beinn na Sroine	636m	126
G191	Glas Bheinn (Loch Eil)	636m	190
G192	Beinn Ghobhlach	635m	250
G193	Glas-chàrn	633m	198
G194	Cruinn a' Bheinn	632m	103
G195	Meall a' Chaorainn (Strath Vaich)	632m	255
G196	Tullich Hill	632m	95
G197	Beinn Dhorain	628m	277
G198	Beinn na Feusaige	627m	235
G199	Beinn a' Chlachain	626m	238
G200	Scaraben	626m	280
G201	Meall nan Caorach	623m (n)	120
G202	Creag Ruadh (Loch Laggan)	622m	176
G203	Creag Ghuanach	621m	140
G204	Tom Meadhoin	621m	139
G205	Beinn Mhòr (South Uist)	620m	312
G206	Meall Reamhar	620m (o)	120
G207	Pressendye	619m	162
G208	Beinn an Eoin	619m	266
G209	Cauldcleuch Head	619m	70
G210	Beinn Bheag (Cowal)	618m	81
G211	Càrn na h-Easgainn	618m	173
G212	Cruach Choireadai	618m	294
G213	Beinn na Gucaig	616m	139
G214	Càrn nan Tri-tighearnan	615m	172
G215	Beinn a' Mheadhoin	613m	223
G216	Meall an Fheur Loch	613m	275
G217	Creag a' Mhadaidh	612m	147
G218	Creag Dhubh Mhòr	612m (p)	233
G219	Stac Pollaidh	612m	267
G220	Cruach nan Capull	611m	79
G221	Cruach nam Mult	611m	86
G222	Corwharn	611m (q)	153
G223	Ben Aslak	610m (r)	300
G224	Ladylea Hill	610m (s)	164

(a) Ratified height of 761.7m which is below 2500ft;
(b) Unratified height of 785.5m;   (c) Unratified height of 753.6m;   (d) Unratified height of 727.8m;   (e) Unratified summit Stuc na Cabaig 708.3m;   (f) Unratified height of 704.9m;   (g) Unratified height of 700.9m;   (h) Unratified height of 688.9m;   (i) Unratified height of 673.7m;   (j) Unratified height of 665.6m;   (k) Unratified height of 644.1m;   (l) Unratified height of 645.9m;   (m) Unratified height of 636.7m;   (n) Unratified height of 623.7;   (o) Unratified height of 617.8m;   (p) Unratified height of 610.9m;   (q) Unratified height of 609.1m;   (r) Unratified height of 609.0m;   (s) Unratified height of 609.1m

Cairnsgarroch, right, and distant Cairnsmore of Carsphairn (Tom Prentice)

Hill No	Name	Height	Page	Hill No	Name	Height	Page
D1	The Merrick	843m	19	D22	Swatte Fell	729m (e)	50
D2	Broad Law	840m	58	D23	Lowther Hill	725m	36
D3	Cramalt Craig	831m (a)	58		Falcon Craig	724m	50
D4	White Coomb	821m	54,56		Nether Coomb Craig	724m	50
D5	Dollar Law	817m	62	D24	Cape Law	722m	56
D6	Corserine	814m	26	D25	Ben Cleuch	721m	73
	Fifescar Knowe	811m	62		Benyellary	719m	19
D7	Hart Fell	808m	50,52		The Scrape	719m	60
D8	Carlin's Cairn	807m	24	D26	Lamachan Hill	717m	16
D9	Lochcraig Head	801m	54	D27	Middle Hill	716m (f)	60
	Firthhope Rig	800m	54,56		Millfire	716m	26
D10	Cairnsmore of Carsphairn	797m	28	D28	Cairnsmore of Fleet	711m	14
D11	Kirriereoch Hill	786m	22	D29	Tinto	711m	40
D12	Molls Cleuch Dod	785m	56		Beninner	710m	28
D13	Shalloch on Minnoch	775m	22	D30	Blackcraig Hill	700m (g)	30
	Great Hill	774m (b)	56	D31	Black Law	698m	62
	Nickies Knowe	761m	54	D32	Garelet Dod	698m	56
	Carrifran Gans	757m	54,56	D33	Windy Standard	698m	30
D14	Culter Fell	748m	42	D34	Queensberry	697m	32
D15	Meikle Millyea	746m (c)	26	D35	Tarfessock	697m	22
D16	Under Saddle Yoke	745m	50	D36	Chapelgill Hill	696m	42
D17	Dun Rig	744m	64	D37	Meaul	695m	24
	Cairn Hill West Top	743m	70	D38	Ettrick Pen	692m	48
D18	Milldown	738m	26	D39	Mullwharchar	692m	19
D19	Pykestone Hill	737m	60	D40	Talla Cleuch Head	691m	58
	Carlavin Hill	736m	56	D41	Erie Hill	690m	56
	Saddle Yoke	735m (d)	50	D42	Ballencleuch Law	689m	34
	Notman Law	734m	62	D43	Gathersnow Hill	688m	44
D20	Glenrath Heights	732m	64	D44	Loch Fell	688m	48
D21	Green Lowther	732m	36		Rodger Law	688m	34

Hill No	Name	Height	Page
	Lairds Cleuch Rig	684m	56
D45	Blacklorg Hill	681m	30
	Garelet Hill	680m	56
D46	Capel Fell	678m	48
D47	Andrewhinney Hill	677m	46
D48	Dun Law	677m	36
D49	Larg Hill	676m	16
D50	Stob Law	676m	64
	Black Cleuch Hill	675m	62
	Cardon Hill	675m	42
D51	Curleywee	674m	16
D52	Wedder Law	672m	34
	West Knowe	672m	48
	Andrew Gannel Hill	670m	73
D53	Drumelzier Law	668m	60
D54	Gana Hill	668m	32
	Din Law	667m	56
D55	Bodesbeck Law	665m (h)	46
D56	Wind Fell	665m	48
D57	Uamh Bheag	664m (i)	77
D58	Scaw'd Law	663m	34
D59	Birkscairn Hill	661m	64
D60	Cairnsgarroch	659m	24
	Caerloch Dubh	659m	22
D61	Windlestraw Law	659m	68
D62	Millfore	657m	16
	Bareback Knowe	657m (j)	68
	Knee of Cairnsmore	657m	14
D63	Hillshaw Head	652m	44
D64	Blackhope Scar	651m	66
D65	Moorbrock Hill	650m	28
D66	King's Seat Hill	648m	73
D67	Comb Law	645m	34
D68	Craignaw	645m	19
D69	Tarmangie Hill	645m	76
	Smidhope Hill	644m	48
D70	Greenside Law	643m	62
	Meikledodd Hill	643m	30
	Whitewisp Hill	643m	76
D71	Alhang	642m	30
	Clockmore	641m	58
	Coomb Hill	640m	44
	Hunt Law	639m	58
	The Law	638m	73
D72	Croft Head	637m	48
D73	Whitehope Heights	637m	52
	Taberon Law	636m (k)	60
	Coomb Dod	635m	44
	Hopetoun Craig	632m	48
D74	Beinn nan Eun	631m	77
D75	Blairdenon Hill	631m	75
D76	East Mount Lowther	631m	36
	Deer Law	629m	62
	Alwhat	628m	30
	Cold Moss	628m	36
	Trowgrain Middle	628m	46
	Beinn Odhar	626m	77
D77	Bowbeat Hill	626m	66
D78	Hudderstone	626m	46
	Conscleuch Head	624m	62

Hill No	Name	Height	Page
D79	Bell Craig	623m	46
D80	Corran of Portmark	623m	24
D81	Dundreich	623m	66
D82	Whitehope Law	623m	68
	Ben Ever	622m	73
	White Shank	622m	48
	Meall Clachach	621m (l)	77
D83	Dungeon Hill	620m	19
	Tarfessock South Top	620m	22
D84	Cauldcleuch Head	619m	70
D85	Windy Gyle	619m	70
D86	Lousie Wood Law	618m	36
	Mid Rig	616m	46
D87	Herman Law	614m	46
	Bow	613m	24
	Glenleith Fell	612m	34
	Meikle Mulltaggart	612m	14
D88	Earncraig Hill	611m	32
	Keoch Rig	611m	28
D89	Innerdownie	610m	76

(a) Unratified height of 830.2m; (b) Unratified height of 774.7m; (c) Harvey map height of 749m; (d) Unratified height of 735.5m; (e) Unratified height of 729.9m; (f) Unratified height of 717.1m; (g) Unratified height of 700.9m; (h) Unratified height of 664.2m; (i) Unratified height of 665.6; (j) Unratified height of 656.0m; (k) Unratified height of 636.7m; (l) Unratified height of 618.9m

Ben Ever, left, The Law and Andrew Gannel Hill from above Mill Glen (Tom Prentice)

SCOTTISH MOUNTAINEERING CLUB
SCOTTISH MOUNTAINEERING TRUST

Prices were correct at time of publication, but are subject to change

HILLWALKERS' GUIDES

The Munros	£23.00
The Corbetts and Other Scottish Hills	£23.00
North-West Highlands	£22.00
Islands of Scotland Including Skye	£20.00
The Cairngorms	£18.00
Central Highlands	£18.00
Southern Highlands	£17.00

SCRAMBLERS' GUIDES

Skye Scrambles	£25.00
Highland Scrambles North	£19.00

CLIMBERS' GUIDES

Inner Hebrides & Arran	£25.00
Northern Highlands North	£22.00
Northern Highlands Central	£25.00
Northern Highlands South	£25.00
Skye The Cuillin	£25.00
Skye Sea-cliffs & Outcrops	£25.00
The Cairngorms	£25.00
Ben Nevis	£22.00
Glen Coe	£22.00
Highland Outcrops	£16.00
North-East Outcrops	£22.00
Lowland Outcrops	£22.00
Scottish Winter Climbs	£25.00
Scottish Rock Climbs	£25.00
Scottish Sport Climbs	£28.00

OTHER PUBLICATIONS

Ben Nevis – Britain's Highest Mountain	£27.50
The Cairngorms – 100 Years of Mountaineering	£27.50
Rising to the Challenge – 100 Years of the LSCC	£24.00
Hostile Habitats – Scotland's Mountain Environment	£17.00
Munro's Tables	£16.00
A Chance in a Million? Avalanches in Scotland	£15.00
The Munroist's Companion	£16.00
Scottish Hill Tracks	£18.00
Scottish Hill Names	£16.00

Visit our website for more details and to purchase online:

www.smc.org.uk

Distributed by:
Cordee Ltd
(t) 01455611185 (w) www.cordee.co.uk